WHAT HANGS

IN THE

BALANCE

THE CASE FOR PRINCIPLED, ETHICAL, COMPETENT,
AND COURAGEOUSY SELFLESS LEADERSHIP

WHAT
HANGS
IN THE
BALANCE

★ ★ ★

Philippe Johnson

RESOLVE
EDITIONS

Published by Resolve Editions, an imprint of Forefront Books, Nashville, Tennessee. Distributed by Simon & Schuster.

Library of Congress Control Number: 2024920329
Print ISBN: 978-1-63763-349-6
E-book ISBN: 978-1-63763-350-2

Cover Design by Studio Gearbox
Interior Design by Mary Susan Oleson, Blu Design Concepts

Printed in the United States of America

Note: The views expressed in this publication are those of the author and do not necessarily reflect the official policy or position of the Department of Defense or the U.S. government. The public release clearance of this publication by the Department of Defense does not imply Department of Defense endorsement or factual accuracy of the material.

To MY PARENTS, who instilled in me the traits
and values I espouse here, and to those officers,
noncommissioned officers, and other public servants
with whom I served whose principled leadership
and selflessness inspired this book

Contents

Preface

★ ★ ★

The decisions made every day by local, state, and federal government elected and appointed leaders determine whether the people they serve flourish or suffer. Their choices dictate not only quality of life but, frequently, life itself.

In the twenty-first century, public institutions will continue to confront wide-ranging public policy challenges that demand selfless leaders of impeccable principle. The stakes are high: domestic and international security threats imperil freedom and the rules-based international order. Political extremism, racial and religious nationalism, and tribalism threaten democratic processes, economic opportunity, social justice, and the attainment of unfulfilled constitutional aspirations. Attacks on truth and science endanger good governance, public health, and environmental sustainability.

Too often, people stumble into leadership positions by chance or due to the absence of robust evaluations of leadership performance and potential.

I was inspired to write this book after observing the forty-fifth president of the United States persistently violate and disparage leadership norms and competencies. The president's social media posts were an aberration—in both style and substance—from the standards that have been successfully employed by public leaders for decades, if not centuries. Power, narcissistic tendencies, and social media coalesced to produce a clear record of President Donald J. Trump's disregard for the institutions that undergird American democracy.

During my twenty-four-year career as an officer in the United States Air Force, I began to appreciate that even flawed and ineffective leaders can provide valuable leadership lessons. Their choices provide both an immediate and an enduring reminder of what not to do and of how leaders should conduct themselves instead.

The deficiencies chronicled in the following chapters—most originating from the zenith of public leadership—deserve attention because of their diversity, their frequency, and their impact. To ignore them is to risk that they be emulated by current or future public servants. Organizational morale and effectiveness are diminished when leaders don't understand their roles, when they behave unethically and abuse authority, when they mistreat subordinates, and when they demand personal loyalty over loyalty to the Constitution. Vital democratic institutions like a free press and independent judiciary are threatened when attacked by the selfish motivations of a leader sworn to protect them. Trafficking in disinformation contributes to an ignorant, easily manipulated electorate and an erosion of trust in electoral processes.

As stated, the stakes are dire. A nation's citizens need and deserve public servants who provide exceptional leadership.

Introduction

This book focuses primarily on former president Trump's leader-ship deficiencies and their consequences. The book does not aim to provide a comprehensive appraisal of the merits of Trump administration policies. For those, I defer to historians and policy experts for a more meaningful and nuanced discussion.

Even for those who have supported or still support Donald Trump, there is much to learn from the former president's conduct and the occasionally courageously principled comportment of his subordinates. Much of what is recounted in the following pages comes directly from the former president and those who worked for him.

Former counselor to President Trump Kellyanne Conway once suggested that her boss needed "to tweet like we need to eat." During his four years in office, the president published over twenty-five thousand tweets covering a multitude of subjects. Those posts, hundreds of which appear in this book, inspired each of the chapter topics and are used to illustrate a wide range of leadership principles and competencies vital to effective public leadership. They are presented as originally posted and therefore contain errors in grammar and spelling. I have occasionally omitted individual posts that were part of a thread (a series of connected posts), and shortened some posts when extraneous content did not further a chapter's subject matter. At times, I **boldface** words in posts merely for emphasis. When I quote other personalities, it is not necessarily to uphold them as exemplars of leadership; many are quoted because their messages illuminate the chosen topic or the events described.

Though the leadership topics I discuss are presented primarily in the context of events occurring during the Trump presidency, they are relevant and applicable to leadership in both public and private organizations.

The book's chapters are grouped into seven sections of over-arching leadership principles, competencies, and traits necessary to inspire integrity and promote successful organizational outcomes. Later chapters build on the material presented in the earlier chapters. The initial section includes a discussion of responsibilities fundamental to leadership in a constitutional democracy and is followed by a selection of topics relevant to organizational leadership and management. A section on effective and responsible communication is followed by sections highlighting the importance of character, trust, and accountability. The penultimate section addresses the consequences of leadership that is ethically challenged, with special emphasis paid to efforts to overturn the 2020 election. The final section contrasts the one immediately prior by emphasizing the importance of service before self.

My relationship to public service arguably began when I was a child. My father served for thirty years in the U.S. Army as an attorney and judge. While living in Europe as a child, I attended the Normandy D-Day commemorations where the value of service and selflessness were indelibly impressed on me. I was raised by parents who instilled in me the value of truth, fairness, justice, and treating others with dignity. I decided at a fairly young age, and absent any parental pressure, to pursue a career in the military. My own career in public service arguably began with four years of leadership training in a Reserve Officers' Training Corps detachment at the University of Florida, followed by twenty-four years of challenging assignments as a pilot, intelligence officer, military diplomat, and safety professional. My daily leadership and managerial experience were supplemented with three rounds of professional military education at various points in my career. Each included a heavy focus on leadership. While serving in the Washington, D.C., area, I completed a master's degree in public policy.

I have had the honor of serving with exceptional leaders from the Defense and State Departments. Their outstanding examples, along with my own experiences and the expertise of renowned leadership organizations and historical luminaries, inform the leadership perspectives and convictions I espouse in this book.

Whether you are currently serving or perhaps contemplating a career in public service, your fellow citizens are counting on you. We need public leaders in local, state, and federal governments to be grounded in the leadership competencies championed in the following chapters. They are also counting on you, through the power of your example, to inspire others to a life of effective leadership in public service.

Part 1

★ ★ ★

A PUBLIC LEADER'S FUNDAMENTAL RESPONSIBILITIES

CHAPTER 1

Defending the Constitution and Key Institutions

*Freedom is never more than one generation away from extinction.
It has to be fought for and defended by each generation.*

—President Ronald Reagan, July 1987

The act of raising one's right hand and taking an oath of office is a simple yet profound act. Unique to public service, this personal commitment requires adherence to certain ideals and standards consecrated at the founding of the American Republic. A public servant's career in one of the three federal branches of government typically begins with a pledge to, among other things, "support and defend the Constitution of the United States against all enemies, foreign and domestic," and to "bear true faith and allegiance to the same." As Representative Liz Cheney (R-WY) explained during a hearing investigating the January 6, 2021, attack on the United States Capitol,

There is a reason why people serving in our government take an oath to the Constitution. As our Founding Fathers recognized, democracy is fragile. People in positions of public trust are duty-bound to defend it, to step forward when action is required. In our country, we don't swear an oath to an individual or a political party. We take our oath to defend the United States Constitution.

We take that oath to safeguard self-governance and the rule of law. We remain vigilant in defending the Constitution because we cherish the freedoms and individual protections that we too often see as unceasing and self-perpetuating. We protect the Constitution because we value a way of life characterized by peace, prosperity, progress, and the opportunity to realize our individual and collective potentials. Representative and former Army Ranger Jason Crow (D-CO) described his own relationship to the oath as "a firm commitment to a life of service, a commitment to set aside your personal interest, your comfort, and your ambition to serve the greater good—and a commitment to sacrifice." In short, service before self and before personal ambition. Crow went on to explain how America was great in part because of the millions of Americans who had taken that oath—and meant it. Many have courageously risked their jobs and careers to honor their oaths. Others followed through on that oath by making the ultimate sacrifice.

Our personal convictions and beliefs—our sense of what is morally right and wrong—may sometimes be in conflict with the nation's laws and judicial decisions. Yet public leaders do not have the luxury of allowing their beliefs to compromise faithful adherence to their oaths of office. South Africa's Nelson Mandela knew that in many instances, his own views on individual issues mattered far less than the democratic process—that it was better to lose on an individual matter and allow democracy to win.

The obligation to defend the U.S. Constitution applies to everyone in federal service, and arguably to those who serve in state and local governments. It especially applies to leaders. The Trump administration's acting director of national intelligence, Joseph Maguire, explained the leadership context as follows: "I view it as a covenant I have with my workforce that I lead, and every American, that I will well and faithfully discharge the duties of my office." Jason Crow echoed that theme when he said the following:

> An oath is also a bond between people who have made a common promise. Perhaps the strongest example is the promise between the Commander in Chief and our men and women in uniform. Those men and women took their oath with the understanding that the Commander in Chief, our President, will always put the interests of the country and their interests above his own, and understanding that his orders will be in the best interest of the country, and that their sacrifice in fulfilling those orders will always serve the common good.

The betrayal of a leader's oath of office risks significant harm to the immediate organization, and in the context of national leadership, national security and the very institutions that undergird the Constitution. As Representative Adam Schiff (D-CA) explained, "The founders were not speaking, of course, of a piece of parchment. Rather they were expressing the obligation of the president to defend the institutions of our democracy, to defend our system of checks and balances...to defend the rule of law, a principle upon which the idea of America was born that we are a nation of laws, not men. If we do not defend the nation, there is no Constitution. But if we do not defend the Constitution, there is no nation worth defending."

Domestic threats to the Constitution have always existed. As Abraham Lincoln proclaimed in 1838, "If destruction be our lot, we must ourselves be its author and finisher." The most dangerous and insidious threats to the Constitution come from those in positions of trust who attack a nation's democratic processes and institutions from within.

> *It is comforting to assume that the institutions*
> *of our Republic will always withstand those who try*
> *to defeat our Constitution from within. But our*
> *institutions are only strong when those who*
> *hold office are faithful to our Constitution.*
> —Representative Liz Cheney

For our democratic system of checks and balances (with separate and coequal branches of government) to function as intended, each branch must respect the constitutional authorities granted to the others. The principle of separation of powers helps ensure that no one branch becomes too powerful, and it relies in part on voluntary compliance or respect for the authorities of the other branches. Whether one considers the powers inherent in the executive branch, the constitutionally vested authority of Congress to investigate corruption and abuse of power, or the judiciary's authority to interpret the law—when one branch ignores or seeks to undermine the legitimate authorities of the other branches, the possibility of tyranny threatens the balance of constitutional democracy.

On January 20, 2017, Donald J. Trump, at seventy years of age, swore for the first time that he would faithfully execute the office of president of the United States and would to the best of his ability preserve, protect, and defend the Constitution of the United States.

Within three weeks of his inauguration, President Trump began challenging the independence and legitimacy of the judiciary. In one example, he attacked a federal judge's decision to temporarily block his executive order banning all foreign nationals (including refugees undergoing extensive vetting) from seven predominantly Muslim countries from entering the United States for a fixed period of time. An appeals court eventually refused to reinstate the president's ban.

> @realDonaldTrump
> What is our country coming to when a judge can halt a Homeland Security travel ban and anyone, even with bad intentions, can come into U.S.?
> 12:44 PM - Feb 4, 2017

> @realDonaldTrump
> Just cannot believe a judge would put our country in such peril. If something happens blame him and court system. People pouring in. Bad!
> 12:39 PM - Feb 5, 2017

A similar pattern emerged when the home and office of Michael Cohen, President Trump's former personal attorney, were searched by the Federal Bureau of Investigation (FBI). As is standard procedure, the search warrant was approved after a federal magistrate evaluated probable cause presented in an affidavit, a process requiring two of the three branches of federal government. The president characterized the search as a "disgraceful situation" and a "total witch hunt." In the following post, President Trump conflates the court-authorized search of Cohen's properties with an alleged episode of breaking and entering.

> @realDonaldTrump
> Remember, Michael Cohen only became a "Rat" after the FBI did something which was absolutely unthinkable & unheard of until the Witch Hunt was illegally started. They BROKE INTO AN ATTORNEY'S OFFICE! Why didn't they break into the DNC to get the Server, or Crooked's office?
> 6:39 AM - Dec 16, 2018

Michael Cohen had been under criminal investigation.

Perceiving a threat to his personal and political interests, the president similarly tried to discredit the Justice Department's investigation into Russian interference in the 2016 election (a topic that will be revisited in later chapters) by referring to it as "an attack on our country, in a true sense. It's an attack on what we all stand for."

> @realDonaldTrump
> The Mueller investigation is totally conflicted, illegal and rigged! Should never have been allowed to begin, except for the Collusion and many crimes committed by the Democrats. Witch Hunt!
> 3:45 PM - Feb 17, 2019

Supporting the Constitution also requires that public leaders defend the foundation of our democracy—the nation's electoral processes. Threatening and potentially deterring citizens from voting—especially without reasonable cause—does not strengthen a democracy.

@realDonaldTrump

Law Enforcement has been strongly notified to watch closely for any ILLEGAL VOTING which may take place in Tuesday's Election (or Early Voting). Anyone caught will be subject to the Maximum Criminal Penalties allowed by law. Thank you!

7:41 AM - Nov 5, 2018

The 2020 election. The most egregious violations of President Trump's presidential oath transpired during his multi-pronged scheme to retain power after losing the 2020 election. His objective, as articulated by the Select Committee to Investigate the January 6th Attack on the United States Capitol, was "to corruptly obstruct, impede, or influence the counting of electoral votes on January 6th, and thereby overturn the lawful results of the election."

The president's schemes involved a concerted disinformation campaign, spurious legal challenges, and a pressure campaign on state election officials. He plotted to send fake slates of electors to Congress and pressured his vice president and members of Congress to ignore the will of the voters. He attacked the Constitution's separation of powers by disrupting the January 6, 2021, congressional certification of electoral votes. He was

23

derelict in his inaction while the Capitol was under attack. Some of these schemes will be revisited in later chapters in different contexts. In the majority of these schemes, the president and his alleged coconspirators were asking and expecting state and federal officials to violate their oaths of office. Halting the counting of ballots, as suggested in the following post, would have violated both state and federal laws.

@realDonaldTrump
STOP THE COUNT!
9:12 AM - Nov 5, 2020

Disinformation and frivolous lawsuits. While serving as vice chair of the committee investigating the attack on the Capitol, Representative Liz Cheney summarized the president's disinformation campaign:

President Trump falsely declared victory...he and his team launched a fraudulent media campaign that persuaded tens of millions of Americans that the election was stolen from him.

Donald Trump intentionally ran false ads on television and social media featuring allegations that his advisors and his Justice Department repeatedly told him were untrue...Donald Trump launched a fraudulent fundraising campaign that raised hundreds of millions of dollars, again based on those same false election fraud allegations.

Likely the most enduring and tragic legacy of his efforts to overturn the election is the continued belief by millions of Americans that massive fraud produced an unjust result in the 2020 presidential election—that one political party successfully conspired to steal an election, thereby invalidating the choices and voices of millions of voters. President Trump may have done irreparable harm to American democracy by undermining faith in its electoral system.

While the disinformation campaign was underway, Trump's legal team was racking up an impressive sixty losses in state and federal courts. United States district court judge Linda Parker, who presided over one of the cases in Michigan, described the case as "a historic and profound abuse of the judicial process....Plaintiffs' attorneys have scorned their oath." Among other sanctions, she determined that the actions of nine Trump attorneys warranted "a referral for investigation and possible suspension or disbarment to the appropriate disciplinary authority for every state bar and federal court in which each attorney is admitted." The attorney general of Texas, on behalf of the Trump campaign, also filed a lawsuit baselessly alleging widespread fraud in four states. The lawsuit was supported by a majority of congressional Republicans and effectively asked the Supreme Court to overturn the election results in those states.

@realDonaldTrump

We will be INTERVENING in the Texas (plus many other states) case. This is the big one. Our Country needs a victory!

8:44 AM - Dec 9, 2020

@realDonaldTrump
Now that the Biden Administration will be a scandal
plagued mess for years to come, it is much easier
for the Supreme Court of the United States to follow
the Constitution and do what everybody knows has to
be done. They must show great Courage & Wisdom.
Save the USA!!!
8:16 AM - Dec 11, 2020

The president had nominated a third of the nine justices on the
Supreme Court, which summarily and decisively rejected the Texas
lawsuit.

@realDonaldTrump
The Supreme Court really let us down.
No Wisdom, No Courage!
11:50 PM - Dec 11, 2020

On January 6, 2021, Senate majority leader Mitch McConnell
(R-KY) addressed the president's disinformation campaign and
spurious legal maneuvers in a speech aimed at his Republican
colleagues:

> President Trump claims the election was stolen. The
> assertions range from specific local allegations to consti-
> tutional arguments, to sweeping conspiracy theories. I
> supported the President's right to use the legal system.
> Dozens of lawsuits received hearings in courtrooms
> all across our country. But over and over the courts

rejected these claims, including all-star judges, whom the President himself has nominated. Every election we know features some illegality and irregularity, and of course, that's unacceptable....But my colleagues, nothing before us proves illegality anywhere near the massive scale that would have tipped the entire election. Nor can public doubt alone justify a radical break when the doubt itself was incited without any evidence.

The pressure campaign. Senator Mitt Romney (R-UT) summarized President Trump's efforts to overturn the election by exerting pressure on state legislators and state election officials: "Having failed to make even a plausible case of widespread fraud or conspiracy before any court of law, the President has now resorted to overt pressure on state and local officials to subvert the will of the people and overturn the election. It is difficult to imagine a worse, more undemocratic action by a sitting American President." As part of the pressure campaign on election officials in selected states, President Trump attempted to coerce the Justice Department into transmitting alleged claims of election fraud that would suggest that the outcomes of those elections were in question (as detailed in chapter 29).

Fake electors. The president worked with the Republican National Committee and others in a plot that resulted in officials in seven targeted states submitting fraudulent slates of electors to federal officials at the National Archives and the U.S. Senate. This scheme—which would have knowingly violated the Electoral Count Act of 1887—was designed to obstruct the joint session of Congress's certification of electoral votes on January 6 by creating uncertainty such that the vice president might either reject both the legitimate and illegitimate slates of electors, or potentially even accept only the fraudulent slates of electors. Michael Luttig, a prominent retired conservative judge, characterized the justifications for these actions as "the most reckless, insidious, and calamitous failures of both legal and political judgment in American history." By April 2024, thirty-six people had been indicted in Georgia, Michigan, Nevada, and Arizona for signing certificates that fraudulently declared them to be their states' electors.

Pressure on the vice president and Congress. After numerous recounts and audits, all fifty states and the District of Columbia certified their election results in early December. Members of the Electoral College cast their votes several days later, cementing Joe Biden's 306 to 232 victory over Donald Trump. In the run-up to the January 6, 2021, certification of the Electoral College vote by a joint session of Congress, President Trump began his campaign of pressuring Republican lawmakers to object to lawful electoral votes from key battleground states. He also pressured Vice President Pence to refuse to count those same votes during the joint session (an episode detailed in chapter 31). On January 6, Senator McConnell addressed certain Republican colleagues who were objecting to the certification of Arizona's electoral votes:

> We're debating a step that has never been taken in American history. Whether Congress should overrule the voters and overturn a presidential election. I've served thirty-six years in the Senate. This'll be the most important vote I've ever cast.... The Constitution gives us here in Congress a limited role.... The voters, the courts,

and the states have all spoken....If we overrule them, it would damage our Republic forever....If this election were overturned by mere allegations from the losing side, our democracy would enter a death spiral. We'd never see the whole nation accept an election again. Every four years would be a scramble for power at any cost....Self-government, my colleagues, requires a shared commitment to the truth and a shared respect for the ground rules of our system....It would be unfair and wrong to disenfranchise American voters and overrule the courts and the States on this extraordinarily thin basis. And I will not pretend such a vote would be a harmless protest gesture while relying on others to do the right thing. I will vote to respect the people's decision and defend our system of government as we know it.

Within hours of McConnell's impassioned plea to respect the Constitution, and in the immediate aftermath of the violence and destruction resulting from the attack on the Capitol, a majority of House Republicans nonetheless voted against recording the election results of two states.

The attack on the Capitol. President Trump flouted the Constitution's separation of powers by arguably inciting an attack on the U.S. Capitol (detailed further in chapter 33) for the purpose of disrupting Congress's certification of the presidential election. As described in the "incitement" article of impeachment, Trump "gravely endangered the security of the United States and its institutions of Government. He threatened the integrity of the democratic system, interfered with the peaceful transition of power, and imperiled a coequal branch of Government. He thereby betrayed his trust as President, to the manifest injury of the people of the United States." The attack also put in danger the top three individuals in the presidential line of succession—the vice president, the Speaker of the House, and the president pro tempore of the Senate.

Within a week of the attack, the military's Joint Chiefs were compelled to provide service members the following reminder:

> The U.S. military will obey lawful orders from civilian leadership…and remain fully committed to protecting and defending the Constitution of the United States against all enemies, foreign and domestic.…The rights of freedom of speech and assembly do not give anyone the right to resort to violence, sedition and insurrection.…We support and defend the Constitution. Any act to disrupt the Constitutional process is not only against our traditions, and values, and oath; it is against the law. On January 20, 2021, in accordance with the Constitution, confirmed by the states and the courts, and certified by Congress, President-elect Biden will be inaugurated and will become our 46th Commander in Chief.

Over 370 congressional staffers signed a letter imploring senators to convict Trump at the conclusion of his second (and incitement-related) impeachment trial. Their letter read, in part:

Our Constitution only works when we believe in it and defend it. It's a shared commitment to equal justice, the rule of law, and the peaceful resolution of our differences. Any person who doesn't share these beliefs has no place representing the American people, now or in the future. The use of violence and lies to overturn an election is not worthy of debate. Either you stand with the republic or against it.

Presidential negligence. Before January 6, the schemes engineered by the president and his supporters to overturn the election had not yet achieved their objective. The mob he had summoned to Washington, D.C., was, however, successfully interrupting the counting of votes in the January 6 joint session of Congress and therefore interfering with the peaceful transfer of power. During a period of almost three hours, President Trump refused to take any action to stop the violence at the Capitol.

Vice President Pence gaveled the Congress into its joint session just after 1 p.m. At the conclusion of his speech at the Ellipse, President Trump traveled to the West Wing of the White House, arriving at 1:21 p.m. He was immediately informed about the ongoing violence at the Capitol. From 1:25 to 4 p.m., the president stayed in the dining room off the Oval Office where he monitored television coverage of the attack. During that time, he purposefully ignored the pleas of senior White House staff, lawmakers at the Capitol, and members of his own family who all desperately wanted him to condemn the violence and instruct the rioters (his supporters) to leave the Capitol. During the same time period, the president's chief of staff was being inundated with messages from current and former administration officials, members of Congress, and conservative media personalities. All were insisting that the president take action to stop the worst attack on the U.S. Congress in over two centuries. The president repeatedly told his advisors that the people at the Capitol were angry because the election had been stolen.

At 1:34 p.m., the House sergeant at arms and the mayor of Washington, D.C., requested additional troops to reinforce the beleaguered Capitol Police and D.C. Metropolitan Police. At 1:49 p.m., the chief of the Capitol Police made an urgent request for National Guard support. At the same time, President Trump posted a video of his inciteful speech at the Ellipse. After more than an hour of violent clashes with police, the rioters entered the Capitol at 2:13 p.m. Members of Congress were forced to flee the Capitol grounds. At 2:24 p.m., the president incited additional outrage by attacking his vice president on social media. The president's former chief of staff commented several minutes later.

@MickMulvaney
Peaceful protests are one thing. Illegally storming the Capitol is another thing entirely. The President needs to discourage any violence immediately.
2:31 PM - Jan 6, 2021

President Trump seemingly attempted to mitigate the ongoing chaos with a post suggested by his daughter Ivanka. Notably absent was any request for his supporters to leave the Capitol grounds onto which they had illegally trespassed. The post also suggested that the rioters had thus far acted peacefully.

> @realDonaldTrump
> Please support our Capitol Police and Law
> Enforcement. They are truly on the side of our
> Country. Stay peaceful!
> 2:38 PM - Jan 6, 2021

At 2:53 p.m., Donald Trump Jr. sent a message to the president's chief of staff insisting that his father needed to "condem [*sic*] this shit. Asap. The captiol [*sic*] police tweet is not enough." Sometime after 3:05 p.m., the president was informed that someone had been shot. The president posted again at 3:13 p.m. but failed to explicitly condemn the violence and demand that the rioters leave.

> @realDonaldTrump
> I am asking for everyone at the U.S. Capitol to remain
> peaceful. No violence! Remember, WE are the Party of
> Law & Order – respect the Law and our great men and
> women in Blue. Thank you!
> 3:13 PM - Jan 6, 2021

> @MickMulvaney
> The best thing @realdonaldtrump could do right now is
> to address the nation from the Oval Office and condemn
> the riots. A peaceful transition of power is essential to
> the country and needs to take place on 1/20.
> 4:07 PM - Jan 6, 2021

By 4 p.m., elected officials at the Capitol were in secure locations. Fox News (watched by the president) had reported that the entire D.C. National Guard had been mobilized and that the FBI was also sending troops to the Capitol. At 4:17 p.m., the president released a video doubling down on his claims of a stolen election. He had been given a scripted message but instead "went off the cuff." He praised his supporters, finally told them to go home, but neglected to condemn the violence at the Capitol:

> I know your pain. I know your hurt. We had an election that was stolen from us. It was a landslide election, and everyone knows it, especially the other side. But you have to go home now. We have to have peace. We have to have law and order. We have to respect our great people in law and order. We don't want anybody hurt. It's a very tough period of time. There's never been a time like this where such a thing happened, where they could take it away from all of us—from me, from you, from our country. This was a fraudulent election, but we can't play into the hands of these people. We have to have peace. So go home. We love you. You're very special. You've seen what happens. You see the way others are treated that are so bad and so evil. I know how you feel. But go home and go home at peace.

By that point, police officers at the Capitol had been in a battle for their lives for over three hours. One of Trump's supporters had been killed in the melee. At no time on January 6 did President Trump place a call to his national security leaders. He also failed to order any of his staff to facilitate a law enforcement response and could not be bothered to check on the welfare of his vice president. Instead, he called senators to encourage them to object to or delay the electoral vote certification. The president also phoned his personal attorney Rudy Giuliani. It was Vice President Pence who ordered a military response from his secure location at the Capitol. Chairman of the Joint Chiefs of Staff, General Mark Milley, would later testify about the president's inaction. "You know, you're the Commander in Chief. You've got an assault going on at the Capitol of the United States of America. And there's nothing? No call? Nothing? Zero?"

Senator Mitch McConnell weighed in after the conclusion of the president's impeachment trial:

> The unconscionable behavior did not end when the violence actually began....It was obvious that only President Trump could end this. He was the only one who could. Former aides publicly begged him to do so. Loyal allies frantically called the Administration. But the President did not act swiftly. He did not do his job. He didn't take steps so federal law could be faithfully executed and order restored. No. Instead, according to public reports, he watched television happily, happily. As the chaos unfolded, he kept pressing his scheme to overturn the election....Later, even when the President did halfheartedly begin calling for peace, he didn't call right away for the riot to end. He did not tell the mob to depart until even later. And even then, with police officers bleeding and broken glass covering Capitol floors, he kept repeating election lies and praising the criminals.

President Trump's former attorney general, William (Bill) Barr, characterized Trump's behavior as a "betrayal of his office and supporters."

In describing Trump's lack of intervention, Representative Liz Cheney declared, "There has never been a greater betrayal by a president of the United States of his office and his oath to the Constitution." She would later remark that "Donald Trump made a purposeful choice to violate his oath of office, to ignore the ongoing violence against law enforcement, to threaten our constitutional order." On the evening of January 6, the president's former campaign manager, Brad Parscale, messaged a White House staffer lamenting that the president's actions were about "pushing for uncertainty in our country. A sitting president asking for civil war. This week I feel guilty for helping him win."

It was not until the next day that the president condemned the attack and its perpetrators in a scripted speech likely motivated by his own potential legal exposure, in addition to the possibility that his cabinet might remove him from office by invoking the 25th Amendment. In that speech, he falsely claimed to have "immediately deployed the National Guard and federal law enforcement to secure the building and expel the intruders."

In August 2023, Mr. Trump was indicted by a federal grand jury. The four counts included conspiracy to defraud the United States and conspiracy to obstruct an official proceeding. The former president was accused of perpetrating three conspiracies for the purpose of overturning "the legitimate results of the 2020 presidential election by using knowingly false claims of election fraud to obstruct the federal government function [established by the Constitution and the Electoral Count Act] by which those results are collected, counted, and certified."

Preserving constitutional democracy. Freedom House, an American organization devoted to the support and defense of democracy around the world, concluded in a 2021 report that global freedom had been in decline for the previous fifteen years. As Ronald Reagan reminded us in the quote opening this chapter, constitutions and democratic norms are not self-perpetuating. When under attack from within, using ostensibly legal processes, they can be eroded and replaced. We cannot assume that what exists during our lifetimes will exist indefinitely.

Germany's Weimar Republic is a prime example of a democracy eroded from within, eventually becoming a totalitarian dictatorship under Adolf Hitler. Timothy Snyder eloquently addressed these contemporarily relevant issues in his book *On Tyranny: Twenty Lessons from the Twentieth Century*. In a passage that should serve as stark warning to freedom-loving people everywhere, Snyder wrote, "The European history of the twentieth century shows us that societies can break, democracies can fall, ethics can collapse, and ordinary men can find themselves standing over death pits with guns in their hands."

The aforementioned democratic institutions under attack have defended the Constitution from enemies foreign and domestic and secured and maintained the rights of generations of Americans. As citizens and patriots, we vote in elections because defending democracy is not a spectator sport. Leaders in public service must actively work to protect those institutions, imperfect as they may be.

A guiding principle in the endeavor to defend democracy is to recall and practice the idea that our primary allegiance belongs to the Constitution and the institutions supporting it rather than specific persons in positions of authority.

To paraphrase former FBI director James Comey, sometimes "No" must be spoken into a storm of crisis with opposing loud voices all around. This can be exceptionally difficult when it is the president of the United States on the receiving end of "No." Elected officials face similar pressures when doing what they believe to be right in the face of intense criticism. Representative Justin Amash (R-MI) was accused at a public event of not representing the will of his constituents with respect to his decision to impeach President Trump. Amash responded by explaining that it was not his job to merely do the will of his constituents but rather to defend the Constitution.

The pressures that elected officials face notwithstanding, Thomas Jefferson suggested that we might "return with joy to that state of things, when the only questions concerning a candidate shall be, is he honest? Is he capable? Is he faithful to the Constitution?" While speaking to MSNBC in 2019, Harvard University's professor of constitutional law emeritus, Laurence Tribe, described what happens when moral courage is lacking. "There is a point when caution becomes cowardice and a point when cowardice becomes betrayal…betrayal of the Constitution." Thomas Jefferson also wrote that "We are likely to preserve the liberty we have obtained only by unremitting labors and perils. But we shall preserve it." Adam Schiff furthered that sentiment when he wrote the following:

> The Constitution is a powerful document, but it's not self-effectuating. It requires vigilance. It requires moral courage. We will do everything in our power to preserve this marvelous experiment in self-governance. America is worth it.

CHAPTER 2

Promoting Core Values
and Principles

★ ★ ★

A n organization is unlikely to succeed if its core values are routinely
neglected or, worse yet, if its leader fails to uphold them. This
failure of leadership creates a cultural ripple effect across the organization, necessitating greater reliance on the professionalism of the
rank and file until its leader can be replaced. Under these circumstances, cynicism and a general distrust of leadership are inevitable.
It is sufficiently distressing when these lapses are witnessed by those
in the organization, but the reputation of the entire organization is
at risk when these lapses impact external customers. Organizations
are much more likely to succeed when their actions—including their
leaders'—are in harmony with their core values.

To secure the respect and trust of subordinates, peers, superiors, and external agencies, one's words and actions must align with
organizational values. Competent public leaders should strive to
make organizational core values their own, becoming the stewards
of those values. They must ensure that those values are ingrained in

the culture of their organizations. To that end, leaders must communicate expectations and, when necessary, condemn attacks on those values while providing corrective guidance.

Public institutions are defined by their underlying values and principles. The core values of the United States Air Force, for example, are *Integrity First, Service Before Self,* and *Excellence In All We Do.* Some of the key values and principles enshrined in America's Constitution include individual liberty, consent of the governed, freedom of speech, equal justice under the law, free and fair elections, freedom of religion, the right to dissent, and the preeminence of the rule of law. America has also traditionally valued pluralism, multilateralism with robust alliances, freedom from foreign interference, the protection of human rights, and a commitment to truth. These values and principles serve to preserve our vital democratic institutions and liberty itself. They also animate the structure of our government by inspiring coherent organizational visions, which in turn promote mission success and provide a unifying context for acceptable conduct.

There are examples in American history when one or more branches of government did not adequately defend constitutional principles and another branch stepped in to provide the necessary moral leadership. When the executive and legislative branches were initially slow to seek full rights for African Americans, it was the judicial branch that took an aggressive lead in this area with the landmark 1954 *Brown v. Board of Education* school desegregation decision.

Colonel Anthony E. Hartle correctly asserted that while people of high ability are important to any organization, people of high integrity are indispensable. Though capability is necessary for success in any endeavor, it is a virtue that cannot prosper in public service without a set of guiding principles. Inherent in the oath of office is an obligation to promote and defend the values and principles explicitly enshrined in the Constitution. The following posts and quotes from President Trump are an affront to the denoted values and principles.

Freedom of speech.

@realDonaldTrump
Nothing funny about tired Saturday Night Live on Fake News NBC! Question is, how do the Networks get away with these total Republican hit jobs without retribution? Likewise for many other shows? Very unfair and should be looked into. This is the real Collusion!
4:52 AM - Feb 17, 2019

What should have been "looked into" is the First Amendment of the U.S. Constitution. Political satire is protected free speech, as unanimously reaffirmed by the U.S. Supreme Court in *Hustler Magazine v. Falwell* (1988).

Principles of American jurisprudence. When President Trump attacked both a foreperson (juror) and judge in the trial of his associate Roger Stone, it was an assault on the principles of equal justice under the law (trial by a jury of one's peers) and the expectation of privacy usually afforded jurors. The following discredited accusations made during the trial necessitated additional security measures in the courtroom to protect the jurors who were performing their obligatory civic duties.

@realDonaldTrump

There has rarely been a juror so tainted as the fore-woman in the Roger Stone case. Look at her background. She never revealed her hatred of "Trump" and Stone. She was totally biased, as is the judge. Roger wasn't even working on my campaign. Miscarriage of justice. Sad to watch!

3:01 PM - Feb 25, 2020

Presiding over the case, Judge Amy Berman Jackson commented, "Any attempt to invade the privacy of the jurors or to harass or intimidate them is completely antithetical to our entire system of justice....They deserve to have their privacy protected." It was not the first and would not be the last time that Trump used authoritarian tactics to intimidate and threaten those who administer the law. When Trump was held in criminal contempt of court during his 2024 New York criminal trial, the judge wrote that the former president "not only called into question the integrity, and therefore the legitimacy of these proceedings, but again raised the specter of fear for the safety of the jurors and of their loved ones. Such concerns undoubtedly threaten to 'interfere with the fair administration of justice and constitutes a direct attack on the Rule of Law.'"

The American system of justice is an adversarial system in which two sides make competing arguments. Though common practice, it does not expect the accused to cooperate or plea-bargain. Nonetheless, the practice of witness cooperation has been an acceptable and essential tool in American jurisprudence. This tool for discerning truth and promoting justice is often used in cases involving conspiratorial crimes (such as organized crime). In 2018, President Trump disparaged the practice of witness cooperation, calling it "not fair" and suggesting that it "almost ought to be outlawed." The president made those comments in the context of his former campaign manager, Paul Manafort, whom he described as being "very brave" because he did not "flip" and because he refused to "break." Manafort had agreed to cooperate with investigators before eventually breaching his plea agreement by lying to prosecutors, and consistently so regarding one particularly consequential subject: his ties to Konstantin Kilimnik. Kilimnik has ties to Russian intelligence and at the time of writing was wanted by the FBI for obstruction of justice.

The 2020 U.S. Senate Select Committee on Intelligence report *Russian Active Measures Campaigns and Interference in the 2016 U.S. Election* described how Manafort "sought to leverage his position [as head of the 2016 Trump campaign] to resolve his multi-million-dollar foreign disputes and obtain new work in Ukraine and elsewhere."

> On numerous occasions over the course of his time on the Trump Campaign, Manafort sought to secretly share internal Campaign information with Kilimnik.… Manafort briefed Kilimnik on sensitive Campaign polling data and the Campaign's strategy for beating Hillary Clinton.…Following the election, Manafort worked with Kilimnik on narratives that sought to undermine information showing that Russia interfered in the 2016 U.S. election.…Manafort's high-level access and willingness to share information with individuals closely affiliated with the Russian intelligence services, particularly Kilimnik, represented a grave counterintelligence threat.

Manafort's interactions represented the single most direct tie between senior Trump campaign officials and Russian intelligence services. President Trump's attacks on witness cooperation should be seen in the context of his own potential obstruction of justice as it relates to both dangling and issuing pardons, topics explored further in chapter 30.

Promoting democratic principles on the world stage. There is a pragmatic need to maintain the moral high ground in today's globally interdependent environment. When we act contrary to our own principles, we diminish our standing in the world, create security risks for our citizens at home and abroad, and embolden authoritarians. This is especially true for fledgling democracies at risk of experiencing a slowdown or reversal of progress with respect to democratic institutions and human rights. Thomas Jefferson wrote, "The flames kindled on the 4th of July, 1776, have spread over too much of the globe to be extinguished by the feeble engines of despotism; on the contrary, they will consume these engines and all who work them." Unfortunately, authoritarianism is currently on the rise in Europe and elsewhere across the globe.

A 2019 U.S. House of Representatives report emphasized the importance of America living up to its historic ideals of human rights and economic and political freedom:

> America remains the beacon of democracy and opportunity for freedom-loving people around the world. From their homes and their jail cells, from their public squares and their refugee camps, from their waking hours until their last breath, individuals fighting human rights abuses, journalists uncovering and exposing corruption,

persecuted minorities struggling to survive and preserve their faith, and countless others around the globe just hoping for a better life look to America. What we do will determine what they see, and whether America remains a nation committed to the rule of law.

American diplomats often volunteer to serve as international election observers in an effort to demonstrate America's commitment to free and fair elections. In contrast, messaging that embraces authoritarian-style politics and praises authoritarian leaders is inconsistent with leadership in a rule-of-law society. In the following post, President Trump may have been trying to persuade North Korea's leader to pursue economic power instead of nuclear technology for military purposes. But a public message is not the place (if there is any) to laud a despot.

@realDonaldTrump
North Korea, under the leadership of Kim Jong Un, will become a great Economic Powerhouse. He may surprise some but he won't surprise me, because I have gotten to know him & fully understand how capable he is. North Korea will become a different kind of Rocket - an Economic one!
4:50 PM - Feb 8, 2019

Likewise, when the leader of what is arguably the world's oldest democracy characterizes standing on North Korean soil with a rogue dictator as "a great honor," it sends the wrong message to fledgling democracies and countries suffering under authoritarian regimes.

@realDonaldTrump

Leaving South Korea after a wonderful meeting with Chairman Kim Jong Un. Stood on the soil of North Korea, an important statement for all, and **a great honor!**

3:21 AM - Jun 30, 2019

The president may have intended this to be more of a personal statement of appreciation, but words matter. Leaders cannot easily divorce public statements like these from the contexts in which they are likely to be perceived. The president would not likely have felt as honored if visiting a North Korean concentration or "reeducation" camp. In the conduct of foreign policy, the example we set determines whether other countries want to be more like us or less like us.

The 2019 *Trump-Ukraine Impeachment Inquiry Report* provided additional examples of acts going directly against the cause of promoting American values abroad. Ambassador Marie Yovanovitch was advancing American policy in Ukraine by vigorously championing anti-corruption reforms. Meanwhile, President Trump's subordinates and civilian associates were orchestrating a scheme to pressure Ukraine's government into announcing an investigation into potential presidential candidate and then former vice president Joe Biden. If successful, the scheme would have benefited Trump personally and politically. The impeachment report explains that "in so doing, the President undermined U.S. policy supporting anti-corruption reform and the rule of law in Ukraine, and undermined U.S. national security."

During his related and infamous July 25, 2019, phone call to President Zelenskyy of Ukraine (who would be lauded for his leadership after the Russian invasion of Ukraine in 2022), President Trump disparaged his own former ambassador to Ukraine (Yovanovitch) while praising a corrupt former Ukrainian prosecutor. Ambassador Yovanovitch would later testify that "our leadership depends on the power of our example and the consistency of our purpose. Both have now been opened to question." In other words, we should not be in the business of exporting corrupt values. If our values strengthen us, then attacking those values weakens us. We would be remiss to neglect instances where these values are attacked from within, as Timothy Snyder addressed in 2019:

> The question is not right now whether Americans can show the world what democracy looks like. The question now is whether Americans can show Americans what democracy looks like. If we can get that taken care of, then maybe at one point we'll resume our role as some kind of model for the rest of the world.

Democratic transition of power. The post-election peaceful transfer of power is one of the Constitution's most fundamental principles and one of America's greatest exports. The process traditionally begins with the loser conceding when the outcome is a mathematical certainty, and sometimes after any legitimate legal challenges have been adjudicated. The concession speech—usually gracious in tone—serves to remind the electorate that the loser respects the legitimacy of the democratic process, that there will be a smooth transition between administrations, and that in the final analysis, we are all citizens of the same country.

In the 2000 presidential election, Al Gore's bid for the White

House came to an end with the controversial *Bush v. Gore* Supreme Court decision that stopped the Florida recount. The following is from Al Gore's concession speech:

> The U.S. Supreme Court has spoken. Let there be no doubt, while I strongly disagree with the court's decision, I accept it. I accept the finality of this outcome, which will be ratified next Monday in the Electoral College. And tonight, for the sake of our unity as a people and the strength of our democracy, I offer my concession. I also accept my responsibility, which I will discharge unconditionally, to honor the new president-elect and do everything possible to help him bring Americans together in fulfillment of the great vision that our Declaration of Independence defines and that our Constitution affirms and defends.

During his 2016 inaugural address, President Trump thanked the former president and first lady for their assistance during the transition. Just prior to Trump's victory in 2016, Harvard University professor Noah Feldman suggested, "Trump probably wouldn't start riots by refusing to concede. But it's not something we should want to find out." In 2019, Trump's former attorney Michael Cohen testified before Congress, warning, "Indeed, given my experience working for Mr. Trump, I fear that if he loses the election in 2020 that there will never be a peaceful transition of power, and this is why I agreed to appear before you today." President Trump would be the first American president not to ensure a peaceful transfer of power. A member of the House committee investigating the

January 6, 2021, attack on the U.S. Capitol stated the following:

> For more than 200 years, our democracy has been distinguished by the peaceful transfer of power. When an American raises their right hand and takes the presidential oath of office, they are transformed from an ordinary citizen, into the most powerful person in the world—the president. This is an awesome power to acquire. It is even more awesome when it is handed on peacefully....Other countries use violence to seize and hold power, but not in the United States. Not in America.

In the early hours of November 4, 2020 (effectively Election Night)—days before any major media outlet had declared a winner—President Trump declared himself the victor in remarks made at the White House. The major media outlets finally declared Trump the loser on November 7. On November 10, Secretary of State Mike Pompeo irresponsibly and perhaps sarcastically suggested that "there will be a smooth transition to a second Trump administration," prompting the president to post, "That's why Mike was number one in his class at West Point!"

Trump's defiance continued:

> @realDonaldTrump
> He only won in the eyes of the FAKE NEWS MEDIA.
> I concede NOTHING! We have a long way to go. This
> was a RIGGED ELECTION!
> 9:19 AM - Nov 15, 2020

A week earlier, the president had requested that his staff look into the feasibility of trademarking the expression "Rigged Election!"

> @realDonaldTrump
> WE HAVE JUST BEGUN TO FIGHT!!!
> 8:47 AM - Dec 12, 2020

As the Electoral College certified each state's electoral votes on December 14, confirming Biden as the winner, many of the president's senior staff and certain members of his family were urging him to concede. On December 15, White House press secretary Kayleigh McEnany defiantly equivocated by suggesting that there would be either a smooth transition or a continuation of power. Trump and his allies were refusing to accept an outcome that had been evident for weeks. To put the following post into context, President Trump lost the 2020 popular vote by just over seven million votes.

> @realDonaldTrump
> @MailOnline. Mitch, 75,000,000 VOTES, a record for a sitting President (by a lot). Too soon to give up. Republican Party must finally learn to fight. People are angry!
> 12:40 AM - Dec 16, 2020

In the days following the January 6 attack on the Capitol, America's European allies denounced Trump for the role his failure to concede likely played in fomenting the violence on that day. Chancellor Angela Merkel of Germany was compelled to remind us that "a ground rule of democracy is that after elections there are winners and losers. Both have their role to play with decency and responsibility so that democracy itself remains the winner." It was not until January 7, the day after the attack on the Capitol, that President Trump finally acknowledged that there would be a smooth and orderly transition of power to a new administration. He did not mention President-elect Biden's name, nor did he acknowledge the legitimacy of the election. He refused to say that the election was over but only that Congress had certified the results. Neither did he place a congratulatory phone call or extend an invitation to the White House in the tradition of his predecessors.

In a final break of precedent that deprived the world the opportunity to witness America's traditional peaceful transition of power, Trump refused to attend the inauguration of his successor. Trump's failure to concede—despite what was almost universally deemed a free and fair election—will have lasting consequences. Authoritarian leaders abroad were likely emboldened to ignore unfavorable results in their own elections. In America's 2022 midterm elections, over a hundred candidates nominated for national or statewide office chose to embrace Trump's "stolen election" narrative. They did so believing that Trump's support would improve their electoral prospects.

Public servants come from diverse cultural and religious backgrounds. They receive disparate levels of guidance and nurturing with respect to ethics and the principles that inform public service. As a result, their personal values may not always harmonize with organizational values. Military organizations, for example, understand the inherent challenge of forming teams of people with diverse backgrounds and dissimilar ethical values and beliefs. Despite these challenges, leaders must ensure through employee training, accountability, and leading by example that everyone subscribes to and upholds organizational core values.

When Thomas Jefferson wrote about the founding values, principles, and freedoms afforded by the Constitution—freedoms that would elude too many generations of Americans—he provided the following advice:

> The wisdom of our sages and the blood of our heroes have been devoted to their attainment. They should be the creed of our political faith—the text of civil instruction—the touchstone by which to try the services of those we trust; and should we wander from them in moments of error or alarm, let us hasten to retrace our steps and to regain the road which alone leads to peace, liberty, and safety.

Historian and author Ron Chernow noted that "we've *always* been fighting for the soul of America. We've *always* fallen short of the hallowed ideals enshrined in our founding documents. America has *always* been a work in progress, a perpetual journey, a freedom ride with no final destination. And it falls to each new generation to renew and rediscover our country's lofty promise." In that context, Thomas Jefferson's timeless wisdom should continue to inspire public leaders to defend America's constitutional values and principles with respect to what President Joe Biden referred to as the ongoing "battle between democracy and autocracy. Between liberty and repression. Between a rules-based order and one governed by brute force."

CHAPTER 3

Freedom of the Press

The architects of the American Constitution considered a free press—enshrined in the First Amendment—to be one of the linchpins of democracy. Thomas Jefferson wrote in 1786 that "our liberty depends on the freedom of the press, and that cannot be limited without being lost." A former head of the United Nations (UN) echoed that sentiment when stating, "Freedom of the press ensures that the abuse of every other freedom can be known, can be challenged, and even defeated." The landmark *New York Times Co. v. Sullivan* Supreme Court decision of 1964 further protected the rights of citizens to criticize public officials without fear of being sued for defamation (providing falsehoods are not expressed knowingly or with malice).

As Princeton University professor Eddie Glaude explained to MSNBC, "The fourth estate [the news media] is absolutely critical... to the functioning of this democracy. It's the way in which the citizenry acquires the information in order to engage in reasoned deliberation about the matters in front of them. It's the way in which we hold elites accountable...doing the investigative research to shed a light on the power operating in dark corners." Critically important, reasoned deliberation cannot occur in the absence of a common set of facts. Ron Chernow hammered this point home during his 2019 White House Correspondents' Dinner speech. "Without the facts, we cannot have agreement in our badly divided nation; more importantly, without the facts we cannot have an honest *dis*agreement." A free press also provides crucial information to the public during crises and amplifies expertise from trusted public institutions.

Journalism has professional and ethical standards that include accuracy and fairness. As with any profession, people can make mistakes or exercise poor judgment. Despite the political polarization that increasingly comes to define some media organizations, I would still contend that the majority of journalists in reputable news organizations take their ethical obligations seriously and correct mistakes quickly to preserve credibility and journalistic integrity. They should also strive for impartiality to retain trust. Being impartial, however, does not mean ignoring the ethical lapses and policy failures of public officials in an effort to appear unbiased. Like military attachés from every nation-state posted at embassies around the world, the role of a journalist, broadly speaking, is to observe and report with depth, context, and understanding.

As human beings, we are all subject to confirmation bias and will invariably approach a story through the filter of our own experiences, values, and beliefs. However, problematic bias thrives when professional journalists broadly choose not to report on an issue of public concern or intentionally emphasize certain facts over others. This intentional omission of facts dilutes context and hinders truth. Knowingly perpetuating demonstrably false narratives is likewise unacceptable. Opinion pieces can be useful, provided they are clearly represented as such. Finally, there are occasions when journalists should consider not printing something that might, in the aggregate, do more harm than good to society. An example might be the publication of a story (especially if unconfirmed) that is likely to incite violence against a minority group incapable of defending itself. As President Biden remarked at the 2022 White House Correspondents' Dinner, the protections granted to a free press by the Constitution come with "a very heavy obligation to seek the truth as best you can, not to inflame or entertain, but to illuminate and educate."

American presidents have historically "enjoyed" a love-hate relationship with the press. While at times unavoidably adversarial, the relationship can still be civil in order to better serve the public. President John F. Kennedy elaborated on the "abrasive quality of the press" when he explained, "Even though we never like it, and even though we wish they didn't write it, and even though we disapprove, there isn't any doubt that we could not do the job at all in a free society without a very, very active press." After the *New York Times* published a Pulitzer Prize–winning investigation about undisclosed civilian deaths resulting from America's military operations in Afghanistan, Iraq, and Syria, Defense Department spokesperson John Kirby acknowledged that the revelations were uncomfortable, unpleasant, and not simple to address. He went on to say, "But I guess that's the whole point. It's not supposed to be. That's what a free press at its very best does. It holds us to account and makes us think, even as it informs. It changes our minds. And it helps us…at our big job of defending this nation." In the Trump era, that included defending the nation from domestic threats to democracy.

The journalists who perform these vital functions often put

themselves at significant risk as they report from areas of armed conflict, natural disasters, or countries where journalists are routinely persecuted, jailed, and even killed by their own repressive governments. The organization Committee to Protect Journalists reported in late 2022 that 363 journalists were imprisoned. Sixty-seven journalists and media workers were killed in 2022. Five employees of the *Capital Gazette* in Annapolis, Maryland, were killed in a 2018 targeted attack. In that same year, CNN's Manhattan offices were evacuated when a pipe bomb mailed by a supporter of President Trump was discovered in the building. The courage exhibited by journalists operating in dangerous areas is arguably similar to the courage displayed by military personnel operating in harm's way. Journalists, however, are typically unarmed.

Some attacks on journalism promote the notion that fact-based reporting no longer exists and that journalism broadly serves only to weaponize information. This dangerous premise primarily serves those in power who work to replace facts with their own self-serving propaganda. One of the ways in which Trump encourages people to distrust information is to equate criticism with untruth. Taking a cue from Hitler, if critique is negative, it must also be a lie or "fake." From that false equivalence flows a natural pattern of denial. Filipino president Rodrigo Duterte also referred to certain outlets covering his government's numerous extrajudicial killings as "fake news" and, like Trump, occasionally banned certain reporters from official events. The kind of journalism we need to worry about is not that which criticizes those in power but rather that which provides propaganda on behalf of those in power. Theodore Roosevelt addressed the topic of presidential criticism, saying, "To announce that there must be no criticism of the President, or that we are to stand by the President, right or wrong, is not only unpatriotic and servile, but is morally treasonable to the American public. Nothing but the truth should be spoken about him or anyone else. But it is even more important to tell the truth, pleasant or unpleasant, about him than about anyone else."

President Trump might be forgiven for having dispensed with the tradition of attending the annual White House Correspondents' Dinner, but we cannot afford to disregard his flagrant attacks on journalism and a free press. The overarching goals of these attacks were to justify a decrease in his own transparency while also limiting the ability of traditional media outlets to provide accountability.

> @realDonaldTrump
> .....So, what the hell has happened to @FoxNews.
> Only I know! Chris Wallace and others should be on
> Fake News CNN or MSDNC. How's Shep Smith doing?
> Watch, this will be the beginning of the end for Fox,
> just like the other two which are dying in the ratings.
> Social Media is great!
> 10:44 AM - Jan 28, 2020

His contempt for more traditional media sources undermined fact-based deliberation, and his embrace of social media allowed him to proliferate his own information, whether factual or not. He did this in the pursuit of his own objectives and interests while attacking a pillar of American democracy: a free and independent press. His tactics for discrediting the media included (1) creating distrust, (2) fostering division, and (3) encouraging some degree of censorship.

Distrust. The following posts demonstrate how Trump hurled accusations of dishonesty and corruption in an effort to foster distrust.

> @realDonaldTrump
> Think how wonderful it is to be able to fight back and show, to so many, how totally dishonest the Fake News Media really is. It may be the most corrupt and disgusting business (almost) there is! MAKE AMERICA GREAT AGAIN!
> 6:27 PM - Aug 10, 2019

> @realDonaldTrump
> The Media is "Fixed" and Corrupt. It bears no relationship to the truth. The @nytimes & @washingtonpost are pure fiction. Totally dishonest reporting!
> 9:49 AM - Oct 5, 2019

The following post's "They get it" statement is an attempt to persuade people—through projection and flattery—that they are regularly being deceived and of course smart enough to know it.

> @realDonaldTrump
> Check out Tweets from last two days. I refer to Fake News Media when mentioning Enemy of the People - but dishonest reporters use only the word "Media." The people of our Great Country are angry and disillusioned at receiving so much Fake News. They get it, and fully understand!
> 5:14 PM - Oct 29, 2018

Division. The following demonstrate attempts to create division and an adversarial relationship between the public and the media.

@realDonaldTrump

The Fake News Media has NEVER been more Dishonest or Corrupt than it is right now. There has never been a time like this in American History. Very exciting but also, very sad! Fake News is the absolute Enemy of the People and our Country itself!

5:24 AM - Mar 19, 2019

@realDonaldTrump

.....ALSO, NOT TRUE! Anything goes with our Corrupt News Media today. They will do, or say, whatever it takes, with not even the slightest thought of consequence! These are true cowards and without doubt, THE ENEMY OF THE PEOPLE!

6:15 PM - Jun 15, 2019

@realDonaldTrump

People are disgusted and embarrassed by the Fake News Media, as headed by the @nytimes, @washingtonpost, @comcast & MSDNC, @ABC, @CBSNews and more. They no longer believe what they see and read, and for good reason. Fake News is, indeed, THE ENEMY OF THE PEOPLE!

4:13 PM - Mar 1, 2020

The expression "enemy of the people" serves to create opposing sides. Though it has been around for centuries, the expression was

WHAT HANGS IN THE BALANCE

used more prominently in the twentieth century by dictators such as Stalin and Mao who were responsible for the deaths of millions of their own citizens. More recently, Vladimir Putin used the terms *fascist* and *Nazi* to refer to Russians who opposed the 2022 invasion of Ukraine. After Trump began labeling much of the media as the "enemy of the people," major media outlets were compelled to use security guards at his political rallies.

President Trump was right to warn about so-called fake news, but he was too often the source of it. His behavior provided ammunition for autocrats around the world. The news reports Trump referred to as "negative stories" were usually based in fact, often using his own words. Trump also employed hypocrisy and projection when attacking the press. With the latter, he aimed to equate his own views with those of the public. "People love it when you attack the press," he once proclaimed. In the following post, he tried to supplant the role of the media with the suggestion that it was he who was providing a "great service" to the public.

> @realDonaldTrump
> The Fake News hates me saying that they are the Enemy of the People only because they know it's TRUE. I am providing a great service by explaining this to the American People. They purposely cause great division & distrust. They can also cause War! They are very dangerous & sick!
> 4:38 AM - Aug 5, 2018

President Trump disparaged reporters and referred to them with unflattering nicknames. He also enjoyed renaming their shows.

60

Examples include "Deface the Nation," "Morning Joke," and "Meet the Corrupt Press."

Censorship. This is one method for a government to attack the press. Within weeks of Russia's invasion of Ukraine in February 2022, Russia's government began dismantling its own free and independent press, resulting in what some experts referred to as a total information blackout regarding the unfolding humanitarian disaster. The Russian parliament went so far as to pass a law criminalizing reporting that it considered disinformation (with sentences up to fifteen years). Examples included referring to the invasion as a "war" instead of the preferred phrase "special military operation." President Putin's propaganda machine was further strengthened as the Russian government censored independent Western media organizations that eventually began removing their journalists from the country in an effort to protect them from the new law. The following Trump post reminds me of the quip that 70 percent of statistics are made up on the spot. More concerning, his suggestion to "take away credentials" highlights the threat of censorship via the restriction of media access as a way to impede legitimate criticism.

@realDonaldTrump

The Fake News is working overtime. Just reported that, despite the tremendous success we are having with the economy & all things else, 91% of the Network News about me is negative (Fake). Why do we work so hard in working with the media when it is corrupt? Take away credentials?

4:38 AM - May 9, 2018

Former Central Intelligence Agency (CIA) analyst, White House briefer, and author Cindy Otis put the president's attacks in perspective: "Trump's continued attacks on our constitutional right to a free press is one of the most alarming things he's doing. It's one of the biggest factors intel analysts look at when analyzing democratic backsliding in foreign countries, and it's a key precursor to authoritarianism."

The sowing of distrust in American mainstream media has yielded a disturbingly widespread skepticism of facts that should not be in dispute, increasing the likelihood that people might proliferate their own potentially dangerous conspiracy theories. That can be disastrous in times of national emergency. The threat to a free press puts nothing less than the accountability of our elected officials and therefore our democracy at risk. It is incumbent upon every leader in public service to vigorously defend the First Amendment's freedom of the press.

Part 2

★ ★ ★

ORGANIZATIONAL LEADERSHIP AND MANAGEMENT

CHAPTER 4

Understanding Your Role

Who Put That in My Job Description?

★ ★ ★

Leadership and management are distinct disciplines, but the competencies required for each are overlapping and complementary. Both disciplines, when skillfully employed, allow public organizations to achieve their stated objectives. While this book focuses primarily on leadership, the following definition of *public management* from G. Edward DeSeve demonstrates the necessity of competent and ethical leadership in public service:

> The stewardship activity that allocates resources to implement public policies in the most economical way possible using people, technology and systems in unique combinations to create delighted customers, to promote public trust and to accomplish pre-determined positive outcomes with requisite integrity.

This chapter briefly addresses a selection of essential leadership *responsibilities* and *competencies.* The responsibilities include:

- providing vision
- defining and prioritizing objectives
- communicating expectations
- taking care of one's people
- being an effective custodian of one's position
- grooming future leaders

The leadership *competencies* addressed include a thorough understanding of:

- one's position
- the limits of one's authority
- obligatory versus optional duties
- subordinate roles
- the relationship between authority and responsibility

Leadership responsibilities. People want to know why their work matters in the context of organizational purpose, but the vast majority of employees in an organization will be necessarily focused on their specialized roles, leaving limited bandwidth for strategic organizational thinking. It is leadership's responsibility to develop and clearly communicate an organization's vision statement.

A bold, aspirational yet realistic vision statement serves to inspire employees of what the organization can achieve in its ideal state. In an organizational context, leaders do not create "miracles" themselves. Rather, their visions for an organization create environments where miracles can happen and where people are motivated to overcome obstacles to success. Leaders must also promote organizational cultures that support the vision, a process that may require shifting peoples' mindsets and behaviors.

Bono (of the rock band U2) has referred to "the right to be ridiculous," which I interpret as the courage to dream big and to persist in the accomplishment of goals most would think unattainable. Bono demonstrated this notion when he facilitated what he once described as getting two people into a room who would normally have no business being together. His vision of bringing together politicians with disparate ideologies (in addition to his own meeting with evangelical senator Jesse Helms) facilitated the George W. Bush administration's implementation and funding of the U.S. President's Emergency Plan for AIDS Relief (PEPFAR). The resulting investments provided antiretroviral drugs that helped to achieve epidemic control of HIV in at least twenty countries. The program is credited for having saved approximately twenty million lives.

Defining and prioritizing objectives. Vision statements are supported by mission statements and realistic organizational objectives that promote mission success. While the development of objectives sometimes falls to an agency's managers and subject matter experts, leaders facilitate the process by providing direction and communicating clear priorities. To foster trust, leaders must also ensure that the mission and objectives of the organization are well understood by external stakeholders (such as the public). This is especially important when an organization is contending with a crisis or proposing the enactment of significant policy reforms.

Communicating expectations. Managers and their subordinates cannot meet leadership expectations for job performance and personal conduct if they do not understand them. Effective leaders first lead by example, then communicate specifically to their teams regarding roles, core competencies, and values. Only then can results be effectively measured against leadership expectations. Subordinates will take cues both from what is spoken explicitly and communicated implicitly through behavior. They will then make corresponding judgments about what is encouraged, permissible, tolerated, and frowned upon.

Caring for your people. Leaders are ultimately responsible for the effectiveness and welfare of their people. If you attend to the needs of your people, empower them, and foster an atmosphere of trust, your people will take care of the mission.

Custodial responsibility. The reputation of a specific leadership position, for better or worse, will transcend the tenure of its short-term occupant. If that reputation is damaged through inappropriate action or incompetence, the result could be diminished subordinate and public trust that extends well beyond the offending leader's tenure. Public organizations that do not enjoy public trust and buy-in tend to perform more poorly, which in turn further erodes public trust. In the following, President Obama addressed the notion that leadership positions outlast their occupants:

> The office [of the presidency] humbles you. You're reminded daily that in this great democracy, you are but a relay swimmer in the currents of history, bound by decisions made by those who came before, reliant on the efforts of those who will follow to fully vindicate your vision.

Grooming leaders. Author and political activist Ralph Nader famously said, "The function of leadership is to produce more leaders, not more followers." We do not need leaders who merely want a cadre of followers. Rather, we need leaders who recognize the importance of developing capable and ethical people who will eventually succeed them. With respect to nurturing those with leadership potential, experts often tout training as more important than recruitment.

In grooming leaders, we should accept that we may never see the fruits of our labors. As the proverb says, "Sometimes leadership is planting trees under whose shade you will never sit." It was in that context that Thomas Jefferson wrote, "But though an old man, I am but a young gardener." It is out of concern for the organization and the beneficiaries of its work that one puts ego aside and accepts the task of grooming leaders. An organization that is unable to effectively train and groom people for leadership will be less effective in implementing cultural transformation, a requirement during times of crisis.

Position-specific competencies. *Understanding your position.* For a wide range of leaders, from military commanders in times of peace or war to elected officials confronting emergencies, incompetence can cost lives. A study conducted by the Center for Creative Leadership—a nonprofit provider of leadership development and a pioneer in the field of global leadership research based in Greensboro, North Carolina—found that 38 to 50 percent of executives in new leadership positions fail during their first eighteen months. They fail primarily because they do not properly assess the needs of their new environments. The extent of one's willingness and ability to adapt to a new position and operating environment will determine success or failure.

One must have the requisite knowledge to perform one's leadership functions effectively, despite having access to advisors who are experts in their fields. Learning is a continuous process, and preparation for a leadership position should begin before actually assuming that post. The process might begin with studying the mission and structure of one's prospective organization as well as any applicable governing directives. Upon assuming a new position, request informational briefings from one's subordinates. This demonstrates intellectual curiosity, humility, and a genuine desire to increase one's professional knowledge. One should strive to obtain a broad span of operational and institutional knowledge, even beyond the scope of one's immediate responsibilities. Aim to thoroughly understand what services the agency provides and to which internal and external customers they are provided. Finally, avoid remaining mentally anchored to the methodologies and assumptions of one's previous position or specialty. That said, consider that some of that previously acquired experience and expertise may prove useful or even necessary as one transfers into the new position.

Limits to authority. Competent leaders have a clear understanding of what their unique authorities are, while also critically grasping the limits of those authorities. Not understanding the latter could result in inappropriate influence or even unlawful actions. While you may legitimately require legal advice in the course of your duties from time to time, your subordinates should not have to regularly remind you that the action you want to take would violate an existing law or treaty. This, according to former secretary of state Rex Tillerson, was a routine occurrence during his interactions with President Trump.

About two months into the COVID-19 pandemic, the governors of many states were reluctant to ease measures they deemed necessary for containing the spread of the virus. In his effort to "reopen" the states, President Trump declared that he had the authority to override governors with respect to lifting stay-at-home orders and restrictions on businesses. "When somebody's the president of the United States, the authority is total, and that's the way it's got to be," he declared, without offering any legal basis for his claim.

@realDonaldTrump
For the purpose of creating conflict and confusion, some in the Fake News Media are saying that it is the Governors decision to open up the states, not that of the President of the United States & the Federal Government. Let it be fully understood that this is incorrect....
....It is the decision of the President, and for many good reasons. With that being said, the Administration and I are working closely with the Governors, and this will continue. A decision by me, in conjunction with the Governors and input from others, will be made shortly!
10:53 AM - Apr 13, 2020

The president had to walk back those claims of authority the next day, conceding that the governors would be running their states.

Obligatory versus optional duties. It is important to understand the difference between roles you are expected to perform and those considered discretionary. Just prior to President Trump's first impeachment trial in the U.S. Senate, several senators expressed an unwillingness to conduct themselves as impartial jurors. That is, they intended to ignore their constitutional duties to evaluate the evidence diligently and objectively before rendering a judgment. As the trial was ending, Senator Mitt Romney addressed those intentions along with similar arguments made by President Trump's defense team:

> The defense argues that the Senate should leave the impeachment decision to the voters. While that logic is appealing to our democratic instincts, it is inconsistent with the Constitution's requirement that the Senate, not the voters, try the president. Hamilton explained that the Founders' decision to invest senators with this obligation rather than leave it to voters was intended to minimize—to the extent possible—the partisan sentiments of the public. This verdict is ours to render. The people will judge us for how well and faithfully we fulfilled our duty. The grave question the Constitution tasks senators to answer is whether the President committed an act so extreme and egregious that it rises to the level of a "high crime and misdemeanor." Yes, he did.

Understanding the roles of your subordinates. Your ability to delineate and successfully deploy subordinate roles, responsibilities, and authorities depends on your understanding of the same. Without that knowledge, you are less likely to effectively empower your subordinates and less likely to know from whom to seek advice and how best to delegate. The head of a racing team may not have the skills to drive or design the car, but by developing a keen understanding of those individual roles and corresponding expertise, he or she can more effectively delegate leadership tasks, provide a framework for team members to perform at their best, and foster an environment of mutual trust.

In February 2020, President Trump stated the following: "I'm actually, I guess, the chief law enforcement officer of the country." Though a president nominates and supervises the chief law enforcement officer (who is appointed with the advice and consent of the Senate), a president is not in fact the attorney general of the United States despite Article II of the Constitution stating that presidents "shall take Care that the Laws be faithfully executed." The president's confusion or potential ignorance highlights the importance of understanding the difference between overseeing certain authorities and actually having those authorities. This is an important concept in public service because of the many authorities that are designed to function with a necessary degree of independence. Justice Department investigations and inspector general programs (discussed in a later chapter) are two such examples.

The relationship between authority and responsibility. In my own career, nothing motivated me more than being personally responsible for mission success and the welfare of others. A leader's given authorities are usually proportional to their given responsibilities. Increased authority or power for its own sake is unfortunately the primary objective and source of fulfillment for some. The primary motivation for receiving additional authority should correlate directly to the fulfillment that comes from a greater sense of responsibility for improving the organization and ensuring mission success.

CHAPTER 5

Understanding Your Organization

★ ★ ★

The caliber of an organization's leadership will often determine if customers experience either profoundly positive or profoundly negative outcomes. With the stakes this high, a leader needs to understand their organization's core functions, limits of authority, internal policies and processes, external agency relationships, and history—including best practices. What you do not know can hurt you. Ignorance in any of these areas can lead to poor decision-making, poor resource allocation, fiscal irresponsibility, regulatory noncompliance, and ethical violations. Any one of these lapses could result in a disruption of services or, worse yet, mission failure.

The examples provided in the following pages highlight the importance of understanding (1) the directives that govern an organization, (2) an agency's relationship to external and subordinate organizations, and (3) an organization's history.

Organizational directives. Public leaders cannot afford to be ignorant about the laws and directives that regulate their organizations. National leadership, in particular, requires an understanding of the major tenets of domestic and international law.

When the United States is a signatory to an international law or treaty, through either executive agreement or Senate ratification, respectively, those laws and treaties become binding upon the United States. When President Trump threatened in the following post to target Iranian cultural sites, he was apparently unaware that such an act would constitute a war crime because it violates prohibitions against targeting cultural property that is devoid of military value.

> @realDonaldTrump
> ....targeted 52 Iranian sites (representing the 52 American hostages taken by Iran many years ago), some at a very high level & important to Iran & the Iranian culture, and those targets, and Iran itself, WILL BE HIT VERY FAST AND VERY HARD. The USA wants no more threats!
> 2:52 PM - Jan 4, 2020

Questioned on the legality of his threat, the president equivocated while stating, "If that's what the law is, I like to obey the law." It is certainly easier to comply with laws when you are aware of them. The commander in chief should have been and was most likely briefed (as are all members of the U.S. military) on the basics of the Law of Armed Conflict and the Geneva Conventions.

The president also demonstrated his ignorance of election laws. Ballots arriving *after* Election Day—primarily mail-in ballots that have been postmarked by Election Day, including those sent by overseas military personnel—can be legally counted in over twenty states.

> @realDonaldTrump
> ANY VOTE THAT CAME IN AFTER ELECTION DAY WILL
> NOT BE COUNTED!
> 10:09 AM - Nov 5, 2020

The Justice Department enjoys a tradition of independence from political interference but is nonetheless part of the executive branch and therefore technically subordinate to the president of the United States, who should be somewhat familiar with the basic tenets of criminal investigation and trial proceedings. In the following post, the president mistakenly suggested that crimes must be proven prior to the initiation of an investigation. It is not clear if he was guilty of ignorance or, alternatively, deliberately attempting to misinform his followers.

> @realDonaldTrump
> "The Lisa Page (FBI) transcript also confirms earlier
> reporting that Page testified Russian Collusion was
> still unproven when Special Counsel Robert Mueller
> was appointed." Catherine Herridge, @FoxNews In
> other words they appointed someone when there was
> (and is) no crime. Bad!
> 3:47 PM - Mar 13, 2019

In the following example, the president appeared not to understand that the crime of obstruction of justice does not require an underlying crime. A person can obstruct an investigation without having committed the crime(s) under investigation.

> @realDonaldTrump
> NO COLLUSION, NO OBSTRUCTION. **Besides, how**
> **can you have Obstruction when not only was there**
> **No Collusion (by Trump),** but the bad actions were
> done by the "other" side? The greatest con-job in the
> history of American Politics!
> 6:03 AM - May 1, 2019

In this final example, the president was keen to share the ridiculous notion that whistleblower programs apparently do not apply to all federal agencies.

> @realDonaldTrump
> "I think it's outrages that a Whistleblower is a CIA
> Agent." Ed Rollins @FoxNews
> 10:12 AM - Oct 4, 2019

External and subordinate agency relationships. Every public organization has relationships with external agencies. They include program beneficiaries, oversight agencies, external stakeholders, foreign entities, the media, and various advocacy organizations. In order to maintain mutually beneficial relationships with external agencies, one must understand their expectations and be clear on respective roles and responsibilities. President Trump, for example, struggled with the reality that Congress does indeed have legitimate oversight responsibilities and authorities vis-à-vis the executive branch.

One must also understand an organization's relationship to subordinate or quasi-subordinate entities and, more specifically, how the organization is expected to support those entities. Support may include guidance, resources, and coordination with other agencies on their behalf. In the following, the president should have known that it is the governor of an affected state who must request a federal declaration of a major disaster.

@realDonaldTrump

At the request of Senator Thom Tillis, I am getting the North Carolina Emergency Declaration completed and signed tonight. Hope you won't need it!

8:43 PM - Sep 3, 2019

Organizational history. A familiarity with organizational history and past performance, as provided through inspection reports and other sources of historical data, provides numerous benefits. Retrospect provides important context and perspective for planning, decision-making, and process improvement. It may also reveal systemic problems. The better one understands organizational lessons learned, the less likely one will be to make "avoidable" mistakes. Likewise, it is important to understand the value of original justifications for processes and best practices still in use. Such knowledge will inform decisions about which processes and policies to keep in place.

For leadership at the national level, a familiarity with national and world history (and the history of policy related to your particular field) provides similar benefits. Leaders must be perpetual learners and be committed to personal growth, which includes the study of history and its patterns. Historical patterns remind us that it is dangerous to believe in the inevitable continuation of current and perhaps favorable conditions.

Historical lessons must be understood and applied to avoid repeating mistakes that lead to tragedies. One example is the importance of understanding the costs of war and the mistakes that lead to avoidable conflict. President Kennedy's reading of *The Guns of August* taught him important lessons about how European empires stumbled into the First World War, a conflict that claimed approximately forty million lives. He was determined that the United States and the Soviet Union avoid similar mistakes, and he allowed those lessons to inform his actions during the Cuban Missile Crisis of 1962.

In another example of the moral utility of studying history, author Jonathan Glover recounts one soldier's heroic actions during the Vietnam War. Hugh Thompson protected defenseless villagers from the wrath of his American compatriots during the My Lai massacre because he "remembered the Nazis also shot people in ditches."

In the following post, a better understanding of the historical significance of lynching in America might have precluded the use of that word.

> @realDonaldTrump
> So some day, if a Democrat becomes President and the Republicans win the House, even by a tiny margin, they can impeach the President, without due process or fairness or any legal rights. All Republicans must remember what they are witnessing here - a lynching. But we will WIN!
> 7:52 AM - Oct 22, 2019

Understanding the history of our national values allows us to recognize when they are being neglected, and also how they might reasonably evolve with changes in societal sentiment. As people took to the streets of America in the summer of 2020 to protest police brutality and demand social justice, there was a renewed emphasis on removing prominently displayed monuments celebrating Confederate generals of the Civil War. The majority of these monuments were created in the late nineteenth and early twentieth centuries to celebrate those who defended slavery in the American South. They are not to be confused with monuments erected during or immediately after the Civil War to commemorate Confederate casualties. The monuments glorifying the Confederate cause also served to intimidate African Americans already suffering under Jim Crow laws. Even the Confederacy's top general, Robert E. Lee, was opposed to the postwar construction of statues honoring him. By 2020, there was still no overwhelming consensus among Americans regarding the appropriateness of these statues in prominent public spaces. President Trump's defense of leaving the monuments in place seemed to ignore the historical record and the concerns of African Americans in particular.

@realDonaldTrump
This is a battle to save the Heritage, History, and Greatness of our Country! #MAGA2020
7:00 PM - Jun 30, 2020

@realDonaldTrump
Very sad to see States allowing roving gangs of wise guys, anarchists & looters, many of them having no

idea what they are doing, indiscriminately ripping
down our statues and monuments to the past. Some
are great works of art, but all represent our History &
Heritage, both....

....the good and the bad. It is important for
us to understand and remember, even in turbulent
and difficult times, and learn from them. Knowledge
comes from the most unusual of places!

11:45 PM - Jun 24, 2020

The president was correct in suggesting that there be an orderly
and legal process to determine the fate of these monuments. But
leaders must be able to differentiate between the need to understand
history and the apparent need to prominently display objects that
are offensive to many because they glorify a previous way of life that
is incompatible with our national values and principles. Monuments
to the Holocaust, for example, do not celebrate the Nazi architects
of genocide. Germans have increasingly not shied away from memo-
rializing the horrors associated with this shameful period in their
history. Their museums serve to educate and perhaps atone for those
episodes. They do not serve to glorify them, unlike the statues of
Civil War generals.

In late 2022, pursuant to a Defense Department order, the
United States Military Academy at West Point began removing
Confederate monuments and symbols from its campus. The
congressionally created commission recommending the removals
emphasized that the intent was not to erase history but rather "to
affirm West Point's long tradition of educating future generations
of America's military leaders to represent the best of our national

ideals." It acknowledged that cadets should continue to learn about the Civil War "with all the quality and complex detail our national past deserves."

Similar to the removal of Civil War statues, a campaign was initiated during President Trump's tenure to change the designations of U.S. military installations named after Confederate generals.

@realDonaldTrump
It has been suggested that we should rename as many as 10 of our Legendary Military Bases, such as Fort Bragg in North Carolina, Fort Hood in Texas, Fort Benning in Georgia, etc. These Monumental and very Powerful Bases have become part of a Great American Heritage, and a...

...history of Winning, Victory, and Freedom. The United States of America trained and deployed our HEROES on these Hallowed Grounds, and won two World Wars. Therefore, my Administration will not even consider the renaming of these Magnificent and Fabled Military Installations...

...Our history as the Greatest Nation in the World will not be tampered with. Respect our Military!
2:40 PM - Jun 10, 2020

@realDonaldTrump
THOSE THAT DENY THEIR HISTORY ARE DOOMED TO REPEAT IT!
10:09 AM - Jun 11, 2020

@realDonaldTrump

"Don't throw the American story into the river, don't throw it into the lake. Be proud of it." @kilmeade @ foxandfriends

7:51 AM - Jul 10, 2020

In a statement explaining the reasons he refused to sign the National Defense Authorization Act for Fiscal Year 2021, President Trump cited a clause supported by America's military leaders to rename some of the bases honoring Confederate leaders. Trump's statement read in part, "I have been clear in my opposition to politically motivated attempts like this to wash away history and to dishonor the immense progress our country has fought for in realizing our founding principles." The president conflated the names of the installations with history and the legacy of the men and women who had served there, as if they were somehow inextricably linked. Replacing the names with those who better represent America's founding values and the present-day, predominant values of the country is not a denial of history. Rather, it is an affirmation of progress, of not embracing the worst in our past, and ultimately an affirmation of who we aspire to be.

As nations, and as people, we cannot choose the history
that we inherit. But we can choose what lessons to draw from it,
and use those lessons to chart our own futures.
—President Barack Obama

CHAPTER 6

Serving Your People

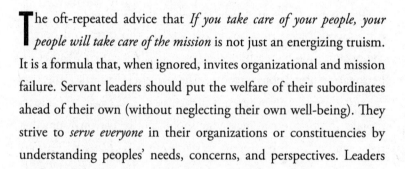

The oft-repeated advice that *If you take care of your people, your people will take care of the mission* is not just an energizing truism. It is a formula that, when ignored, invites organizational and mission failure. Servant leaders should put the welfare of their subordinates ahead of their own (without neglecting their own well-being). They strive to *serve everyone* in their organizations or constituencies by understanding peoples' needs, concerns, and perspectives. Leaders also serve their people through *respect* and *empowerment*.

Serving everyone. In the context of social, economic, and environmental justice, U2's Bono reminded us that *where* you live should not determine *if* you live. Thomas Jefferson promoted the idea—clearly aspirational at the time—that "when brought together in society, all are perfectly equal, whether foreign or domestic, titled or untitled, in or out of office." Ensuring equal and fair access to opportunities and resources promotes unity of purpose. Paraphrasing what former presidents Truman and Kennedy stated more eloquently in the context of being "everyone's president," organizational leaders serve everyone, because they are by virtue of their positions uniquely responsible for everyone's welfare.

Being "everyone's leader" sometimes requires transcending one's background, experiences, and beliefs. President Harry Truman transcended his own cultural and political upbringing by eventually deciding to integrate the U.S. military and promote civil rights. Similarly, Benjamin Franklin changed his long-standing prejudices regarding the potential of African Americans after visiting a classroom of Black children. Franklin described this successful evolution of belief as exceptionally difficult and a test of one's humanity. He would become in his final years an ardent abolitionist.

Good leaders must avoid the tendency to cater to people in the organization with whom they more easily identify, whether for personal or professional reasons. The perception that a leader has "favorites" (especially when not merit-based) can negatively impact morale. In this context, messaging should not be narrowly aimed at those who perform best, more fervently support their leader, or are presumed to be more receptive to the message. A recurring element in President Trump's messaging was an exaggerated focus on his base of support versus his general constituency.

@realDonaldTrump

My supporters are the smartest, strongest, most hard working and most loyal that we have seen in our countries history. It is a beautiful thing to watch as **we win** elections and gather support from all over the country. **As we get stronger,** so does our country. Best numbers ever!

6:12 AM - Jun 16, 2018

There is a time and a place for campaign-style rhetoric. The previous post more closely resembles something I would expect to see from the fan club of my favorite rock band. In contrast, unifiers attempt to reach even those least likely to be receptive to their messaging. They appeal to peoples' best instincts with the understanding that they cannot always please or even reach everyone.

Another practice that weakens organizational unity is unnecessarily categorizing subordinates or constituents, as demonstrated in the following post:

> @realDonaldTrump
> As our Country rapidly grows stronger and smarter, I want to wish all of my friends, supporters, enemies, haters, and even the very dishonest Fake News Media, a Happy and Healthy New Year. 2018 will be a great year for America!
> 2:18 PM - Dec 31, 2017

When you serve all Americans, there is no justifiable reason to separate them by their level of enthusiasm for you. In an organizational context, *consciously* categorizing people (on top of potential implicit or unconscious bias) promotes favoritism toward some and potentially even unwarranted mistrust of the "others." I witnessed this phenomenon firsthand in the military when some married leaders subtly provided considerations to married officers not afforded to single officers. I similarly observed another leader appear to favor those whose religious beliefs more closely aligned with his own.

Serving everyone sometimes requires protecting minority interests in the face of significant opposition, especially when the majority sentiment is unjust. An oft-cited example is Chief Justice Earl Warren's 1954 decision in *Brown v. Board of Education*, which ended legalized segregation in schools. Despite the fact that some Southern states actively resisted integration and that American opinion on the issue was essentially split, Warren was guided by the Constitution's core values and principles and worked to ensure the landmark decision was unanimous (8-0, with one abstention). Public support for the decision continued to grow in subsequent decades.

Understanding your people. Maintaining the pulse of your subordinates or constituents is an important facet of serving everyone. You cannot effectively influence others if you do not understand them. To know your people is to understand their values, their aspirations, their motivations, their challenges, and the state of their well-being. You should also understand what they expect from the organization's leaders and managers and the degree to which they approve of the overall direction of the organization.

> *Leaders in every field need more than anything else to know*
> *human nature, to know the needs of the human soul.*
> —THEODORE ROOSEVELT

A study of executives in senior leadership positions identified its subjects as either "arrivers" (those who succeeded) or "derailers" (those who did not). The study noted that "the ability—or inability—to understand other people's perspectives was the most glaring difference between the two groups." It is important to understand the perspectives of others when marshaling teams toward a common goal, especially when those teams are personally, culturally, and professionally diverse. President Abraham Lincoln was renowned for his ability to grasp the emotional and professional needs of the members of his politically and geographically diverse cabinet. His social awareness and empathy—components of emotional intelligence (EQ)—enabled him to manage and influence the cabinet such that they supported his policies at critical junctures during the Civil War. A high EQ is what distinguishes successful leaders from their less successful peers.

The art of respectfully addressing disparate perspectives sometimes requires that one step away from the views and opinions informed by one's own experiences.

> @realDonaldTrump
> Our Country is Free, Beautiful and Very Successful. If you hate our Country, or if you are not happy here, you can leave!
> 5:17 AM - Jul 16, 2019

An alternative to President Trump's binary "love it or leave it" approach would have been a sincere effort to understand why some people are not satisfied with their personal circumstances or, more generally, the state of the union. The president's post implicitly suggested that displeasure with the president's policies, priorities, or values corresponded to irrational or unjustified grievance. Other than for exceptions like extreme or dangerous beliefs, one need not devalue the sentiments of others when addressing differences. As with leader-subordinate relationships, government agencies should also strive to understand the requirements, expectations, and preferences of the people and stakeholders they serve. These efforts will go a long way toward earning and maintaining public trust and support.

A leader who is tone-deaf or out of touch with the needs or desires of his or her subordinates will erode trust and morale. As my classmates and I were about to graduate from Air Force pilot training, we were informed that we would soon be choosing from a list of available assignments (top in class chose first, and so on). I learned that it was our commander's intent to keep the options (aircraft choices and base locations) secret until the entire class was gathered for the formal selection process. I informed him that this "game show" format was unacceptable to me and my classmates. We were appalled that he somehow thought it was either desirable or appropriate for people to make instantaneous selections (for themselves and their families) from a list of disparate jobs whose locations spanned the globe. To his credit, he was eventually persuaded to provide us the list of available assignments in advance, affording us the opportunity to research and evaluate the options while also discussing among ourselves what choices we intended to make.

Being out of touch unfortunately happens at the highest levels of leadership. On the first full day of President Trump's presidency, millions of people across the United States participated in what was generally known as the Women's March. The demonstrations addressed perceived threats to, among other issues, women's rights, reproductive rights, and the president's demonstrated (and recorded) history of misogyny. Their concerns were apparently lost on him.

@realDonaldTrump

Watched protests yesterday but was under the impression that we just had an election! Why didn't these people vote? Celebs hurt cause badly.

4:47 AM - Jan 22, 2017

After invading Iraq in 2003, the U.S. military learned how ethnocentrism and a lack of cultural awareness could hamper local cooperation and, ultimately, operational success. In an episode involving cultural considerations in the United States nearly two decades later, there was mounting pressure to rename American sports teams whose names and mascots had long offended Native American groups. President Trump, however, seemed unable or unwilling to understand those concerns.

@realDonaldTrump

They name teams out of STRENGTH, not weakness, but now the Washington Redskins & Cleveland Indians, two fabled sports franchises, look like they are going to be changing their names in order to be politically correct. Indians, like Elizabeth Warren, must be very angry right now!

2:13 PM - Jul 6, 2020

Following an avoidable government shutdown in early 2019, many federal employees (including more than forty-two thousand personnel in the United States Coast Guard) were temporarily required to work without pay for over five weeks. Some were forced to rely on food pantries and other forms of financial assistance. Their hardship was involuntary and avoidable. The president might have apologized instead of thanking them.

@realDonaldTrump
To all of the great people who are working so hard for your Country and not getting paid I say, THANK YOU - YOU ARE GREAT PATRIOTS! We must now work together, after decades of abuse, to finally fix the Humanitarian, Criminal & Drug Crisis at our Border. WE WILL WIN BIG!
5:25 PM - Jan 20, 2019

Accessibility. Accessibility provides a crucial window into what is happening in your organization. It also allows your people to seek clarification and assistance. Open-door policies and organizational town hall meetings promote accessibility. Another way to make oneself accessible to others is to spend time with one's people in their work environments. A leader's presence can have an enormous impact on morale, demonstrating to subordinates that they and their efforts are valued. Never think of yourself as too important to interact with subordinates in a situation as fleeting as a passing "Hello" or "How are you?" Momentary and simple displays of kindness, concern, and decency go a long way toward building respect, trust, and loyalty.

Our country needs a commander in chief who takes care of our troops in the same way he would his own family.
— FORMER SECRETARY OF STATE
(AND RETIRED GENERAL) COLIN POWELL

You should also, to some degree, feel personally responsible for your subordinates' well-being. Though leaders may not be able to influence the majority of their personal choices, they should be well equipped to provide support and advice and refer subordinates to professional resources that can provide the help they need.

Respect. Studies suggest that the ability to show respect is the key behavioral trait necessary for achieving positive organizational outcomes, promoting healthy work cultures, and securing the commitment of subordinates.

> *If we just take people as they are, we make them worse;*
> *If we treat them as if they were meant to be,*
> *we get them where they need to be.*
> —Johann Wolfgang von Goethe

A work environment devoid of respect for others will result in the loss of your best people—that is, the people who respect themselves. Respect is necessarily practiced as a means to an end, though it should also be practiced as a means unto itself. While those who contribute more to an organization deserve more professional respect and recognition, personal respect should be afforded to everyone. Being accessible and seeking to understand the concerns of others (listening), even when there are major disagreements, are two ways to show respect. The Center for Creative Leadership suggests cultivating respect through recognition, through transparency with respect to policies and procedures, by clarifying decision-making processes, and by seeking input regarding those processes.

One of the simplest ways to model respectful behavior involves the manner in which one addresses subordinates. When President Lincoln wrote to General Grant during the Civil War, the letter was addressed to "Major General Grant," and the opening line began with, "My dear general." Lincoln was technically entitled to use Grant's first name (though not likely the custom at the time) but chose to respect Grant's position and authority. Effective leaders similarly model respect in the way they address subordinate leaders and managers who have their own subordinates present. For example, despite holding the lowest officer rank (second lieutenant) in my first Air Force assignment, my boss understood the importance of addressing me as "lieutenant" or "LT" in front of my enlisted subordinates. He was simultaneously setting the example for how I should respectfully address my own subordinate managers.

There were countless instances where President Trump did not afford his subordinates the respect they deserved. As mentioned, while serving as U.S. ambassador to Ukraine, Marie Yovanovitch championed Ukrainian anti-corruption reforms. At the same time, President Trump's personal attorney, Rudy Giuliani, along with corrupt Ukrainian prosecutor Yuriy Lutsenko, were orchestrating a concerted smear campaign against Yovanovitch. This unfortunate episode was detailed in the *Trump-Ukraine Impeachment Inquiry Report*:

> The attacks against Ambassador Yovanovitch were amplified by prominent, close allies of President Trump, including Mr. Giuliani and his associates, Sean Hannity, and Donald Trump Jr....In the face of attacks driven by Mr. Lutsenko and the President's allies, Ambassador Yovanovitch and other senior State Department officials

asked Secretary of State Mike Pompeo to issue a statement of support for her and for the U.S. Embassy in Ukraine. The Secretary declined, fearing that President Trump might publicly undermine those efforts, possibly through a tweet.

As explained publicly by both Giuliani and his associate Lev Parnas, the primary objective of the smear campaign was to have Yovanovitch removed (as requested by Lutsenko). Her removal would have made it easier for corrupt Ukrainian prosecutors to announce an investigation into Trump's political rival, then former vice president Joe Biden.

In early 2019, Yovanovitch was told that she needed to return to the United States immediately. No one in her supervisory chain was able (or had the courage) to provide an explanation for the recall. She was eventually told by the State Department that the president had lost confidence in her, but she was never provided a substantive justification for her removal. Several months later, during Trump's July 25, 2019, phone call to newly elected Ukrainian president Zelenskyy, he disparaged and threatened Yovanovitch, telling Zelenskyy, "The former ambassador from the United States, the woman, was bad news and the people she was dealing with in the Ukraine were bad news, so I just want to let you know that…Well, she's going to go through some things." During her testimony to Congress, Yovanovitch acknowledged that she felt threatened after learning of the president's phone call. A final act of disrespect in this episode was Trump's direction to Yovanovitch and other executive branch officials to risk their careers by defying legitimate congressional subpoenas issued during the course of his first impeachment inquiry.

Empowerment. Entrusting employees with a reasonable degree of independence and meaningful decision-making authority builds confidence and motivation. Empowerment is the polar opposite of micromanagement and an important way to prepare people for increased responsibility and positions of leadership. Trust is reciprocal. Leaders who demonstrate trust are more likely to be trusted by their followers, something essential for leadership success, employee productivity and satisfaction, and, therefore, organizational effectiveness. Giving subordinates the tools and support they need will strengthen that trust.

Leaders also provide empowerment by mentoring their subordinates, which includes providing authentic performance feedback. As with one's own leadership development, the goal is to have individuals (and therefore organizations) operating with more of their strengths and fewer of their weaknesses. Thomas Jefferson addressed more generally the need to promote a more educated and better-informed electorate when he proclaimed, "Every government degenerates when trusted to the rulers of the people alone. The people themselves, therefore, are its only safe depositaries. And to render even them safe, their minds must be improved to a certain degree." In an organizational context, professional development can also serve as a check on ineffective or unethical leadership.

On my final day of active duty in the U.S. Air Force, a two-star general asked if I had any final feedback for him or the organization. The question alone communicated a degree of respect and demonstrated that he actually valued the input of someone who worked several organizational levels below him. I replied by addressing the need for supervisors at all levels to be more diligent in providing their subordinates feedback as part of the mentoring process.

Formal professional development programs are well-defined in the military. Though periodic one-on-one supervisor-subordinate performance feedback sessions are mandatory in the Air Force, meaningful feedback (if any) is largely dependent on the motivation and dedication of individual supervisors. I attribute this inconsistency in commitment to a variety of reasons. Paraphrasing leadership expert and author John C. Maxwell, to improve your people, you must first value them. Supervisors with poor relationship management skills (which are part of emotional intelligence) may simply lack the courage to give subordinates honest feedback if they fear potential conflict. Others rationalize that their subordinates do not deserve it, though respect demands it. Some tell themselves that certain subordinates do not need feedback, rationalizing that the person would not have made it this far without already possessing all the necessary skill sets. Others are simply lazy or believe they are too busy to invest in their people. And finally, some supervisors may see their own success as "self-made," having convinced themselves that they never benefited from mentoring. We tend to forget about the formal and informal guidance we have received along the way, in the same way that we forget that performing at a certain level (in whatever discipline) once required much greater effort. Providing honest and meaningful feedback is an important component of serving, respecting, and empowering your subordinates. This demonstration of genuine interest in the development and well-being of one's subordinates is crucial for promoting greater trust in leadership.

CHAPTER 7

How Not *to* Undermine Your Organization

★ ★ ★

A poor leader's influence can undermine and create chaos through incompetence or, in perhaps the ultimate act of disloyalty, through the intentional subversion of the organization. Undermining an organization creates a toxic workplace that adversely affects morale, recruiting, productivity, innovation, the retention of competent people, and, ultimately, public confidence and mission accomplishment.

I previously identified nonadherence to core values as a contributor to organizational dysfunction, and in later chapters I will address the abuse of power, retaliation, undue influence, and deception. In this chapter I touch on six broad means of undermining organizations: (1) harmful staffing and personnel practices, (2) denigrating and disrespecting subordinate organizations and their leaders, (3) failing to uphold the law, (4) suppressing information flow, (5) illegitimately using an organization, and (6) compromising organizational continuity.

Staffing and personnel practices. There is a clear relationship between the diligence that goes into vetting people and the likelihood that the right people are hired. Proper vetting curbs unnecessary turnover by thoroughly evaluating experience, any history of ethical abuses, and potential financial and personal conflicts of interest.

During the first two years of the Trump administration, sixty-one nominations requiring Senate confirmation were withdrawn—double the number withdrawn by the previous administration for the same period of time. Many withdrawals stemmed from legal and ethical problems or insufficient experience. For positions requiring Senate confirmation, considerable time and resources were required to nominate replacements as a result of poor vetting.

Established and effective vetting processes already exist for public organizations. Nonetheless, when reporters asked President Trump in August 2019 about his vetting process, he responded by saying, "I think the White House has a great vetting process. You vet for me....You're part of the vetting process...I give out a name to the press, and they vet for me. We save a lot of money that way."

Contrary to what is suggested in the following largely retaliatory post, one should not select someone for one of the most critical positions in government (national security advisor) in order to "give someone a chance."

@realDonaldTrump
I gave John Bolton, who was incapable of being Senate confirmed **because he was considered a wacko, and was not liked, a chance.** I always like

hearing differing points of view. He turned out to be
grossly incompetent, and a liar. See judge's opinion.
CLASSIFIED INFORMATION!!!
8:34 AM - Jun 22, 2020

An arena in which one flavor of cronyism triumphed over sound vetting was diplomacy. U.S. ambassadors are on the front lines of defending American values and national security interests abroad. The Trump administration selected a historically high number of political appointees for ambassadorships in lieu of experienced career diplomats with regional expertise. Though some political appointees arrive with ample experience and perform admirably, an inexperienced political appointee (sometimes a campaign donor) who faces off against foreign professional diplomats may end up inadvertently compromising American interests. Similarly, the experience and competence of President-elect Trump's transition team was an issue addressed in the August 2020 Senate report *Russian Active Measures Campaigns and Interference in the 2016 U.S. Election.*

The existence of a cadre of informal advisors to the Transition Team with varying levels of access to the President-elect and varying awareness of foreign affairs presented attractive targets for foreign influence, creating notable counterintelligence vulnerabilities. The lack of vetting of foreign interactions by Transition officials left the Transition open to influence and manipulation by foreign intelligence services, government officials, and co-opted business executives.

Excessive turnover. One consequence of poor vetting is excessive turnover, which impairs continuity and creates organizational disruptions. Presidency scholar Dr. Kathryn Dunn Tenpas tracked turnover at the senior level of the White House staff and cabinet over the course of Trump's term. Among her findings, Trump replaced 35 percent of his most senior staff members within the first year, an unprecedented rate of turnover. That number rose to 92 percent by the end of his four-year term. Forty-five percent of those positions turned over twice or more. Fourteen cabinet-level officials (representing eleven of the fifteen Senate-confirmed heads of federal executive departments who are in the presidential line of succession) were replaced by the end of Trump's term. Shortly after the three-year point, President Trump was on his fourth chief of staff and his fourth national security advisor and still had a third of Department of Defense (DoD) Senate-confirmed civilian positions either vacant or filled by temporary leaders. As Senator Jack Reed (D-RI) noted, those vacancies continued "to challenge the [Defense] department's ability to effectively respond to national security challenges and undermine civilian inputs into the decision-making process."

A large number of dismissals and resignations result in a detrimental number of vacancies of varying lengths. These vacancies are often filled by temporary replacements who tend to have less authority and influence while serving in an "acting" capacity. In 2019, the United States had an acting secretary of defense for almost six months. When a "whole of government" response is needed during a national crisis and excessive turnover has resulted in an unusually high number of vacancies and temporary leaders, the national response will likely be compromised.

The act of purging or encouraging the departures of dedicated public servants from an organization can have lasting effects. This was the case with the State Department under the Trump administration, where there was an exodus of senior and mid-level career professionals representing decades of knowledge and experience. Described as a "hollowing out of the foreign service," officers who voluntarily and involuntarily departed represented the current and future leadership of the department. Recruitment also suffered during this time period, with fewer applicants taking the foreign service exam in 2018 than each of the previous nine years. In a more specific example, the aforementioned abrupt removal of Ambassador Yovanovitch left a vacuum in the leadership of the U.S. embassy in Ukraine, hampering rapport with the newly elected Ukrainian president. There was also no deputy chief of mission (second in charge) assigned to the embassy at the time of her removal. Her temporary replacement arrived more than a month later. All of this came at a time when Ukraine was defending itself against ongoing Russian military aggression while also preparing itself for a worst-case scenario—the eventual Russian invasion in early 2022.

Denigrating and disrespecting. A surefire means of undermining a subordinate organization is to denigrate its leadership and workforce.

Making spurious public accusations is one way to denigrate and disrespect subordinate organizations and their leaders. The smear campaign (described in the previous chapter) that preceded Ambassador Yovanovitch's departure provides a lesson in how undermining her ability to lead within the embassy likely compromised the organization's diplomatic efforts in Ukraine. In her own words:

It makes it hard to be a credible ambassador in a country....

Ukrainians were wondering whether I was going to be leaving, whether we really represented the President, U.S. policy, et cetera. And so I think it was—you know, it really kind of cut the ground out from underneath us....If our chief representative is kneecapped it limits our effectiveness to safeguard the vital national security interests of the United States.

During her testimony to Congress, Yovanovitch also described the chilling effect of her removal on the embassy's staff and the State Department more generally. Her unexplained removal caused many of her colleagues to question if they would continue to be supported in furthering stated U.S. policy objectives. They felt that their efforts were being undermined by their own chain of command.

President Trump's treatment of the FBI and Department of Justice (DOJ) before and after the release of the report on Russian interference in the 2016 election provides additional examples of hurling false accusations at subordinate organizations. Trump's claims in the following regarding "collusion" and spying are further addressed in chapters 20 and 23, respectively.

@realDonaldTrump

As the House Intelligence Committee has concluded, there was no collusion between Russia and the Trump Campaign. As many are now finding out, however, **there was tremendous leaking, lying and corruption at the highest levels of the FBI, Justice & State.** #DrainTheSwamp

10:11 AM - Mar 17, 2018

@realDonaldTrump

Wow, word seems to be coming out that **the Obama FBI "SPIED ON THE TRUMP CAMPAIGN WITH AN EMBEDDED INFORMANT."** Andrew McCarthy says, "There's probably **no doubt that they had at least one confidential informant in the campaign.**" If so, this is bigger than Watergate!

5:45 AM - May 17, 2018

Absent evidence from an official investigation, it is almost unfathomable that a leader would try to tarnish the reputation of his subordinate organizations in such a manner—organizations vital to national security and upholding the nation's laws. An investigation conducted by Trump's own DOJ inspector general (IG) in 2019 failed to substantiate the claims that Trump chose to recklessly proliferate. The IG's report "found no evidence that the FBI attempted to place any CHSs [confidential human sources] within the Trump campaign, recruit members of the Trump campaign as CHSs, or task CHSs to report on the Trump campaign." While the report did determine that there was insufficient oversight by FBI and DOJ leaders with respect to case agents failing to comply with, or not being aware of, FBI policy, that lack of oversight (if not incompetence) did not constitute "corruption at the highest levels," as suggested in the president's first post above.

A very small proportion of employees in every government organization occasionally break the law, as happens in nearly every private entity. In the following post, President Trump seemed to relish publicizing what was at the time merely speculation—that someone in the FBI had broken the law. His intent was primarily

105

to invalidate the Russia investigation and its findings.

@realDonaldTrump

New Fox Poll: 58% of people say that the FBI broke the law in investigating Donald J. Trump. @ foxandfriends

4:05 AM - May 17, 2019

In August 2020, an attorney who had worked for the FBI for four years pleaded guilty to doctoring an email that provided advice to investigators regarding a surveillance application. That isolated act—while unacceptable—also did not constitute high-level corruption. The aforementioned DOJ IG report concluded that there was no evidence that political bias influenced the opening of the investigation into the Trump campaign's potential involvement in Russian election interference. In fact, it concluded that the FBI was justified in launching the investigation.

Trump took additional swipes at the FBI and DOJ after his 2020 election loss in the form of unfounded claims of election fraud. The president described both organizations as "missing in action. Can't tell you where they are" and even suggested that they might be complicit in having perpetrated the election fraud he was alleging.

Another way to denigrate the people in your organization is to embrace a fringe conspiracy theory that alleges the existence of a "deep state" of public servants (or shadowy government within the government) plotting to undermine you. This QAnon conspiracy, labeled a potential domestic terror threat by the FBI, also subscribes to the notion that the same government employees are involved in satanic pedophilia. QAnon adherents also believe that Trump appointees who eventually resigned or were fired were intentionally brought into the administration so that Trump could expose them as disloyal deep state operators. It is a paranoia and distrust reminiscent of Joseph Stalin, who had thirty thousand of his military personnel arrested and executed, devastating Soviet readiness before the eventual Nazi invasion of 1941. President Trump's failure to disavow the so-called deep state conspiracy theory (and his self-serving embrace of it) likely contributed to his distrust of his intelligence agencies, the activities of his law enforcement agencies, and the advice provided by his public health experts. The following posts represent just a handful of the president's deep state attacks.

@realDonaldTrump
Look how things have turned around on the **Criminal Deep State.** They go after Phony Collusion with Russia, a made up Scam, and end up **getting caught in a major SPY scandal** the likes of which this country may never have seen before! What goes around, comes around!
3:54 AM - May 23, 2018

@realDonaldTrump
Some of the best Economic Numbers our Country has ever experienced are happening right now. This is despite a **Crooked and Demented Deep State**, and a probably illegal Democrat/Fake News Media Partnership the likes of which the world has never seen. MAKE AMERICA GREAT AGAIN!
3:28 PM - Sep 21, 2019

@realDonaldTrump

The deep state, or whoever, over at the FDA is making it very difficult for drug companies to get people in order to test the vaccines and therapeutics. Obviously, they are hoping to delay the answer until after November 3rd. Must focus on speed, and saving lives! @SteveFDA

7:49 AM - Aug 22, 2020

In the final post above, the president was gracious enough to include the Twitter handle of his Food and Drug Administration (FDA) commissioner as a means of ensuring that he received the message.

With the exception of a comparatively small number of political appointees selected by each new administration, the federal government largely comprises career civil servants who serve nonpartisan institutions. Their longevity and expertise are needed to tackle the enormous challenges faced by government agencies. They address a myriad of issues with time horizons greater than an annual budget or the policy priorities of any given administration. And they are generally too busy implementing existing programs in pursuit of agency objectives to engage in political sabotage. During my time in the Air Force, I served leaders (and presidents) whose policies I did not embrace. Nonetheless, it never occurred to me to actively undermine their lawful directives. For the vast majority of public servants, the more likely response would be appropriate dissent or resignation. In a post referencing three civil servants who testified before Congress in the president's first impeachment inquiry, Donald Trump Jr.'s disdain for public servants was on full display.

@DonaldJTrumpJr
America hired @realDonaldTrump to fire people like the first three witnesses we've seen. **Career govern-ment bureaucrats and nothing more**.
11:37 AM - Nov 15, 2019

President Trump also disparaged whistleblowers and the entire system of exposing fraud and potential criminal wrongdoing in government by associating them with the deep state conspiracy.

@realDonaldTrump
The first so-called second hand information "Whistleblower" got my phone conversation almost completely wrong, so now word is they are going to the bench and another **"Whistleblower" is coming in from the Deep State**, also with second hand info. Meet with Shifty.
Keep them coming!
9:17 PM - Oct 5, 2019

During a campaign rally for his 2024 presidential bid, the former president vowed to "totally obliterate the deep state." Trump's inten-tion to greatly expand the number of political appointees would unduly politicize American bureaucracies.

Inappropriate or unfounded public criticism and intimida-tion of a subordinate organization undermine its leader's ability to command respect from within the organization. It also undermines public confidence. As usual, the president's criticisms in the following posts were very loosely based in fact.

@realDonaldTrump

Why is the United States Post Office, which is losing many billions of dollars a year, while charging Amazon and others so little to deliver their packages, making Amazon richer and the **Post Office dumber and poorer?** Should be charging MUCH MORE!

5:04 AM - Dec 29, 2017

@realDonaldTrump

Wow! **The NSA** has deleted 685 million phone calls and text messages. **Privacy violations?** They blame technical irregularities. **Such a disgrace. The Witch Hunt continues!**

7:18 AM - Jul 3, 2018

@realDonaldTrump

Now it looks like the fore person in the jury, in the Roger Stone case, had significant bias. Add that to everything else, and this is not looking good for the **"Justice" Department.** @foxandfriends @FoxNews

7:57 AM - Feb 13, 2020

President Trump's own attorney general acknowledged that the president's posts about the DOJ's pending and ongoing cases "make it impossible for me to do my job and to assure the courts and the department that we're doing our work with integrity....I cannot do my job here at the department with a constant background commentary that undercuts me." Trump admitted as much in an interview, stating, "Yeah, I do make his job harder. I do agree with that." The president also worked hard to "motivate" the FBI.

@realDonaldTrump
The truth is that we have a nation that is disgusted with the FBI. We have a crisis of confidence in the number one law enforcement agency in this country (thanks Comey!). @LouDobbs **"It's a scandal."** @AlanDersh
8:53 PM - Sep 3, 2019

In the following post, which indirectly references the DOJ IG report on the FBI's Russia investigation, the president made a veiled threat of termination by referring to Christopher Wray as the "current Director."

@realDonaldTrump
I don't know what report current Director of the FBI Christopher Wray was reading, but it sure wasn't the one given to me. With that kind of attitude, he will **never be able to fix the FBI, which is badly broken** despite having some of the greatest men & women working there!
7:16 AM - Dec 10, 2019

When the leader of an agency intentionally misrepresents or contradicts the work of his own people, the victims will be organizational morale and public confidence in the agency's leader. Just before the report on Russian interference in the 2016 election (also referred to as the Mueller report) was publicly released in March 2019, Attorney General William Barr, for political expediency, misrepresented its conclusions regarding President Trump's numerous potential acts of obstruction of justice. A federal judge later concluded that Barr had made "misleading public statements" and had shown a "lack of candor." When Trump's DOJ IG released its report in 2019 on the origins of the Russia investigation, Barr similarly contradicted the findings by suggesting that the FBI investigation was initiated on a "bogus narrative."

An agency's leadership should not be pressured to contradict its own (correct) position. When President Trump erroneously suggested that Hurricane Dorian (2019) would affect the state of Alabama, the National Weather Service quickly reassured the public via Twitter that Alabama would not see any impacts. The president doubled down days later by displaying a forecast map that had been obviously (and poorly) edited from the original to show how Alabama was allegedly threatened by the storm. Days later, the National Oceanic and Atmospheric Administration disavowed the National Weather Service position that Alabama was never at risk. Alleged pressure from the commerce secretary was to blame for the reversal, which resulted in a considerable amount of consternation within the National Weather Service. Episodes like these have the potential to compromise public confidence in an agency's ability to provide information with scientific integrity and free of political influence.

Another way to disrespect an organization is to publicly communicate a lack of trust or confidence. President Trump's treatment of his intelligence agencies undermined credibility and morale and provides a clear example of what not to do.

@realDonaldTrump

The Intelligence people seem to be extremely passive and naive when it comes to the dangers of Iran. **They are wrong!** When I became President Iran was making trouble all over the Middle East, and

beyond. Since ending the terrible Iran Nuclear Deal,
they are MUCH different, but....
5:50 AM - Jan 30, 2019
  ...a source of potential danger and conflict.
They are testing Rockets (last week) and more, and
are coming very close to the edge. There economy
is now crashing, which is the only thing holding them
back. Be careful of Iran. **Perhaps Intelligence should
go back to school!**
5:56 AM - Jan 30, 2019

The most disturbing episode, however, occurred in Helsinki, Finland, on day 543 of the Trump presidency. As a general rule, disputes about national security information should not be aired outside of the national security establishment, and especially not to an international audience. Nonetheless, President Trump managed to cast doubt on the unanimous findings of his own intelligence agencies and the investigation that indicted twelve Russians for interfering in the 2016 presidential election. The episode was effectively a betrayal that played out before a global audience. With Russian president Vladimir Putin standing at Trump's side, the Associated Press's Jonathan Lemire posed the following question:

President Trump, you first. Just now President Putin denied having anything to do with the election interference in 2016. Every U.S. intelligence agency has concluded that Russia did. My first question for you, sir, is who do you believe? My second question is would you now with the whole world watching tell President

Putin—would you denounce what happened in 2016 and would you warn him to never do it again?

In what was a propaganda coup for the Russians, the president included the following snippet in his long-winded and somewhat incoherent response:

> My people came to me, Dan Coats [director of national intelligence] came to me and some others and said they think it's Russia. I have President Putin. He just said it's not Russia. I will say this. I don't see any reason why it would be....So I have great confidence in my intelligence people, but I will tell you that President Putin was extremely strong and powerful in his denial today.

Despite evidence of extensive Russian interference, Trump effectively sided with Putin—a former KGB officer skilled in the art of deception and a geopolitical adversary bent on destabilizing the North Atlantic Treaty Organization (NATO) and the post-WWII/Cold War order. Months later, Trump would further undermine his intelligence services by repeating a debunked Russian talking point about alleged Ukrainian interference in America's 2016 election.

Failing to uphold the law. *Another means of disrespecting an institution is refusing to uphold its laws.* In 2019, President Trump told a reporter that he would be inclined to accept dirt on a political opponent from a foreign power (likely flouting U.S. election laws). When FBI director Wray stated that such offers should be reported to the FBI, Trump publicly contradicted and undermined

Wray by stating that he was "wrong." In addition to a likely blow to morale in federal law enforcement agencies, it was also an invitation to America's enemies to meddle in future elections by offering information that could compromise American officials and therefore America's national security. What are other countries to think, especially our allies, when the president says publicly that he is willing to break the law? It unfortunately sends the message that the United States may no longer value the rule of law. Career foreign service officer Chuck Park, who resigned during Trump's tenure, expressed a similar sentiment in an editorial.

> Over three tours abroad, I worked to spread what I believed were American values: freedom, fairness, and tolerance. But more and more I found myself in a defensive stance, struggling to explain to foreign peoples the blatant contradictions at home.

It is illegal to vote more than once in an election. Nonetheless, President Trump encouraged his supporters to potentially do so during campaign rallies in North Carolina and Pennsylvania in the run-up to the 2020 presidential election. When asked about his comments, Trump stated, "So let them send it in [by mail] and let them go vote [in person], and if their system's as good as they say it is, then obviously they won't be able to vote. If it isn't tabulated, they'll be able to vote. So that's the way it is. And that's what they should do." Election officials in North Carolina, where the president first suggested this "test" of the system, were quick to push back on Trump's efforts to undermine absentee or mail-in voting: "The State Board office strongly discourages people from showing up at the polls on Election Day to check whether their absentee ballot was counted. That is not necessary, and it would lead to longer lines and the possibility of spreading COVID-19." Voting twice in Pennsylvania is a third-degree felony, and its chief election official was also quick to discourage it. "Needless to say, this is not the message that we are sending. Nobody should vote twice. Nobody should try to vote twice. We all have one fundamental vote that we should all exercise once and once only." The president repeated his suggestion on Twitter. The following example (one of many) was accompanied by the following message on Twitter: "This Tweet violated the Twitter Rules about civic and election integrity."

> @realDonaldTrump
> NORTH CAROLINA: To make sure your Ballot COUNTS, sign & send it in EARLY. When Polls open, go to your Polling Place to see if it was COUNTED. IF NOT, VOTE! Your signed Ballot will not count because your vote has been posted. Don't let them illegally take your vote away from you!
> 9:10 AM - Sep 12, 2020

Unnecessarily suppressing information flow. *Unnecessarily suppressing or discouraging information flow to oneself or to outside agencies (including the public) can undermine an organization's efficacy and credibility.* When a leader creates an atmosphere where important information on a particular topic is regarded as "bad news," subordinates are conditioned to restrict the upward flow of that information. A secondary and unfortunate consequence of this conditioning is that subordinates will be rewarded for providing the leader with what is perceived to be good news. Neither practice provides the leader with the information needed for sound decision-making. When a leader's ability to protect organizational interests is compromised due to a lack of information, one would hope that others in the organization would bridge the gaps. But you cannot always count on subordinates to work priority issues that are not receiving the attention they deserve from leadership.

Suppressing the outflow of information can have unintended economic and security implications and may allow significant policy challenges to go unaddressed. One example involved Trump administration officials who refused to publicize peer-reviewed Department of Agriculture studies that contained specific warnings about the effects of climate change on certain crops. In this instance, researchers were working in an environment where they felt censored. Similarly, when Trump's own agencies published the latest version of the national climate assessment that contained findings important to American farmers, Trump told reporters, "I don't believe it," which had the effect of suppressing the report's circulation. Thankfully, federal employees are encouraged to report censorship related to research, analysis, and technical information.

After leaders from the intelligence community briefed Congress on Russia's efforts to interfere in a manner benefiting Trump in the upcoming 2020 presidential election, the president suggested that their analysis was the product of partisan conspiracy theories. This was despite Putin admitting—only feet away from him in Helsinki in 2018—that Russia had favored Trump in the 2016 election.

@realDonaldTrump
Another misinformation campaign is being launched
by Democrats in Congress saying that Russia prefers
me to any of the Do Nothing Democrat candidates
who still have been unable to, after two weeks, count
their votes in Iowa. **Hoax number 7!**
10:36 AM - Feb 21, 2020

Trump was reportedly furious that the briefing had been provided
to members of Congress, who were cleared to receive it *and* had
a need to know. Trump's perception of disloyalty resulted in the
early dismissal of Acting Director of National Intelligence Joseph
Maguire, along with a ripple effect of other departures from
Maguire's office and consternation throughout the intelligence
community. In a similar turn of events, Maguire's predecessor, Dan
Coats, had been forced out after he apparently refused to modify
an intelligence assessment about Russia's preference for Trump.
Retired admiral William McRaven addressed the firing of Maguire
and others in an opinion piece:

> When good men and women can't speak the truth,
> when facts are inconvenient, when integrity and
> character no longer matter, when presidential ego
> and self-preservation are more important than
> national security—then there is nothing left to stop
> the triumph of evil.

Former CIA director John Brennan also addressed this attempt
to curtail the flow of intelligence to national decision-makers.

@JohnBrennan

We are now in a full-blown national security crisis. By trying to prevent the flow of intelligence to Congress, Trump is abetting a Russian covert operation to keep him in office for Moscow's interests, not America's.

7:17 PM - Feb 20, 2020

Seven months later, a Department of Homeland Security (DHS) whistleblower reprisal complaint submitted by Brian Murphy exposed additional actions taken by senior national security officials to censor, unjustifiably alter, and limit the dissemination of vetted intelligence reports.

> In mid-May 2020, Mr. [Chad] Wolf [Acting Secretary of Homeland Security] instructed Mr. Murphy to cease providing intelligence assessments on the threat of Russian interference in the United States, and instead start reporting on interference activities by China and Iran. Mr. Wolf stated that these instructions specifically originated from White House National Security Advisor Robert O'Brien. Mr. Murphy informed Mr. Wolf he would not comply with these instructions, as doing so would put the country in substantial and specific danger.
>
> …the concern raised pertained to abuse of authority, willfully withholding intelligence information from Congress, and the improper administration of an intelligence program.
>
> On July 7, 2020, DHS Chief of Staff John Gountanis sent an e-mail to Mr. Murphy directing

him to cease any dissemination of an intelligence notification regarding Russian disinformation efforts....Mr.
Wolf stated to Mr. Murphy the intelligence notification
should be "held" because it "made the President look
bad." Mr. Murphy objected, stating that it was improper
to hold a vetted intelligence product for reasons [of]
political embarrassment.

During multiple meetings between the end
of May 2020 and July 31, 2020, Mr. Murphy made
protected disclosures to Messrs. Wolf and Cuccinelli
regarding abuse of authority and improper administration of an intelligence program with respect to intelligence information on ANTIFA and "anarchist" groups
operating throughout the United States. On each occasion, Mr. Murphy was instructed by Mr. Wolf and/or
Mr. Cuccinelli to modify intelligence assessments to
ensure they matched up with the public comments by
President Trump on the subject of ANTIFA and "anarchist" groups. Mr. Murphy declined to modify any of
the intelligence assessments based upon political rhetoric, and advised both officials he would only report
accurate intelligence information as collected by DHS
I&A [Office of Intelligence and Analysis].

Murphy was also instructed to edit several sections of a
Homeland Threat Assessment dealing with white supremacy and
Russian influence in the United States. Murphy's superiors were once
again concerned about how the report would reflect on President
Trump.

Illegitimate use of an organization. *Yet another means of undermining an organization is to use it for inappropriate or illegitimate purposes.* Two broad examples include exceeding an agency's mandate or jurisdiction and politicizing a government agency. An example of the latter is weaponizing the Justice Department to "prove" one's conspiracy theories about the alleged wrongdoing of political rivals and to "validate" baseless claims of widespread election fraud (as discussed in later chapters).

When Attorney General Barr ordered Washington, D.C., National Guard personnel and agents from various federal agencies to disperse a group of protestors in Lafayette Square, numerous retired generals expressed their concern about what appeared to be a military use of force for political purposes. The dispersal was immediately followed by the president's walk through the same area, accompanied by Secretary of Defense Mark Esper and Chairman of the Joint Chiefs of Staff General Mark Milley. At risk was the perception and arguably the reality that American military forces were being used inappropriately against their own people. General Milley apologized within days while addressing the National Defense University.

> I should not have been there. My presence in that moment and in that environment created a perception of the military involved in domestic politics. As a commissioned uniformed officer, it was a mistake that I have learned from, and I sincerely hope we all can learn from it. We who wear the cloth of our nation come from the people of our nation, and we must hold dear the principle of an apolitical military that is so deeply rooted in the very essence of our republic.

Compromising organizational continuity. One of my pet peeves is poor continuity—that is, managers and leaders who neglect ensuring the success of their successors (and thereby the organization they are leaving) by neglecting to provide accurate and useful continuity materials. Neglect can take the form of insufficient continuity, and occasionally the opposite—maintaining an abundance of unnecessary records.

Immediately following the 2020 election, President-elect Biden's transition effort was delayed by approximately three weeks. The primary cause of the delay was Donald Trump's unwillingness to concede defeat. Timely and effective transitions are especially critical for continuity and policy formulation in matters involving national security. In just one example of a development that raised concerns even among Senate Republicans, President-elect Biden and Vice President–elect Harris were denied access to the President's Daily Brief (intelligence report) until they were in their fourth week of the eleven-week presidential transition period. Promoting organizational success by serving one's successors is one manifestation of principled loyalty, a topic addressed in chapter 28.

CHAPTER 8

Seeking Counsel
and Expertise

Even When You Know It All

One of the great challenges in this world is knowing
enough about a subject to think you're right,
but not enough about the subject
to know you're wrong.

—NEIL DEGRASSE TYSON

I heard someone correctly observe that when you are ill-informed and undisciplined, you need advisors. Even the well-informed and disciplined require advice and expertise. Those who think they do not need advice often do not value lifelong learning and lack intellectual curiosity. They are to be contrasted with those who appreciate, after having gained some new knowledge on a subject, just how much *more* there usually is to learn. Even leaders whose knowledge and decisiveness inspire confidence necessarily benefit from the collective expertise that cannot reside with just one person. It takes a team to ensure a leader's success. Expertise matters, and the attitude that "I alone can fix it" has no place in public service.

> *I think the people of this country*
> *have had enough of experts...*
> —MICHAEL GOVE,
> BRITISH MEMBER OF PARLIAMENT, 2017

Public institutions employ experts in part to inform decision-makers who can then make sound policy choices. The greater the authority, the smaller the likelihood that leader will have *all* of the institutional knowledge and experience necessary to make effective, ethical, and lawful decisions. Consequently, advisors and subject matter experts must understand the importance of providing knowledge that may not always be appreciated (as with inconvenient truths). Providing inaccurate or incomplete information will likely result in poor decision-making. But leaders, too, are expected to be well versed on a wide variety of subjects and to possess a requisite amount of expertise in their own fields. Having great advisors does not absolve one of the responsibility of attempting to independently understand all sides of an issue. Well-informed leaders better anticipate opposing viewpoints and more easily assess the value of the advice and expertise they are provided.

Choosing advisors. In a *Saturday Night Live* portrayal, the actor playing President Trump advised 2020 graduates to surround themselves with the worst people they could find. That way, they would always shine. Yet in reality, leadership does not require you to be the most intelligent or knowledgeable person but rather the person best suited to lead because of some combination of experience, temperament, ethics, an ability to communicate and motivate, and of course an ability and willingness to benefit from the advice and expertise of others. President Nelson Mandela often aligned himself with those he thought were brighter and quicker than he. Good leaders understand their limitations and compensate by recruiting people with complementary strengths and talents.

Leaders tend to make better decisions when they receive input from a diverse range of stakeholders. There are times when you may be the most knowledgeable person in the room, but that does not mean that you should not make the effort to hear other points of view. In *Mandela's Way*, Richard Stengel describes how President Mandela was aware that Lincoln had put some of his fiercest rivals in his cabinet—and Mandela likewise put members of the opposition party in his own first cabinet. He was impressed with the way Lincoln used persuasion rather than force in managing his cabinet. Having a "team of rivals" may serve to generate a broader range of solutions and more spirited policy debate. However, leaders who relish ongoing internal conflict between advisors—in the spirit of Trump's former reality television show *The Apprentice*—risk hurting morale by introducing unnecessary chaos into the decision-making process.

Choose your advisors and sources of information carefully. "I'm not the smartest fellow in the world, but I can sure pick smart colleagues," proclaimed Franklin D. Roosevelt. Thomas Jefferson wrote about how he would in times of personal difficulty consider what certain esteemed colleagues would do under similar circumstances. As those working in the discipline of human intelligence appreciate, the quality and accuracy of the information you receive corresponds directly to your source's access and reliability. Having good advisors increases the likelihood of remaining connected to what is objectively true—a prerequisite for sound decision-making. Leaders should also welcome external perspectives as provided through audits, inspections, and customer feedback.

Following his 2020 election loss, President Trump spent his final weeks surrounded by unofficial advisors who pushed conspiracy theories and proposed outlandish means of keeping him in office. He too often sought the counsel of his private attorneys over that of his White House legal advisors and the leadership of the Justice Department. A small contingent of official advisors were fortunately able to counter many of the conspiracy-driven narratives, thereby preventing the president from following through on some of his worst instincts. As the president continued to publicly question the outcome of the election, his secretary of labor urged him in a letter to use his cabinet for decision-making, in lieu of the private citizens who were serving him poorly.

Despite the considerable official resources at his disposal, President Trump too often sought advice from his favorite cable news show hosts:

> I watched Lou Dobbs last night, Sean Hannity last night, Tucker last night, Laura. I watched *Fox and Friends* in the morning. You watch these shows, you don't have to go too far into the details. They cover things. It's really an amazing thing. They got caught in the biggest political scandal in the history of our country. They were spying on their opponent's campaign.

In his book *Hoax: Donald Trump, Fox News, and the Dangerous Distortion of Truth*, Brian Stelter details how the president used those Fox News "advisors." As recounted by former administration officials, those unofficial advisors directly influenced unvetted White House hires, inspired improper and potentially illegal policy choices, and encouraged controversial pardons. They also inspired bogus accusations of treason against public servants. The following two posts provide examples of misinformation that the president consumed and then proliferated.

@realDonaldTrump

I have asked Secretary of State @SecPompeo to closely study the South Africa land and farm seizures and expropriations and the large scale killing of farmers. "South African Government is now seizing land from white farmers." @TuckerCarlson @FoxNews

7:28 PM - Aug 22, 2018

@realDonaldTrump

Patrick Moore, co-founder of Greenpeace: "The whole climate crisis is not only Fake News, it's Fake Science. There is no climate crisis, there's weather and climate all around the world, and in fact carbon dioxide is the main building block of all life." @foxandfriends Wow!

5:29 AM - Mar 12, 2019

Similarly, when Trump's acting deputy attorney general assured him during a phone call in late December 2020 that there was no evidence of widespread election fraud, the president responded with, "You guys may not be following the internet the way I do."

A short case study in choosing one's advisors poorly is the 2019 saga in which President Trump initially froze military assistance to Ukraine. In 2014, Russia illegally annexed the Crimean Peninsula of Ukraine and in 2019 was still engaged in armed conflict in the country's Donbas region. The conflict had already killed thirteen thousand and displaced over 1.4 million people. President Trump was receiving negative information about Ukraine and its president-elect (Zelenskyy) from Rudy Giuliani. Trump was also getting advice from Russian president Vladimir Putin, as detailed in the first of the following two passages from the *Trump-Ukraine Impeachment Inquiry Report*:

> The President reportedly discussed Ukraine with Russian President Vladimir Putin when they spoke by phone on May 3. President Trump posted on Twitter that he "[h]ad a long and very good conversation with President Putin of Russia" and discussed "even the 'Russian Hoax'"—an apparent reference to the unanimous finding by the U.S. Intelligence Community that Russia interfered in the 2016 election with the aim of assisting President Trump's candidacy....President Putin also expressed negative views about Ukraine to President Trump.
>
> ...[Deputy Assistant Secretary of State George] Kent said he understood President Trump's discussions about Ukraine with President Putin and [Hungary's] Prime Minister Orbán "as being similar in tone and approach." He explained that "both leaders" had "extensively talked Ukraine down, said it was corrupt, said Zelenskyy was in the thrall of oligarchs," the effect of

which was "negatively shaping a picture of Ukraine, and even President Zelenskyy personally." The veteran State Department diplomat concluded, "[T]hose two world leaders [Putin and Orbán], along with former Mayor Giuliani—their communications with President Trump shaped the President's view of Ukraine and Zelenskyy, and would account for the change from a very positive first call on April 21 to his negative assessment of Ukraine."

The flow of hundreds of millions of dollars of security assistance to Ukraine had already been bipartisan policy since 2014. In 2019, both the DoD and State Department intended to deliver security assistance to Ukraine after having certified that the country had implemented sufficient anti-corruption reforms.

> The United States has an interest in providing security assistance to Ukraine to support the country in its long-standing battle against Russian aggression and to shore it up as an independent and democratic country that can deter Kremlin influence in both Ukraine and other European countries.
>
> *...U.S. Officials Briefed President Trump About their Positive Impressions of Ukraine.* Ambassadors [Kurt] Volker and [Gordon] Sondland left Kyiv with "a very favorable impression" of the new Ukrainian leader. They believed it was important that President Trump "personally engage with the President of Ukraine in order to demonstrate full U.S. support for him," including by

inviting him to Washington for a meeting in the Oval Office. It was agreed that the delegation would request a meeting with President Trump and personally convey their advice. They were granted time with President Trump on May 23.

...President Trump reacted negatively to the positive assessment of Ukraine. Ambassador Volker recalled that President Trump said Ukraine is "a terrible place, all corrupt, terrible people" and was "just dumping on Ukraine." This echoed Mr. Giuliani's public statements about Ukraine during early May.

According to both Ambassadors Volker and Sondland, President Trump also alleged, without offering any evidence, that Ukraine "tried to take me down" in the 2016 election. The President emphasized that he "didn't believe" the delegation's positive assessment of the new Ukrainian president, and added "that's not what I hear" from Mr. Giuliani. President Trump said that Mr. Giuliani "knows all of these things" and knows that President Zelenskyy has "some bad people around him."

President Trump froze the military assistance to Ukraine without providing meaningful justification. In late August 2019, Trump's national security advisor, secretary of state, and defense secretary met with him to convince him that releasing the assistance to Ukraine was in America's interests. Despite evidence to the contrary, Trump communicated his skepticism about meaningful reforms in a country he continued to characterize as corrupt.

The aid was finally released in September after committees in the House of Representatives launched investigations into allegations that President Trump and his associates had pressured the Ukrainian government into announcing an investigation into presidential candidate and then former vice president Joe Biden.

A study in contrasts is President John F. Kennedy's use of advisors during the Cuban Missile Crisis in October 1962. During thirteen days in which the world was arguably never closer to nuclear war, Kennedy was faced with deciding how the United States would respond to evidence of Soviet nuclear-capable missiles in Cuba. In contrast to his use of advisors in the April 1961 Bay of Pigs debacle, Kennedy on this occasion assembled a team from a wide range of agencies that included voices with which he was likely to disagree. He occasionally withdrew from deliberations in the knowledge that some advisors would be reluctant to present dissenting views in his presence. He was also able to see through his advisors' self-interest. He listened to his military advisors with an open mind, despite skepticism stemming from the Bay of Pigs fiasco. His military advisors vigorously advocated air strikes, arguing that a naval quarantine was a weak response. Dissatisfied and not caving to pressure, Kennedy consulted other advisors, adjusted his strategy as he received new information, and eventually chose the naval quarantine option along with negotiated concessions. His skilled use of advisors resolved the crisis and eventually resulted in the removal of Soviet missiles from Cuba.

How to solicit, encourage, and take advice. When seeking advice, you must be willing to have others challenge your preconceived notions (in addition to challenging them yourself). It may be more comfortable to surround yourself with like-minded people, but hearing a different perspective might lead you to justifiably revise your position on an issue. As Air Force Lieutenant Colonel Henry Staley pointed out, "A truly effective leader has the strength of character to realize that his or her intuitive judgment is usually a poor substitute for the collective wisdom of the staff." Even when your original intuition is sound, hearing a different point of view may allow you to better articulate your original position.

One challenge leaders face is the reluctance of subordinates to provide honest and dissenting advice or feedback. As Staley noted, leaders must demand and reward honest feedback, struggling against their subordinates' subservience training and career survival instincts.

Nelson Mandela understood that there is nothing that ingratiates you with someone else as asking his help—that when you defer to others, you increase their allegiance to you. Being receptive to advice or new ideas from any level of an organization builds trust by demonstrating to subordinates that you value their knowledge, experience, and perhaps differing perspectives. It requires humility to acknowledge you are not an expert on something and modesty when you want advice despite your expertise. A leader possessing those traits is more likely to attract quality advisors.

Encouraging advice. The country team meeting at a typical American embassy is chaired by the ambassador and includes the most senior representatives from various State Department sections as well as representatives from other U.S. government departments and agencies. While serving as the assistant air attaché at the U.S. embassy in Manila, I occasionally attended the country team meeting when the defense attaché was unavailable. During one of those meetings, I was listening to another participant's opinion on some agenda item. I was not known for having a poker face. The ambassador picked up on my perplexed facial expression. When the other person had finished speaking, she zeroed in on me and asked if I had anything to add. I did not, but her query alone demonstrated how perceptive she was and how she valued hearing what could have been an alternative view. Good leaders understand that reluctant voices are sometimes a source of valuable input.

Taking and evaluating advice. By the time one has reached a position of leadership, one should have on numerous occasions received and processed constructive performance-related feedback from superiors. When leaders receive blunt and critical feedback from subordinates about a decision or the state of the organization, it is important to differentiate critical assessments of a personal or general nature intended to improve an organization from personal attacks that serve no real purpose. This can be challenging for some leaders because they feel responsible (and should) for everything that happens in their organizations, especially as it concerns the consequences of their own decisions. After ego is set aside, one should consider constructive criticism from a subordinate (unless communicated publicly) as an act of loyalty. Nelson Mandela was more comfortable with those who confronted him than those who hid their feelings. Disagreement should not be confused with disrespect. Good leaders can even educate their subordinates on how and when they prefer to receive criticism.

Taking advice requires a certain amount of humility regarding our ignorance. We should withhold judgment until we have all (or most) of the facts. This idea speaks to the importance of listening with an open mind. Doing so requires that we not mentally shut down (in

133

order to remain "right") when our assumptions are challenged. If we indeed learn more when we are listening than when we are talking, then we should take former news anchor Chris Matthews's advice to himself and avoid listening with our mouths. Leaders who spend too much time lecturing subordinates are unlikely to get the information they need from those who might be reluctant to interrupt their bosses.

During one of my Air Force assignments, I felt strongly that our unit's supervisory structure, while technically permissible, was unacceptable due to its conflicts of interest. It allowed junior officers to rate other junior officers (write their annual performance reports, which are eventually used to evaluate promotion potential). The conflict of interest was that the rater (supervisor) could eventually be competing for promotion against his ratee (subordinate). I brought this to my commander's attention. He was not particularly interested in my arguments and informed me that it was a problem only because I was making it a problem. The operations officer (second in charge of the squadron) was thankfully more receptive to my concerns. Despite his skepticism, as expressed during several occasionally heated exchanges, he was nonetheless willing to hear all of my apprehensions. Knowing that he would be taking command of the squadron in a few months' time, he assured me that he would adjust the supervisory structure such that all junior officers would be rated by the unit's more senior officers. This episode highlights a leader's willingness—despite the clear position of his own immediate supervisor (the original commander)—to consider with an open mind the concerns of a subordinate, evaluate the different sides of an argument, and eventually make meaningful and principled organizational reforms.

Another episode of evaluating advice that required keeping an open mind (and a dose of humility) involved an unusual in-flight emergency. What is known as a functional check flight—a flight conducted after specific maintenance is performed on various aircraft systems—was required for our C-12C (Beechcraft Super King Air 200) aircraft. Given the nature of the flight, our mechanic supplemented the typical crew of two pilots. My copilot was an officer from my organization who happened to outrank me.

After completing the necessary in-flight checks, we proceeded back to our base of operations, an international airport. While on final approach to the airport's primary runway, we received notification on the instrument panel that we had a main landing-gear malfunction. That left us with the nose and left main landing gear down, and the right main landing gear still stowed in the aircraft's belly.

One cannot be sure how an emergency gear-up landing (touching down with all landing gear retracted) will play out until it actually happens. It is an emergency procedure that can be rehearsed only in a flight simulator (if at all, given such malfunctions are rather uncommon and not heavily emphasized in training).

We broke off the approach and spent the next hour troubleshooting with our stellar mechanic and with colleagues via satellite phone. In the end, we correctly concluded that nothing could be done to lower the right main landing gear, even with the manual pump mechanism normally available for such emergencies. Our best option was to raise the landing gear, burn fuel until sunset, and then perform a gear-up landing. Attempting a landing with the main landing gear down on just one side—while perhaps entertaining to spectators on the ground—is likely to provide more "adventure" for the crew than desired. As an emergency landing of this nature would have likely shut down the international airport for several hours, we proceeded instead toward another nearby airport with an inactive runway alongside its primary, active runway.

I had been designated aircraft commander (or pilot in command, in civilian parlance) for this particular flight. At some point, my senior-in-rank copilot informed me that he would be performing the emergency gear-up landing. I acknowledged that I would entertain his suggestion, but that as aircraft commander, the decision would ultimately be mine to make. In that moment, I felt that he was challenging my aircraft commander authority (though he would years later explain that he intended it more as a suggestion). I was, after all, ultimately responsible for whatever might happen to the aircraft and crew—regardless of his seniority back in the office. I would not have the luxury of later explaining that I had chosen a particular course of action because my copilot had insisted on it. I felt that my judgment—informed by all available input—had to prevail.

Objectively evaluating his "suggestion" would require putting ego aside, keeping an open mind, and not allowing myself to be overly influenced by what I considered to be a potential challenge to my authority. My eventual decision was made easier by his factual assertion that he had more fixed-wing experience than I, as I had accumulated most of my flight time in helicopters. I was also unusually tired that day. I finally informed him that I had decided that he would perform the landing. In truth, success for this partic- ular maneuver requires both pilots to simultaneously perform a series of choreographed, critically timed actions just prior to touchdown. On our relatively uneventful touchdown performed beautifully by the copilot, the airplane slid approximately five thousand feet on its belly and flaps, sustaining minimal damage. My willingness to objectively evaluate my copilot's advice under challenging circumstances contributed to the successful conclusion of this once-in-a-career emergency.

Barriers to receiving, evaluating, and accepting advice. The barriers to receiving and accepting advice include self-interest, arrogance, inability to suppress personal bias, and the tendency to censor, contradict, and criticize your advisors.

Self-interest. Self-interest can unfortunately be the root cause of ignoring otherwise sound advice and reliable information. During President Trump's first impeachment trial, a House impeachment manager warned about the threat to national security that results from someone being made to disbelieve his own intelligence experts regarding Russian election interference:

> Now, why would Donald Trump believe a man like Rudy Giuliani over a man like Christopher Wray? Okay. Why would anyone in their right mind believe Rudy Giuliani over Christopher Wray? Because he wanted to and because what Rudy was offering him was something that would help him personally. And what Christopher Wray was offering him was merely the truth. What Christopher Wray was offering him was merely the information he needed to protect his country and its elections, but that's not good enough. What's in it for him? What's in it for Donald Trump?

Robert Cardillo, who headed the National Geospatial-Intelligence Agency from 2014 to 2019, described this dynamic in a 2020 interview with CNN:

> As an intelligence professional, we often confront policymakers who come into a situation or an issue with a bias, or their own experience, of course, but then they take on new information and they use that to either challenge or adjust their thinking. This president has a way to deflect new information, even scientific data in a way that allows him to be more comfortable, and to sustain, as I said, that internal view and to think about what the best outcome is for himself. . . . What he doesn't want to believe and chooses not to believe is the fact that Russia did interfere in our election in 2016, and its intent was to get him elected. Because he feels that that delegitimizes his presidency, he will deflect anything, again, that conflicts with that view. And so when Vladimir Putin says "I didn't do it," that fits and thus he would align with that, vice the Intelligence Community's assessment.

Arrogance. As a young second lieutenant in my first operational assignment, I was responsible for rating a handful of noncommissioned officers. The most important discriminator on their annual enlisted performance reports (EPR) was a block showing their overall rating on a scale of one to five, with five being the highest possible evaluation. Likely overconfident in my understanding of the enlisted evaluation system, I devised what seemed to be a reasonable method of determining the overall rating by simply averaging the numerical ratings for the various performance subcategories. Thankfully, the unit's senior enlisted member, a chief master sergeant, was charged with reviewing all EPRs before they were signed/finalized. He patiently explained to me that my method would likely unduly compromise the promotion prospects of my subordinates. He was correct based on what the rest of the Air Force was doing. Though I initially resisted his logic (perhaps because a lowly second lieutenant technically outranks a highly experienced chief master sergeant), I eventually concurred and modified my evaluation process. It was an important lesson in humility and remaining receptive to expertise.

Some leaders, and often those of the charismatic variety, tend to claim unique and unparalleled expertise where they have none. This unfortunate tendency is often accompanied by the need to dismiss those with actual expertise. When asked during his 2016 campaign with whom he was consistently consulting on foreign policy matters, Mr. Trump responded, "I'm speaking with myself, number one, because I have a very good brain...so I know what I'm doing and I listen to a lot of people, I talk to a lot of people, and at the appropriate time I'll tell you who the people are...but my primary consultant is myself." The following post is another example of arrogance or overconfidence.

@realDonaldTrump

The Democrats are trying to belittle the concept of a Wall, calling it old fashioned. The fact is there is nothing else's that will work, and that has been true for thousands of years. It's like the wheel, there is nothing better. **I know tech better than anyone, & technology**.....

3:58 AM - Dec 21, 2018

Whether he actually believed what he was saying or not, the president also claimed that nobody understood the following subjects as well as he: money, debt, taxes, trade, campaign finance, drones, infrastructure, renewables, and finally, courts. He may have been experiencing a phenomenon known as the Dunning–Kruger effect, in which people with low expertise or experience in a particular area tend to underestimate their own incompetence. Arrogance and unwarranted confidence may also inhibit leaders from soliciting the feedback they need, creating a pernicious cycle of mistakes and lessons unlearned.

> *We don't have time for a meeting of the Flat Earth Society.*
> —PRESIDENT BARACK OBAMA

The inability to suppress personal bias. A leader technically has the luxury of asking for advice without the obligation of properly evaluating or accepting it. Some simply do not want to be encumbered with information that contradicts their preexisting viewpoints.

President Obama and Governor Chris Christie (R-NJ) advised President-elect Trump not to hire Lieutenant General Mike Flynn (U.S. Army, retired) as national security advisor. Christie later claimed that his warning about Flynn contributed to his dismissal as the head of Trump's transition team. Representative Elijah Cummings (D-MD), in a November 2016 letter to Vice President–elect Pence, warned about Flynn's conflicts of interest. Flynn had been lobbying on behalf of Turkish government interests while simultaneously receiving classified briefings during the presidential transition. President Trump nonetheless hired Flynn—and then subsequently fired him for dishonesty.

@realDonaldTrump

It now seems the General Flynn was under investigation long before was common knowledge. **It would
have been impossible for me to know this but,** if that
was the case, and with me being one of two people
who would become president, why was I not told so
that I could make a change?

7:35 AM - May 17, 2019

People are typically under criminal investigation long before it is "common knowledge," out of fairness to the person being investigated and because a degree of secrecy is required to avoid compromising the investigation's integrity. Nonetheless, Flynn had reportedly informed Trump's transition team that he was under investigation.

In a July 2020 interview with Fox's Chris Wallace, Trump was asked about the possibility of renaming military bases named after Confederate leaders. As Trump began defending the status quo, Wallace stated, "But the military says they're for this." Trump responded with, "Excuse me, excuse me. I don't care what the military says." When you stop valuing the advice of subordinates—especially those charged with providing advice based on their expertise and vast experience—they will begin to feel undervalued and ineffective. Secretary of Defense James Mattis resigned when it was clear that President Trump was largely impervious to his counsel on matters of national security.

As urged by former secretary of defense and director of the CIA Leon Panetta, leaders must appreciate the facts as they are presented, versus trying to create their own view of what the world should be. When President Trump insulted intelligence professionals who presented "unwelcome" information, one is left with the impression that he confused the shared conclusions of his intelligence agencies with what he deemed to be merely personal views (especially if those "views" happened to contradict his own). Though Robert Cardillo acknowledged that it is natural for humans to arrive with their own perspectives and experiences and that Trump's instincts may have served him well in other capacities, he described the dynamic in which Trump struggled to align new information with "initial or enduring bias":

> What is exceptional, though, about this president is that...he bases so much of his judgments about his view of the reality on his internal guidance, that he takes in very little external input to that guidance, that it becomes more than just a tension, it's a disconnect. And that disconnect is what I worry about, because if you disconnect, you know, our most senior leaders from the valued input from the intelligence community, what you risk are making uninformed, ill-advised, and ultimately dangerous decisions.

Another potential consequence of Trump's uncontrolled personal bias was a potential reluctance by intelligence professionals to provide crucial information that perhaps did not comport with their leader's biases.

> *Good government depends on public servants*
> *being able to give full and frank advice.*
> —Prime Minister Theresa May

Censoring, contradicting, and criticizing your experts. On January 28, 1986, the space shuttle *Challenger* broke apart seventy-three seconds into its flight, killing all seven of its crew members. The subsequent accident investigation revealed that NASA officials exerted extreme pressure on contractors, including Morton Thiokol (MTI). Consequently, MTI regularly overrode internal dissent, as it unfortunately did on the eve of *Challenger*'s final flight. This tragic episode highlights the need for leaders to recognize when subordinate leaders and managers are impeding the upward flow of crucial information. Subordinate advisors must feel psychologically safe to speak up in the interests of safety and innovation and, more generally, to challenge a problematic status quo.

During President Trump's first 2020 presidential debate against Joe Biden, the moderator asked him if he would be willing to condemn white supremacist groups and to publicly state that they needed to stand down. During the exchange Trump stated, "I would say almost everything I see is from the left wing, not from the right wing." Trump's statement directly contradicted FBI Director Christopher Wray's testimony to Congress that the predominant domestic terrorism threat emanated from right-wing (largely white supremacist) hate groups. When brought to Trump's attention that Director Wray had also testified that Antifa was a movement or ideology versus a group or organization (though Wray did characterize Antifa as a serious concern), Trump responded by saying, "Well, then you know what—he's wrong."

The ability to effectively solicit and evaluate information and advice, along with critical thinking, are skills needed for effective decision-making, the topic of the next chapter.

CHAPTER 9

Considered
Decision-Making

★ ★ ★

The ability to make good decisions in a timely and reasoned manner is arguably a public servant's most valuable skill. Poor decision-making can lead to embarrassment and short-term setbacks or, worse, calamitous strategic international blunders with unintended second- and third-order effects. Foundational to sound decisiveness are the organizational and ethical principles that inform both judgment and logic. This chapter addresses some of the *mental processes* one brings to decision-making: the management of *inputs* to decision-making, additional considerations such as *timing* and *post-decision analysis*, and, finally, a learning example—President Trump's decision to abandon the 2015 agreement on Iran's nuclear program.

Mental processes. Decision-making in public service requires, first and foremost, that one subordinate *self-interest* in favor of public or shared interests. One must guard against the instincts of self-preservation and personal gain. In *The Room Where It Happened*, former national security advisor John Bolton described how personal motives and political aspirations consistently informed President Trump's decision-making on issues of national significance.

When it comes to public service decision-making, leaders ought to exercise the same degree of diligence for those whom they've never met as they would for themselves or their loved ones.

The role of instinct. Rarely does impulse substitute for knowledge, experience, and robust decision-making processes.

President Trump's May 2017 decision to fire FBI Director James Comey could be an example of someone acting largely on impulse, purportedly out of self-interest, yet the president did not anticipate the consequences to his own presidency. Comey's firing was the catalyst for the appointment of Special Counsel Robert Mueller, who took over the investigation into Russian election interference. Comey's firing also opened the door to the related inquiry into the president's potential obstruction of justice of the Russia investigation. It was perhaps an example of what journalist and author Fareed Zakaria referred to as "the triumph of gut over brain, of emotion over intelligence."

Another example of supplanting logic with emotion comes courtesy of the New Mexico county commissioners who refused to certify election results in June 2022. The commissioners' concerns stemmed from unsubstantiated fears promoted by conspiracy theorists claiming that Dominion Voting Systems machines were compromised. Commissioner Vickie Marquardt felt "dishonest" certifying the election "because in my heart, I don't know if it is right." Her colleague Couy Griffin, who was sentenced for his presence at the U.S. Capitol on January 6, 2021, similarly admitted that his refusal to certify was not "based on any evidence." "It's only based on my gut, my gut feeling, and my own intuition, and that's all I need to base my vote on the elections." Facing possible criminal charges and removal from office, Marquardt and another colleague eventually provided the two-vote majority needed to certify the county's election results.

Instinct and intuition can still play a useful role in decision-making for someone who is well informed and open to advice. Experience and knowledge can fuel beneficial gut reactions, even if one does not fully understand the process. Thomas Jefferson's statement that "experience alone brings skill" could apply to the utility of "informed intuition" for better decision-making.

Critical thinking. A certain degree of conformism is necessary in any organization to promote teamwork and achieve unity of purpose. Intellectual conformism, however, is antithetical to the critical-thinking skills needed by decision-makers. The majority opinion does not always represent the best answer. In the following, Thomas Jefferson made clear his disdain for undisciplined intellectual conformity:

> I never submitted the whole system of my opinions to the creed of any party of men whatever, in religion, in philosophy, in politics, in anything else, where I was capable of thinking for myself. Such an addiction, is the last degradation of a free and moral agent.

Critical thinking is essentially the use of logic, reason, objectivity, and creativity to analyze evidence, separate fact from assumption and opinion, and distill the essential elements into information useful for forming a position. To think critically, one must also possess a certain amount of knowledge. Dr. John Hnatio described the critical thinker as someone who thinks about objections and analyzes positions by probing assumptions and consequences. The critical thinker understands that emotions and prejudices can impact decisions and therefore demands clarity where there is vagueness. It is also important to examine one's prejudices or preferred solutions, especially when they run counter to evidence.

Experts on critical thinking warn about the potential traps in which even good leaders may find themselves. One trap is positive or negative bias associated with the person providing the information. This trap leaves leaders vulnerable to readily accepting bad information or, conversely, rejecting sound input. An example of the former was Donald Trump's propensity to treat dubious information provided by President Vladimir Putin as factual. Another trap involves wishful thinking—believing in a desired outcome without critically evaluating its likelihood.

Keeping an open mind. An open mind allows one to see all sides by evaluating a broader field of facts and opinions. Intellectual humility encourages a person to ask lots of questions, prevents attachment to a particular position, and, when appropriate, allows one to assume a new or revised position based on new evidence.

Decision-makers also need to develop *comfort with ambiguity*— that is, they need to make decisions with confidence despite some degree of uncertainty. Additionally, one should not limit one's evaluations to just the positions at the polar extremes of an issue. Doing so may result in failing to evaluate a more nuanced, and perhaps more appropriate, solution. For example, say two people are fighting over the same orange. Though splitting the orange in half would be the "logical" solution, a better understanding of each person's needs might reveal that one person desires only the rind, while the other wants only flesh.

A leader's lack of expertise on a particular subject can create uncertainty, which can result in indecision, stymying, or stalling. When your own knowledge and experience are insufficient, you must learn to rely on your experts while still challenging their assumptions.

Inputs. One must be able to assimilate the inputs to decision-making in a manner that allows one to make effective, timely, and ethical choices. Effectively analyzing the likely costs and benefits of a decision may require one to embrace the nuance and complexity of a particular issue. Furthermore, as artificial intelligence is increasingly used as an input to decision-making, leaders must remain mindful of when human judgment is required to prevent tech-provided solutions from trampling organizational values.

Balancing available inputs. The knowledge and opinions of any one leader are insufficient for understanding complex issues and formulating coherent policy. Consequently, agencies in the executive branch of the U.S. government have formal processes that detail the use of specific personnel and procedures to facilitate sound decision-making. These processes stand in contrast to the closed and hierarchical decision-making found in most dictatorships. Good leaders seek all available and relevant guidance. It is important to understand what information is available, what information is unknown

("known unknowns"), and with which advisors and stakeholders one should consult. Even for decisions that do not seem particularly complex, consulting with a subordinate, peer, or even a superior may reveal an otherwise overlooked input or solution.

For most issues, there is likely a healthy balance between the need to achieve consensus among your advisors and the tendency to make decisions with minimal input. This balance can be adjusted according to the complexity of the issue and the time available. While consensus is a worthy goal, leaders are expected to make informed decisions without it. It is poor practice, however, to make major decisions with no or limited input from advisors and then expect subordinates (or allies) to scramble to implement or react to those decisions.

President Trump, on several occasions, rebuffed consulting with experts. Instead, he announced major decisions via social media without consulting his advisors and, in some cases, before consulting America's international allies. What could have been a well-defined process often degenerated into chaos management for the president's staff.

Reality and objectivity. Experiential reality—encompassing the senses, intuition, beliefs, and experiences—tends to reinforce one's perceptions of reality. It also distorts facts to fit preexisting notions, thus constraining thinking. This phenomenon is thwarted by the input of advisors. Agreement reality—involving concepts that do not necessarily represent reality but make our lives easier when we collectively buy into them (like time zones)—can also affect our thinking. Experiential and agreement reality challenge our capacity to remain objective or impartial with respect to inputs that do not already neatly fit into our existing worldviews. Consequently, public institutions must have access to objective data that allow leaders to effectively confront issues related to an organization's mission, readiness, and relationships.

Leaders must of course have an interest in receiving objective data. As former attorney general William Barr stated regarding President Trump's claim in December 2021 that there was definitive evidence of fraud associated with Dominion voting machines, "There was never an indication of interest in what the actual facts were."

Filtering out noise. In order to avoid the "garbage in, garbage out" phenomenon, one must learn to filter out the distracting and irrelevant inputs that can hinder judgment and objectivity. The biases associated with our aforementioned realities represent some of that noise. When we obtain more input than necessary, the surplus and potentially irrelevant information (or noise) can unnecessarily and unacceptably delay decision-making. German philosopher Friedrich Schiller warned that one "who reflects too much will accomplish little." Similarly, a general for whom I worked made a habit of reminding us that most decisions can be made with about 80 percent of the available information. The remaining 20 percent of available information often just confirms or validates the information we already have. That is, the pursuit of "perfection" is often the enemy of "good enough" and may result in analysis paralysis. Knowing one's job well also helps to filter out the noise.

Doing your homework. Performing one's due diligence involves looking carefully at an issue from every perspective. In May 2020, President Trump fired the State Department's inspector general, who was in good company as Trump had recently fired several IGs from other executive branch agencies. This particular IG had reportedly been investigating alleged improprieties involving Secretary of State Mike Pompeo and his wife. When asked by reporters about his decision to fire the State Department IG, Trump said, "I don't know him at all. I never even heard of him. But I was asked to by the State Department, by Mike [Pompeo]." If his response is taken at face value, Trump really did not understand why he was firing the IG. A willingness and need to understand the salient details of an issue should not be conflated with micromanagement. Pompeo's conduct was eventually found by the State Department to be "inconsistent with the Standards of Ethical Conduct and related Department policies." The president had a duty to understand the circumstances and justifications associated with Pompeo's request.

Additional considerations. The appropriate or necessary *time* required to decide can vary greatly. In emergency, time-sensitive situations, the decision-maker will have limited opportunity to receive and consider input from colleagues. Using an aviation example, when a helicopter experiences sudden catastrophic gearbox failure, there is no time to form a committee to explore potential responses. The pilot must recognize the condition and take the necessary steps within the first two to three seconds to ensure a survivable landing. A more strategic example involves the time available for the U.S. government to determine a response after detecting the launch of a nuclear warhead from Russia. Based on the flight time of an intercontinental ballistic missile, the decision-making window would be under thirty minutes. In scenarios where time is limited, decision-making is aided by well-developed processes, checklists, and situation-specific training.

Decision-making in public service generally requires a rather deliberate approach. One should not make snap decisions in order to appear decisive, especially when there is time to fully leverage the resources at one's disposal. Staffs exist to present decision-makers with well-researched courses of action. Even for large-scale and relatively slow-moving public health emergencies such as a pandemic, plans exist to guide the more urgent decisions and to ensure the participation and input of all relevant players. Nelson Mandela believed that most of the mistakes he had made in his life came from acting too hastily rather than too slowly. There are some decisions that benefit from delay. But if you are delaying or avoiding saying no because it is unpleasant, better to do it right away and clearly.

Thomas Jefferson wrote about his admiration for George Washington's resistance to unnecessary haste. "Perhaps the strongest feature of his character was prudence, never acting until every circumstance, every consideration, was maturely weighed; refraining if he saw a doubt, but, when once decided, going through with his purpose, whatever obstacles opposed." The Cuban Missile Crisis of 1962 is a good case study for considered decision-making. Having lived through two world wars, Soviet leader Nikita Khrushchev understood that one rash action could trigger an exaggerated, catastrophic response. By being intentionally deliberate, both Kennedy and Khrushchev allowed the other to "step back from the brink" while searching for an exit. They avoided pushing the other into a corner by allowing the initial response of anger to evolve into a rational fear of nuclear war. Consequently, some decisions were intentionally postponed.

Vertical empathy versus independent decisiveness. Leaders must consider organizational relationships when making decisions. The notion of vertical empathy encourages leaders to consider what impact their decisions will have several echelons up the chain and whether those decisions align with the priorities of their superiors.

There are times, however, when leaders must show decisiveness in lieu of deferring to actual or perceived guidance from senior leaders. While subordinate organizations must generally comply with higher directives, they often have the latitude to enact more restrictive measures as needed.

Leaders should also consider their successors and the future of their organizations as they deliberate. Impacts should be evaluated not just in the short-term context of a leader's tenure but also in the context of an organization's enduring policy objectives.

Anticipating responses. Before a decision is made, one should anticipate how stakeholders and even casual observers will respond to the initial announcement and the likely consequences of the decision. Example: President Trump should not have expressed surprise at the level of pushback that resulted from his initial decision to host a meeting of the G7 at one of his Trump-branded properties. It was a clear conflict of interest.

Post-decision considerations. In a manner consistent with providing feedback to subordinates or conducting an after-action review, decisions on significant issues should be critically examined after the fact. Tools such as the OODA loop cycle of decision-making (observe, orient, decide, act), developed by Air Force colonel John Boyd, can be used in post-decision analysis so that lessons learned and newly acquired data can be fused to inform future decision-making.

One trap to avoid in post-decision analysis is the tendency to judge the merits of a decision based only on the outcome. People routinely get away with bad decisions. Similarly, good decisions will occasionally yield undesired outcomes because of extreme, unusual, or unforeseen factors or circumstances. Finally, it is important to have the willingness or agility to change course when a decision or series of decisions is not producing the desired result.

Pulling out of the Iran nuclear agreement. The Iran nuclear agreement, or Joint Comprehensive Plan of Action (JCPOA), was a 2015 agreement between Iran, the United States, China, France, Germany, and the United Kingdom. The UN Security Council endorsed the agreement (implemented in January 2016) that required Iran to take key steps to restrict its nuclear program while also agreeing to intrusive inspections (up to twenty-five years in some cases). Iran's compliance was monitored by the International Atomic Energy Agency (IAEA) and confirmed by the intelligence services of the United States and the plan's other signatories. Presidential candidate Trump repeatedly disparaged the hard-won deal before the 2016 election.

Despite clear evidence of Iran's compliance, President Trump announced in May 2018 that the United States was withdrawing from the agreement and would reinstate nuclear sanctions on the Iranian regime. Trump was gambling that the resulting economic hardship would force Iran to accept a more restrictive agreement. Instead, Iran began violating the JCPOA in May 2019, citing how the new sanctions negated a key component of the original plan—sanctions relief tied to their nuclear activities. Pulling out of the deal also vanquished the extraordinary verification measures that had been used by international inspectors. Meanwhile, President Trump continued to spread falsehoods about the original agreement.

> @realDonaldTrump
> President Obama made a desperate and terrible deal with Iran - Gave them 150 Billion Dollars plus 1.8 Billion Dollars in CASH! Iran was in big trouble and he bailed them out. Gave them a free path to Nuclear Weapons, and SOON. Instead of saying thank you, Iran yelled.....
> ....Death to America. I terminated deal, which was not even ratified by Congress, and imposed strong sanctions. They are a much weakened nation today than at the beginning of my Presidency, when they were causing major problems throughout the Middle East. Now they are Bust!....
> 6:03 AM - Jun 21, 2019

As former secretary of energy Ernest Moniz explained on CNN, the Trump administration's so-called maximum-pressure campaign on Iran, which started in 2018, had no material effect on the country's regional adventures or mischief. Furthermore, Iran was not given $150 billion (a high estimate) but rather was allowed through the agreement to access its own money that had been frozen largely in foreign banks (outside of the United States) when Iran was previously sanctioned. The $1.8 billion referenced by Trump was unrelated to the JCPOA and stemmed from a claim Iran had filed against the United States in international courts. The Trump administration's criticisms often revolved around issues involving Iran that were never intended to be resolved in the context of the JCPOA.

President Trump's loathing of his predecessor's role in securing the agreement likely contributed to a decision guided more by impulse than reason. Objectivity and critical thinking did not have a chance. Trump's rhetorical criticism of the deal does not provide any insight into the interagency process that may have influenced his decision. His criticism does not appear to be informed by an understanding of the JCPOA's merits, its basic provisions, or, of course, the consequences of terminating America's involvement in the deal. President Trump appears to have been unwilling to do his homework. Fareed Zakaria provided the following commentary on the administration's post-decision justifications:

> The best illustration of the incoherence of the Trump administration's strategy toward Iran came last week in a White House press release. It read, "There is little doubt that even before the deal's existence, Iran was violating its terms." The White House has not subsequently explained how a country can violate the terms of a deal before that deal existed.

Prior to 2018, Iran had no highly enriched uranium. It has since very effectively used the time to increase its nuclear capacity. As of 2022, Iran had produced tons of enriched uranium. A November 2021 IAEA report suggested that Iran had developed the ability to produce enough weapon-grade uranium for a single nuclear weapon in as little as three weeks. This so-called breakout period was at least one year when the agreement was in effect.

While other consequences of President Trump's decision may have been unintended, they were certainly foreseeable. Prior to the agreement, Europe's support of America's stance regarding Iran's nuclear program had created enough pressure to force Iran to the negotiating table. When President Trump pulled the United States out of the deal, it undercut America's credibility and standing in the world by sending the message, to both allies and adversaries, that it could not be trusted to abide by the terms of a negotiated agreement—even one it had championed. Trump's decision predictably deepened a humanitarian crisis in Iran, increased tensions in the region, and provided Iran an excuse to violate the terms of the deal. It also pushed Iran further into the arms of Russia and China.

CHAPTER 10

Things You Don't Do Publicly

★ ★ ★

Millions of public servants wake up each workday with the intention of doing their best to further the missions of their agencies. When they or their leaders are unnecessarily publicly disparaged, the adverse effects are felt throughout those organizations.

There are some actions—unless justified by exceptional circumstances—that should simply not be undertaken publicly (that is, organization-wide or external to the organization). They include personal admonishments and notifications of termination.

I am disappointed in you, and the world needs to know about it. There are protocols to ensure that employees put their egos and personal feelings aside in a manner that affords their superiors a commensurate degree of respect and courtesy. But respect must flow both ways. In the same way that subordinates should not publicly criticize their superiors, leaders must treat their subordinates with decency and dignity. To praise in public and admonish in private is a basic rule of leadership. Nonetheless, publicly belittling, bullying, and humiliating subordinates is surprisingly common both in public and private organizations.

Holding subordinates accountable for their conduct and performance is crucial for individual professional development and organizational effectiveness. In most instances, it should be done discreetly to avoid embarrassment or humiliation. Communicating a lack of belief in someone—especially publicly—compromises a person's ability to learn from their mistakes. Likewise, one should avoid making overarching judgments about a person and instead focus on criticizing the problematic behavior or outcome. The goal should be behavior modification and performance enhancement versus guilt or shame that the subordinate might project into the future. We all have *self-imposed* limitations. Leaders should not impose additional limitations on someone's potential by responding with unnecessarily harsh criticism or discipline, especially when mentoring is likely the more appropriate tool.

There are some instances, however, where public admonishment serves as an effective deterrent or lesson for others. One example is the public release of information relating to convictions or significant administrative proceedings, especially for the purpose of showing that even senior officials are being held to account. Another example might include calling out a subordinate's inappropriate behavior in real time when it is witnessed by the offender's peers (behavior such as insubordination or bigotry).

Judgment is sometimes needed to determine whether public or semi-private counseling is more fitting. While practicing Air Force ROTC marching maneuvers at the University of Florida, our flight commander (a more senior cadet) told my friend and fellow cadet

Mike to instruct about ten of us on a particular marching maneuver. With the flight commander observing from about thirty feet away, Mike stood before us and explained that there were two ways to perform the maneuver: the flight commander's way and the correct way. We struggled to control our nervous laughter after this brash display of bravado and disrespect (even if he was technically correct). To her enormous credit, the flight commander watched silently for several minutes until Mike had completed his instruction. She then called him over to where she was standing, out of earshot for the rest of us, and administered some necessary counseling. She would have been completely justified in stopping him immediately and publicly dressing him down, providing us a lesson in respect for authority. She instead exercised judgment and provided us a lesson in discipline, personal security, and restraint by allowing him to continue before eventually providing a verbal reprimand that we could see but not hear. A less confident leader might not have handled the situation so professionally. It is worth noting that she had been, and continued to be, one of the most respected cadet leaders in the organization.

Insecurity and narcissism can fuel unnecessary public admonishment, sometimes resulting in the deflection of blame onto subordinates. Whatever the motivation, the end result will likely be resentful employees who dread going to work. Those subordinates may also acquire a newfound "excuse" to thwart their leaders' agendas. Leaders should also understand that their own inappropriate behaviors will have ripple effects. Humiliated subordinates may in turn take it out on their own subordinates. They may also bring that anger home. Finally, employees with self-respect will not tolerate a toxic work environment. They may even leave public service for more lucrative opportunities in the private sector.

The most inappropriate form of public admonishment may be the trashing of a subordinate leader in front of his or her own subordinates. One such example came courtesy of President Trump's acting secretary of the Navy, Thomas Modly. Captain Brett Crozier was relieved of his command of the USS *Theodore Roosevelt* by Modly for actions resulting in the leak of a memorandum. Crozier's memo warned about the unabated spread of COVID-19 on his aircraft carrier. Shortly thereafter, Secretary Modly flew to Guam to address the crew of the ship, a crew that by most accounts had been enamored with their leader. In his remarks before a gathering of the crew that was also transmitted ship-wide, Modly characterized Crozier as "too naive or too stupid" to be in command. A sailor in attendance was immediately heard exclaiming "What the fuck?" in response to Modly's comment. Modly eventually apologized to the Navy for "any confusion this choice of words may have caused," insisting that "the spoken words were from the heart." Controlling his heart and mouth with his brain would have been more appropriate and less detrimental to good order and morale. Secretary Modly resigned shortly after the incident.

President Trump was particularly fond of publicly questioning, antagonizing, and humiliating his immediate subordinates.

@realDonaldTrump

I told Rex Tillerson, our wonderful Secretary of State, that he is wasting his time trying to negotiate with Little Rocket Man...

7:30 AM - Oct 1, 2017

...Save your energy Rex, we'll do what has to be done!

7:31 AM - Oct 1, 2017

The following post was in response to FBI Director Christopher Wray's testimony to Congress. Wray had warned about the "very active efforts by the Russians to influence our election in 2020...to both sow divisiveness and discord and...to denigrate Vice President Biden."

> @realDonaldTrump
> But Chris, you don't see any activity from China, even though it is a FAR greater threat than Russia, Russia, Russia. They will both, plus others, be able to interfere in our 2020 Election with our totally vulnerable Unsolicited (Counterfeit?) Ballot Scam. Check it out!
> 8:20 PM - Sep 17, 2020

During an October 2020 town hall event, a journalist confronted President Trump about his election fraud conspiracy theories. When the president was reminded that his FBI director (who has about thirty-five thousand people under him) had stated that there was no evidence of widespread fraud, Trump responded with, "Well, then he's not doing a very good job."

One of President Trump's favorite punching bags was his first attorney general, Jeff Sessions. His complaints in the following posts were largely without merit.

> @realDonaldTrump
> Why is A.G. Jeff Sessions asking the Inspector General to investigate potentially massive FISA abuse. Will take forever, has no prosecutorial power and already late with reports on Comey etc. Isn't the I.G. an Obama guy? Why not use Justice Department lawyers? **DISGRACEFUL!**
> 6:34 AM - Feb 28, 2018

@realDonaldTrump

....Do you believe Nelly worked for Fusion and her husband STILL WORKS FOR THE DEPARTMENT OF "JUSTICE." I have never seen anything so Rigged in my life. **Our A.G. is scared stiff and Missing in Action.** It is all starting to be revealed - not pretty. IG Report soon? Witch Hunt!

11:54 AM - Aug 11, 2018

@realDonaldTrump

"They were all in on it, clear Hillary Clinton and FRAME Donald Trump for things he didn't do." Gregg Jarrett on @foxandfriends **If we had a real Attorney General,** this Witch Hunt would never have been started! Looking at the wrong people.

5:06 AM - Aug 14, 2018

@realDonaldTrump

Two long running, Obama era, investigations of two very popular Republican Congressmen were brought to a well publicized charge, just ahead of the Mid-Terms, **by the Jeff Sessions Justice Department.** Two easy wins now in doubt because there is not enough time. **Good job Jeff......**

11:25 AM - Sep 3, 2018

Not content with demeaning agency heads and cabinet officials who reported directly to him, President Trump occasionally unleashed his wrath onto other senior and even mid-level executive branch personnel. His victims included Army lieutenant colonel

Alexander Vindman, who had testified to Congress about the president's infamous call to Ukrainian president Zelenskyy.

> @realDonaldTrump
> Fake News @CNN & MSDNC keep talking about "Lt. Col." Vindman as though I should think only how wonderful he was. Actually, I don't know him, never spoke to him, or met him (I don't believe!) but, **he was very insubordinate, reported contents of my "perfect" calls incorrectly, &...**
> **....was given a horrendous report by his superior,** the man he reported to, who publicly stated that Vindman **had problems with judgement, adhering to the chain of command and leaking information.** In other words, "OUT".
> 9:41 AM - Feb 8, 2020

Though he was effectively the leader of his political party, the president was not shy about publicly disparaging congressional Republicans.

> @realDonaldTrump
> Great news for the Republican Party as **one of the dumbest & most disloyal men** in Congress is "quitting" the Party. No Collusion, No Obstruction! Knew he couldn't get the nomination to run again in the Great State of Michigan. Already being challenged for his seat. **A total loser!**
> 6:05 AM - Jul 4, 2019

President Trump was also happy to humiliate those who did not work for him (though he had nominated this individual for Senate confirmation):

@realDonaldTrump

Our pathetic, slow moving Federal Reserve, headed by Jay Powell, who raised rates too fast and lowered too late, should get our Fed Rate down to the levels of our competitor nations. They now have as much as a two point advantage, with even bigger currency help. Also, stimulate!

10:00 AM - Mar 10, 2020

@realDonaldTrump

....My only question is, **who is our bigger enemy, Jay Powell or Chairman Xi?**

10:57 AM - Aug 23, 2019

No termination without humiliation. Or as Trump liked to say, "Fired like a dog." Leaders should have the courage to personally and discreetly inform their immediate subordinates that they are being terminated, replaced, or asked to resign. In most cases, relying on subordinates to deliver that information is cowardly. President Trump's chief of staff phoned Veterans Affairs (VA) Secretary David Shulkin to inform him of his firing just before Trump posted the announcement. Worse yet, Trump had reportedly had a phone conversation with the VA secretary just hours earlier, making no mention of his imminent termination.

FBI Director James Comey learned that President Trump

had fired him in May 2017 through a television news report he happened to notice while addressing employees at a Los Angeles FBI field office. The initial news report claimed that Comey had resigned, leading Comey to initially believe it was an elaborate prank perpetrated by his FBI colleagues. He later learned that an official termination letter, sent by Trump to his office in Washington, D.C., explained that he was being fired based (somewhat disingenuously) on the recommendation of the deputy attorney general. Trump's chief of staff reportedly threatened to resign in disgust over the way Comey was treated. Adding insult to injury, the president told the Russian foreign minister in the Oval Office just days later, "I just fired the head of the FBI. He was crazy, a real nut job."

It was not beneath the president to provide initial notice of termination to his cabinet officials via tweet.

@realDonaldTrump

Mike Pompeo, Director of the CIA, **will become our new Secretary of State.** He will do a fantastic job! **Thank you to Rex Tillerson for his service!** Gina Haspel will become the new Director of the CIA, and the first woman so chosen. Congratulations to all!

5:44 AM - Mar 13, 2018

Wanting to contribute in real time, President Trump conveniently issued the following termination post on the very day I was writing this chapter.

@realDonaldTrump

I am pleased to announce that Christopher C.
Miller, the highly respected Director of the National
Counterterrorism Center (unanimously confirmed by
the Senate), **will be Acting Secretary of Defense,
effective immediately..**

    **...Chris will do a GREAT job! Mark Esper
has been terminated.** I would like to thank him
for his service.

12:54 PM - Nov 9, 2020

CHAPTER 11

Diplomacy and Professional
Interpersonal Relationships

★ ★ ★

I t is not only accredited diplomats who represent their countries abroad. All government employees working abroad or interacting with foreign counterparts at home are engaging in diplomacy to some degree. They are not just representing themselves or their organizations; they are representing their country and the character of their fellow citizens.

When interacting with foreign counterparts, one should strive to preserve a counterpart's dignity by avoiding displays of arrogance. This is especially true when one represents a more powerful and influential country. Consider the example of a wealthy and arrogant restaurant patron who treats their server poorly. The server is not only likely to resent the obnoxious customer but may also come to resent *all* wealthy people. The same phenomenon can occur in international diplomacy when a bad experience results in someone unnecessarily internalizing a negative stereotype.

Discretion is a valuable tool in diplomacy. Similar to the

principle of praising in public and admonishing in private, diplomacy is more effective when more forceful language (such as a warning) is communicated privately. Though there may be times when it is appropriate for governments to publicly condemn objectionable behavior, *publicly* criticizing a counterpart can have the effect of backing someone into a corner and compromising cooperation.

Communicating on the world stage. Because communication is the primary tool of diplomacy, it is of utmost importance to strive for clarity and authenticity when presenting one's positions and intentions with foreign counterparts. Doing so will minimize misunderstandings and prevent unnecessary provocation. Likewise, strive to fully understand the positions and concerns of your counterparts.

Foreign counterparts are not oblivious to how our leaders characterize their own predecessors and other domestic colleagues. To a practical degree, and consistent with the notion that politics end at "the water's edge," one should avoid highlighting domestic fissures or insulting domestic peers when communicating to a global audience. Trashing a former (or future) administration is still trashing one's own government.

@realDonaldTrump
Does the Fake News Media remember when Crooked Hillary Clinton, as Secretary of State, was begging Russia to be our friend with the misspelled reset button? Obama tried also, but he had zero chemistry with Putin.
4:43 PM - Nov 11, 2017

@realDonaldTrump
I was actually sticking up for Sleepy Joe Biden while on foreign soil. Kim Jong Un called him a "low IQ idiot," and many other things, whereas I related the quote of Chairman Kim as a much softer "low IQ individual." Who could possibly be upset with that?
2:58 PM - May 28, 2019

It should go without saying that making false claims can irreparably damage credibility and compromise the trust that international partnerships require. For example, when President Trump contradicted the findings and public testimony of his own intelligence agencies, falsely asserting early in his tenure that Iran was not complying with the JCPOA, the credibility of American leadership abroad was tarnished. One indicator of a more general erosion of trust abroad was reflected in a 2020 Pew Research Center poll of citizens in thirteen countries allied with the United States. When asked about the international reputations of six world leaders, only 16 percent of respondents indicated that President Trump could be trusted to do the right thing regarding world affairs. The poll results likely reflected the policy positions and choices of each of the six world leaders. At 16 percent, President Trump had the lowest confidence rating, finishing just behind Russia's president Putin and China's president Xi. In contrast, Germany's chancellor Angela Merkel had a confidence rating of 76 percent.

Professional interpersonal relationships. In the conduct of diplomatic activities, maintaining the quality of the bilateral, country-to-country relationship takes precedence over the standing of any personal diplomatic relationship. Policy objectives cannot take a back seat to maintaining excellent personal rapport. That said, establishing and nurturing productive interpersonal relationships with foreign counterparts is essential for influencing behavior, facilitating cooperation, and finding common understanding in pursuit of mutually beneficial policy solutions. That same focus on productive relationships, albeit with domestic counterparts, can also facilitate intragovernmental or interagency problem-solving.

Diplomatic relationships are more than mere transactional engagements. There is inherent value in maintaining good relations. For example, the trust I cultivated with the heads of various Filipino government agencies proved to be instrumental. On one occasion, my relationship with the head of the Civil Aviation Authority of the Philippines permitted me to secure critical, short-notice support for the launch of U.S. aircraft in support of counterterrorism operations.

Strong personal connections focused on mutual respect and cooperation can produce mutually beneficial outcomes that would otherwise prove elusive. I would describe this type of relationship as a *healthy* diplomatic friendship—warm and yet professional. Though primarily a means to an end, such a friendship might be considered a secondary goal with its own inherent value. It is certainly more pleasant to work with a counterpart whose company you enjoy. After four years of working closely with my Philippine Air Force counterpart on a variety of bilateral security issues, we had developed a genuine friendship that continues to this day. Nonetheless, one should not feel obligated to characterize a counterpart as a "friend."

@realDonaldTrump

Such an honor to have my good friend, Israel PM @ Netanyahu, join us w/ his delegation in NYC this afternoon.

4:31 PM - Sep 18, 2017

@realDonaldTrump

Why would Kim Jong-un insult me by calling me "old," when I would NEVER call him "short and fat?" Oh well, I try so hard to be his friend - and maybe someday that will happen!

4:48 PM - Nov 11, 2017

@realDonaldTrump

President Xi and I will always be friends, no matter what happens with our dispute on trade. China will take down its Trade Barriers because it is the right thing to do. Taxes will become Reciprocal & a deal will be made on Intellectual Property. Great future for both countries!

5:12 AM - Apr 8, 2018

As previously stated, mere friendship should not be the driving force behind the wider diplomatic partnership. While interpersonal skills are certainly important, strategy and preparation are needed to deal with complex and consequential issues. President Trump was often accused of relying excessively on his personal relationships with counterparts in lieu of making full use of his cadre of seasoned diplomats.

@realDonaldTrump

I agree with Kim Jong Un of North Korea that our
personal relationship remains very good, perhaps the
term excellent would be even more accurate, and that
a third Summit would be good in that we fully understand where we each stand. North Korea has tremendous potential for.......

4:54 AM - Apr 13, 2019

One can have a good personal relationship with a foreign
counterpart who still does not respect your nation's values and has
no interest in furthering your nation's interests. President Trump was
fond of pointing out his allegedly good relationships with authoritarian leaders such as Turkey's president Erdoğan, China's president
Xi, and North Korea's supreme leader Kim. Having a good working
relationship with an adversary or competitor is not inherently bad.
But emphasizing the closeness of those relationships over those with
more traditionally allied leaders betrays what should be a robust
defense of one's own national values and interests. In the following
post, President Trump may have assumed that one of his more adversarial counterparts was, like him, flattery operated.

@realDonaldTrump

...Got along great with Kim Jong-un who wants to
see wonderful things for his country. As I said earlier
today: Anyone can make war, but only the most courageous can make peace! #SingaporeSummit

1:40 PM - Jun 12, 2018

It would have been preferable for Trump to brag (if warranted) about good relations with members of the opposition party at home rather than autocrats abroad.

Just prior to the 2016 election, then presidential candidate Trump publicly suggested he would get along well with Russian president Putin, whom he described as a "strong leader." Candidate Trump also publicly questioned NATO's relevance—music to Putin's ears. During a military town hall event, he praised Vladimir Putin for having "very strong control over a country." Candidate Trump's attempt to clarify the previous comment was perhaps more problematic. "Now, it's a very different system, and I don't happen to like the system, but certainly in that system, he's been a leader. Far more than our president has been a leader." For many reasons, Russian political analysts at the time perceived Trump as favorable to Russia. When Russia interfered in the 2016 election to discredit Hillary Clinton and bolster Trump's chances for success, it was acting in what it believed to be its national interests.

Narcissistic diplomacy. A diplomatic relationship conducted with narcissistic tendencies will inevitably subordinate the national interest to self-interest and the need for personal validation. Another consequence is the development of inappropriately close ties that can compromise rational decision-making. That undue familiarity can result in unwarranted trust that makes one more susceptible to manipulation. This dynamic can lead to compounding personal and professional compromises.

The notion that you destroy your enemies when you make them your friends has limitations. At a September 2018 rally in West Virginia, President Trump described his relationship with North

Korean dictator Kim Jong Un: "I was really being tough, and so was he. And we would go back and forth. And then we fell in love, okay? No, really. He wrote me beautiful letters, and they're great letters. We fell in love." As an attaché in Manila, I was required to formally report (for counterintelligence purposes) any close and continuing personal relationships I had with foreign nationals. Though Trump was not describing an actual romantic relationship, a U.S. president's musings about a warm and close relationship with a brutal and murderous dictator—one who had recently issued nuclear threats against the United States—were inappropriate. His sentiments did not support America's promotion of democratic principles.

In 2020, when Kim finally emerged after a multiweek hiatus from public events that had caused speculation about a serious health issue, President Trump was quick to publicly express his relief.

@realDonaldTrump
I, for one, am glad to see he is back, and well!
5:24 PM - May 2, 2020

While President Trump might be applauded for his uncharacteristic "love thy enemy" approach, a private message might have been more appropriate. Similarly, the following post might have seemed like a warning but more likely bolstered the North Korean dictator's image.

@realDonaldTrump
Kim Jong Un is in good health.
Never underestimate him!
8:45 AM - Sep 10, 2020

Thomas Jefferson wrote the following about trust: "I had rather be the victim of occasional infidelities, than relinquish my general confidence in the honesty of man." Ronald Reagan modified that sentiment with his use of the Russian maxim "Trust, but verify." A trustful nature can be healthy and appropriate in diplomacy. But dealing with foreign governments that often pursue their own interests at the expense of others requires more than naive optimism. A narcissistic approach to diplomacy tends to erode one's necessary skepticism, leaving one open to the manipulative charm and charisma of a skilled adversary. President Trump's excessive admiration and trust allowed him to take and act on advice from Presidents Putin and Erdoğan at the expense of his own institutions. As mentioned, in Helsinki, Trump publicly accepted Putin's denials about Russian interference in the 2016 election (contradicting the conclusions of his own intelligence agencies). In early 2020, Trump was also quick to accept President Xi's assurances that the Chinese had adequately controlled the spread of the COVID-19 virus.

In *Talking to Strangers*, author Malcolm Gladwell described a phenomenon in which people are more likely to place unwarranted trust in someone they have met face-to-face. Gladwell provided the example of how Britain's Neville Chamberlain was inclined to take Hitler at his word after meeting with him. It was the people who spent time with Hitler who were more likely to get him wrong, ignoring the obvious warnings found, for example, in his writings. Gladwell explained that when meeting a charismatic person like Hitler, you tend to overvalue the information from that encounter at the expense of more useful and readily available information that reveals that person's past behavior and future intentions. In contrast, those who had not met Hitler—Prime Minister Churchill and President Roosevelt, to name a few—did not trust him. In another example, George W. Bush famously said after meeting Vladimir Putin that he "looked the man in the eye. I found him to be very straightforward and trustworthy. We had a very good dialogue. I was able to get a sense of his soul; a man deeply committed to his country and the best interests of his country." It is dangerous to have too much faith in one's own ability to read someone's character and intentions.

Excessive deference to foreign counterparts is another symptom and unfortunate result of narcissistic diplomacy. Two of Trump's cabinet members reportedly had concerns about the president granting inappropriate personal favors to autocratic leaders (including undue influence in a DOJ investigation of foreign companies). When President Trump was not threatening his counterparts, he was often extending unwarranted courtesy and accommodation toward them in lieu of a more pragmatic approach. For example, after the president's personal meetings with Kim Jong Un, Trump began minimizing the significance of North Korean missile tests that potentially bolstered the regime's ability to strike targets in South Korea and Japan.

@realDonaldTrump
Kim Jong Un and North Korea tested 3 short range missiles over the last number of days. These missiles tests are not a violation of our signed Singapore agreement, nor was there discussion of short range missiles when we shook hands. There may be a United Nations violation, but..

.....Chairman Kim does not want to disappoint me with a violation of trust, there is far too much for North Korea to gain - the potential as a Country, under Kim Jong Un's leadership, is unlimited. Also, there is far too much to lose. I may be wrong, but I believe that......

....Chariman Kim has a great and beautiful vision for his country, and only the United States, with me as President, can make that vision come true. He will do the right thing because he is far too smart not to, and he does not want to disappoint his friend, President Trump!

11:05 AM - Aug 2, 2019

Trump's unwarranted faith in and excessive deference toward Kim in these posts was likely the result of evaluating Kim's actions through the lens of their personal interactions and correspondence. If President Trump had understood that Kim's provocative actions did not necessarily reflect negatively on himself, Trump might have reacted more objectively and in line with the national interest. But when one makes the focus of international diplomacy one's apparent influence over a counterpart, one begins to rationalize—even when the facts on the ground are counter to the national interest. An inordinate need to appear accommodating or to be liked opens the door to manipulation. No American president before Trump had crossed into North Korea when visiting the demilitarized zone separating it from South Korea. When Trump did so with Kim, he gave Kim's regime what it wanted most—a perception of increased legitimacy. Counterparts can also manipulate with excessive flattery. When

Trump heard that Kim had "unwavering faith in President Trump," it was music to the ears of someone with narcissistic tendencies. The likely effect was that Trump felt pressure to avoid angering or disappointing Kim.

While most diplomatic relationships are likely authentic and transparent with respect to goals and intentions, one has to be on guard for the relationships in which gratuitous flattery, gifts, and unsolicited favors belie less transparent motives. In other words, one has to have diplomatic street smarts. A few of my professional contacts in Manila were masquerading as friends, showering me with unexpected "kindness." The motivation became clear: to obtain diplomatic favors—some appropriate, others questionable. On several occasions during social events organized by my foreign counterparts, I would be discreetly handed an envelope containing a request for a professional favor or courtesy. The requests were usually prepared in a manner suggesting I had advance knowledge of it and furthermore was willing to accommodate it. In some instances, I was able to provide the requested assistance, thereby almost ensuring future reciprocal cooperation on matters of importance to my government. In other cases, it was easy to maintain good relations while explaining that my government's rules simply did not authorize me to facilitate the request.

There can be a real temptation to ignore established professional boundaries (meant to protect you and national interests) when trying to further a professional relationship with a foreign national. There is a human tendency to conflate excellent personal relations with diplomatic success. This need to please—to feel as though you are "coming through" for someone—can result in questionable acts that may be unethical or even illegal by the standards of one's own government. This very scenario played out, almost entirely unbeknownst to me at the time, with a senior colleague with whom I enjoyed working. My colleague's repeated lapses in judgment eventually resulted in a prison sentence.

Intelligence officers serving in diplomatic positions around the globe are trained in the art of eliciting sensitive information from their counterparts. This dynamic raises the stakes when one feels the need to please or impress one's counterpart. President Trump reportedly revealed sensitive and possibly classified information about operations in Syria to the Russian foreign minister during a 2017 meeting in the Oval Office. The incident rattled allies and Trump's own national security team, who wondered whether the president could be trusted to meet with certain foreign leaders without compromising national security. The need to maintain an inappropriately close personal relationship can also result in one wittingly or unwittingly amplifying foreign propaganda and co-opting an adversary's talking points. In the following posts, President Trump managed again to denigrate a former vice president (and future president) and criticize military exercises conducted with South Korea, a key American ally.

@realDonaldTrump

North Korea fired off some small weapons, which disturbed some of my people, and others, but not me. I have confidence that Chairman Kim will keep his promise to me, & also smiled when he called Swampman Joe Biden a low IQ individual, & worse. Perhaps that's sending me a signal?

6:32 PM - May 25, 2019

@realDonaldTrump
In a letter to me sent by Kim Jong Un, he stated,
very nicely, that he would like to meet and start
negotiations as soon as the joint U.S./South Korea
joint exercise are over. It was a long letter, much of it
complaining about the ridiculous and expensive exercises. It was.....
       ....also a small apology for testing the short
range missiles, and that this testing would stop when
the exercises end. I look forward to seeing Kim Jong
Un in the not too distant future! A nuclear free North
Korea will lead to one of the most successful countries in the world!
7:58 AM - Aug 10, 2019

In this final example of undue loyalty stemming from narcissistic self-interest and a need to please, President Trump again contradicted the conclusions of his own intelligence agencies. In this case,
he downplayed Crown Prince Mohammed bin Salman's complicity
in ordering the 2018 murder and dismemberment of U.S.-based
journalist and Saudi Arabian dissident Jamal Khashoggi.

@realDonaldTrump
Just spoke with the Crown Prince of Saudi Arabia
who totally denied any knowledge of what took place
in their Turkish Consulate. He was with Secretary of
State Mike Pompeo...
11:40 AM - Oct 16, 2018

CHAPTER 12

Retaliation

T he U.S. Equal Employment Opportunity Commission (EEOC), along with the U.S. Office of Special Counsel (OSC), investigates allegations of workplace discrimination along with other prohibited personnel practices. Per the EEOC, retaliation[1] is the most frequently alleged basis of discrimination by federal employees. Consequently, the EEOC and OSC protect employees who disclose wrongdoing or otherwise cooperate in their investigations via statutes such as the Whistleblower Protection Act.

Supervisors retaliate for a host of reasons. Some retaliate when their subordinates refuse to agree with their public statements or similarly refuse to refute facts they know to be true. Supervisors might also retaliate when their inappropriate comments or physical advances are rebuffed. Leaders who are unable to tolerate even

....

1 Some government agencies use the terms *retaliation* and *reprisal* interchangeably (as I do here). Others distinguish between the two. Retaliation is sometimes described as the verbal or physical mistreatment of employees by peers or supervisors, whereas reprisal is often associated with adverse personnel actions or, conversely, the withholding of favorable personnel actions.

183

reasonable levels of dissent or disagreement sometimes retaliate with unrelated adverse personnel actions. Others retaliate due to what they incorrectly perceive as disloyalty. Such was the case in President Trump's public and persistent harassment of Attorney General Jeff Sessions over his appropriate recusal from the investigation into Russian interference in the 2016 election (an episode covered further in chapter 28).

Government officials who feel that they must publicly disagree with their bosses—especially regarding potentially reckless policies or illegal conduct—often choose anonymity precisely because they fear some form of retaliation.

> @realDonaldTrump
> Does the so-called "Senior Administration Official" really exist, or is it just the Failing New York Times with another phony source? If the GUTLESS anonymous person does indeed exist, the Times must, for National Security purposes, turn him/her over to government at once!
> 4:40 PM - Sep 5, 2018

> @realDonaldTrump
> When the Failing @nytimes or Amazon @washingtonpost writes a story saying "unnamed sources said", or any such phrase where a person's name is not used, don't believe them. Most of these unnamed sources don't exist. They are made up to defame & disparage. They have no "source"...
> 2:43 PM - Apr 11, 2020

Whistleblower programs, while often imperfectly executed, are designed to encourage employees to report violations of laws, rules, and regulations; gross mismanagement or a gross waste of funds; abuses of authority; substantial and specific dangers to public health or safety; and censorship related to research, analysis, or technical information. In the absence of these programs, misconduct would often go unchecked and likely become more pervasive.

In federal government agencies, whistleblowers are generally expected to submit their reports using procedures and oversight mechanisms internal to their own agencies. This is typically accomplished through a department's inspector general program or, occasionally, with the OSC. In return for the courage displayed in performing this vital role for our institutions, they are protected from forms of retaliation that include termination, demotion, transfer, and loss of security clearance. The disclosure process is also designed to provide some degree of confidentiality.

The Ukraine whistleblower saga. On September 9, 2019, the inspector general of the U.S. government's intelligence community notified Congress that an individual had filed a complaint which appeared credible and addressed an "urgent concern" regarding President Trump's conduct (addressed further in chapters 20 and 29). The complaint was declassified and made available a few weeks later by the House Permanent Select Committee on Intelligence. On the day of its release, President Trump, speaking to a gathering of staffers with the U.S. Mission to the United Nations, suggested that the person who had provided the whistleblower with information had perhaps committed treason—a crime punishable by death:

I want to know who's the person who gave the whistleblower the information because that's close to a spy. You know what we used to do in the old days when we were smart with spies and treason, right? We used to handle it a little differently than we do now.

The president's veiled threats were justifiably condemned by many in Congress. Ambassador Michael McFaul reminded the president in a post that whoever spoke to the whistleblower was not a spy but rather a member of his own national security team who had taken an oath to defend not the president but the United States of America (that is, the Constitution). What followed was a public and persistent effort by the president to expose, question the motive of, threaten, and dispute the accuracy of the whistleblower's report in over one hundred public statements. They included the following sampling of posts demonstrating the president's ignorance on whistleblower programs and the laws that govern them.

> @realDonaldTrump
> ....In addition, I want to meet not only my accuser, who presented SECOND & THIRD HAND INFORMATION, but also the person who illegally gave this information, which was largely incorrect, to the "Whistleblower." Was this person SPYING on the U.S. President? Big Consequences!
> 6:53 PM - Sep 29, 2019

@realDonaldTrump
The Fake Whistleblower complaint is not holding up.
It is mostly about the call to the Ukrainian President
which, in the name of transparency, I immediately
released to Congress & the public. The Whistleblower
knew almost nothing, its 2ND HAND description of the
call is a fraud!
8:03 AM - Sep 30, 2019

Whistleblower complaints must be substantiated through additional investigation, something apparently lost on the president. Ultimately, additional testimony from other officials during the eventual impeachment hearings would negate the need for the whistleblower and original source to testify before Congress.

@realDonaldTrump
Adam Schiff now doesn't seem to want the
Whistleblower to testify. NO! Must testify to explain
why he got my Ukraine conversation sooo wrong, not
even close. Did Schiff tell him to do that? We must
determine the Whistleblower's identity to determine
WHY this was done to the USA..
6:39 AM - Oct 14, 2019

Based on the following posts, President Trump also failed to understand that even if the initial complaint had not been substantiated, there could be no punishment of any kind if the initial complaint had been made in good faith.

@realDonaldTrump
The Whistleblower gave false information & dealt with corrupt politician Schiff. He must be brought forward to testify. Written answers not acceptable! Where is the 2nd Whistleblower? He disappeared after I released the transcript. Does he even exist? Where is the informant? Con!
7:50 AM - Nov 4, 2019

These types of efforts to expose, intimidate, and punish witnesses create environments in which future witnesses to serious misconduct might hesitate to do the right thing, because the message is very clear: you should expect some form of retaliation if you report potential wrongdoing. House impeachment manager Schiff elaborated on this risk during the impeachment trial in January 2020, though his comments remain relevant for misconduct at any level of government:

> I can't tell you who the whistleblower is, because I don't know. But I can tell you who the whistleblower should be. It should be every one of us. Every one of us should be willing to blow the whistle on presidential miscon-duct....I worry that future people that see wrongdoing are going to watch how this person's been treated, the threats against this person's life, and say, "Why stick my neck out? Is my name going to be dragged through the mud?"

There is unfortunately more at stake than just reputations and careers. With a president's public following, labeling someone a traitor could put that person's safety at risk. Furthermore, the threat of retaliation could cause government employees to choose to leak sensitive information to the press in lieu of using established reporting protocols.

Impeachment testimony retaliation. As government witnesses responded to lawfully issued congressional subpoenas (despite inappropriate executive branch direction to ignore them) and began testifying in the initial hearings for President Trump's first impeachment, a familiar pattern of behavior emerged from the retaliator in chief. One lawmaker referred to Trump's actions as "the President's personal retribution tour." The retaliation consisted of a combination of public attacks, personnel transfers, and threats of dismissal for most of the primary witnesses (and effectively any potential future witnesses). Among the career public servants who suffered retaliation were Ambassador William Taylor, Marie Yovanovitch, and Alexander Vindman. They had all served honorably to advance their country's interests under both Republican and Democratic administrations, and occasionally did so abroad under perilous conditions.

@realDonaldTrump
"My support for Donald Trump has never been greater than it is right now. It is paramountly obvious watching this, these people have to go. You elected Donald Trump to drain the Swamp, well, dismissing people like Yovanovitch is what that looks like. Dismissing people like Kent..
....and Taylor, dismissing everybody involved from the Obama holdover days trying to undermine Trump, getting rid of those people, dismissing them,

this is what it looks like. It was never going to be claen, they were never going to sit by idly and just let Trump do this!" Rush L

10:38 AM - Nov 16, 2019

The following post about Ambassador Yovanovitch—who had already been removed from her post in Ukraine—was posted at the exact moment she was testifying on Capitol Hill.

@realDonaldTrump

Everywhere Marie Yovanovitch went turned bad. She started off in Somalia, how did that go? Then fast forward to Ukraine, where the new Ukrainian President spoke unfavorably about her in my second phone call with him. It is a U.S. President's absolute right to appoint ambassadors.

10:01 AM - Nov 15, 2019

The president also targeted Jennifer Williams, an advisor to Vice President Mike Pence. The following post about Williams was posted two days *before* her testimony.

@realDonaldTrump

Tell Jennifer Williams, whoever that is, to read BOTH transcripts of the presidential calls, & see the just released ststement from Ukraine. Then she should meet with the other Never Trumpers, who I don't know & mostly never even heard of, & work out a better presidential attack!

2:57 PM - Nov 17, 2019

The posts targeting Yovanovitch and Williams had their intended effect—to intimidate these witnesses and potentially dissuade others from cooperating with investigators. During his opening statement, Vindman characterized the attacks coming from the president, other politicians, and various media personalities:

> I want to take a moment to recognize the courage of my colleagues who have appeared and are scheduled to appear before this Committee. I want to state that the vile character attacks on these distinguished and honorable public servants is reprehensible.

Several months after his testimony, Vindman was selected by the Department of Defense for promotion to the rank of colonel. After reports surfaced that the White House was inclined not to approve his promotion, members of Congress threatened to hold up all promotions unless Vindman's promotion was approved. As the controversy swirled, Vindman opted instead for retirement, citing months of bullying from the president and his proxies.

In the aforementioned November 16, 2019, Trump post, conservative commentator Rush Limbaugh questioned the loyalty of career public servants largely because they happened to have also served under Democratic administrations. Notably, Ambassador Taylor had been appointed to his most recent post by President Trump. Absent real evidence that people are trying to undermine an administration's policies, these types of purges punish those who prioritize loyalty to an institution or country over any one individual.

Retaliation against other subordinates. FBI Director James Comey and other career professionals also fell victim to this type of loyalty test, both during and after the investigation into Russian interference in the 2016 election.

> @realDonaldTrump
> James Comey will be replaced by someone who will do a far better job, bringing back the spirit and pres-tige of the FBI.
> 4:19 AM - May 10, 2017

> @realDonaldTrump
> ....big, fat, waste of time, energy and money - $30,000,000 to be exact. It is now finally time to turn the tables and bring justice to some very sick and dangerous people who have committed very serious crimes, perhaps even Spying or **Treason.** This should never happen again!
> 1:47 PM - Apr 19, 2019

Presidential historian Jon Meacham commented on the frequent misuse of the word *treason* in President Trump's posts, noting that it is constitutionally relevant only in times of war:

> It's an attempt to stoke fear. It's an attempt to take his opponents and put them in the un-American cate-gory....He's criminalizing dissent....With the FBI folks, he's attempting rhetorically to criminalize the execu-tion and the mechanics of the rule of law....The folks he

mentioned this week—Comey and [his deputy Andrew] McCabe—these are FBI agents—these are sworn officers of the United States, who, we can debate if they're doing the right thing or not....He's using a charged term to create a sense of anxiety and paranoia in order to get his supporters in a place where assent for Trump is a patriotic act. And by doing so, he's throwing 243 years or so of constitutional history away. And that's a precious thing. The framers had this right. They were worried about demagogues. They were worried about exactly this kind of person.

Inspectors general are considered apolitical fact-finders charged with rooting out malfeasance and mismanagement in their agencies. When dedicated and competent public servants such as Inspector General of the Intelligence Community Michael Atkinson, who handled the Ukraine whistleblower complaint, are fired, the message sent is that if you do your job, you may lose it. Within six weeks of Atkinson's firing, President Trump removed three more inspectors general from the Defense, State, and Health and Human Services Departments. This leads to another consequence of retaliation: purges from unwarranted personnel dismissals, transfers, and resignations cause organizational disruption and adverse effects on mission accomplishment.

The moral courage of those on whom we depend to do the right thing will inevitably be compromised when the threat of reprisal comes from the very top of an organization. It is bad enough to be betrayed by someone in your chain of command; even more devastating is the realization that you cannot trust the highest levels of leadership in your organization. During my twenty-four years in the Air Force, I was confident that I could appeal to a higher and more just authority if I were ever subjected to some sort of personal injustice. A lack of confidence in leadership is lamentable. It causes public servants to lose faith in the integrity of their institutions. It may also lead them to question the purpose, and ultimately the value, of their service.

Michael Cohen, Donald Trump's former personal attorney, was still serving a three-year prison sentence in the summer of 2020 when he was released to home confinement as the COVID-19 pandemic raged through America's prisons. He then announced he would be releasing a book about his time working for Trump. The announcement resulted in corrections officials pressuring Cohen to abstain from any media engagement, including on social media platforms. When Cohen demurred, he was returned to the federal penitentiary in Otisville, New York. In his book *Disloyal: A Memoir*, Cohen describes how the reprisal continued as he suffered psychological abuse at the hands of overtly pro-Trump prison guards. After thirty-five days in solitary confinement, a judge ordered his release in an order that included Attorney General William Barr as one of the respondents. The court found that the "Respondents' purpose in transferring Cohen from release on furlough and home confinement back to custody was retaliatory in response to Cohen desiring to exercise his First Amendment rights to publish a book critical of the President and to discuss the book on social media."

If leaders find themselves wanting to retaliate against subordinates when an official complaint has been lodged against them, then they have likely already failed miserably, betraying their organizations and their employees. Acting on their worst impulses to engage in reprisal would constitute the second betrayal.

Retaliating against former subordinates. People who value the esteem of their subordinates and peers do not publicly air their grievances about *former* subordinates—especially while continuing to lead the organization. An exception would be a reasoned and factual rebuttal in response to a patently false claim made by a former subordinate.

However pathetic it may have been, President Trump's retaliation against his former subordinates (most of whom had already left public service) was not as legally problematic as his expressions of reprisal against current subordinates. With respect to his former subordinates, the president was often responding to personal criticism or factual testimony. For Trump, winning was everything, and when confronted with unpleasant criticism or inconvenient facts, winning took the form of revenge. Thomas Jefferson wrote, "I tolerate with the utmost latitude the right of others to differ from me in opinion without imputing to them criminality. I know too well the weakness and uncertainty of human reason to wonder at its different results." That philosophy stands in stark contrast to Trump's notion that someone who disagrees with him or exposes him in a principled manner is necessarily a corrupt enemy. A prospective employer would likely deem such public retaliation as disqualifying, especially for someone seeking a position in management or leadership.

If for some, being trashed by President Trump on social media was a badge of honor, then former FBI director James Comey and former deputy director Andrew McCabe were some of Trump's most decorated former subordinates. As mentioned earlier, Special Counsel Robert Mueller was appointed to lead the Russia election-interference investigation in large part because Trump had fired Comey, a consequence of Trump's dissatisfaction with not securing what would have been inappropriate personal loyalty from Comey. Mueller's report details the manner in which the president and his press secretary handled the immediate aftermath of Comey's removal in May 2017:

> The President said he had received "hundreds" of messages from FBI employees indicating their support for terminating Comey. The President also told McCabe that Comey should not have been permitted to travel back to Washington, D.C. on the FBI's airplane after he had been terminated and that he did not want Comey "in the building again," even to collect his belongings. When McCabe met with the President that afternoon, the President, without prompting, told McCabe that people in the FBI loved the President, estimated that at least 80% of the FBI had voted for him, and asked McCabe who he had voted for in the 2016 presidential election.
>
> In the afternoon of May 10, 2017, deputy press secretary Sarah Sanders spoke to the President about his decision to fire Comey and then spoke to reporters in a televised press conference. Sanders told reporters that…"the rank and file of the FBI had lost confidence in their director."…When a reporter indicated that the "vast majority" of FBI agents supported Comey, Sanders said, "Look, we've heard from countless members of the FBI that say very different things."…Sanders told this Office [Special Counsel] that her reference to hearing from "countless members of the FBI" was a "slip of the tongue." She also recalled that her statement in a separate press interview that rank-and-file FBI agents had lost

confidence in Comey was a comment she made "in the heat of the moment" that was not founded on anything.

President Trump continued throughout his presidency to disparage Comey.

> @realDonaldTrump
> James Comey is a disgrace to the FBI & will go down as the worst Director in its long and once proud history. He brought the FBI down, almost all Republicans & Democrats thought he should be FIRED, but the FBI will regain greatness because of the great men & women who work there!
> 8:00 PM - May 9, 2019

> @realDonaldTrump
> A Dirty Cop at the highest level. Scum!
> 5:15 PM - Dec 28, 2019

A similar pattern emerged in Trump's grossly exaggerated demonization of Andrew McCabe and the FBI.

> @realDonaldTrump
> Andrew McCabe FIRED, a great day for the hard working men and women of the FBI - A great day for Democracy. Sanctimonious James Comey was his boss and made McCabe look like a choirboy. He knew all about the lies and corruption going on at the highest levels of the FBI!
> 9:08 PM - Mar 16, 2018

After leaving office, Trump and one of his attorneys were ordered by a judge to pay nearly $1 million for filing a lawsuit claiming that Comey, McCabe, and dozens of others had conspired to damage Trump in the 2016 election. The presiding judge determined that the lawsuit was "completely frivolous, both factually and legally...brought in bad faith for an improper purpose... in order to dishonestly advance a political narrative." "This is a deliberate attempt to harass; to tell a story without regard to facts," the judge concluded.

Former FBI attorney Lisa Page drew Trump's ire when her 2016 text messages disparaging then candidate Trump were leaked by the FBI. The president frequently attacked her in the context of his discredited claims of law enforcement "spying" on his campaign.

> @realDonaldTrump
> Wow, Strzok-Page, the incompetent & corrupt FBI lovers, have texts referring to a counter-intelligence operation into the Trump Campaign dating way back to December, 2015. SPYGATE is in full force! Is the Mainstream Media interested yet? Big stuff!
> 5:37 PM - Jun 5, 2018

In a 2019 interview, Page described the immediate and even lasting emotional toll of being personally and professionally demeaned in public by someone who had also publicly and falsely accused her of treason. Those accusations are even more intimidating when made by someone with considerable power and influence.

President Trump often bragged prior to his 2017 inauguration that he would assemble the "best people" for his administration. Leaders are responsible for their personnel choices. The targets of Trump's retaliation in the following posts had been hired by the president himself and also reported directly to him. None of the following "post-employment feedback" posts should be confused with principled criticism. The former subordinates featured here include former chief strategist and senior counselor to the president Steve Bannon, former secretary of state Rex Tillerson, retired Marine Corps four-star general and former secretary of defense James Mattis, retired Army four-star general and former White House chief of staff John Kelly, and, finally, former national security advisor John Bolton.

@realDonaldTrump
Michael Wolff is a total loser who made up stories in order to sell this really boring and untruthful book. He used Sloppy Steve Bannon, who cried when he got fired and begged for his job. Now Sloppy Steve has been dumped like a dog by almost everyone. Too bad!
8:32 PM - Jan 5, 2018

@realDonaldTrump
Mike Pompeo is doing a great job, I am very proud of him. His predecessor, Rex Tillerson, didn't have the mental capacity needed. He was dumb as a rock and I couldn't get rid of him fast enough. He was lazy as hell. Now it is a whole new ballgame, great spirit at State!
12:02 PM - Dec 7, 2018

@realDonaldTrump

Mattis was our Country's most overrated General. He talked a lot, but never "brought home the bacon." He was terrible! Someday I will tell the real story on him and others - both good and bad!

9:24 AM - Jun 9, 2020

@realDonaldTrump

When I terminated John Kelly, which I couldn't do fast enough, he knew full well that he was way over his head. Being Chief of Staff just wasn't for him. He came in with a bang, went out with a whimper, but like so many X's, he misses the action & just can't keep his mouth shut,.

11:04 AM - Feb 13, 2020

@realDonaldTrump

President Bush fired him also. Bolton is incompetent!

12:13 AM - Jun 18, 2020

@realDonaldTrump

John Bolton was one of the dumbest people in government that I've had the "pleasure" to work with. A sullen, dull and quiet guy, he added nothing to National Security except, "Gee, let's go to war." Also, illegally released much Classified Information. A real dope!

2:20 PM - Nov 15, 2020

Character assassination in the service of one's ego is not in a leader's job description. Gratuitous retaliation comes with consequences: an atmosphere of fear and intimidation and a diminished ability to recruit quality employees. There are more responsible approaches to dealing with former subordinates who criticize your policies or expose questionable professional conduct. The best option is to ignore their comments. Narcissistic tendencies, however, make the silent approach very unlikely.

Part 3

★ ★ ★

COMMUNICATION
AND
MESSAGING

CHAPTER 13

Communication Befitting
a Leader

★ ★ ★

Words matter. Competent and effective communication plays an important role in establishing credibility and trust within an organization or constituency. Leaders should project confidence when communicating, and their messaging should bolster the confidence of subordinates. Physical limitations should likewise not deter one from communicating with confidence. President Franklin D. Roosevelt, who suffered from paralytic polio, led the United States through the Second World War largely confined to a custom-built wheelchair. When standing, he generally required an aide to hold his arm. He was nonetheless regarded as a symbol of strength and perseverance.

In the context of how a national leader shapes the public character of a nation, Senator Mitt Romney expressed concern about President Trump's inability to "elevate the national discourse with comity and mutual respect." Based on the following posts, it is not difficult to understand how he came to that conclusion.

@realDonaldTrump

Federal Judge throws out Stormy Danials lawsuit
versus Trump. Trump is entitled to full legal fees."
@FoxNews Great, now I can go after Horseface and
her 3rd rate lawyer in the Great State of Texas. She
will confirm the letter she signed! She knows nothing
about me, a total con!

8:04 AM - Oct 16, 2018

@realDonaldTrump

Howard Schultz doesn't have the "guts" to run for
President! Watched him on @60Minutes last night and
I agree with him that he is not the "smartest person."
Besides, America already has that! I only hope that
Starbucks is still paying me their rent in Trump Tower!

5:41 AM - Jan 28, 2019

Anyone reading the writings or speeches of eighteenth- or nineteenth-century American statesmen will have noticed the degree to which our written and spoken political discourse has been dumbed down over the last two centuries. Historian Jon Meacham addressed this phenomenon in the context of more recent presidents:

> We had a fairly coherent political conversation in this country for about seventy-five to eighty years. It was ferocious…and virulent and even violent, but Franklin Roosevelt and Barack Obama governed in the same vernacular, more or less. Donald Trump doesn't. And we have to figure out, do we want that vernacular to take root or do we not?

Though being understood is the primary aim of communication, substance—and to a lesser degree, eloquence—also matter. Though prosecutors cannot indict a sitting president for butchering the English language, a self-proclaimed "stable genius" should have a better grasp (if not mastery) of the mechanics of his native language. The following post, while devoid of spelling errors, fails to conform to general rules of capitalization, includes colorful language and factual errors (the electoral count), and ends with a run-on sentence.

@realDonaldTrump

The Do Nothing Democrats should be focused on building up our Country, not wasting everyone's time and energy on BULLSHIT, which is what they have been doing ever since I got overwhelmingly elected in 2016, 223-306. Get a better candidate this time, you'll need it!

11:48 AM - Oct 2, 2019

Shortly after his inauguration, an American president chose a relatively new technology to communicate directly to the public. He used carefully crafted messages to reach as many as sixty million people simultaneously. He explained to them, in language resembling casual conversation, how the nation would collectively tackle its most dire problems during a period of great economic turmoil. His advice was trusted and heeded because it was frank and necessarily honest. The preceding sentences do not describe Donald Trump's embrace of social media but rather the novelty and efficacy of President Franklin D. Roosevelt's use of radio to deliver his "fireside chats."

In contrast, President Trump's use of social media more

closely resembled remarks heard at the annual White House Correspondents' Dinner, in which presidents are known and even expected to level humor and sarcasm at the media and political foes. President Trump refused to attend those dinners, instead serving his Twitter feasts at any hour of the day. Jon Meacham compared Trump's Twitter battles to a "24/7 professional wrestler who happens to have the nuclear codes."

> @realDonaldTrump
> While I know it's "not presidential" to take on a lowlife like Omarosa, and while I would rather not be doing so, this is a modern day form of communication and I know the Fake News Media will be working overtime to make even Wacky Omarosa look legitimate as possible. Sorry!
> 7:21 AM - Aug 13, 2018

> @realDonaldTrump
> My use of social media is not Presidential - it's MODERN DAY PRESIDENTIAL. Make America Great Again!
> 3:41 PM - Jul 1, 2017

His use of social media was modern-day "presidential" in the same way that trying to illegally overturn an election might be considered modern-day "safeguarding democracy." The president also likely recognized that the substance of his social media posts could not be directly challenged as they might be during a live press conference.

@realDonaldTrump

What is the purposice of having White House News Conferences when the Lamestream Media asks nothing but hostile questions, & then refuses to report the truth or facts accurately. They get record ratings, & the American people get nothing but Fake News. Not worth the time & effort!

6:01 PM - Apr 25, 2020

The answer to Mr. Trump's rhetorical question in the previous post is that leaders have a responsibility to communicate vision, set the tone, and impart critical information to their subordinates or constituents. The press conferences also gave him the opportunity to counter, in real time, press narratives he believed to be false. Having direct access to such a large audience, as evidenced by his claim of "record ratings," provided an opportunity to influence not to be squandered.

@realDonaldTrump

I use Social Media not because I like to, but because it is the only way to fight a VERY dishonest and unfair "press," now often referred to as Fake News Media. Phony and non-existent "sources" are being used more often than ever. Many stories & reports a pure fiction!

2:36 PM - Dec 30, 2017

President Trump's own staff reportedly wanted him to curtail his use of social media. As president, Trump benefited from Twitter privileges only afforded to public officials. His more dishonest and subversive posts were often flagged instead of being immediately removed for violating Twitter's rules. A leader's public messaging should not require special dispensation.

The president was also in the habit of posting readily available facts along with his personal opinions on a wide range of subjects. These "journalistic" posts could have fit neatly into the various segments of a nightly news broadcast's coverage of current events, politics, finance, and even sports and weather. The president's lack of discipline in that regard had real consequences for his subordinates as he showed little regard for conventional work hours or sleep schedules. As social media was the president's primary means of digital communication, even cabinet secretaries felt obligated to read his posts in real time, whatever the hour. These disruptions resulted from Trump's propensity for pairing his "journalistic" and editorial posts with those that actually contained consequential criticism, directives, and even policy declarations. Adding insult to inconvenience, the public nature of the posts also meant his own subordinates were sometimes blindsided when media outlets and the general public were first to see and comment on the more consequential messages.

Context and clarity. In order to further the interests of the organization or state, a public leader must use knowledge—honestly and responsibly—to inform, influence, and persuade both internal and external audiences. To be persuasive, one must communicate with sincerity and conviction. To effectively influence, one's messaging must also be coherent and intelligible. It must also have discernable context. Policy memos drafted for senior decision-makers are often only one to two pages in length. Consequently, they require a high degree of clarity, accuracy, and enough context to effectively frame and justify the proposed solution or course of action. Similarly, when leaders direct specific actions or mandate specific policies, proper attention to detail ensures adequate clarity and context to avoid misunderstandings.

When communicating to the general public, one should consider the diversity of the audience with respect to background and experience. Depending on the subject matter and the audience's corresponding general and technical knowledge, one may need to adjust the level of detail and use of jargon.

"Great leaders are almost always great simplifiers, who can cut through argument, debate, and doubt to offer a solution everybody can understand." This quote, often attributed to Colin Powell (who was paraphrasing the writer Michael Korda), speaks to the need to discern obscurity in speech or writing and transform it into clear and concise language. In that regard, simplicity and eloquence need not be mutually exclusive.

Clarity is important, even when the facts are uncomfortable. For example, when making a difficult decision that will likely be unpopular with subordinates, one should clearly explain one's rationale. While that clarity may not assuage the disappointment of some, it is more likely to engender respect for both the leader and the decision. It will also promote trust.

While leaders cannot provide certainty, they must provide clarity despite the uncertainty inherent in crisis situations. Under stressful and confusing circumstances, directions and intentions must be clearly understood. Poorly chosen words may just add to the confusion.

Trump's erratic and informal use of social media to make unexpected and undercoordinated pronouncements occasionally blindsided domestic stakeholders and foreign allies. Social media is an inappropriate vehicle for communicating significant national security policy positions and decisions, as demonstrated in the following post.

> @realDonaldTrump
> These Media Posts will serve as notification to the United States Congress that should Iran strike any U.S. person or target, the United States will quickly & fully strike back, & perhaps in a disproportionate manner. Such legal notice is not required, but is given nevertheless!
> 12:25 PM - Jan 5, 2020

Countries have stumbled into armed conflict as a result of intentions misinterpreted and goals misunderstood. In conducting foreign policy, governments must clearly communicate their goals and intentions to both allies and adversaries.

Clear and concise messaging is also important when communicating to media outlets, as they invariably serve as the filters between a government organization and its citizenry. They also play a role in garnering public support for specific government programs and policies.

President Trump's rambling style often lacked clarity or coherence. He was an enthusiastic practitioner of the art of using intentionally obscure or vague language, as demonstrated in the following posts, forecasted as cloudy with a chance of confusion and irrelevance.

> @realDonaldTrump
> We are doing very well with China, and talking!
> 2:27 PM - Aug 18, 2019

@realDonaldTrump
Something very big has just happened!
9:23 PM - Oct 26, 2019

The president also used obscurity to spread disinformation, make exaggerated claims, and level unsubstantiated allegations of wrongdoing to diminish others and deflect from his own scandals and political difficulties. He used vague phrasing to create innuendo with casual phrases such as "You look at what they've done" and "When you look at what's happening."

President Trump also practiced the art of talking a lot without saying much. As articulated by journalist David Corn, Trump often spoke for effect rather than to communicate ideas. Phrases such as "We'll see what happens," "Interesting things are happening," and "We're looking at a lot of things" were used in isolation of the substance that would normally precede or follow such statements. His words lacked utility and often served to mislead.

@realDonaldTrump
So many amazing things happened over the last three days. All, or at least most of those things, are great for the United States. Much was accomplished!
8:17 PM - Jun 30, 2019

Consistency. Consistent and reliable messaging breeds confidence, reinforces expectations, and promotes desired behaviors and outcomes. Inconsistent messaging produces uncertainty (a lack of clarity), promotes a lack of discipline, and undermines unity of purpose. Inconsistency can occur within one person's messaging or, for example, when members of the same organization engage in inconsistent messaging on a particular issue. Inconsistent messaging also diminishes internal and external organizational credibility and trust. Consistency for its own sake, however, is not a virtue. New evidence or changing circumstances ought to justify an evolution of one's position and a corresponding change in policy.

Whether communicating formally or informally, the message should be consistent. A scripted speech, for example, should generally mirror the substance and tone of remarks on the same topic delivered through less formal means. This consistency was noticeably missing when comparing "teleprompter" Trump to freewheeling "political rally" or "Twitter" Trump.

In the following pairings, President Trump has provided examples of inconsistent or contradictory messaging that are not likely attributable to genuine or principled evolutions in perspective.

To talk or not to talk:

@realDonaldTrump
The U.S. has been talking to North Korea, and paying them extortion money, for 25 years. **Talking is not the answer!**
5:47 AM - Aug 30, 2017

@realDonaldTrump
...its commitment to denuclearize." @FoxNews This is a big and very positive statement from North Korea. Thank you To Chairman Kim. We will both prove everyone wrong! **There is nothing like good dialogue from two people** that like each other! Much better than before I took office.
8:31 AM - Sep 9, 2018

A perceived lack of loyalty (and the president's evolving legal exposure) quickly changed his perspective on the value of his longtime employee Michael Cohen.

> @realDonaldTrump
> ....non-existent "sources" and a drunk/drugged
> up loser who hates Michael, a fine person with a
> wonderful family. Michael is a businessman for
> his own account/lawyer who I have always liked &
> respected. Most people will flip if the Government lets
> them out of trouble
> 6:10 AM - Apr 21, 2018

> @realDonaldTrump
> If anyone is looking for a good lawyer, I would strongly
> suggest that you don't retain the services of Michael
> Cohen!
> 5:44 AM - Aug 22, 2018

In the following posts, former secretary of state "T-Rex" eventually received the Trump post-employment "extinction" treatment. From first-round draft pick...

> @realDonaldTrump
> The thing I like best about Rex Tillerson is that he has
> vast experience at dealing successfully with all types
> of foreign governments.
> 7:44 AM - Dec 13, 2016

@realDonaldTrump
Congratulations to Rex Tillerson on being sworn in as
our new Secretary of State. He will be a star!
3:18 AM - Feb 2, 2017

...to persona non grata:

@realDonaldTrump
Rex Tillerson, a man who is "dumb as a rock" and
totally ill prepared and ill equipped to be Secretary
of State, made up a story (he got fired) that I was
out-prepared by Vladimir Putin at a meeting in
Hamburg, Germany. I don't think Putin would agree.
Look how the U.S. is doing!
5:29 AM - May 23, 2019

Following the 2016 election, President-elect Trump did not object to the media declaring him the winner within hours of the last polls closing. His hypocrisy shone clearly when the same media outlets declared his opponent the winner a full four days after Election Day 2020.

@realDonaldTrump
Since when does the Lamestream Media call who our
next president will be? We have all learned a lot in the
last two weeks!
1:52 PM - Nov 8, 2020

In the following, inconsistency might suggest a lack of competence, which could result in what I call "earned distrust."

@realDonaldTrump

Under my Administration, we are restoring @NASA to greatness and we are going back to the Moon, then Mars. I am updating my budget to include an additional $1.6 billion so that we can return to Space in a BIG WAY!

2:34 PM - May 13, 2019

@realDonaldTrump

For all of the money we are spending, NASA should NOT be talking about going to the Moon - We did that 50 years ago. They should be focused on the much bigger things we are doing, including Mars (of which the Moon is a part), Defense and Science!

10:38 AM - Jun 7, 2019

Inconsistent or unreliable *behavior* is also detrimental with respect to communicating values and standards. With respect to leadership best practices, you do not want your annual appraisal to read, "When the occasion demands, Smith can pass for a leader." In personnel matters, for example, one can avoid perceptions of favoritism by rewarding and disciplining subordinates fairly and uniformly. There must be harmony and integrity in the relationship between a leader's words and deeds.

Communicating through surrogates. Senior leaders often communicate through a select group of subordinates. These surrogates are typically made up of subordinate agency heads, expert advisors, and those with specifically honed skills, such as press secretaries and public affairs personnel. The principal leader, however, is ultimately responsible for the content of subordinate messaging.

Senior government leaders have access to a wealth of official resources, including subject matter experts, official studies, and investigative reports. Consequently, they should avoid relying on and communicating through unofficial surrogates—especially through those who do not broadly represent the public interest. They should also avoid using unofficial envoys, as President Trump did when he directed his personal attorney and private citizen Rudy Giuliani to travel to Ukraine to purportedly represent U.S. government interests. On that occasion, Giuliani was an illegitimate and mostly unaccountable surrogate serving the corrupt personal and political interests of the president. He was also (hopefully unwittingly) furthering Russian propaganda.

When it served his purposes, President Trump was fond of amplifying messaging from a host of unofficial surrogates. They included media pundits, political allies, celebrities, and even fanatical supporters. In so doing, he was essentially allowing them to communicate on his behalf. The distinction here is important: when you amplify someone else's message, it effectively becomes your own. It is inexcusable to rebroadcast unsubstantiated, demonstrably false, or extremist content—especially from unverified social media accounts. Trump often suggested that he was merely sharing other points of view. The judge in Trump's 2024 New York criminal trial saw it differently when he found, beyond reasonable doubt, the former president to be in criminal contempt on ten occasions for violating a gag order designed to protect the integrity of the trial. Trump had posted about known witnesses and made public statements about jurors. With respect to posting a surrogate's comments, the judge considered context and determined that "a repost, whether with or without commentary by the Defendant, is in fact a statement of the Defendant....there can be no doubt whatsoever, that Defendant's intent and purpose when reposting, is to communicate to his audience that he *endorses and adopts* the posted statement as his own." President Trump frequently used unofficial surrogates to communicate opinions and claims that were apparently beyond his responsibility to clarify or defend. President Trump also used these unofficial surrogates to promote personal exoneration through disinformation, to slander government witnesses and critics, and to spread self-serving conspiracy theories.

Cyberbullying. Most of the senior leaders for whom I worked had a good sense of humor. This intangible is important for the morale of leaders and their followers. Unnecessary ridicule or cruelty, however, are not the tools of self-respecting leaders (or people in general). Nonetheless, President Trump subscribed to the notion that the best defense is a strong offense, and then wasted no opportunity to offend during his internet trolling sprees.

@realDonaldTrump

I must admit that Lyin' Brian Williams is, while dumber than hell, quite a bit smarter than Fake News @CNN "anchorman" Don Lemon, the "dumbest man on television". Then you have Psycho Joe "What Ever Happened To Your Girlfriend?" Scarborough, another of the low I.Q. individuals!

12:23 AM - Apr 30, 2020

@realDonaldTrump

She was thrown off The View like a dog, Zero T.V.
Personas. Now Wallace is a 3rd rate lapdog for Fake
News MSDNC (Concast). Doesn't have what it takes!

5:51 PM - May 2, 2020

Responding to this brand of communication, children at a political demonstration held homemade signs proclaiming "Tweet others the way you want to be tweeted" and "I'm not allowed to act like the president." At issue was decency. Congressman Adam Schiff addressed its importance during closing arguments in President Trump's first impeachment trial:

> Truth matters, right matters, but so does decency. Decency matters. When the president smears a patriotic public servant like Marie Yovanovitch in pursuit of a corrupt aim, we recoil. When the president mocks the disabled, a war hero who was a prisoner of war, or a Gold Star father, we are appalled. Because decency matters here.

CNN commentator Van Jones echoed those sentiments on the day Joe Biden was projected as the winner of the 2020 election. "Well, it's easier to be a parent this morning. It's easier to be a dad. It's easier to tell your kids, 'Character matters. It matters. Telling the truth matters. Being a good person matters.'"

CHAPTER 14

Staying above the Fray

As president of our country and commander in chief of our military,
I accept that people are going to call me awful things every day.
And I will always defend their right to do so.

—President Barack Obama

President Obama's remark was made in the context of defending free speech, but it also speaks to the need and ability to avoid overreacting to criticism that may be justified, unjustified, or perhaps even deeply offensive. The late Supreme Court justice Ruth Bader Ginsburg once suggested that "when a thoughtless or unkind word is spoken, best tune out. Reacting in anger or annoyance will not advance one's ability to persuade."

I like to use the analogy of the obnoxious dog barking at someone minding their own business. While annoying, we do not take the "verbal" assault personally. It is not an attack on one's ego or self-esteem, in part because we do not fully understand the nature of or motivation for the "verbal abuse." If we see people's rude behavior in the same light, understanding that it may stem more from their issues than ours, then we can more easily suppress our ego's reflexive reaction, exercise some degree of emotional self-control, and avoid "barking" back. It was long after trying to put this analogy to use in my own life that I witnessed a real canine exercising what was essentially self-management—a component of emotional intelligence that allows us to manage our emotions, and especially in stressful situations. Unlike most of the other dogs at my local humane society, when removed from her enclosure, Penny would completely ignore the other dogs that were loudly and aggressively reacting to her as she made her way past their enclosures. Penny was instead focused on her goal—getting outside for a walk. Her behavior also likely revealed a certain self-assuredness that allowed her to remain above the fray.

Staying above the fray does not require suppressing a healthy passion for your people and their mission. There will be occasions when unjustified or slanderous personal attacks must be refuted to preserve the reputations of your people and your agency. On the other hand, legitimate criticism that you happen to find unpleasant does not justify or excuse rhetorical attacks on others, especially personal attacks unrelated to the original, substantive criticism.

"Winning" was paramount for President Trump. Too often that meant winning at all costs or, put another way, ensuring his opponents "lost" in the worst possible way. Winning at all costs is never acceptable, whether in business, sports, or politics. It involves lowering one's standards, and unacceptably so. His emphasis on winning, or getting the last word, fueled his retaliation and promoted unnecessary friction. It was the antithesis of staying above the fray.

Billionaire investor Warren Buffett is fond of recommending

that people take the high road as it is less crowded. In lieu of remaining silent if you have nothing nice to say, President Trump preferred instead to share his over-the-top insults with his approximately fifty million Twitter followers. Then presidential candidate Pete Buttigieg was asked how he would handle Trump's social media attacks if he were to become the Democratic nominee. In his response, he described Trump's posts as "mesmerizing and hard for anyone to look away. Me too. It is the nature of grotesque things that you can't look away." Buttigieg tangentially addressed the danger stemming from the inordinate attention President Trump's posts were receiving from the media, thereby diverting public attention from more pressing matters. The sampling of Trump posts in this chapter represents more than a mere inability by Trump to avoid a figurative street fight. They more accurately reflect the slow and deliberate process of donning scuba gear before submerging oneself into the sewer.

Some of Trump's defenders suggested that he had "the right to defend himself." It is less an issue of rights and more about what is necessary, what is proper, and what best serves the public interest. When serving in a significant leadership position, your personal remarks and opinions are largely inseparable from your official capacity. In that context, you should avoid using your bully pulpit to insult private citizens who object to your policies or your conduct.

@realDonaldTrump

Robert De Niro, a very Low IQ individual, has received too many shots to the head by real boxers in movies. I watched him last night and truly believe he may be "punch-drunk."

2:40 AM - Jun 13, 2018

@realDonaldTrump

Lebron James was just interviewed by the dumbest man on television, Don Lemon. He made Lebron look smart, which isn't easy to do. I like Mike!

8:37 PM - Aug 3, 2018

If former president Thomas Jefferson had posted about the importance of polite and tolerant political discourse, it might have included these words from his letter to Maryland governor John Henry.

@realThomasJefferson

I feel extraordinary gratification in addressing this letter to you, with whom shades of difference in political sentiment have not prevented the interchange of good opinion, nor cut off the friendly offices of society and good correspondence. This political tolerance is the more valued by me, who considers social harmony as the first of human felicities, and the happiest moments, those which are given to the effusions of the heart.

Dec 31, 1797

For President Trump, there was no inappropriate time or place to demean his political foes. He saw no reason to hold back during an interview on the hallowed grounds of the American Cemetery and Memorial in Normandy, France. Nor during an Independence Day speech. And certainly not during a ceremony at the White House honoring Native American code talkers who had served their country during the Second World War. His pettiness knew few if any bounds, often personally disparaging people who in no way could be considered his peers (that is, punching down). Examples included scores of American mayors and, in the following posts, London's mayor, in addition to teenage environmental activist Greta Thunberg.

> @realDonaldTrump
> .@SadiqKhan, who by all accounts has done a terrible job as Mayor of London, has been foolishly "nasty" to the visiting President of the United States, by far the most important ally of the United Kingdom. He is a stone cold loser who should focus on crime in London, not me......
> ....Kahn reminds me very much of our very dumb and incompetent Mayor of NYC, de Blasio, who has also done a terrible job - only half his height. In any event, I look forward to being a great friend to the United Kingdom, and am looking very much forward to my visit. Landing now!
> 12:51 AM - Jun 3, 2019

> @realDonaldTrump
> So ridiculous. Greta must work on her Anger Management problem, then go to a good old fashioned movie with a friend! Chill Greta, Chill!
> 7:22 AM - Dec 12, 2019

President Trump likely would not have known just how prophetic and self-descriptive this next post would be in the context of his 2020 firing by the American people and his subsequent efforts to remain in office at any cost.

@realDonaldTrump
Arnold Schwarzenegger isn't voluntarily leaving the
Apprentice, he was fired by his bad (pathetic) ratings,
not by me. Sad end to great show
5:19 AM - Mar 4, 2017

During a 2019 My Brother's Keeper event with basketball great Steph Curry, former president Obama said the following to the young men gathered before them: "If you're confident about your strength, you don't need to show me by putting somebody else down. Show me by lifting somebody else up."

Frederick Douglass—enslaved person, abolitionist leader, statesman, and informal advisor to President Lincoln—suffered a lifetime of abuse and indignity. He left us with the following reflection on the nature of personal disparagement:

They cannot degrade Frederick Douglass. The soul that is within me no man can degrade. I am not the one that is being degraded on account of this treatment, but those who are inflicting it upon me.

CHAPTER 15

Patriotism

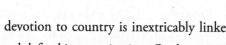

A patriot's devotion to country is inextricably linked to a duty to support and defend its constitution. One's patriotism is therefore informed by a combination of ideology and principle. Furthermore, devotion to the U.S. Constitution requires a commitment to the notion that its rights and protections apply to everyone equally. Patriotism also tempers the more self-serving motivations for the pursuit of power and influence. This sentiment is sometimes expressed as "country over party and politics."

Patriotism should not be confused with the toxic strains of nationalism that serve to elevate certain groups over others. Nor is patriotism, in the context of international relations, the xenophobic nationalism that tramples shared principles and morality in the alleged pursuit of national self-interest. Patriotism has been misappropriated for nefarious means in several categories.

Conflating principled dissent with a lack of patriotism. Political leaders have historically weaponized their notions of patriotism to brand opponents as less than faithful to their countries. In contrast, it is unconventional for a national leader to attack the patriotism of private citizens and corporate entities. President Trump was happy to make an exception. When he was not busy attacking the underpinnings of American democracy, he was lambasting athletes of the National Football League who through peaceful protests sought to raise awareness regarding social inequality and disproportionate police violence against minorities.

@realDonaldTrump
At least 24 players kneeling this weekend at NFL stadiums that are now having a very hard time filling up. The American public is fed up with the disrespect the NFL is paying to our Country, our Flag and our National Anthem. Weak and out of control!
4:45 AM - Nov 28, 2017

@realDonaldTrump
I am a big fan of Drew Brees. I think he's truly one of the greatest quarterbacks, but he should not have taken back his original stance on honoring our magnificent American Flag. OLD GLORY is to be revered, cherished, and flown high...
...We should be standing up straight and tall, ideally with a salute, or a hand on heart. There are other things you can protest, but not our Great American Flag - NO KNEELING!
4:08 PM - Jun 5, 2020

The president's criticism brings to mind Mark Twain's characterization of a patriot as "the person who can holler the loudest without knowing what he is hollering about." During my military career, I understood and gladly fulfilled my obligation to pay respect to America's colors and its national anthem. While serving abroad, I was also required to pay the same respects to the flags and anthems of America's foreign allies. Professional athletes (contractual responsibilities aside) are not similarly obligated. Substantive patriotism should transcend the relatively superficial and largely visceral public displays of devotion to one's country expected at sporting events. The president was focused almost exclusively on what was, in his view, disrespect of a national symbol. He was questioning the patriotism of athletes who were expressing legitimate dissent and conveniently ignoring the principled stand they were taking to further the substantive and consequential aspirations enshrined in the Constitution. He was also, in effect, suggesting that those paid to entertain should not always be allowed to exercise their freedom of speech.

President Trump also questioned the patriotism of political foes who stood in principled opposition to him and sought to hold him accountable.

@realDonaldTrump
The Never Trumper Republicans, though on respirators with not many left, are in certain ways worse and **more dangerous for our Country** than the Do Nothing Democrats. Watch out for them, **they are human scum!**
1:48 PM - Oct 23, 2019

@realDonaldTrump

"This isn't about Ukraine. This isn't about
Impeachment. This is about subverting Democracy!"
@BillOReilly So true, and led by angry and dishonest
people who hate themselves, and **must hate our
Country!**

7:57 PM - Nov 11, 2019

Patriotism and policy differences. Patriotism can also be
weaponized against those who support different policies, as in the
following post suggesting that anyone not supporting President
Trump's Supreme Court pick was necessarily unpatriotic.

@realDonaldTrump

Thank you to @RandPaul for your YES on a future
great Justice of the Supreme Court, Brett Kavanaugh.
Your vote means a lot to me, **and to everyone who
loves our Country!**

3:36 PM - Jul 30, 2018

In the following example, the President questioned the patriotic legitimacy and authenticity of four ethnic minority members of
Congress. All four are American citizens, and three of the four were
born in the United States.

@realDonaldTrump

So interesting to see "Progressive" Democrat
Congresswomen, who originally came from countries whose governments are a complete and total
catastrophe, the worst, most corrupt and inept

anywhere in the world (if they even have a functioning government at all), now loudly......

....and viciously telling the people of the United States, the greatest and most powerful Nation on earth, how our government is to be run. **Why don't they go back** and help fix the totally broken and crime infested places from which they came. Then come back and show us how....

....it is done. These places need your help badly, **you can't leave fast enough.** I'm sure that Nancy Pelosi would be very happy to quickly work out free travel arrangements!

5:27 AM - Jul 14, 2019

In a related post, Trump suggested that the same women were likely not "capable of loving our country." Britain's Boris Johnson—no stranger to making controversial statements—characterized Trump's posts as "totally unacceptable." He further stated, "If you are the leader of a great multiracial, multicultural society, you simply cannot use that kind of language about sending people back to where they came from." Two days later, the U.S. House of Representatives passed a resolution addressing Trump's nativism that included the following excerpts:

Immigration of people from all over the Earth has defined every stage of American history and propelled our social, economic, political, scientific, cultural, artistic, and technological progress as a people, and all Americans, except for the descendants of Native people and enslaved African Americans, are immigrants or descendants of immigrants;...American patriotism is defined not by race or ethnicity but by devotion to the Constitutional ideals of equality, liberty, inclusion, and democracy and by service to our communities and struggle for the common good;...this is "one of the most important sources of America's greatness: we lead the world because, unique among nations, we draw our people—our strength—from every country and every corner of the world, and by doing so we continuously renew and enrich our nation";...President Donald Trump's racist comments have legitimized fear and hatred of new Americans and people of color.

At a rally in North Carolina the following day, the president suggested that one of the congresswomen should leave the country if she did not love it. The inevitable result was a "Send her back" chant from a crowd he would later characterize as "incredible patriots."

@realDonaldTrump
As you can see, I did nothing to lead people on, nor was I particularly happy with their chant. Just a very big and **patriotic crowd. They love the USA!**
3:57 AM - Jul 20, 2019

Their chants echoed historically shameful notions that certain immigrants, ethnic and religious minorities, and even African Americans with countless generations of American ancestors do not belong and should return to their "countries of origin." This type of discrimination and harassment in the workplace violates Title VII of the Civil Rights Act of 1964 and is enforced by the U.S. Equal Employment Opportunity Commission.

Inappropriate appeals to patriotism can also be used to further religio-centric narratives that may encourage intolerance of minority religions.

> @realDonaldTrump
> As Christians throughout this great Country celebrate All Souls Day, let's remember those who went before us and built this great nation. May their legacy inspire us as we keep our nation what it has always been: blessed and great!
> 5:12 PM - Nov 2, 2020

This country will not be a permanently good place for any of us to live in unless we make it a reasonably good place for all of us to live in.
—THEODORE ROOSEVELT

Conflating principle with politics. Elected officials too often abandon principle in their pursuit of power. When that practice becomes habitual, they become callous to circumstances when others are actually acting out of principle. In the following post, the president was surprised to learn that his notions of political obligation, reciprocity, and loyalty do not always override principle.

@realDonaldTrump

I was very surprised & disappointed that Senator Joe Manchin of West Virginia voted against me on the Democrat's totally partisan Impeachment Hoax. No President has done more for the great people of West Virginia than me (Pensions)

10:25 AM - Feb 14, 2020

In the early months of the COVID-19 pandemic, former president George W. Bush released a video calling for national unity. President Trump then characterized Bush's plea to abandon partisan divides as inconsistent because the former president (and fellow Republican) likely chose principle (or discretion) over party affiliation with respect to Trump's first impeachment.

@realDonaldTrump

.@PeteHegseth "Oh bye the way, I appreciate the message from former President Bush, but where was he during Impeachment calling for putting partisanship aside." @foxandfriends He was nowhere to be found in speaking up against the greatest Hoax in American history!

7:42 AM - May 3, 2020

Several days before the 2020 general election, a caravan of vehicles driven by Trump supporters on a Texas highway surrounded and intentionally slowed a Biden campaign bus. The incident, eventually investigated by the FBI, nearly caused several potentially serious accidents and resulted in a canceled campaign event for a Biden surrogate. President Trump chose not to condemn the irresponsibility of his supporters. He instead posted a video of the incident (adding music) and conflated political allegiance with principle and patriotism.

@realDonaldTrump

In my opinion, these patriots did nothing wrong.
Instead, the FBI & Justice should be investigating the terrorists, anarchists, and agitators of ANTIFA, who run around burning down our Democrat run cities and hurting our people!
8:18 PM - Nov 1, 2020

Patriotism and the study of history. On July 3, 2020, President Trump delivered a speech at the foot of Mount Rushmore. Anyone expecting a unifying Independence Day message would have been disappointed. In one portion of his speech, he sought to make American history "great again."

Against every law of society and nature, our children are taught in school to hate their own country, and to believe that the men and women who built it were not heroes but villains. The radical view of American history is a web of lies, all perspective is removed, every virtue is obscured, every motive is twisted, every fact is distorted, and every flaw is magnified until the history is purged and the record is disfigured beyond all recognition. This movement is openly attacking the legacies of every person on Mount Rushmore.

The president's notion of eliminating historical nuance and disregarding the darker moments in American history had parallels to the Lost Cause, in which Southerners after the Civil War sought to reframe their defense of slavery as just and heroic. Trump seemed to have been offended by, among other things, The 1619 Project—a journalistic effort that commemorated the four-hundredth anniversary of the first arrival to America of enslaved people from Africa. The project also sought to reframe America's history through the lens of slavery. More broadly, Trump seemed to be offended by historical accounts that necessarily revealed ugly truths.

> @realDonaldTrump
> Just signed an order to establish the 1776
> Commission. We will stop the radical indoctrination of
> our students, and restore **PATRIOTIC EDUCATION** to
> our schools!
> 2:22 PM - Nov 2, 2020

> @realDonaldTrump
> Over the next 4 years, we will teach our children
> to love our Country, honor our history, and always
> respect our great American Flag—and with God's help,
> we will defend the right to life, religious liberty, and
> the right to KEEP AND BEAR ARMS!
> 7:43 PM - Nov 2, 2020

The Trump administration's 1776 Commission sought to provide "a definitive chronicle of the American founding, a powerful description of the effect the principles of the Declaration of Independence have had on this Nation's history, and a dispositive rebuttal of reckless 're-education' attempts that seek to reframe American history around the idea that the United States is not an exceptional country but an evil one."

"Patriotic education" should be at most a discrete subset of a country's historical record, focusing, for example, on constitutional principles and those who labored diligently to further them. Any historical account deemed "definitive" should invite skepticism. The historical record of a nation should ideally consist of the unvarnished truth as presented from a variety of perspectives. Its primary purpose is not to make us feel good, further a particular tribal narrative, or portray our national heroes as flawless human beings. Our history should look more like a matter-of-fact after-action report and less like the obituary that seeks to purge anything unflattering. Furthermore, the process of reminding ourselves of our darker moments can serve as an ongoing truth and reconciliation exercise in which we recognize that healing and progress require acknowledgment and perhaps even atonement. We study those episodes because we have a moral obligation to understand and learn from our failures while simultaneously promoting love for country by celebrating and drawing inspiration from our collective ongoing efforts to improve. We honor our history by examining it with eyes wide open in order to become that "more perfect Union."

Part 4

★ ★ ★

CHARACTER MATTERS

CHAPTER 16

Humility, Validation, and Recognition

Please Acknowledge My Brilliance

Humility is essential to good character—and to our country.
Only a humble nation—with humble leaders—
will respect the people's natural rights…humility is
at the core of our national creed of equality and liberty.

—Paul Ryan

In 1819, Thomas Jefferson founded the University of Virginia, which still thrives today. Donald J. Trump founded Trump University, which was shuttered after five years and forced to pay millions to its victims due to fraud. Jefferson, in response to his selection for higher office, expressed gratitude for "the favor with which they have been pleased to look toward me, to declare a sincere consciousness that the task is above my talents, and that I approach it with those anxious and awful presentiments which the greatness of the charge and the weakness of my powers so justly inspire." His rare and commendable display of humility stands in stark contrast to the following display of arrogance and unjustified confidence.

> @realDonaldTrump
>
> As I have stated strongly before, and just to reiterate, if Turkey does anything that I, **in my great and unmatched wisdom,** consider to be off limits, I will totally destroy and obliterate the Economy of Turkey (I've done before!).
>
> 11:38 AM - Oct 7, 2019

President Trump posted the following in response to speculation that the White House may have reached out to the governor of South Dakota about having Trump's likeness added to those of former presidents Jefferson, Washington, Lincoln, and Roosevelt on the face of Mount Rushmore.

> @realDonaldTrump
>
> This is Fake News by the failing @nytimes & bad ratings @CNN. Never suggested it although, based on all of the many things accomplished during the first 3 1/2 years, perhaps more than any other Presidency, **sounds like a good idea to me!**
>
> 9:07 PM - Aug 9, 2020

In the following, we see the modesty in Jefferson's letter to the Reverend William Smith, presented here as an eighteenth-century social media post.

@realThomasJefferson

The succession to Doctor [Benjamin] Franklin, at the court of France, was an excellent school of humility. On being presented to any one as the minister of America, the commonplace question used in such cases was "C'est vous, Monsieur, qui remplace le Docteur Franklin?" I generally answered, "No one can replace him, sir; I am only his successor."

Feb 19, 1791

Returning to examples of twenty-first-century "leadership":

@realDonaldTrump

Congratulations to @loudobbs , Number One. Lou has shown the Fake News what happens when you cover **"America's Greatest President"** fairly & objectively! #MAGA #KAG

8:14 AM - Feb 1, 2020

@realDonaldTrump

When I decided to go to Ohio for Troy Balderson, he was down in early voting 64 to 36. That was not good. **After my speech on Saturday night, there was a big turn for the better. Now Troy wins a great victory during a very tough time of the year for voting.** He will win BIG in Nov.

7:59 PM - Aug 7, 2018

Humility can be defined as the absence of pride and arrogance with respect to how you see yourself and others. As Malcolm

Gladwell suggested, there are an infinite number of reasons for why we are better human beings when humble. Humility allows us to get along with others more easily and better appreciate the world around us. It also facilitates learning. In spiritual matters, humility is fundamental to one's relationship with a higher power.

The chapter's introductory quote by Paul Ryan was written in praise of David J. Bobb's *Humility: An Unlikely Biography of America's Greatest Virtue*. Bobb explored the temptation of unhealthy pride and the relationship between humility and greatness, for both individuals and nations. He revealed through the lives of George Washington, James Madison, Abigail Adams, Abraham Lincoln, and Frederick Douglass how both healthy pride and humility are essential for the survival of democracy and self-governance. They are the antidotes to arrogance, unchecked ambition, and an unhealthy love of self—attributes of a tyrant.

Cultivating humility. Roman statesman Marcus Tullius Cicero is credited with providing the following advice: "The higher we are placed, the more humbly we should walk." Admittedly, even great public leaders do not attain those "higher" positions without principled ambition. Though humility is occasionally and incorrectly associated with weakness and passivity, it can coexist with a merited confidence in one's abilities and a healthy pride in one's accomplishments. As expressed by former General Electric CEO Jack Welch, "To possess self-confidence and humility at the same time is called maturity."

Humility is cultivated in the simple act of serving others. In an unexpected display of humility, I was once surprised when an Air Force general asked a small group gathered in his office for a meeting if he could make anyone a cup of coffee. I alone accepted, and the general eventually served me before taking his place at the table.

The leadership topics presented in this book serve to remind us of how and why humility is required. They also showcase how a lack of humility contributes to leadership failures. Though humility may not come to us as naturally as pride, it can nonetheless be cultivated in the following ways:

- A humble and respectful approach to the Constitution, along with organizational core values and public ethics, promotes their preservation.

- Humble leaders strengthen the commitment of subordinates and encourage innovation.

- Humility frees us to admit what we do not know, to benchmark, to seek counsel when necessary, and to remain open to different points of view.

- Humility allows us to change course when our actions and decisions fail to deliver.

- Humility makes room for more persuasive diplomacy and greater influence because we are able to take a genuine interest in others, learn from them, and practice empathy.

- It builds trust through clear, respectful, confident, and authentic communication.

- Humility is present when we exercise self-control and choose to treat others with respect.

- It is essential for the meaningful introspection and self-awareness needed to understand our own contexts within larger issues and also to appreciate the inherent value of others.

- Humility allows us to examine and understand our strengths and weaknesses and to seek continuous self-improvement.

- It prevents us from taking ourselves too seriously, while simultaneously ensuring that we still take our responsibilities seriously.

- Humility encourages accountability and transparency when we make mistakes.

- Humility insists that we not demand that to which we are not entitled.

Validation. Leaders lacking humility will express their arrogance through self-praise and boasting. Their thirst for validation will grow and cause them to neurotically amplify external praise, encourage praise from subordinates, and make public their requests for validation.

> *And whosoever shall exalt himself shall be abased;*
> *and he that shall humble himself shall be exalted.*
> —MATTHEW 23:12 (KJV)

Self-praise. In March 2020, President Trump was asked how he rated his initial response to the COVID-19 pandemic. He gave himself a ten out of ten while also acknowledging the efforts of his administration. If your default self-assessment is that you could not have done better, you are unlikely to acknowledge mistakes and even less likely to seek improvement.

While perhaps more necessary for elected officials, praising one's own leadership is generally unnecessary and reveals a degree of insecurity. Worse yet, if the claims are without merit, it reveals exceptional arrogance. If a leader has to tell their people what a great job they are doing, they may be camouflaging their failures.

Boasting. American patriot John Adams's reputation for arrogance preceded him. Had he been able to share his thoughts on social media, we might have seen the following excerpt from his diary in which he expresses his yearning for greater humility.

@realJohnAdams

Oh! that I could wear out of my mind every mean and base affectation, conquer my natural Pride and Self Conceit, expect no more deference from my fellows than I deserve, acquire that meekness, and humility, which are the sure marks and Characters of a great and generous Soul, and subdue every unworthy Passion and treat all men as I wish to be treated by all. How happy should I then be, in the favour and good will of all honest men, and the sure prospect of a happy immortality!

Feb 16, 1756

President Trump was not burdened by the need to conquer pride and self-conceit, as evidenced in the following pleas for validation.

@realDonaldTrump

Time Magazine called to say that I was PROBABLY going to be named "Man (Person) of the Year," like last year, but I would have to agree to an interview and a major photo shoot. I said probably is no good and took a pass. Thanks anyway!

2:40 PM - Nov 24, 2017

@realDonaldTrump

...Actually, throughout my life, my **two greatest assets have been mental stability and being, like, really smart.** Crooked Hillary Clinton also played these cards very hard and, as everyone knows, went down in flames. I went from **VERY successful businessman, to top T.V. Star.....**

4:27 AM - Jan 6, 2018

....to President of the United States (on my first try). I think that would qualify as not smart, but genius.... and a very stable genius at that!

4:30 AM - Jan 6, 2018

Encouraging praise from subordinates. While it is certainly human nature to desire the approval and admiration of others—especially from those we respect—attaining a respectable position of leadership would provide sufficient validation for most. When the need for praise becomes excessive and unhealthy, the absence of persistent external validation creates an emotional response similar to an addict's withdrawal symptoms. The lack of validation is then perceived as unjustifiably cruel and unfair. One might then have to resort to encouraging and expecting—practically as a condition of employment—praise from one's subordinates. Former FBI director James Comey described this Trumpian dynamic:

> From the private circle of assent, it moves to public displays of personal fealty at places like cabinet

meetings. While the entire world is watching, you do what everyone else around the table does—you talk about how amazing the leader is and what an honor it is to be associated with him.

The actual cabinet meeting "lovefest" referenced by Comey was likely intended for an external audience, as it was aired on cable news. In a separate March 2020 White House COVID-19 press briefing, almost every speaker appeared obligated to praise the president's leadership, seemingly relegating vital public health information to the background. In a similar event on the White House lawn, successive administration officials treated the American public to successive displays of praise for the president's "decisiveness." Vice President Pence set an especially poor example at the event by heaping praise on his boss while referring to all of his "unprecedented" actions. The president's subordinates understood what he wanted to hear, as evidenced in their sycophantic comments that have no place in a public organization or a healthy democracy. It is expected in places like North Korea, where subordinate commentary had better be flattering and in complete agreement with the leader if one wishes to remain unconfined and "healthy."

With only a few exceptions, praise should flow from superior to subordinate. The exceptions might include discreet displays of appreciation for personal or professional support. Leaders who publicly respond to and amplify the intended or unintended praise of their subordinates are clearly communicating their approval and encouragement of such displays.

@realDonaldTrump

"Mattis Says Trump's Warning Stopped Chemical
Weapons Attack In Syria"

2:13 PM - Jun 29, 2017

By praising their superiors and having that praise amplified, subordinates might become conditioned to seeking their own public
recognition.

@realDonaldTrump

Thank you Brock – it is my honor! "We (@FEMA) have
never had the support that we have had from this
President." Administrator @FEMA_Brock

1:41 PM - Sep 15, 2018

@realDonaldTrump

"In 22 years of patrolling our Southern Border, I have
never seen Mexico act like a true Border Security
Partner until President Trump got involved, and now
they are stepping up to the plate and doing what they
need to do." Brandon Judd, National Border Patrol

9:14 AM - Sep 7, 2019

Requesting validation and appreciation. If leaders take the
extraordinary step of requesting validation, they have hit rock
bottom and begun to dig. On the subject of expecting immediate
validation, Thomas Jefferson wrote the following: "I have ever found
in my progress through life, that, acting for the public, if we do
always what is right, the approbation denied in the beginning will
surely follow us in the end. It is from posterity we are to expect

remuneration for the sacrifices we are making for their service, of time, quiet, and good will."

> @realDonaldTrump
> When will people start saying, "thank you, Mr.
> President, for firing James Comey?"
> 8:10 AM - Jun 7, 2018

> @realDonaldTrump
> Stock Market Up Big. Do I get no credit for this?
> Never even mentioned by the Fake News. A New
> Record for Stocks and Jobs Growth. Remember, "it's
> the Economy Stupid". VOTE!!!
> 10:16 AM - Oct 12, 2020

Requesting validation is perhaps the polar opposite of welcoming critical feedback, something encouraged here by Thomas Jefferson:

> I would be glad to know when any individual member
> of Congress thinks I have gone wrong in any instance. If
> I know myself, it would not excite ill blood in me, while
> it would assist to guide my conduct, perhaps to justify it,
> and to keep me to my duty, alert.

A leader should react to such criticism with reasoned consideration in lieu of assuming a posture of "defend and retaliate."

Recognition. Taking the time to publicly identify individuals and teams for their achievements is an important part of taking care of one's subordinates. Acknowledging outstanding performers provides motivation, creates healthy competition, and serves to identify those with potential for advancement and increased responsibility. Employees often place more value on public recognition than more tangible, albeit anonymous, forms of reward.

One form of recognition is empowerment in the form of additional authority or responsibility. Allowing a subordinate to be the public face of a project promotes individual growth and also highlights the organization's depth of talent. In contrast, the boss who hovers too closely to an expert or subordinate presenting on behalf of the organization communicates either a craving for the limelight or a lack of trust.

> *A good leader takes a little more*
> *than his share of the blame,*
> *a little less than his share of the credit.*
> —ARNOLD GLASOW

The leader's role. While those in elected office may occasionally need to highlight their own accomplishments for their constituents and party leaders, unelected public servants should strive for some degree of personal anonymity when touting the accomplishments of their organizations and personnel. Using a sports analogy, coaches are not on the field, but they provide the vision, inspiration, and strategy that enable their teams to succeed. Overall mission success will inherently be attributed to leadership, but humble leaders will focus attention onto the accomplishments of others. No one achieves great success in a vacuum.

Understanding that no one person is responsible for wins, they will characterize successes with a collective pronoun such as *we*. When leaders receive recognition for their success from their superiors, they can in turn demonstrate humility by recognizing the contributions of subordinates along with the influence of mentors, family members, and friends. The following post from President Trump *almost* qualifies as an excellent example of how to distribute recognition.

> @realDonaldTrump
> Thank you to Bahamian Prime Minister Hubert
> Minnis for your very gracious and kind words in
> saying that without the help of the United States
> **and me,** their would have been many more casual-
> ties. I give all credit to FEMA, the U.S. Coast Guard,
> & the brave people of the Bahamas..
> 6:39 AM - Sep 7, 2019

The president did an excellent job of acknowledging his subordinate organizations but still could not resist amplifying the personal praise he received ("and me").

A phenomenon I have witnessed in developing countries is the practice of politicians prominently plastering their names on every public infrastructure project with which they are associated. I was surprised (even in an election year) to see over fifty posts from President Trump describing how he was personally responsible for providing infrastructure funds to a host of municipalities across America.

@realDonaldTrump

Good news for Florida! **I'm awarding** $27.8M from @ USDOT in federal infrastructure funds to five areas including Orlando, Jacksonville, Ft. Myers/Naples, St. Petersburg, and Tampa. Happy to support bus service for the people in beautiful Florida!

2:44 PM - Aug 12, 2020

It may be gratifying to the ego to believe that you have accomplished something independently, but one should avoid taking all the credit or proclaiming that "I alone can fix it." To quote former president Ronald Reagan, "The greatest leader is not necessarily the one who does the greatest things. He is the one that gets the people to do the greatest things." It can be disheartening for people of an organization to see their leader take disproportionate credit for their ideas and their efforts. These final posts, representing "all of the things you could not have done without me," demonstrate how one can sometimes neglect an opportunity to share credit with—or perhaps more accurately, give proper credit to—the organizations and individuals largely responsible for various successes.

@realDonaldTrump

It wasn't the White House, it wasn't the State Department, it wasn't father LaVar's so-called people on the ground in China that got his son out of a long term prison sentence - **IT WAS ME.** Too bad! LaVar is just a poor man's version of Don King, but without the hair. Just think..

2:25 AM - Nov 22, 2017

@realDonaldTrump

Since taking office **I have been** very strict on Commercial Aviation. Good news - it was just reported that there were Zero deaths in 2017, the best and safest year on record!

6:13 AM - Jan 2, 2018

@realDonaldTrump

I built the greatest economy in the World, the best the U.S. has ever had. **I am** doing it again!

6:08 PM - Jun 7, 2020

Avoid putting yourself before others
and you can become a leader among men.

—LAO TZU

CHAPTER 17

Respecting the Dignity
of Others

★ ★ ★

E ffective leaders understand the value of treating their colleagues with respect. Respecting the dignity of others is just something decent people do. Barack Obama was one of several former presidents who delivered remarks at the July 2020 funeral of civil rights icon John Lewis:

> He believed that in all of us there exists the capacity for great courage. And in all of us, there's a longing to do what is right, that in all of us there's a willingness to love all people and extend to them their God-given rights to dignity and respect. So many of us lose that sense. It's taught out of us. We start feeling as if, in fact, we can't afford to extend kindness or decency to other people, that we're better off if we're above other people and looking down on them.

As Lewis lay in state in the U.S. Capitol Rotunda, Senate majority leader Mitch McConnell remarked that he "lived and worked with urgency because the task was urgent. But even as the world around him gave him every cause for bitterness, he treated everyone with respect and love."

There are specific institutional norms and traditions that exist to promote professional courtesy and respect among public servants. For example, it is customary—even for a person in a position of authority—to refer to a peer or subordinate with the professional title that properly reflects that person's accomplishments and status within the organization. Familiarity breeds contempt. Despite their partisan battles and a likely degree of personal contempt, Senate leaders Mitch McConnell and Charles (Chuck) Schumer still usually referred to each other publicly using the other's formal title (such as Leader McConnell).

When American presidents leave office, they customarily leave a personal letter in the Oval Office for their successors. The last line of President Obama's 2017 letter to President-elect Trump read, "Michelle and I wish you and Melania the very best as you embark on this great adventure, and know that we stand ready to help in any way in which we can. Good luck and Godspeed." After the major media outlets projected that Joe Biden was the winner of the 2020 election, George W. Bush phoned both Biden and Vice President–elect Kamala Harris to congratulate them. He also issued a public statement that included the following: "Though we have political differences, I know Joe Biden to be a good man, who has won his opportunity to lead and unify our country....The challenges that face our country will demand the best of President-elect Biden and Vice President–elect Harris—and the best of us all. We must come together for the sake of our families and neighbors, and for our nation and its future."

Given Trump's demonstrated lack of respect for institutional norms and traditions, he was not exactly a member in good standing in the "presidents' club." As discussed, three weeks after Biden was domestically and internationally recognized as president-elect, President Trump had still not conceded the race. Nor had he congratulated Biden or extended the customary invitation to the White House. He chose instead to disrespect and undermine the president-elect.

@realDonaldTrump
Joe Biden was a total disaster in handling the H1N1 Swine Flu, would never have produced a Vaccine in record time (years ahead of schedule), and would do a terrible job of Vaccine delivery - But doesn't everybody already know that!
5:13 PM - Nov 21, 2020

Trump's disrespect of Biden was entirely consistent with his previous treatment of elected officials from both political parties as well as apolitical career public servants. On the day he assumed the office of the presidency, Biden imparted the following to his subordinates: "I'm not joking when I say this: if you ever work with me and I hear you treat another colleague with disrespect—talk down to someone—I promise you I will fire you on the spot. On the spot. No ifs, ands, or buts. Everybody, everybody is entitled to be treated with decency and dignity. That's been missing in a big way the last four years."

Considering the stakes associated with potential public policy outcomes, one should strive to elevate discourse and practice personal respect in all of one's professional relationships. Comity serves the interests of government by facilitating two difficult but necessary pursuits—interpersonal and interagency cooperation and, for elected officials, political compromise. In the following passage, Thomas Jefferson expressed this need for compromise and tolerance in the pursuit of the common good:

> I see too many proofs of the imperfection of human reason to entertain wonder or intolerance at any difference of opinion on any subject; and acquiesce in that difference as easily as on a difference of feature or form; experience having long taught me the reasonableness of mutual sacrifices of opinion among those who are to act together for any common object, and the expediency of doing what good we can, when we cannot do all we would wish.

Magazine publisher Malcolm Forbes addressed the occasionally transactional nature of respect: "You can easily judge the character of a man by how he treats those who can do nothing for him." Building on that theme, there are notable examples of people such as Nelson Mandela, who despite being mistreated during his twenty-seven years of imprisonment, refused to see only the worst in people. In treating others with some degree of unconditional respect, he set a powerful example for those less inclined to do so.

One's personal feelings about someone need not translate into corresponding professional dispositions. Unfortunately,

President Trump often conflated principled differences over policy and process—such as legitimate oversight and accountability—with personal animus. He viewed his first impeachment as a largely personal and partisan attack, predictably responding with personal insults.

> @realDonaldTrump
> Nervous Nancy is an inherently "dumb" person. She wasted all of her time on the Impeachment Hoax. She will be overthrown, either by inside or out, just like her last time as "Speaker". Wallace & @FoxNews are on a bad path, watch!
> 12:58 PM - Apr 19, 2020

A maxim associated with Abraham Lincoln reads, "We should be too big to take offense and too noble to give it." Paraphrasing President John F. Kennedy in the context of Cold War relations, civility in professional relationships is not a sign of weakness. One must be able to criticize policies and actions without personally disrespecting the people behind them. One can be simultaneously blunt *and* respectful. Decent people and successful leaders aim for this balance.

The art of slander. President Trump was fond of leveling unsubstantiated accusations against his numerous "rivals." His occasionally entertaining yet juvenile and repetitive use of slanderous nicknames was far from harmless. While that kind of behavior merely lands elementary school children in the principal's office, Trump's slanderous behavior as president diminished political discourse while grossly distorting the truth about various national leaders. He was quick to slander when criticized or when confronted with evidence of wrongdoing that threatened his presidency. Trashing opponents was also a way of endearing himself to supporters who likewise failed to appreciate the need for decency and professional courtesy.

In *Humility*, David J. Bobb explained how James Madison reacted to the painful rejection of some of his ideas by his colleagues at the Constitutional Convention of 1787. Madison resisted the temptation to publicly or privately slander his colleagues in the midst of contentious disagreement, demonstrating instead an appreciation for the importance of their collective work. His mature and measured approach earned him the respect of his peers. In contrast, President Trump did not seem to appreciate the benefits of comity. His comments and posts provide us with exceptional examples of what *not* to do.

> @realDonaldTrump
> Why is so much money sent to the Elijah Cummings district when it is considered the worst run and most dangerous anywhere in the United States. No human being would want to live there. Where is all this money going? How much is stolen? Investigate this corrupt mess immediately!
> 7:24 AM - Jul 27, 2019

> @realDonaldTrump
> LYIN' SHIFTY SCHIFF!
> 6:15 PM - Oct 4, 2019

Prior to a debate with then presidential opponent Joe Biden, Trump suggested that Biden had been using performance-enhancing drugs.

@realDonaldTrump

I will be strongly demanding a Drug Test of Sleepy Joe
Biden prior to, or after, the Debate on Tuesday night.
Naturally, I will agree to take one also. His Debate
performances have been record setting UNEVEN,
to put it mildly. Only drugs could have caused this
discrepancy???

9:34 AM - Sep 27, 2020

@realDonaldTrump

Joe Biden just announced that he will not agree to a
Drug Test. Gee, I wonder why?

10:33 AM - Sep 28, 2020

Two weeks before Election Day 2020, Trump once again
unleashed an avalanche of accusations against his rival, telling a group
of journalists, "He is a criminal. He's a criminal. He got caught. Read
his [Hunter Biden's] laptop. And you know who's a criminal? You're a
criminal for not reporting it....Let me tell you something. Joe Biden
is a criminal, and he's been a criminal for a long time." Similarly-
themed posts were inevitable.

@realDonaldTrump

Corrupt politician Joe Biden makes Crooked Hillary
look like an amateur!

2:14 PM - Oct 18, 2020

Sarcasm and schadenfreude. Some people practice cruelty for
its own sake and perhaps also out of self-hate or a lack of self-respect.
Trump's use of sarcasm and schadenfreude are evident in the following:

@realDonaldTrump

Really bad news! The Baltimore house of Elijah
Cummings was robbed. Too bad!

7:58 AM - Aug 2, 2019

@realDonaldTrump

Oh no, really big political news, perhaps the biggest
story in years! Part time Mayor of New York City, @
BilldeBlasio, who was polling at a solid ZERO but had
tremendous room for growth, has shocking dropped
out of the Presidential race. NYC is devastated, he's
coming home!

8:02 AM - Sep 20, 2019

@realDonaldTrump

Oh no, Beto just dropped out of race for President
despite him saying he was "born for this." I don't
think so!

5:51 PM - Nov 1, 2019

@realDonaldTrump

Really Big Breaking News (Kidding): Booker, who
was in zero polling territory, just dropped out of the
Democrat Presidential Primary Race. Now I can rest
easy tonight. I was sooo concerned that I would
someday have to go head to head with him!

8:13 AM - Jan 13, 2020

Insults and humiliation. In a study referenced earlier in the
book regarding executives who "derailed," insensitivity to others

(an abrasive, intimidating, bullying style) was frequently a cause for derailment. Good leaders respect themselves, their colleagues, and even their competitors.

> @realDonaldTrump
> Joe Biden got tongue tied over the weekend when he was unable to properly deliver a very simple line about his decision to run for President. Get used to it, another low I.Q. individual!
> 6:14 AM - Mar 18, 2019

> @realDonaldTrump
> "PELOSI STAMMERS THROUGH NEWS CONFERENCE"
> 6:09 PM - May 23, 2019

> @realDonaldTrump
> ....Paul Ryan almost killed the Republican Party. Weak, ineffective & stupid are not exactly the qualities that Republicans, or the CITIZENS of our Country, were looking for. Right now our spirit is at an all time high, far better than the Radical Left Dems. You'll see next year!
> 2:19 PM - Jul 13, 2019

> @realDonaldTrump
> Jay Powell and the Federal Reserve Fail Again. No "guts," no sense, no vision! A terrible communicator!
> 2:25 PM - Sep 18, 2019

@realDonaldTrump

Crazy "Nancy Pelosi, you are a weak person. You are a poor
leader. You are the reason America hates career politicians,
like yourself." @seanhannity She is totally incompetent
& controlled by the Radical Left, a weak and pathetic
puppet. Come back to Washington and do your job!

9:33 AM - Apr 16, 2020

In April 1865, General Ulysses S. Grant wrote a letter encouraging his military opponent—fellow West Point alumnus and Confederate leader General Robert E. Lee—to surrender. By this time, over six hundred thousand Americans had died during the course of the five-year civil war. Grant's signature on the letter was preceded by the words "very respectfully," in part because he understood that respect and the preservation of dignity would contribute to lasting peace. In the less consequential but perhaps more relatable world of sports, there is a stark contrast between the football player who tries to humiliate his opponent with trash talk after a momentary triumph and the athlete who plays with intensity but does not mind occasionally helping to his feet the quarterback he has just sacked. The need to degrade and humiliate is sometimes a projection of one's own fear of failure.

@realDonaldTrump

Lightweight Senator Kirsten Gillibrand, a total flunky
for Chuck Schumer and someone who would come to
my office "begging" for campaign contributions not so
long ago (and would do anything for them), is now in
the ring fighting against Trump. Very disloyal to Bill &
Crooked-USED!

5:03 AM - Dec 12, 2017

@realDonaldTrump

Beto (phony name to indicate Hispanic heritage) O'Rourke, who is embarrassed by my last visit to the Great State of Texas, where I trounced him, and is now even more embarrassed by polling at 1% in the Democrat Primary, should respect the victims & law enforcement - & be quiet!

11:57 PM - Aug 6, 2019

@realDonaldTrump

I don't know who Joaquin Castro is other than the lesser brother of a failed presidential candidate (1%) who makes a fool of himself every time he opens his mouth. Joaquin is not the man that his brother is, but his brother, according to most, is not much. Keep fighting Joaquin!

8:23 PM - Aug 7, 2019

In the following post, the president managed to weave slander and personal insults into his preferred nicknames.

@realDonaldTrump

Our case against lyin', cheatin', liddle' Adam "Shifty" Schiff, Cryin' Chuck Schumer, Nervous Nancy Pelosi, their leader, dumb as a rock AOC, & the entire Radical Left, Do Nothing Democrat Party, starts today at 10:00 A.M. on @FoxNews, @OANN or Fake News @ CNN or Fake News MSDNC!

9:37 AM - Jan 25, 2020

He also resorted to the infantile practice of mocking his opponents' physical attributes.

> @realDonaldTrump
> Mini Mike is a 5'4" mass of dead energy who does not want to be on the debate stage with these profes- sional politicians. No boxes please. He hates Crazy Bernie and will, with enough money, possibly stop him. Bernie's people will go nuts!
> 8:23 AM - Feb 13, 2020

> @realDonaldTrump
> The least effective of our 53 Republican Senators, and a person who truly doesn't have what it takes to be great, is Little Ben Sasse of Nebraska, a State which I have gladly done so much to help. @SenSasse was as nice as a RINO can be until he recently won the Republican....
> ...Nomination to run for a second term. Then he went back to his rather stupid and obnoxious ways. Must feel he can't lose to a Dem. Little Ben is a liability to the Republican Party, and an embarrass- ment to the Great State of Nebraska. Other than that, he's just a wonderful guy!
> 9:39 AM - Oct 17, 2020

Author Jonathan Glover describes the "cold joke" as one of the strongest expressions of disrespect. It mocks and humiliates the victim with added cruelty, while also serving as a display of power. In one example that occurred during the 1990 Iraqi invasion of

Kuwait, the family of a boy killed by Iraqi forces was billed for the bullet. Glover cites even more disturbing examples that highlight the role that humiliation and slights to self-respect and dignity can play in starting the "spiral of conflict" between two groups. People who are repeatedly disrespected are more likely to commit atrocities. Glover describes respect for dignity as "one of the greatest barriers against atrocity and cruelty. To acknowledge our shared moral status makes it harder for us to torture or kill each other. The erosion of the protective barrier creates danger." While the disrespect for dignity found in Trump's posts do not reach the level of the "cold joke," they still have the potential to further erode the respect that affirms our shared humanity.

Human kindness has never weakened the stamina
or softened the fiber of a free people. A nation does not
have to be cruel in order to be tough.
—FRANKLIN D. ROOSEVELT

CHAPTER 18

Discipline and
Self-Control

★ ★ ★

President Trump's secretary of the Navy, Richard Spencer, resigned in the wake of White House interference in naval judicial proceedings. In his letter of resignation, he highlighted the importance of promoting a culture of discipline and compliance:

> One [of] the most important responsibilities I have to our
> people is to maintain good order and discipline throughout
> the ranks.... Good order and discipline is what has enabled
> our victory against foreign tyranny time and again.

Subordinates and constituents count on their leaders to practice discipline and self-control in their professional endeavors and, to some extent, in their personal lives. Those who are unable to control their problematic impulses, emotions, and desires—especially those that clash with organizational core values—have no business leading people or controlling resources.

Mark Twain made the following assertion: "Laws control the lesser man. Right conduct controls the greater one." Adhering to notions of "right conduct" requires discipline and self-control in order to avoid making statements or engaging in conduct that can compromise one's reputation and credibility. Discipline and self-control are also needed for the following:

- To avoid engaging in favoritism, inappropriate professional relationships, and a host of other self-serving abuses of power or violations of the law

- To avoid getting sucked into the orbit of unscrupulous peers and superiors, and to avoid being personally compromised

- To avoid security lapses (such as the compromise of sensitive or classified information)

- To prevent mishaps (the loss of people and resources)

- To carry out lawful orders that one may find personally objectionable

- To tell the truth, even when personally inconvenient

- To stay the course during a frustrating yet consequential negotiation

- To complete difficult or unpleasant tasks or projects

- To practice persistent attention to detail when performing mundane yet important duties

Noncompliance, stemming from a lack of personal discipline, is very often the root cause of mishaps. The human behaviors and conditions that contribute to a breakdown in discipline include apathy, laziness, inattention, excessive fatigue, ignorance (of rules and procedures), bravado, poor judgment, and an unhealthy need for approval or recognition. Alone or in combinations, these behaviors and conditions will erode personal discipline to the point that effective leadership—and likely operational and organizational success—will be compromised.

Donald Trump's presidency was arguably a nonstop illustration of what happens when one is unable to exercise a requisite modicum of self-control. With respect to emotional intelligence, he was lacking the self-management or self-regulation skills that help to keep one's impulses in check. The vast majority of the posts featured in this book point to a lack of discipline and restraint. They are also likely symptoms of more profound personal shortcomings, including personality disorders and enduring ethical challenges—topics addressed in later chapters.

When it came to avoiding personal pettiness, for example, the president's instinct for restraint was consistently off duty. Leaders should understand that not every attack or criticism requires a response and that they do not always have the luxury of indulging their own emotions.

@realDonaldTrump
Going to the White House is considered a great honor for a championship team. Stephen Curry is hesitating, therefore invitation is withdrawn!
5:45 AM - Sep 23, 2017

In response to the preceding post, I envision over the painting of Abraham Lincoln in the Oval Office a word bubble containing words actually attributed to him: "You can tell the greatness of a man by what makes him angry." The practice of setting aside something written in anger or spite for a period of time before deciding whether or not to send it—one requiring self-control and favored by Lincoln himself—was clearly not embraced by everyone.

> @realDonaldTrump
> George Conway, often referred to as Mr. Kellyanne Conway by those who know him, is VERY jealous of his wife's success & angry that I, with her help, didn't give him the job he so desperately wanted. I barely know him but just take a look, a stone cold LOSER & husband from hell!
> 4:51 AM - Mar 20, 2019

> @realDonaldTrump
> Watched @billmaher last week for the first time in a long time. He's totally SHOT, looks terrible, exhausted, gaunt, and weak. If there was ever a good reason for no shutdown, check out this jerk. He never had much going for him, but whatever he did have is missing in action!
> 8:11 AM - Aug 12, 2020

President Trump's lack of discipline was unfortunately also evident in matters related to national security. His propensity to blurt out sensitive, even classified information (at inappropriate places or to inappropriate audiences) reportedly caused staffers to consider what information they should include in his intelligence briefings. Subordinates should not have to regularly police their leaders' actions due to a lack of self-control. The following post alarmed administration officials because it may have compromised intelligence sources and methods.

> @realDonaldTrump
> The United States is learning much from the failed missile explosion in Russia. We have similar, though more advanced, technology. The Russian "Skyfall" explosion has people worried about the air around the facility, and far beyond. Not good!
> 5:26 PM - Aug 12, 2019

In a similar episode, the president posted a photo of an explosion at an Iranian space launch facility. In doing so, he ignored the concerns of his aides regarding what the photo might reveal about America's surveillance capabilities.

The conduct of foreign policy also requires discipline. The disingenuous and unsophisticated threats made in the following posts—some of which predate the "falling in love" episode between Trump and Kim Jong Un—demonstrate a profound lack of discipline in communication. Such displays of bravado can potentially threaten national security by eliciting responses opposite to those intended. These posts also flout the doctrine of proportional response, which aims to avoid escalation and prevent further attacks.

> @realDonaldTrump
> The USA has great strength & patience, but if it is forced to defend itself or its allies, we will have no choice but to totally destroy #NoKo.
> 1:22 PM - Sep 19, 2017

@realDonaldTrump
Just heard Foreign Minister of North Korea speak at
U.N. If he echoes thoughts of Little Rocket Man, they
won't be around much longer!
8:08 PM - Sep 23, 2017

@realDonaldTrump
...caused over so many years. Any attack by Iran, in
any form, against the United States will be met with
an attack on Iran that will be 1,000 times greater in
magnitude!
11:04 PM - Sep 14, 2020

An implicit aim of terrorism is to provoke a highly disproportionate response from a more powerful adversary. Such a response might then culminate in various self-destructive effects. Discipline and self-control are needed to avoid reacting in a manner that results in unnecessary friendly casualties, the squandering of national resources, and self-imposed political or legal measures that could unnecessarily curtail civil liberties.

Discipline and self-control *can* be cultivated within organizations. To that end, individuals and teams should set goals, promote good habits, insist on compliance and ethical conduct, and practice mutual accountability. The leader's primary role is to consistently set the example through disciplined communication and conduct.

CHAPTER 19

Empathy

What more sublime delight than to mingle tears with
one whom the hand of heaven hath smitten!
To watch over the bed of sickness,
and to beguile its tedious and its painful moments!
To share our bread with one whom misfortune has let none!
This world abounds indeed with misery; to lighten its burden,
we must divide it with one another.

—Thomas Jefferson

Thomas Jefferson viewed empathy, a key component of what is contemporarily referred to as emotional intelligence, as a necessary element of the social contract. Practicing empathy is also necessary for effective communication and collaboration.

Empathy is generally divided into three distinct types. *Affective* empathy allows us to experience the emotions of others, while *cognitive* empathy allows us to understand their thoughts and feelings. *Behavioral* empathy generally refers to how we communicate affective and cognitive empathy to others through verbal and nonverbal behaviors.

In *Humanity: A Moral History of the Twentieth Century*, Jonathan Glover describes respect for dignity and sympathy as the moral resources and human responses that promote self-restraint, allow us to care for others, and work against narrowly selfish behavior. Per Glover, the empathy apparent in everyday acts of decency is even more necessary for confronting what he terms "moral emergencies." "These small acts reinforce the ordinary, everyday human decencies, out of which the large heroic acts grow."

Sources of empathy. As depicted in *Saturday Night Live*'s twist on the actual 5-hour ENERGY beverage, there is unfortunately no "5-hour Empathy" drink. Despite evidence that some psychopathic traits can be detected in early childhood, the body of research on empathy suggests that one's upbringing plays a larger role than genetics. Though we may not be able to control the environment in which we are raised, empathy can be learned. We can, to some extent, choose who we want to be and attune our actions—one choice at a time—to that ideal. Because empathy is largely a learned behavior, it is even more incumbent on leaders to model it for their subordinates.

Franklin D. Roosevelt's polio is believed to have made him a more empathetic leader. Firsthand suffering—whether mental, emotional, physical, or financial—can enhance one's general capacity for empathy and allow one to empathize with forms of suffering one has not personally experienced. That said, the ability to genuinely identify with and empathize with a specific kind of suffering can be exceptionally difficult absent similar personal experiences. For example, someone who has not personally experienced poverty or mental illness might be limited in their ability to relate to someone experiencing homelessness or clinical depression.

Another source of empathy is *awareness.* Former president Jimmy Carter believed that his commitment to human rights grew from his personal knowledge of the devastating effects of racial segregation in the American South.

Barriers to empathy. Certain personality disorders, characterized by the tendency to feel only one's own pain, can easily inhibit empathetic responses. Tribalism is another barrier to empathy when it results in less concern for people outside of "our own group." Jonathan Glover described how the moral resources can be overwhelmed by pressures to obey or conform. Using the Nazi practice of deliberately cultivated hardness as an example, he warned about how the combination of belief and tribalism can create a psychological distance, thereby weakening moral responses such as sympathy and empathy. Another barrier to empathy is privilege. In contrast to President Carter's example of awareness, the more isolated we are from tragedy or injustice, the easier it is to dismiss it.

Expressing empathy. Empathy is most often expressed through communication and perspective-taking.

Communication. We practice empathy when we actively listen, ask questions with a sincere desire to understand another person's point of view, and acknowledge their responses. In the wake of tragedy, leaders are occasionally expected to assume the role of mourner-in-chief, a role that requires one to give voice to what others are feeling while simultaneously imparting a reasonable degree of hope.

When Brazil's president was confronted with what was to date his country's highest one-day death toll during the COVID-19 pandemic, he responded with, "We are sorry for all the dead, but that's everyone's destiny." After a catastrophic winter storm exposed weaknesses in Texas's power grid in early 2021, leaving millions without power and water for days, the mayor of Colorado City chose to lecture his constituents on self-reliance, as demonstrated in this excerpt from his Facebook post:

> Let me hurt some feelings while I have a minute!! No one owes you [or] your family anything; nor is it the local government's responsibility to support you during trying times like this! Sink or swim it's your choice! The City and County, along with power providers or any other service owes you NOTHING!...Only the strong will survive and the weak will parish [*sic*]...Am I sorry that you have been dealing without electricity and water; yes! But I'll be damned if I'm going to provide for anyone that is capable of doing it themselves...

The mayor resigned shortly thereafter. President Trump also struggled to win awards in the consoler-in-chief category. While Trump's rebuke of gun violence in American cities was justified (though often inconsistently characterized depending on the governing political party), the families of shooting victims in Chicago deserved better from their president.

@realDonaldTrump
Seven people shot and killed yesterday in Chicago.
What is going on there - totally out of control. Chicago
needs help!
4:01 PM - Feb 23, 2017

After observing the repatriation of the remains of two American soldiers killed in Afghanistan, the president tried his best to express solemnity.

@realDonaldTrump
Just returned to White House from Dover. Very sad!
1:32 AM - Feb 11, 2020

Seemingly forgetting that Puerto Rico is a U.S. territory, the president also struggled to express empathy after the island was devastated by successive hurricanes.

@realDonaldTrump
Texas & Florida are doing great but Puerto Rico, which
was already suffering from broken infrastructure &
massive debt, is in deep trouble..
5:45 PM - Sep 25, 2017

@realDonaldTrump
Puerto Rico got 91 Billion Dollars for the hurricane,
more money than has ever been gotten for a hurricane before, & all their local politicians do is complain
& ask for more money. The pols are grossly incompetent, spend the money foolishly or corruptly, & only
take from USA....
4:33 AM - Apr 2, 2019

Perspective-taking. Perspective-taking is the empathetic skill that constrains hasty judgment by allowing us to be receptive to and tolerant of other viewpoints and experiences. Putting oneself in someone else's shoes can help one understand both sides of an issue. It can even allow us to empathize with the struggles of an opponent. Consider the newly crowned tennis champion who instead of gloating personifies class by rightfully acknowledging their opponent's efforts.

At the outset of the American Civil War, President Lincoln saw that Ulysses S. Grant possessed a critical leadership skill—the ability to understand others. At the war's conclusion, General Grant understood the importance of winning the peace with respect to the terms of his opponents' surrender. During the surrender at Appomattox, Grant prohibited his soldiers from gloating or celebrating in front of Confederate troops. He understood that empathy and respect for dignity were needed to suppress resentment and secure lasting peace.

Events that required more empathy than Donald Trump could muster included an alleged sexual assault and a movement to further social justice. During the 2018 Supreme Court confirmation hearing of Trump nominee Brett Kavanaugh, Dr. Christine Blasey Ford alleged that Kavanaugh had sexually assaulted her thirty-six years earlier.

@realDonaldTrump

I have no doubt that, if the attack on Dr. Ford was as bad as she says, charges would have been immediately filed with local Law Enforcement Authorities by either her or her loving parents. I ask that she bring those filings forward so that we can learn date, time, and place!

6:14 AM - Sep 21, 2018

In the president's singular focus to defend his nominee, he failed to understand or acknowledge that the majority of sexual assaults are not reported to police. Empathy, or perhaps just intellectual curiosity, was needed to understand how victims of sexual assault often behave. In May 2023, a jury in a civil trial found Donald J. Trump liable for sexually abusing (in the mid-1990s) and later defaming E. Jean Carroll.

In the summer of 2020, Americans from all walks of life took to the streets in support of the Black Lives Matter movement for social justice and police reform. The protests came in response to the deaths of several unarmed Black Americans at the hands of police officers over the course of several months. An empathetic leadership response was needed to acknowledge and address the pain and anger of African Americans regarding the systemic racism and lack of accountability that contributed to and followed, respectively, each of the deaths. The president instead focused on isolated episodes of violence and looting that occasionally accompanied the generally peaceful protests. He promoted a "law and order" theme in lieu of a more necessary, nuanced approach.

@realDonaldTrump
Get tough police!
6:47 AM - Jun 3, 2020

@realDonaldTrump
Our great National Guard Troops who took care of the area around the White House could hardly believe how easy it was. "A walk in the park", one said. The protesters, agitators, anarchists (ANTIFA), and others, were handled VERY easily by the Guard, D.C. Police, & S.S. GREAT JOB!
8:49 AM - Jun 11, 2020

@realDonaldTrump
LAW & ORDER!
7:19 AM - Jun 3, 2020

Trump would repost the "Law & Order" tweet an additional fourteen times over the following four months. In describing the actions of police officers who use excessive force, the president suggested that those who shoot unarmed suspects—such as the officer who shot Jacob Blake in the back seven times in front of his children—choke like a golfer missing a three-foot putt.

When a garage door pull rope fashioned as a noose was found in the Talladega Superspeedway team garage of racing driver Bubba Wallace, fellow drivers were quick to support NASCAR's only Black driver. Further investigation determined that the "noose" had been installed long before the garage had been assigned to Wallace's team, indicating that Wallace was not likely targeted. Nonetheless, the NASCAR organization eventually took steps that included banning Confederate flags from all of its facilities. Despite the fact that Wallace had no role in discovering the "noose," President Trump decided that unjustly shaming Wallace and NASCAR was more important than acknowledging the problems of pervasive racism and white nationalism.

@realDonaldTrump
Has @BubbaWallace apologized to all of those great NASCAR drivers & officials who came to his aid, stood by his side, & were willing to sacrifice everything for him, only to find out that the whole thing was just another HOAX? That & Flag decision has caused lowest ratings EVER!
8:33 AM - Jul 6, 2020

Empathy in the workplace. Leaders skilled in empathetic perspective-taking are less likely to derail, because they positively influence the mental health and output of their workers, retain talent, increase cooperation between individuals, and promote more effective problem-solving within teams. They are also better decision-makers.

One should strike a healthy balance between empathy and firmness or decisiveness, as they are not mutually exclusive. Leaders who do not deal with misconduct or gross incompetence appropriately (by disciplining, reassigning, or firing) will appear ineffective and risk losing the confidence of their people. That said, empathy should not be confused with weakness.

Employees want to be understood and valued by their leadership. They should feel safe sharing their personal or professional struggles without fear of being perceived as weak (especially regarding mental health issues). With respect to personal challenges, empathy allows one to understand that subordinates will have disparate experiences and personal support systems. One may need to transcend one's lack of personal experience regarding a subordinate's particular problem, and to consult relevant experts—as permitted—to ensure the person's needs are adequately met.

Empathy and public organizations. Bono delivered the keynote address at the 2006 National Prayer Breakfast, attended by President George W. Bush, First Lady Laura Bush, King Abdullah of Jordan, and other distinguished guests. He reminded his audience that Washington was a town with a reputation for coming together on behalf of "the least of these." Assisting those most in need requires first that we have the courage to not look away, even at the risk of personal discomfort.

Public organizations can be effective in promoting empathetic policies at home and abroad. As with individual expressions of empathy and kindness, humanitarian aid provided by public agencies need not be conditioned on reciprocity.

@realDonaldTrump
Just spoke to President Nayib Bukele of El Salvador. Will be helping them with Ventilators, which are desperately needed. They have worked well with us on immigration at the Southern Border!
10:20 AM - Apr 24, 2020

Implicit in the above post (and similar ones referencing Ecuador, Indonesia, Honduras, and Ethiopia) is that lifesaving equipment was provided in the context of a quid pro quo.

Cultivating empathy. President Trump suggested during a speech to law enforcement officers that they were demonstrating excessive care when placing restrained people into police vehicles (by guiding their heads to prevent injury). "Please don't be too nice," he said. Not only was he sending the wrong message but he was also seemingly oblivious to public sentiment and the valid concern—especially among minorities—that excessive force was already too prevalent.

Public leaders can foster empathy through the power of their own examples. Empathy can be fostered through seemingly small gestures like a sympathy card circulated for signatures in support of a sick or grieving colleague or the promotion of an organization's annual charity drive. Formal training is also available. The study of history and other cultures also tends to grow empathy. Leaders can boost empathetic responses by simply practicing the basic principles of compassionate communication and perspective-taking during routine professional and personal interactions.

From Jamestown forward, our story has become fuller and fairer because of people who share a conviction that Dr. King articulated on that Sunday half a century ago: The arc of the moral universe is long, but it bends toward justice. Bending that arc requires all of us. It requires we the people, and it requires a president of the United States with empathy, grace, a big heart, and an open mind.
—JON MEACHAM

Part 5

★ ★ ★

TRUST
AND
ACCOUNTABILITY

CHAPTER 20

Responsibility and Accountability

★ ★ ★

In June 1944, General Dwight Eisenhower—the supreme commander of Allied forces in Europe and leader of the D-Day invasion of Normandy—drafted a letter in the event the invasion against Nazi Germany failed. The letter ended with the words, "If any blame or fault attaches to the attempt, it is mine alone."

Following the 2024 assassination attempt on former president Trump in Butler, Pennsylvania, the head of the Secret Service characterized the episode as "the most significant operational failure of the Secret Service in decades....On July thirteenth, we failed. As the Director...I take full responsibility for any security lapse of our agency."

During a press conference in March 2020, President Trump was asked if he took any responsibility for disbanding (in 2018) the White House office responsible for coordinating pandemic responses. He immediately deflected responsibility to his subordinates. "When you say me, I didn't do it. We have a group of people..." When asked if he took responsibility for not having sooner resolved bureaucratic issues affecting the Centers for Disease Control and Prevention (CDC) COVID-19 response, the president's response was similar. "No. I don't take responsibility at all."

Whether the president would have had any direct, personal involvement in resolving the aforementioned issues is beside the point. A leader should take responsibility for the actions of subordinates and subordinate organizations. Leaders who are incapable of admitting their mistakes and failures are unlikely to learn from them. If not held accountable, they are likely to repeat those mistakes and may grow emboldened to engage in new misdeeds. The ability to share lessons from one's own mistakes is a key component of building trust.

Admitting responsibility. Speaking at the 2019 White House Correspondents' Dinner, Ron Chernow addressed the importance of admitting mistakes:

> We've fought horrific wars, weathered massive depressions, and ended the unspeakable cruelty of slavery and Jim Crow. America has always been great, not when it boasted, not when it blustered, but when it admitted its mistakes and sought to overcome them.

During a screening of Kevin Costner's Western *Open Range*, the actor/director similarly expressed the notion that America could only achieve something close to its full potential when it had fully reckoned with the sins of its past. He was referring specifically to the near-extinction of Native Americans and the moral peril associated with whitewashing that chapter of America's history. Accountability is not always about punishment or restitution. Sometimes it is just about having the courage to acknowledge what transpired. Similarly, and on a smaller scale, public institutions and their leaders must willingly accept responsibility for the consequences of their actions. During the COVID-19 pandemic, the officer responsible for vaccine distribution, General Gustave Perna, took personal responsibility for disruptions that resulted in states receiving fewer allocations than expected. "I failed, nobody else failed....It was my fault. I gave guidance....It was a planning error and I am responsible."

Owning one's mistakes requires humility and a little courage. It may also require a degree of resilience sufficient to see beyond recent setbacks, disappointments, and outright failures. As one newscaster liked to say, some people seem to never suffer a single minute of self-doubt with respect to their performance or conduct. These types of leaders are incapable of learning from their mistakes because they work hard to avoid the first step—admitting them. Denial is sometimes expressed as outrage.

@realDonaldTrump
The call to the Ukrainian President was PERFECT.
Read the Transcript! There was NOTHING said that
was in any way wrong. Republicans, don't be led
into the fools trap of saying it was not perfect, but is
not impeachable. No, it is much stronger than that.
NOTHING WAS DONE WRONG!
2:43 PM · Nov 10, 2019

@realDonaldTrump
I JUST GOT IMPEACHED FOR MAKING A PERFECT
PHONE CALL!
12:39 PM - Jan 16, 2020

To believe the call was perfect would require finding it acceptable to solicit foreign interference in an election by asking a foreign leader to investigate your primary political rival, smear a U.S. ambassador, and undermine Ukraine's anti-corruption efforts by praising one of its corrupt prosecutors.

We do not often see the level of humility displayed by President Abraham Lincoln in the following letter to Major General Ulysses S. Grant regarding the latter's victory at the 1863 siege of Vicksburg:

> My dear General—I do not remember that you and I ever met personally. I write this now as a grateful acknowledgment for the almost inestimable service you have done the country. I wish to say a word further. When you first reached the vicinity of Vicksburg, I thought you should do, what you finally did—march the troops across the neck, run the batteries with the transports, and thus go below; and I never had any faith, except a general hope that you knew better than I, that the Yazoo Pass expedition, and the like, could succeed. When you got below, and took Port-Gibson, Grand Gulf, and vicinity, I thought you should go down the river and join Gen. Banks; and when you turned Northward East of the Big Black, I feared it was a mistake. I now wish to make the

personal acknowledgment that you were right, and I was wrong. Yours very truly—A. Lincoln

Such an admission appears almost effortless for Lincoln. Admitting mistakes and apologizing are signs that you possess the requisite humility and confidence to avoid the trap of projecting inauthentic perfection. Even a small amount of contrition can yield a great deal of understanding, forgiveness, and cooperation and foster a culture of trust and respect. The need to apologize does not wane with increased seniority or authority. Furthermore, acts of contrition do not diminish one's authority.

Most leaders—and especially elected officials—understand that in the long run, quickly admitting one's wrongdoing works better than remaining unremorseful or, worse yet, deceitful. The study of executives categorized as either "arrivers" or the "derailed" handled mistakes very differently. Though neither group made many mistakes, the arrivers almost always "admitted the mistake, forewarned others so that they wouldn't be blindsided by it, then set about analyzing and fixing it." The arrivers notably did not blame others, nor did they dwell on their mistakes.

As described in an earlier chapter, what began as a minor misstatement or inaccurate description by President Trump— that Hurricane Dorian was forecasted to threaten the state of Alabama—could have been corrected in a matter of seconds. It was instead transformed into a days-long attempt by the president to prove that the storm had indeed been forecasted to threaten the state.

@realDonaldTrump

The Fake News Media was fixated on the fact that I properly said, at the beginnings of Hurricane Dorian, that in addition to Florida & other states, Alabama may also be grazed or hit. They went Crazy, hoping against hope that I made a mistake (which I didn't). Check out maps.....

....This nonsense has never happened to another President. Four days of corrupt reporting, still without an apology. But there are many things that the Fake News Media has not apologized to me for, like the Witch Hunt, or SpyGate! The LameStream Media and their Democrat.....

....partner should start playing it straight. It would be so much better for our Country!

10:29 AM - Sep 6, 2019

A phenomenon often observed with politicians is the tendency to take credit when things are going well and to scapegoat or cast blame on outside forces during times of difficulty. As Jeffrey Kluger explained in his entertaining book *The Narcissist Next Door*, "Blaming outside circumstances suggests you'll always be buffeted by random events." In contrast, taking responsibility when things go wrong—by communicating what went wrong and how it can be fixed—conveys a certain degree of control. Kluger cited psychologist Ben Dattner, whose research suggested that "companies that make a habit of shouldering responsibility for problems outperform the stock market year to year."

As mentioned earlier, President Trump initially proposed hosting the G7 Summit at one of his Trump-branded properties, a clear conflict of interest. Despite a fair amount of pushback from even his Republican allies in Congress, the president was unrepentant and opted to blame outside entities for eventually having to change course.

> @realDonaldTrump
> ....Therefore, based on both Media & Democrat Crazed and Irrational Hostility, we will no longer consider Trump National Doral, Miami, as the Host Site for the G-7 in 2020. We will begin the search for another site, including the possibility of Camp David, immediately. Thank you!
> 9:52 PM - Oct 19, 2019

Similar to admitting a mistake is changing one's position after receiving new evidence or additional introspection. This requires open-mindedness, self-confidence, and the humility to admit that the appearance of having initially been mistaken or having "flip-flopped" is outweighed by the adoption of the preferred position or course of action. The Center for Creative Leadership cites the *inability to adapt* as the most frequently cited reason for career derailment among North American managers. This is true in part because "inflexible leaders limit the workplace adaptability of others." Additionally, "Resistance to change may undermine critical projects or system-wide implementation....Employee enthusiasm, cooperation, morale, and creativity are jeopardized, making it all the more difficult to run the business or organization." As Richard Stengel explained in *Mandela's Way*, "When Nelson Mandela reverses himself, you would never know he had ever felt differently. He goes over to the other side and embraces it with the zeal of the newly converted."

When one shares lessons learned from one's own mistakes, it gives subordinates the freedom to critically evaluate their own short-comings. During what would have been a routine introduction of himself while addressing subordinates during a newcomer's orientation session, a particular Air Force colonel drew from his own marital issues to convey some very personal lessons on being more attuned to the needs of others. His demonstrated vulnerability likely contributed to his being one of the most trusted and revered leaders in the organization.

Accountability. A ninety-three-year-old former Nazi SS concentration camp guard was finally brought to justice in 2020 for his role in the murder of more than five thousand prisoners between 1944 and 1945 at the Stutthof camp in occupied Poland. Two years later, a German court convicted a 101-year-old former guard of being an accessory to over 3,500 murders at the Sachsenhausen concentration camp.

I was deployed in support of NATO operations in Kosovo when one of my subordinates made a credible accusation against one of our officers. It had not taken long for me to conclude that this officer rated highly for a lack of professionalism. His accuser was alleging inappropriate advances (verbal sexual harassment) and reprisal for reporting the incidents. Efforts to raise the issue to the appropriate senior U.S. officer on the base, a colonel, had resulted in no meaningful action. The allegations eventually came to a head when the colonel called for a meeting in his office that included the accused, the accuser, and a few others familiar with the unfortunate series of events. What happened next took us all by surprise. The colonel opened his desk drawer, produced a Bible, and began reading a passage about forgiveness. While I believe in the power of forgiveness, forgiveness and accountability are not mutually exclusive.

A few weeks later, the colonel was forced to choose accountability after another serious breach of discipline by the accused officer. Perhaps needing a break from the demands of harassing his subordinates, he had engaged in consensual, yet rather inappropriate, public fraternization with an enlisted subordinate. The incident was apparently witnessed and reported by his own subordinates. Unable to ignore this incident, the colonel ended his deployment and returned him to his permanent duty station. The accuser who had made the original sexual harassment allegation eventually filed an inspector general complaint against the accused officer.

Accountability does more than just demand certain levels of job performance and standards of behavior. It also allows for corrective training and deters unacceptable behavior by holding organizations and individuals to account. When leaders are not held to account, subordinates will become more cynical of their leaders and of leadership generally. Promising subordinates may even be dissuaded from pursuing leadership roles.

Trust is crucial for the success of a public organization—trust between the organization and the public, and trust between organizational leaders and their followers. Without trust, leadership is generally ineffective and a leader's ability to influence is compromised. A lack of trust also diminishes the ability of followers to influence their leaders. In contrast, a climate of trust encourages two-way constructive communication, mutual cooperation, and empowerment—all increasing the likelihood of mission or program success.

One does not have to violate a regulation or break a law to abuse or violate trust. A failure to hold people accountable can also erode trust, both within and external to an organization. Acting Secretary of Defense Patrick Shanahan addressed the external relationship in a 2019 memorandum to all Department of Defense personnel:

> Congress and the Nation have placed their trust in us— trust that we will deliver high performance results and remain accountable to the American people as good stewards of their tax dollars. As we continue translating strategy into action, we must demonstrate our commitment as leaders in carrying this trust forward.

As compared to their private sector counterparts, public organizations and their leaders are arguably more exposed to public scrutiny with respect to performance expectations and policy outcomes. This is due to the checks and balances inherent in American government, the role of a free press, and the expectations of citizens whose taxes fund the government. This additional scrutiny requires that organizations be more transparent with respect to accountability.

Self-accountability. Leaders play a crucial role in promoting self-accountability. Who one is in the face of failure is one of the greatest tests of leadership. Holding subordinates accountable but not oneself is hypocritical. Equally troubling is the leader who refuses to hold others to account because they do not hold themselves to account and do not want others holding them to account. Leaders should foster a culture where people not only hold themselves accountable but also expect their fellow colleagues to hold them accountable.

At a certain point in my flying career, I adjusted my mindset about the moderately stressful periodic flight evaluations (a.k.a. checkrides) administered to Air Force aircrew every seventeen months. As with many things and especially checkrides, it was better to give than receive. Instead of approaching it as a threatening ordeal in which the evaluator pilot was out to expose any potential weaknesses, I slowly shifted from an adversarial mindset to one in which I welcomed the challenge and would accept in its proper context that potentially poor performance demanded certain consequences. That is, I began to see the experience in more of an organizational context—evaluation for the sake of organizational and mission success as opposed to an experience intended to threaten my ego or flying career. That mental shift allowed me to co-opt the evaluator's viewpoint. That attitude might also be expressed in a variation of the Golden Rule. In lieu of "Do unto others as you'd have them do unto you," it might instead read, "Expect for yourself that which you believe is deserved for others for similarly inadequate performance or inappropriate behavior."

Leaders should not take credit for the accomplishments of their subordinates if they cannot also feel responsible for their subordinates' failures. While leaders may not be directly responsible for most subordinate deficiencies, they should nonetheless feel accountable. Adopting a mindset of complete responsibility and accountability will animate one's efforts to shape organizational performance and behavior by providing the necessary resources, training, and guidance.

Introspection. Introspection is another practice that promotes personal accountability. It is useful to examine your thoughts, feelings, and actions through the lens of an outside and disinterested observer. Leaders must become comfortable living with their imperfections, along with the imperfections of others. Musician Carlos Santana refers to this as "naked awareness"—the ability to see yourself fully and make changes. The unwillingness to examine one's own fallibilities has parallels to the flawed notion that one cannot be critical of one's own organization or country. The insistence that one should "love it or leave it," for example, suggests an inability to live with imperfection and an unwillingness to confront and fix faults. After making a mistake, one should—at the appropriate time— perform a postmortem of sorts, similar to a mishap investigation that uncovers causes and provides recommendations. The following post, related to the president's first impeachment, weds a lack of introspection to fanciful rationalization.

@realDonaldTrump
They are trying to stop ME, because I am fighting for YOU!
5:14 PM - Sep 28, 2019

As an Air Force officer, I was required to provide periodic, structured feedback sessions to my subordinates. Rather than addressing expectations in a one-way conversation, I chose instead to promote introspection and self-assessment. In sessions usually lasting close to an hour, I would ask my subordinates to evaluate themselves with respect to each performance criterion before providing my own, previously prepared feedback. Near the end of the session, I would also ask my subordinates for feedback on the leadership and support I was providing. We all have blind spots regarding our own performance and behaviors. Giving and receiving feedback is also a key component of building trust, and it likely made me a more accessible supervisor.

A leadership skill that requires some finesse is understanding when subordinates independently understand the causes and consequences of their mistakes. This understanding can remove or diminish the need for condemnation. Leaders secure in themselves can also keep subordinates' mistakes in perspective by understanding that not all of those mistakes reflect on their own leadership. Furthermore, leaders must avoid promoting a mistake-averse culture in which subordinates must choose between honesty (publicly owning their mistakes) and career progression. If subordinates feel that they cannot demonstrate initiative and take reasonable risks, innovation will be stifled.

Though the book *Difficult Conversations* focuses primarily on interpersonal relationships, its discussion of shifting from *blame* to *contribution* can apply to organizational accountability. Blame—focused on fault-finding and punishment—is differentiated from contribution, which is focused on understanding what occurred in order to effect meaningful change. Blame can hinder problem-solving and leave systemic issues undiscovered. With respect to personal accountability, blame is also likely to inhibit the process of understanding how your own actions contributed to a problem. Using Air Force mishap investigations as an example, a Safety Investigation Board determines the causes of a mishap in order to prevent similar mishaps (contribution), while the Accident Investigation Board (if deemed necessary) focuses on accountability (blame). The two investigations are essentially identical processes serving different purposes. The advantage of the contribution model is that it promotes candidness and is more likely to serve the long-term interests of an organization. However, blame in the form of punitive accountability is sometimes necessary and is built into the Constitution and all three branches of federal government.

The consequences of neglecting accountability. Once President Trump understood that his conduct with respect to the ongoing investigation into Russian election interference was under scrutiny, he responded to the potential of future personal accountability with outrage.

> @realDonaldTrump
> Study the late Joseph McCarthy, because we are now in period with Mueller and his gang that make Joseph McCarthy look like a baby! Rigged Witch Hunt!
> 5:24 AM - Aug 19, 2018

The president frequently characterized the investigation as a "witch hunt" and "the Russia hoax." He did so at the expense of its primary focus—understanding Russia's extensive interference in the 2016 election. With respect to the nexus between Russian government interference and members of his own campaign, the president adopted the "no collusion" refrain. Regarding the investigation into his obstruction of the investigation itself (volume 2 of the Mueller report), President Trump adopted the "no obstruction" tagline. A "no collusion, no obstruction" placard was even affixed to his White House lectern.

> @realDonaldTrump
> NO COLLUSION, NO OBSTRUCTION, TOTAL EXONERATION. DEMOCRAT WITCH HUNT!
> 6:15 PM - Jul 27, 2019

As Special Counsel Robert Mueller testified to Congress, his investigation examined criminal conspiracy versus "collusion," the latter not technically a legal term. The investigation "did not establish that members of the Trump Campaign conspired or coordinated with the Russian government in its election-interference activities." While there was not sufficient evidence found to charge anyone for conspiring with the Russian government, the report cited numerous contacts between Trump campaign officials and individuals with ties to the Russian government. They included Paul Manafort's passing of sensitive polling data to an individual assessed to have ties to Russian intelligence.

On the issue of obstruction, the report documented ten distinct incidents in which President Trump may have committed obstruction of justice (discussed further in chapter 30). The president's claim of "total exoneration," in concert with Attorney General William Barr's disingenuous exculpatory interpretation of the report, are both contradicted in the investigation's findings. Members of his campaign, his national security advisor, and other associates were convicted of lying, in addition to other crimes discovered during the course of the investigation. The DOJ policy stating that a sitting president cannot be indicted informed the careful wording used by Mueller and his team in the conclusion of the report:

> If we had confidence after a thorough investigation of the facts that the President clearly did not commit obstruction of justice, we would so state. Based on the facts and the applicable legal standards, however, we are unable to reach that judgment....Accordingly, while this report does not conclude that the President committed a crime, it also does not exonerate him.

When the unrepentant are not held accountable, they become emboldened. They also set a poor example for and reduce the inhibitions of subordinates who may come to believe that they, too, can act with impunity. Because of the aforementioned DOJ policy, President Trump was not indicted for what the evidence showed were likely multiple acts of obstruction of justice of the Russia investigation. His unrelated attempt to extort Ukraine quickly followed.

> @realDonaldTrump
> The Radical Left Democrats and their Fake News Media partners, headed up again by Little Adam Schiff, and batting Zero for 21 against me, are at it again! They think I may have had a "dicey" conversation with a certain foreign leader based on a "highly partisan" whistleblowers..
> 8:27 AM - Sep 20, 2019

It was also a case of the president failing to absorb the Russia investigation's broader lessons about election interference, as described in the House Permanent Select Committee on Intelligence's *Trump-Ukraine Impeachment Inquiry Report*:

> Having witnessed the degree to which interference by a foreign power in 2016 harmed our democracy, President Trump cannot credibly claim ignorance to its pernicious effects. Even more pointedly, the President's July call with Ukrainian President Zelenskyy, in which he solicited an investigation to damage his most feared 2020 opponent, came the day after Special Counsel Robert Mueller

testified to Congress about Russia's efforts to damage his 2016 opponent and his urgent warning of the dangers of further foreign interference in the next election. With this backdrop, the solicitation of new foreign intervention was the act of a president unbound, not one chastened by experience. It was the act of a president who viewed himself as unaccountable and determined to use his vast official powers to secure his reelection....President Trump publicly declared anew that other countries should open investigations into his chief political rival, saying, "China should start an investigation into the Bidens," and that "President Zelenskyy, if it were me, I would recommend that they start an investigation into the Bidens."

During the course of the Trump–Ukraine impeachment inquiry, the president employed a variety of tactics to thwart accountability. In the following posts, he used denial (self-deception), distraction and disinformation, and a rationalized appeal to sympathy, respectively.

@realDonaldTrump
Breaking News: Unemployment Rate, at 3.5%, drops to a 50 YEAR LOW. Wow America, lets impeach your President (even though he did nothing wrong!).
8:47 AM - Oct 4, 2019

@realDonaldTrump
Why isn't the IG investigating his so-called Whistleblower? All bad info!
9:42 AM - Oct 10, 2019

> @realDonaldTrump
> Despite all of the great success that our Country
> has had over the last 3 years, it makes it much more
> difficult to deal with foreign leaders (and others) when
> I am having to constantly defend myself against the
> Do Nothing Democrats & their bogus Impeachment
> Scam. Bad for USA!
> 9:36 AM - Dec 26, 2019

With a personal history of avoiding accountability, it is perhaps not surprising that another of his posts began with, "I never in my wildest dreams thought my name would in any way be associated with the ugly word, Impeachment!" On this occasion, President Trump was impeached for abuse of power and obstruction of Congress. During the Senate trial, the president continued to characterize the impeachment as a solely partisan exercise intended to compromise his electoral prospects.

> @realDonaldTrump
> The Impeachment Hoax is interfering with the 2020
> Election - But that was the idea behind the Radical
> Left, Do Nothing Dems Scam attack. They always
> knew I did nothing wrong!
> 7:50 AM - Jan 24, 2020

Following the Senate impeachment trial, Senator Lamar Alexander (R-TN) conceded that the House managers had proved their case against Trump but argued that his acts were somehow not impeachable:

It was inappropriate for the president to ask a foreign leader to investigate his political opponent and to withhold United States aid to encourage that investigation. When elected officials inappropriately interfere with such investigations, it undermines the principle of equal justice under the law. But the Constitution does not give the Senate the power to remove the president from office and ban him from this year's ballot simply for actions that are inappropriate.

Harvard Law professor Noah Feldman had testified in the House impeachment hearings with regard to what the framers of the Constitution intended with respect to impeachment and presidential abuses of power.

> The framers provided for impeachment of the president because they feared that a president might abuse the power of his office to gain personal advantage; to corrupt the electoral process and keep himself in office; or to subvert our national security.

> ...The essential definition of high crimes and misdemeanors is the abuse of office. The framers considered the office of the presidency to be a public trust. Abuse of the office of the presidency is the very essence of a high crime and misdemeanor.

> To be clear, when the framers chose these words "high crimes and misdemeanors," there was no longer any

meaningful difference between "high crimes" and "high misdemeanors." The words were used interchangeably in the Hastings impeachment. The distinction in criminal law between felonies and misdemeanors is not implicated in the framers' phrase.

...It is important to note that the traditional meaning of high crimes and misdemeanors was *not* restricted to acts defined as ordinary crimes by statute. The language was deliberately meant to be flexible enough to incorporate a range of abuses of power that endanger the democratic process, because the Framers understood that they could not perfectly anticipate every possible abuse of power by the president.

A barrier to accountability during the Senate trial was the publicly declared unwillingness of some senators to act as impartial jurors. Some of them clearly feared electoral backlash. It is difficult to understand how U.S. senators—some of whom had experienced combat or had voted to put American troops into harm's way—could not muster the political courage to hold another elected official accountable in order to safeguard their constitutional democracy. Journalist and author Peter Baker described the president's demeanor after his acquittal by the Senate: "A triumphant Mr. Trump emerges from the biggest test of his presidency emboldened, ready to claim exoneration, and take his case of grievance, persecution and resentment to the campaign trail."

The lead House impeachment manager had warned that if not held accountable, President Trump would again violate his oath of office. Twelve months later—unable to accept his 2020 electoral defeat—the president attempted to illegitimately retain power by engaging in various schemes to overturn the results of the election (as detailed in other chapters). As a second impeachment loomed for "incitement of insurrection," Trump and his allies suggested it was a time for healing and unity. In contrast, Senator Mitt Romney recognized that unity requires "accountability, for truth and justice." Even in restorative justice—where the victim and victimizer are brought together for healing—accountability is a necessary first step. Some of the president's allies in the Senate questioned the need for impeachment, given the president's imminent departure from office. Senator Bernie Sanders provided the answer: "Some people ask: Why would you impeach and convict a president who has only a few days left in office? The answer: Precedent. It must be made clear that no president, now or in the future, can lead an insurrection against the U.S. government."

In his second impeachment trial—unprecedented for an American president—Trump was once again acquitted. Though fifty-seven senators (including seven Republicans) voted to convict, the vote fell short of the two-thirds majority needed for a conviction. It was perhaps a case of too many spinal columns experiencing simultaneous collapse. Senate Minority Leader Mitch McConnell partially justified his vote to acquit on the grounds that the president was no longer in office (though a conviction could have permanently barred Trump from ever again holding public office). McConnell nonetheless declared, "There's no question—none—that President Trump is practically and morally responsible for provoking the events of the day. No question about it."

Accountability also serves as a deterrence. In response to a motion in the Senate to dismiss the 2021 (January 6 riot) impeachment proceedings, House Manager David Cicilline (D-RI) explained that "we have a common interest in making clear that there are lines that nobody can cross, especially the President of the United States." House Manager Ted Lieu (D-CA) stressed that "President Trump's lack of remorse and refusal to take accountability after the attack poses its own unique and continuing danger. It sends the message that it is acceptable to incite a violent insurrection to overthrow the will of the people and that a President of the United States can do that and get away with it." As House Manager Diana DeGette (D-CO) put it, "Impeachment is not to punish but to prevent. We are not here to punish Donald Trump. We are here to prevent the seeds of hatred he planted from bearing any more fruit." Another lawmaker characterized the impeachment as an effort to protect the public from further wrongdoing. These remarks were echoed by Senate Chaplain Barry Black, who had prayed for the senator jurors. "Remind them that the seeds they plant now will bring a harvest. May the choices they make bring blessings, healing, and prosperity to our land."

A leader's seniority does not diminish the need for accountability. On the contrary, lack of accountability for increasing levels of authority will correlate to the amount of harm done to an organization and its reputation for consistency and fairness. Senior leaders in the military are regularly held accountable for their actions. The alternative would be disastrous for good order, morale, and mission accomplishment. If a government cannot hold its leaders accountable, its efforts to promote the rule of law and fight corruption abroad will ring hollow.

In a January 2024 social media post aimed at the Supreme

Court in the context of his federal criminal charges related to alleged conspiracies to overturn the 2020 election, Donald Trump suggested that presidents cannot function properly without complete and total immunity from criminal prosecution. In their unanimous February 2024 decision, the D.C. Circuit Court of Appeals rejected Trump's claim that "a President has unbounded authority to commit crimes that would neutralize the most fundamental check on executive power—the recognition and implementation of election results." As the Supreme Court was about to hear arguments resulting from Trump's appeal of the D.C. Circuit Court decision, a group of nineteen retired four-star generals and admirals, along with former secretaries of the Army, Navy, and Air Force, submitted an amicus brief arguing that presidential immunity "would undermine our nation's foundational commitment to civilian control of the military" and would "undermine the military's adherence to the rule of law and thus its orderly functioning and public trust." They further asserted that immunity had the potential to severely undermine the commander in chief's legal and moral authority to lead the military forces, as it would signal that they but not he must obey the rule of law.

On July 1, 2024, the Supreme Court concluded in a six to three decision along ideological lines that presidents are immune from criminal prosecution when exercising their "core" constitutional powers and are entitled to presumptive immunity for all other official acts. This immunity does not extend to unofficial acts. The court also determined that "in dividing official from unofficial conduct, courts may not inquire into the President's motives." In her dissent, Justice Sonia Sotomayor noted that "this new official-acts immunity now 'lies about like a loaded weapon' for any President that wishes to place his own interests, his own political survival, or his own financial gain, above the interests of the Nation....Never in the history of our Republic has a President had reason to believe that he would be immune from criminal prosecution if he used the trappings of his office to violate the criminal law." Justice Ketanji Brown Jackson's dissent described a departure from the traditional model of individual accountability in that "the majority has concocted something entirely different: a Presidential accountability model that creates immunity—an exemption from criminal law—applicable only to the most powerful official in our Government.... Consequently, our Nation has lost a substantial check on Presidents who would use their official powers to commit crimes with impunity while in office." The court's decision decreased the likelihood that President Trump will ever be held accountable for his efforts to overturn the 2020 election.

> *Without accountability, it all becomes normal, and it will recur.*
> —LIZ CHENEY

CHAPTER 21

Promises and Commitments

Undertake not what you cannot perform
but be careful to keep your promise.

—Sixteenth-century French maxim

E mpty, unfulfilled promises erode credibility and trust. Once leaders squander that trust, their tenures are typically too short to regain it.

Those seeking elected office can entice voters with promises that provide hope and project future success. Once in office, however, they may feel constrained to fulfill those campaign pledges, despite new evidence or changing circumstances. That obligation to make good on what was likely an unrealistic or unwise promise can become an impediment to good governance.

By raising taxes after vowing not to propose additional taxation, President George H.W. Bush broke a campaign promise that likely cost him reelection. But he did so with principled

315

courage, believing he was acting in the national interest. While one should strive to honor one's promises and commitments, the Bush example demonstrates that they are to be made judiciously and responsibly.

Making assurances about policy outcomes may play well during a political campaign, but leading and governing require a more sober approach.

> @realDonaldTrump
> Despite what you hear in the press, healthcare is coming along great. We are talking to many groups and **it will end in a beautiful picture!**
> 9:01 AM - Mar 9, 2017

That beautiful picture never materialized, despite at least five public assurances from President Trump between March 2017 and October 2020 that a national health-care plan would be imminently released and signed into law.

One should also not make promises on behalf of others.

> @realDonaldTrump
> **Republican Senators will not let the American people down!** ObamaCare premiums and deductibles are way up - it was a lie and it is dead!
> 5:49 AM - May 7, 2017

The senators may not have let down the majority of Americans when they failed to repeal the Affordable Care Act, but they certainly disappointed the president.

In what may have also been intended as a motivational speech for a dictator, the president assured Americans that he understood the North Korean leader's desires and intentions.

@realDonaldTrump
Anything in this very interesting world is possible, but I believe that Kim Jong Un fully realizes the great economic potential of North Korea, & will do nothing to interfere or end it. **He also knows that I am with him & does not want to break his promise to me. Deal will happen!**
6:42 AM - May 4, 2019

No substantive deal was ever reached.

@realDonaldTrump
The Democrats should get together with their Republican counterparts and work something out on Border Security & Safety. **Don't wait until after the election because you are going to lose!**
5:49 PM - Jun 17, 2018

Hollow threats can bring about unintended consequences. Basketball great Michael Jordan's rivals discovered that taunting him usually resulted in an undesired and pronounced boost in his performance. In this case, contrary to Trump's prediction, the Democrats won control of the House of Representatives in the 2018 midterm elections.

A more consequential and dangerous form of promise-making is wishful thinking. Making assurances with no regard for science during a pandemic, for example, may influence people to conduct themselves in a manner that unnecessarily elevates their risk of sickness or death.

> @realDonaldTrump
> The Invisible Enemy **will soon be in full retreat!**
> 11:15 AM - Apr 10, 2020

If by "soon" he meant before the end of the year, then the virus was not listening. In the following, it is not clear if the president was prophesying or declaring victory.

> @realDonaldTrump
> ....And then came a Plague, a great and powerful Plague, and the World was never to be the same again! But America rose from this death and destruction, always remembering its many lost souls, and the lost souls all over the World, and became greater than ever before!
> 10:43 AM - May 3, 2020

The weekly COVID-19 death toll would not reach its peak for another nine months.

The distinction between promises and commitments is an especially important one. When President Kennedy in May 1961 called for human exploration of the moon, he communicated his vision in the language of commitment and realism.

I believe that this nation should commit itself to

achieving the goal, before this decade is out, of landing a man on the moon and returning him safely to the earth. No single space project…will be more impressive to mankind, or more important…and none will be so difficult or expensive to accomplish.

In a related speech made twelve months later, Kennedy insisted that as Americans, we would do the work required to accomplish that goal. His commitment gave the thousands tasked with realizing his vision the courage to weather the numerous struggles that eventually culminated in the successful moon landing in July 1969. Kennedy's goal was aspirational yet grounded in a realistic optimism.

One must exercise caution when communicating generalized aspirations that resemble assurances.

@realDonaldTrump
Things will work out fine between the U.S.A. and Russia. At the right time everyone will come to their senses & there will be lasting peace!
6:16 AM - Apr 13, 2017

CHAPTER 22

Perceptions and
Conflicts of Interest

★ ★ ★

Perceptions. Leaders should always consider themselves in the spotlight at center stage. Subordinates are continuously observing and judging their words and deeds. If subordinates perceive something untoward—even in the absence of actual wrongdoing, acts of favoritism, or conflicts of interest—confidence in leadership is diminished. Without trust and respect, the ability to lead is severely compromised.

My first Air Force assignment provided some immediate lessons in perception issues. Running late for work one day, I decided to use a front-row parking spot reserved for an enlisted quarterly award winner whom I knew to be out of town. My boss gently explained to me that despite the "owner's" absence, my decision to use the spot created a negative perception of privilege. This was especially true because I was one of only four officers in a squadron of 130 people.

Another example involved my participation in organized sports in the local community. As some of my subordinates played on the same team, it was important for me—once back in the office—to maintain a formal relationship with those subordinates because of our more casual interactions outside of the office. I avoided any perception of undue familiarity that could be wrongly interpreted as preferential treatment in the workplace.

Decision-making in personnel matters can also provoke perceptions of favoritism. Even so, a fair and objective personnel decision will withstand scrutiny. It is beneficial, though, to examine whether one's behavior outside of the decision itself—such as one's demeanor around certain subordinates—may contribute to any perception issues.

While speaking at an event for American veterans, President Trump told one of the recipients of the highest individual military decoration—the Medal of Honor—that he had earlier joked with his staff about whether he could give the award to himself. The Medal of Honor is "conferred only upon members of the United States Armed Forces who distinguish themselves through conspicuous gallantry and intrepidity at the risk of life above and beyond the call of duty." Actual or perceived undue personal privilege is incompatible with command. Leaders can and must choose who they are being with respect to the perceptions they create. They must possess enough self-awareness to see themselves as others see them.

The Justice Department has a long-standing policy that restricts all but its most senior leaders from communicating with the White House. The policy seeks to avoid the perception (or reality) of political influence on the activities of the department. That policy was violated when the DOJ's Jeffrey Clark attended a meeting with President Trump following the 2020 election. Clark did not inform his boss, Acting Attorney General Jeffrey Rosen, before or after the

Oval Office meeting. When Rosen discovered Clark's actions, Clark assured him he would comply with the policy. Clark then violated the policy within five days during a phone call with the president, and then again during another in-person meeting with the president. Clark's actions went beyond mere perception issues. He was at the White House because the president and his allies in Congress were pushing for him to be installed as acting attorney general. Once installed, Clark could further Trump's agenda of using the department to assist in overturning the results of the 2020 presidential election.

Conflicts of interest. In the executive branch, federal statutes (specifically 18 U.S. Code, section 208) can impose criminal penalties on those who refuse to recuse themselves when their official roles might conflict with their financial interests. Though this provision is not legally binding on the president and vice president, presidents have generally divested themselves of certain financial interests to avoid even the perception that private financial gain is driving policy decisions. In his 1941 annual message to Congress, President Franklin D. Roosevelt stated, "We must especially beware of that small group of selfish men who would clip the wings of the American eagle in order to feather their own nests." Thomas Jefferson made clear his personal philosophy with respect to financial influence on public service.

My public proceedings were always directed by a single view to the best interests of our country. I had no motive to public service but the public satisfaction. I preferred public benefit to all personal considerations and retired much poorer than when I entered the public service. If, in the course of my life, it has been in any degree useful to the cause of humanity, the fact itself bears its full reward.

Properties owned or branded by the Trump Organization became almost synonymous with the concepts of perceived and real conflicts of interest. The Mueller report detailed how Trump attorney Michael Cohen recalled conversations with then candidate Trump in which Trump suggested that his 2016 presidential campaign would be a significant infomercial for Trump-branded properties. As president, he visited Trump-owned, -managed, or -branded properties on over 415 of his approximately 1,460 days in office. This was significant because of the revenue generated at these properties when Secret Service personnel and other support staff were required to accompany the president. When foreign leaders, their delegations, and American members of Congress visited Trump properties, they at the very least furthered perceptions of paying for political access and influence. These conflict-of-interest issues were exacerbated when the properties were featured in the president's conspicuous public communications.

@realDonaldTrump

After Turkey call I will be heading over to **Trump National Golf Club, Jupiter, to play golf (quickly) with Tiger Woods and Dustin Johnson. Then back to Mar-a-Lago** for talks on bringing even more jobs and companies back to the USA!

4:10 AM - Nov 24, 2017

@realDonaldTrump

I have arrived in Scotland and will be at **Trump Turnberry** for two days of meetings, calls and hopefully, some golf - my primary form of exercise! The weather is beautiful, **and this place is incredible!** Tomorrow I go to Helsinki for a Monday meeting with Vladimir Putin.

2:43 AM - Jul 14, 2018

@realDonaldTrump

I thought I was doing something very good for our Country by using **Trump National Doral, in Miami,** for hosting the G-7 Leaders. **It is big, grand, on hundreds of acres, next to MIAMI INTERNATIONAL AIRPORT, has tremendous ballrooms & meeting rooms,** and each delegation would have...

9:18 PM - Oct 19, 2019

By September 2020, the organization known as Citizens for Responsibility and Ethics in Washington had documented 3,403 conflicts of interest related to President Trump's businesses. A multi-year investigation by the Democratic staff of the U.S. House of Representatives Committee on Oversight and Accountability determined that President Trump received, through entities he owned and controlled, at least $7.8 million in foreign payments from at least twenty countries. Their report concluded that these payments violated the U.S. Constitution's foreign emoluments clause, producing "the exact kinds of presidential corruption and conflicts between the President's personal financial interests and the public interest that this constitutional provision was designed to prevent."

At the outset of the 2020 COVID-19 outbreak in the United States, four U.S. senators were urged to explain why they had dumped millions of dollars in stocks shortly after receiving a sensitive briefing on the pandemic and its likely economic impacts. Though some of the senators explained that they were not directly involved in investment decisions affecting their portfolios, it was too late to prevent the widespread perception (if not reality) that the stock sales were genuine conflicts of interest.

If a leader feels the need to justify an action *after* the fact, the damage has likely already been done. A better practice is to explain the rationale for a course of action that could cause perception issues *prior* to implementation. The following examples should not be considered "innocent explanations" for likely conflicts of interest.

> @realDonaldTrump
> I know nothing about an Air Force plane landing at an airport (which I do not own and have nothing to do with) near Turnberry Resort (which I do own) in Scotland, and filling up with fuel, with the crew staying overnight at Turnberry (they have good taste!). NOTHING TO DO WITH ME
> 9:43 AM - Sep 9, 2019

> @realDonaldTrump
> I had nothing to do with the decision of our great @ VP Mike Pence to stay overnight at one of the Trump owned resorts in Doonbeg, Ireland. Mike's family has lived in Doonbeg for many years, and he thought that during his very busy European visit, he would stop and see his family!
> 9:52 AM - Sep 9, 2019

Nepotism and cronyism. In 1967, Congress passed legislation addressing nepotism, the prohibited personnel practice of people in positions of authority exercising favoritism on behalf of their relatives. The statute applies primarily to hires, appointments, and promotions pertaining to public officials in all three federal branches of government—including the president and members of Congress. Nepotism and cronyism (the hiring of friends or associates) understandably create perceptions of unfairness, a sense of entitlement by the beneficiaries, and resentment among the employees who do not benefit. While President Trump's hiring of his daughter and son-in-law as special advisors may not have technically run afoul of the nepotism statute based on some interpretations, it certainly violated the spirit and intended purpose of the law. The perception of favoritism was made stronger by what comes across as reluctant restraint regarding what would have been, in the following, a clear-cut case of nepotism:

> @realDonaldTrump
> So nice, everyone wants Ivanka Trump to be the new United Nations Ambassador. She would be incredible, but I can already hear the chants of Nepotism! We have great people that want the job.
> 6:54 AM - Oct 12, 2018

Using one's position to provide other types of advantages to friends or supporters is also a form of cronyism. In the following post, the president encouraged a state agency to ignore its internal staff recommendation to close a specific coal burning plant. The particular plant in question reportedly bought its coal from a company owned by someone who made significant financial contributions to the president's campaign.

> @realDonaldTrump
> Coal is an important part of our electricity generation mix and @TVAnews should give serious consideration to all factors before voting to close viable power plants, **like Paradise #3 in Kentucky!**
> 2:03 PM - Feb 11, 2019

If subordinates are inspired to emulate a leader's commendable actions, they may also unfortunately emulate a leader's deplorable behaviors. The boss sets the tone for the entire organization. It is therefore perhaps no surprise that a record number of Trump administration appointees either resigned or were under scrutiny for conflict-of-interest or ethics violations. Subordinates are more likely to engage in questionable behavior if they perceive that the behavior is acceptable to their superiors.

I love to see honest and honorable men at the helm,
men who will not bend their politics to their purses,
nor pursue measures by which they may profit,
and then profit by their measures.
—THOMAS JEFFERSON

CHAPTER 23

Dishonesty and Deception

*It is of great importance to set a resolution,
not be shaken, never to tell an untruth.
There is no vice so mean, so pitiful, so contemptible.*

—Thomas Jefferson

Dishonesty is defined as a lack of honesty or integrity, with a disposition to defraud or deceive. In a passage reminiscent of The Police's "Murder by Numbers," Thomas Jefferson noted how dishonesty progressively corrupts:

> He who permits himself to tell a lie once, finds it much easier to do it a second and third time, till at length it becomes habitual; he tells lies without attending to it, and truths without the world's believing him. This falsehood of the tongue leads to that of the heart, and in time depraves all its good dispositions.

Lying, however, does not necessarily result in deception. Deception occurs when someone intentionally misleads in order to cause another to accept as true what is false or invalid.

Deception has grave implications for the survival of democracy and freedom. Though spoken in the context of education and learning, Franklin D. Roosevelt's suggestion that "the truth is found when men are free to pursue it" also speaks to the notion that truth and freedom need each other in order to flourish. Representative Adam Schiff echoed this sentiment during his closing arguments in President Trump's first impeachment trial:

> America believes in a thing called truth. She does not believe that we're entitled to our own alternate facts. She recoils at those who spread pernicious falsehoods. To her, truth matters. There is nothing more corrosive to a democracy than the idea that there is no truth.

Jon Meacham posed the following question: "Will facts actually continue to be a governing principle in our political affairs, or is it going to be what people want to believe, [versus] what's on the page?" In *On Tyranny: Twenty Lessons from the Twentieth Century*, Timothy Snyder warned that "to abandon facts is to abandon freedom. If nothing is true, then no one can criticize power, because there is no basis upon which to do so." Without truth, there is no trust. As Snyder also cautioned, "When people don't believe in truth, they fall back on belief. Charismatic politicians fill the void with a myth, with a story, with their own personality. And that's when you start moving towards fascism."

According to astrophysicists, there may be no objective reality in quantum physics. In public service, however, we must concede that facts are necessary for the general efficiency and effectiveness of public agencies. Good governance, meaningful public opinion, and domestic and foreign policymaking rely on facts. Similar to the debasement of a nation's currency when printed in excess, a national leader who invents "facts" debases the national conversation and frustrates necessary deliberation on consequential matters. As then senator Obama put it, "Politics depends on our ability to persuade each other of common aims based on a common reality."

Likewise, the rule of law cannot exist without facts and therefore truth. In the criminal justice system, there is a public interest in arriving at the truth for the purposes of accountability and preventing crime. During the 2020 sentencing of Trump associate Roger Stone, Judge Amy Berman Jackson addressed threats to democracy and sound policy in the context of Stone's obstruction of the congressional investigation into Russian election interference:

> The truth still matters. Roger Stone's insistence that it doesn't, his belligerence, his pride in his own lies are a threat to our most fundamental institutions, to the very foundation of our democracy.

> And if it goes unpunished, it will not be a victory for one party or another. Everyone loses because everyone depends on the representatives they elect to make the right decisions on a myriad of issues... based on the facts.

Everyone depends on our elected representatives to protect our elections from foreign interference based on the facts....

This effort to obstruct the investigation was deliberate, planned, not one isolated incident, and conducted over a considerable period of time. And Stone lied and sought to impede production of information to whom? Not to some secret anti-Trump cabal, but to Congress. To the elected representatives of both parties who were confronted with a matter of grave national importance.

...he was not convicted and is not being sentenced for exercising his First Amendment rights, his support of the President's campaign or his policies. He was not prosecuted, as some have complained, for standing up for the President. He was prosecuted for covering up for the President.

In *Humanity: A Moral History of the Twentieth Century,* Jonathan Glover described the disastrous societal consequences stemming from the abandonment of objective truth. There are dire implications for moral identity when individuals abandon a commitment to truth. This abandonment happens in two stages. The first stage involves someone intentionally lying for some purpose while still retaining a private grip on the truth. The second and more dangerous stage of abandonment—which Glover likens to crossing a crucial boundary—occurs when "the tension involved in conscious deception of others can lead to self-deception and denial." That is, a

lie stated repeatedly becomes truth for the speaker, and then potentially for others. The nineteenth-century Russian novelist Fyodor
Dostoyevsky also warned about self-deception:

> Above all, do not lie to yourself. A man who lies to himself
> and listens to his own lie comes to a point where he does not
> discern any truth either in himself or anywhere around him,
> and thus falls into disrespect towards himself and others.

Glover also warned about the civic consequences of self-deception:

> As self-deception feeds on itself, there is less and less
> to stop beliefs about one's moral identity becoming
> systematically false. The growth of such a delusional
> system is a personal moral disaster. It can also be a
> political disaster.

Indeed, democratic systems depend on *individuals* selecting
their leaders with what should ideally be a shared set of facts. It is in
this context that Timothy Snyder addressed the personal abandonment of truth:

> You submit to tyranny when you renounce the differ-
> ence between what you want to hear and what is actually
> the case. This renunciation of reality can feel natural and
> pleasant, but the result is your demise as an individual—
> and thus the collapse of any political system that depends
> upon individualism.

People engage in dishonesty and deception for a variety of reasons, including self-aggrandizement, accountability avoidance, and to achieve objectives unobtainable with the truth. Rationalizations for dishonesty and deceit abound. Admiral John Poindexter and Lieutenant Colonel Oliver North lied to Congress during the 1987 Iran–Contra affair hearings. Their (baseless) justification was secrecy in the interest of national security. During congressional testimony in late 2019, former Trump campaign manager Corey Lewandowski explained that his lying to reporters was acceptable because he believed the media to be dishonest. In the same year, a prominent former governor argued that with respect to honesty, elected officials such as the president of the United States should be held to a different standard than unelected public servants. He rationalized that elected officials are only accountable to voters for their dishonesty, or to bodies like Congress that have the power to impeach. While he may have been correctly describing the disparate legal mechanisms for holding these two groups of public servants to account, if a senior *elected* leader cannot be expected to model a culture of honesty, then we should not be surprised if that leader's unelected subordinates also engage in dishonesty and deceit.

A dishonest leader can have a corrupting influence on subordinates, especially when they are directed to lie or are willingly complicit in furthering a lie. Former FBI director James Comey addressed this corrupting influence along with the personal compromise that occurs when a leader's lies go unchallenged.

This president [Trump], because he's an amoral leader, shapes those around him. And that shaping sometimes pushes out someone who is a strong person of integrity

who stands up and says, "Not going to have it," but far
more often it shapes and bends and pulls in weaker souls.

Denial can infect those subjected to a leader's deceit. Most people
would prefer to believe what their leaders tell them, in part because
being distrustful and cynical requires more effort and creates discomfort. This desire or inclination to trust makes the dishonest leader
or authority figure that much more loathsome. The insistence of
German soldiers after the conclusion of World War II that Hitler
had never lied is a phenomenon that has reverberated through time.
When a reporter asked a Trump supporter at a rally if the president's
relationship with the truth bothered him, he proudly declared that
Trump "never lies."

A topic debated in both military and civilian institutions is to
what extent duplicity in someone's personal affairs is an indication of
potentially similar behavior in that person's professional endeavors.
There are limits to one's ability to compartmentalize deceit, as deceit
is more likely the product of character versus circumstance.

A related debate involves the question of whether one's professional standing should suffer because of duplicity in personal affairs.
Should marital infidelity, for example, result in professional admonishment? There is less consensus on this issue, but increased scrutiny
regarding personal misconduct may be justified depending on the
level of professional trust required (for example, the national security
arena) and the potential for blackmail. In both personal and professional affairs, one should be willing and able to accept the consequences of being truthful and therefore conduct oneself in a manner
that precludes the temptation to deceive. Very few people will ever
experience circumstances under which lying is necessary to protect

WHAT HANGS IN THE BALANCE

their lives or the lives of others.

According to Paul Simon, there are fifty ways to leave your lover. For the unscrupulous, there are also many ways to deceive.

Repetition (or saturation) operates on the principle that a lie told repeatedly becomes the truth. The volume of lies told might operate in the same manner, in that some of the many lies might be believed. The *big lie*, as espoused by Hitler, operates on the notion that a lie of greater significance often carries more credibility compared to so-called smaller lies. Even when it lacks credibility, the big lie has the effect of making less significant lies more acceptable.

Unreasonable optimism (or wishful thinking) is sometimes used to deceive when the facts do not justify said optimism. Examples include unrealistic budget projections or the following statement made by President Trump about COVID-19 infections at the outset of the pandemic: "We're going to be pretty soon at only five people, and we could be at just one or two people over the next short period of time. So we've had very good luck."

Reversing the truth is essentially accusing the other side of that of which you are guilty.

The *use of the media* is less a type of lying versus a means to propagate lies with the help of sympathetic news outlets. It is one thing for a media organization to discuss policy through the lens of its particular political or ideological viewpoint. When it knowingly repeats an untruth, however, the deception grows exponentially.

President Trump's dishonesty and deception. A common cynical cliché is that all elected officials occasionally lie. There is episodic lying, and there are virtuoso levels of dishonesty. President Trump had an exceptionally adversarial relationship with the truth.

Former president Harry Truman suggested that people who make mistakes eventually correct themselves with the passage of time and when faced with the facts. President Trump's falsehoods were rarely mistakes, and he seldom if ever made corrections. While Hitler's quotes should be used sparingly, the notion that "it is not truth that matters, but victory" seems appropriate for a president who was obsessed with winning.

The *Washington Post*, in what seemed out of necessity to become a full-time job, began tallying President Trump's false or misleading claims shortly after his inauguration. By day 1,000 of his presidency, the tally had reached 13,438, with the daily count increasing with each year in office. During a single rally in Wisconsin in April 2019, The *Washington Post* cited sixty-one false claims by a president who was clearly unencumbered by facts. By his last day in office, the total had reached 30,573. When a reporter asked White House Press Secretary Kayleigh McEnany in May 2020 if the president had ever lied, she responded, "His intent is always to give truthful information to the American people."

The illustrations of President Trump's dishonesty and deceit presented in the following pages involve five specific topics: the origins of the FBI's investigation into Russian election interference, attempts to fire Special Counsel Robert Mueller, claims that Trump's 2016 campaign was spied on, claims that James Comey leaked classified information to the press, and the president's big lie regarding the outcome of the 2020 presidential election.

The Russia investigation. Trump expended considerable effort attacking the origins of the FBI's investigation into Russian interference in the 2016 election. The president claimed that the so-called

Steele dossier initiated the investigation (known in the FBI as Crossfire Hurricane) that began in July 2016. The DOJ inspector general report published in late 2019 determined that "Steele's reports played no role in the Crossfire Hurricane opening." The FBI's investigation was initiated based on reporting from a friendly foreign government.

President Trump also misrepresented the findings of the DOJ IG report with respect to the legitimacy of the investigation's inception.

> @realDonaldTrump
> ....It has now been determined that the Mueller Scam should never have been set up in the first place, there were no grounds. It was all an illegitimate Witch Hunt, & a big price must be paid. How different my life would have been if this fraud on America was never committed!!!
> 9:03 AM - Sep 12, 2020

The IG report instead concluded that Assistant Director E. W. Priestap's "exercise of discretion in opening the investigation was in compliance with Department and FBI policies, and we did not find documentary or testimonial evidence that political bias or improper motivation influenced his decision. While the information in the FBI's possession at the time was limited, in light of the low threshold established by Department and FBI predication policy, we found that Crossfire Hurricane was opened for an authorized investigative purpose and with sufficient factual predication."

The Russia investigation also "established that several individuals affiliated with the Trump Campaign lied to the Office [of

Special Counsel], and to Congress, about their interactions with Russian-affiliated individuals and related matters. Those lies materially impaired the investigation into Russian election interference. The Office charged some of those lies as violations of the federal false-statements statute." With all of the complaining by Trump and his supporters about the investigation into the Trump campaign, there seemed to be no acknowledgment of how a clear pattern of dishonesty invited additional scrutiny. That pattern of conduct, as detailed in the Mueller report, was summarized by the chairman of the House Intelligence Committee during Special Counsel Robert Mueller's testimony to Congress:

> The Russians made outreach to the Trump campaign... the campaign welcomed the Russian help....The president himself called on the Russians to hack Hillary's emails.... The president praised the releases of the Russian-hacked emails through WikiLeaks...Paul Manafort was trying to make money or achieve debt forgiveness from a Russian oligarch...Michael Flynn was trying to make money from Turkey...Mike Flynn lied...George Papadopoulos was convicted of lying...Paul Manafort was convicted of lying...[and] went so far as to encourage other people to lie...Manafort's deputy, Rick Gates, lied....The Trump Campaign officials built their strategy—their messaging strategy around those stolen documents [stolen by the Russians]....And then they lied to cover it up.

Attempts to fire the Special Counsel. The portion of the Russia investigation dealing with President Trump's potential obstruction of justice of the investigation itself included an examination of the president's efforts to have White House Counsel Don McGahn remove Special Counsel Robert Mueller.

@realDonaldTrump

As has been incorrectly reported by the Fake News Media, I never told then White House Counsel Don McGahn to fire Robert Mueller, even though I had the legal right to do so. If I wanted to fire Mueller, I didn't need McGahn to do it, I could have done it myself.

4:47 AM - Apr 25, 2019

The testimony that informed Mueller's report concluded otherwise:

In early 2018, the press reported that the President had directed McGahn to have the Special Counsel removed in June 2017 and that McGahn had threatened to resign rather than carry out the order. The President reacted to the news stories by directing White House officials to tell McGahn to dispute the story and create a record stating he had not been ordered to have the Special Counsel removed. McGahn told those officials that the media reports were accurate in stating that the President had directed McGahn to have the Special Counsel removed. The President then met with McGahn in the Oval Office and again pressured him to deny the reports. In the same meeting, the President also asked McGahn why he had told the Special Counsel about the President's effort to remove the Special Counsel and why McGahn took notes of his conversations with the President. McGahn refused to back away from what he remembered happening and perceived the President to be testing his mettle.

It is standard practice to take notes when meeting with a superior in order to accurately document leader intent and required actions. Notes are also used to produce official records of deliberations and decisions. With President Trump, however, it had become common practice for private attorneys, subordinates, and other government officials to take notes, make contemporaneous records, and even record conversations out of fear that Trump would later lie about his own statements or misrepresent the statements of others. Prominent examples include an in-person recording by his personal attorney, Michael Cohen; contemporaneous notes made by FBI Director James Comey after dining with the president; and a phone conversation recorded by Georgia's secretary of state while President Trump was pressuring him to "find" the votes he needed to win the state in the 2020 election.

Allegations of spying on the Trump campaign. Another charge made obsessively by the president was that the previous administration, using its law enforcement and intelligence agencies, had in 2016 spied (implying illegal surveillance) on members of the Trump campaign during the course of the Russia investigation.

@realDonaldTrump
Terrible! Just found out that Obama had my "wires tapped" in Trump Tower just before the victory. Nothing found. This is McCarthyism!
3:35 AM - Mar 4, 2017

@realDonaldTrump
My Campaign for President was conclusively spied on. Nothing like this has ever happened in American Politics. A really bad situation. TREASON means long jail sentences, and this was TREASON!
4:11 AM - May 17, 2019

The crime of treason, often mentioned by Trump in relation to the Russia investigation, is roughly defined as providing aid or comfort to an enemy during a conflict.

The DOJ under President Trump confirmed, pursuant to a Freedom of Information Act lawsuit, that there was no evidence the Obama administration had ordered any such surveillance. A 2019 DOJ IG report addressed the FBI's use of confidential human sources during the investigation:

> Shortly after the FBI opened the Crossfire Hurricane investigation, the FBI conducted several consensually monitored meetings between FBI confidential human sources (CHS) and individuals affiliated with the Trump campaign, including a high-level campaign official who was not a subject of the investigation. We found that the CHS operations received the necessary approvals under FBI policy; that an Assistant Director knew about and approved of each operation, even in circumstances where a first-level supervisory special agent could have approved the operations; and that the operations were permitted under Department and FBI policy because their use was not for the sole purpose of monitoring activities

protected by the First Amendment or the lawful exercise of other rights secured by the Constitution or laws of the United States. We did not find any documentary or testimonial evidence that political bias or improper motivation influenced the FBI's decision to conduct these operations. Additionally, we found no evidence that the FBI attempted to place any CHSs within the Trump campaign, recruit members of the Trump campaign as CHSs, or task CHSs to report on the Trump campaign.

Despite the report's findings, the president continued to deceive. The following posts are merely a sampling but nonetheless demonstrate the technique of deception through repetition.

@realDonaldTrump
A lot of very good people were taken down by a small group of Dirty (Filthy) Cops, politicians, government officials, and an investigation that **was illegally started** & that **SPIED on my campaign.** The Witch Hunt is sputtering badly, but still going on (Ukraine Hoax!).
5:58 AM - Jan 2, 2020

@realDonaldTrump
So we catch Obama & Biden, not to even mention the rest of their crew, **SPYING on my campaign,** AND NOTHING HAPPENS? I hope not! If it were the other way around, 50 years for treason. NEVER FORGET!!!!
1:14 PM - Jul 19, 2020

@realDonaldTrump

BIG NEWS! The Political Crime of the Century is unfolding. **ObamaBiden illegally spied on the Trump Campaign,** both before and after the election. Treason!

2:10 PM - Aug 5, 2020

@realDonaldTrump

HE SPIED ON MY CAMPAIGN, AND GOT CAUGHT!

10:33 PM - Aug 19, 2020

@realDonaldTrump

Obama, Biden, Crooked Hillary and many others got caught in a **Treasonous Act of Spying** and Government Overthrow, a Criminal Act. How is Biden now allowed to run for President?

8:15 PM - Oct 7, 2020

Allegations against James Comey. Following his dismissal by President Trump in early 2017, former FBI director Comey shared four memos with his attorneys. The memos documented one-on-one interactions with the president, including what Comey believed to be improper requests to drop the investigation into former national security advisor Michael Flynn. It was the contents of those memos, in addition to President Trump's firing of Comey, that hastened the DOJ's appointment of Special Counsel Mueller to take over the Russia investigation. A 2019 DOJ IG report chastised Comey for violating department policy on the handling of these memos but determined that there was "no evidence that Comey or his attorneys released any of the classified information contained in any of the Memos to members of the media." Nonetheless, the president claimed otherwise before and after the release of the IG report.

> @realDonaldTrump
> James Comey leaked CLASSIFIED INFORMATION to the media. That is so illegal!
> 6:40 AM - Jul 10, 2017

President Trump's big lie—the 2020 election. Trump's crusade to further delegitimize American democracy began in the early hours of November 4, just hours after the last polls had closed. His campaign manager, Bill Stepien, understood that vote-counting would continue for days and advised the president that it was far too early to declare victory. He suggested that the president instead express pride in the race that was run and strike a tone of optimism with regard to the eventual outcome. President Trump disagreed. In reality, the plan to declare victory had been in place long before Election Day.

> @realDonaldTrump
> I will be making a statement tonight. A big WIN!
> 12:45 AM - Nov 4, 2020

While ballots were still being counted, the president declared from the White House, "This is a fraud on the American public. This is an embarrassment to our country. We were getting ready to win this election. Frankly, we did win this election." Within days of the election, the Trump campaign's lead data analyst informed the president in blunt terms that he was going to lose.

For the next three months, the president would use repetition to unjustly undermine critical and necessary faith in America's electoral system. The Electoral College vote was 306 to 232 in Biden's favor. Biden won the popular vote by just over seven million votes.

> @realDonaldTrump
> I WON THIS ELECTION, BY A LOT!
> 10:36 AM - Nov 7, 2020

> @realDonaldTrump
> NO WAY WE LOST THIS ELECTION!
> 10:05 PM - Nov 29, 2020

By late November, the president was using his big lie to pressure state lawmakers to overturn their election results and select alternate (fraudulent) slates of electors.

> @realDonaldTrump
> A total FRAUD. Statehouse Republicans, proud, strong and honest, will never let this travesty stand!
> 3:42 PM - Nov 26, 2020

Trump also targeted Republican members of Congress.

> @realDonaldTrump
> That's because he is a great champion and man of courage. More Republican Senators should follow his lead. **We had a landslide victory,** and then it was swindled away from the Republican Party - but we caught them. Do something!
> 8:46 PM - Dec 17, 2020

@realDonaldTrump

.@senatemajldr and Republican Senators have to
get tougher, or you won't have a Republican Party
anymore. **We won the Presidential Election, by a lot.**
FIGHT FOR IT. Don't let them take it away!

9:14 AM - Dec 18, 2020

@realDonaldTrump

**He didn't win the Election. He lost all 6 Swing
States, by a lot.** They then dumped hundreds of
thousands of votes in each one, and got caught. Now
Republican politicians have to fight so that their great
victory is not stolen. Don't be weak fools!

9:41 AM - Dec 19, 2020

@realDonaldTrump

The lie of the year is that Joe Biden won! Christina
Bobb @OANN

2:59 PM - Dec 19, 2020

By mid-December, there were "Stop the Steal" demonstrations in
numerous states. The president's lies had already begun sowing the
seeds of the January 6 attack on the U.S. Capitol.

The true cost of Trump's big lie may not be evident for years or
even decades to come. Within six months of the 2020 election, the
myth of massive voter fraud was weaponized by lawmakers in dozens
of states. Some states passed laws empowering partisan legislatures
to intervene in election processes traditionally supervised by state
and county election officials. During the 2022 midterm election

cycle, embracing the big lie and related conspiracy theories became a loyalty test for Republican candidates desperate for Trump's endorsement and the support of his followers.

Jon Meacham addressed this fraying of the social contract in America, where there has been "this flight from fact…from evidence… from truth…to a self-serving vision of reality where power is more important than principle." Timothy Snyder had warned about the effects of Trump's big lie just a week after the election.

> And insofar as he gets people to believe this lie, he's transforming democratic politics which is about facts, interests, and values, into authoritarian politics which is about faith—faith in the leader, believing what the leader says despite everything. And it's dangerous that the particular form the big lie takes is the idea of the stab in the back, that somehow we didn't win when we should have won. And who's fault is this? Well, it's the fault of the other side…The problem with the stab-in-the-back myth is that it says that the other side doesn't really belong to the nation.

In the months following President Biden's inauguration, several national polls suggested that a majority of Republicans believed that the election was stolen. The logical extension of those beliefs is an electoral system rife with fraud and an illegitimate president in the White House—a recipe likely to increase cynicism, further erode trust in elections, and produce more political violence. The FBI has warned that the greatest domestic terrorism threat comes from extremists who believe that the 2020 election was stolen.

When lying becomes acceptable, we become blind to the threat it poses to our institutions. Also problematic is the individual subordinate or supporter who becomes indifferent to a leader's dishonesty or, worse, actively supports it. During a May 2019 interview, James Comey spoke to the danger of becoming numb to dishonesty.

> I think the Trump presidency risks sending a message that leadership doesn't have to have a moral component, that it's not important in this country for a leader to have external ethical reference points, and that it's okay for a leader to only have one reference point, which is, "What will be good for me?" Leaders matter because of what they say, but most importantly, they matter like parents do, because of the way in which they're watched....as a parent, you shape a family. As a leader, you shape a company, a part of a government, or the entire country. We really risk sending a message that it is okay to act in the way this president acts. We are becoming numb to the fact that the leader of the free world lies constantly. And even if you support him, you have to look in the mirror and say, yeah, he lies constantly. We're so numb to it that we're forgetting it's not okay. And that's a recipe for a melting of our standards much more broadly.

If the value of a leader's words is diminished because of a history of dishonesty, it may become much more difficult for that leader to obtain needed support from subordinates, the public, another branch of government, or foreign allies. Cynicism, skepticism, and distrust are the consequences of deceit. When someone lacking either the requisite education or sophistication to understand an issue decides that no one is believable—or that they simply cannot differentiate between reason and nonsense—that person will discount or simply ignore reasonable arguments and useful advice. A lack of trust in one leader, even if that leader is removed for dishonesty, could produce a ripple effect with respect to subordinate trust and support for successive leaders in the same organization.

Defending truth. President Biden addressed the scourge of deceit during his inaugural address. "There is truth and there are lies. Lies told for power and for profit. And each of us has a duty and responsibility, as citizens, as Americans, and especially as leaders—leaders who have pledged to honor our Constitution and protect our nation—to defend the truth and to defeat the lies."

Defending truth in a public organization can be challenging. Police unions, for example, are sometimes able to prevent the disciplining of employees who have been dishonest and who have abused their authorities. Organizational leaders should nonetheless strive to remove these individuals in order to prevent further abuses, protect the reputations of compliant employees, and limit the erosion of public trust.

When a leader engages in deception, subordinates can choose to either further those lies or refute them. Refusing to support the lies is in itself an act of leadership. In May 2017, President Trump had decided to fire FBI Director James Comey without input from the Justice Department. Nonetheless, White House staffers chose to publicly push the president's narrative that the decision to fire Comey came solely from a DOJ recommendation, and more specifically, from Deputy Attorney General Rod Rosenstein. Rosenstein had submitted a memorandum to his boss (Attorney General Jeff Sessions) that was highly critical of Comey's public announcements related to the conclusion of the 2016 Hillary Clinton email investigation. Unlike White House staffers such as Press Secretary Sean Spicer, Rosenstein fought to defend the truth, as demonstrated in this excerpt from the Mueller report:

> That night, the White House Press Office called the Department of Justice and said the White House wanted to put out a statement saying that it was Rosenstein's idea to fire Comey. Rosenstein told other DOJ officials that he would not participate in putting out a "false story." The President then called Rosenstein directly and said he was watching Fox News, that the coverage had been great, and that he wanted Rosenstein to do a press conference. Rosenstein responded that this was not a good idea because if the press asked him, he would tell the truth that Comey's firing was not his idea. Sessions also informed the White House Counsel's Office that evening that Rosenstein was upset that his memorandum was being portrayed as the reason for Comey's termination.

An idea attributed to Friedrich Schiller is that *truth lives on in the midst of deception.* For truth to survive requires the collective efforts of public servants willing to sacrifice for the principle that a commitment to truth will best serve public institutions and the citizens they serve.

CHAPTER 24

Disinformation

(Trafficking in Bullshit)

When a swarm of bees decides that it is time to find a new place to live, it sends out scouts (worker bees) to evaluate potential sites. The scouts return to accurately communicate their findings through an intricate dance. Though some bees display a healthy skepticism of the reported information and fly to the scouted sites for verification, the bees eventually reach consensus on the best location for their new home. What is notable is that the scouts do not try to deceive in order to have their particular locations chosen. It is a risk they cannot take, as their survival depends on the adequacy of their new home. Sound public policy formulation and implementation (and potentially the survival of American democracy) also depend on truthfully presented empirical evidence.

The distinction between misinformation and disinformation is an important one. Misinformation is false information that is disseminated regardless of intent to mislead. If someone is unknowingly spreading false information, they are technically spreading misinformation. Disinformation, on the other hand, requires intent. Described as the actual art of deception, disinformation is misleading or false information that is deliberately weaponized. Per former Cybersecurity and Infrastructure Security Agency (CISA) director Christopher Krebs, the three objectives of disinformation campaigns are power, money, and influence.

Tactics used in spreading disinformation include the use of hyperbole, innuendo, deliberately vague claims, intentional omission, embellished outrage, half-truths, and sophism—invalid arguments that seem correct in form. A tactic referred to as censorship through noise involves the deliberate obscuration of the truth with the use of excessive information.

The best-known vehicle for disinformation is probably the conspiracy theory. Though the phrase has been used as a term of propaganda to marginalize people challenging legitimate conspiracies, I use the phrase here to portray what historian Kathleen Belew describes as "distortions of the factual landscape." Conspiracy theories easily exploit ignorance and prejudice by offering fraudulently simple solutions to complex problems. They feed the psychological needs of those who feel powerless and seek community. They often provide their adherents with the belief that they have been let in on a secret regarding a cause that requires their support. The alleged conspiracies also identify the supposed perpetrators.

The dangers of disinformation. As with many myths, the best lies are said to have a reasonably considered basis in fact. Even disinformation that is partly true can be exceptionally damaging in the hands of a motivated demagogue or autocrat who might exploit it to vilify opponents, deceive the public, and replace reasoned deliberation with whipped-up passion. On the level of the individual, it can infiltrate and attach to core beliefs. When presented with new (and factual) information that challenges those core beliefs, individuals experience stress and employ defense mechanisms to reject the new information (they experience cognitive dissonance). For many, it becomes exceptionally difficult to admit that they once believed something that they now know to be false.

Anne Applebaum, the author of *Autocracy, Inc.: The Dictators Who Want to Run the World*, described the political use of the conspiracy theory: "It organizes your followers around this set of ideas and puts them in opposition to reality. [It] gives them something that keeps them together, creates their identity, and makes them different from others." She explained how autocracies around the world are dependent on a set of conspiracy theories or lies to maintain power. Autocrats necessarily distract people with culture wars or conspiracy theories to "keep them away from the real business of politics." In contrast, when people are able to focus on real political issues, they invariably desire democratic solutions, justice, and the rule of law. The danger of spewing nonsense and conspiracy theories is that they often become a narrative that can weaken democratic institutions.

Modern disinformation does more than just deceive. According to David Patrikarakos, the author of *War in 140 Characters*, it aims to sow confusion, thereby making it more difficult for people to recognize the truth when they see it. In *The Origins of Totalitarianism*, philosopher Hannah Arendt wrote, "The ideal subject of totalitarian rule is not the convinced Nazi or the convinced Communist, but people for whom the distinction between fact and fiction (i.e., the reality of experience) and the distinction between true and false (i.e., the standards of thought) no longer exist." Disinformation corrupts rational, fact-based discourse.

Technology (social media in particular) has unfortunately enhanced the ease and efficacy of using disinformation to confuse people and exploit their fears. Tactics include coordinated bot attacks, anonymous mass texting, deepfake videos, microtargeted Internet ads, supposedly local Internet news sites, and the use of troll farms to create fake social media profiles bent on creating division and even organizing rallies. Researchers looking at disinformation on Twitter found that "falsehood diffused significantly farther, faster, deeper, and more broadly than the truth in all categories of information." In just one example, the use of disinformation on social media has been tied to the rise and election of former Filipino president Rodrigo Duterte, whose administration stands accused of condoning thousands of extrajudicial killings as part of its war on drugs.

Far-right media personality and conspiracy theorist Alex Jones (who also promoted the "Stop the Steal" movement on behalf of President Trump) for years profited from his absurd claims. He played a role in propagating the "Pizzagate" conspiracy theory, which suggested that children were being held in a Washington, D.C., restaurant as part of a sex trafficking ring. It resulted in one "believer" driving from North Carolina and firing a weapon inside the restaurant. Jones's most egregious act was probably his contention that the massacre of twenty first graders and six educators at Sandy Hook Elementary School in 2012 was a government hoax perpetrated to promote gun control policies. The conspiracy theory's adherents accused grieving parents of being actors and posted their addresses and other personal information online. The family members of the victims endured online harassment, personal confrontations, and threats of rape and death and received messages threatening to defile the victims' graves. Some family members were consequently forced to relocate and hire security. Jones was finally held accountable in a series of civil trials in 2022. He was ordered to pay the families of eight of the shooting victims a sum totaling nearly $1.5 billion.

Using a similar tactic in 2022, the Russian government accused Ukraine of using crisis actors to fabricate the well-documented wartime atrocities committed in Bucha. Vladimir Putin's spokesperson, Dmitry Peskov, characterized Russia's war crimes as a "well-staged insinuation, nothing else," and "simply a well-directed—but tragic—show….It is a forgery aimed at denigrating the Russian army."

Online conspiracy theories about the source and relative danger of COVID-19 resulted in threats aimed at one of America's preeminent immunologists, Dr. Anthony Fauci, who had advised seven presidents on HIV/AIDS and other domestic and global health issues. Another consequence of the COVID-19 conspiracy theories was the preventable sickness and death that resulted from people not adequately protecting themselves against the spread of the virus.

In yet another example, the man who broke into the home of House Speaker Nancy Pelosi in 2022 and fractured her husband's skull with a hammer was an adherent of numerous conspiracy theories, including those related to the 2020 presidential election.

The principal adversaries of Western liberal democracy, the governments of China and Russia, have exported disinformation in an effort to create confusion, indifference, and distrust. False messages have reached millions of Americans via cell phone, social media, and even Russian Radio Sputnik broadcasts originating from American cities. This external propaganda is sometimes amplified wittingly or unwittingly by American politicians, whose public positions of trust unfortunately lend credibility and allow outside disinformation to subvert from within. A glaring example of this was the previously examined 2018 incident in Helsinki in which President Trump, standing next to Russian president Putin, essentially told the world that despite the clear and detailed conclusions of his own intelligence agencies, he had no reason to disbelieve President Putin's claim that Russia did not meddle in the 2016 American presidential election.

As described in the U.S. intelligence community's (IC) February 2022 threat assessment, the Russian government "presents one of the most serious foreign influence threats to the United States, using its intelligence services, proxies, and wide-ranging influence tools to try to divide Western alliances, and increase its sway around the world, while attempting to undermine U.S. global standing, amplify discord inside the United States, and influence U.S. voters and decision-making." It aims to convince the citizens of open societies that democracies are inherently flawed and ineffective. The resulting disorientation and apathy can discourage political participation (voting) and can also result in an unwarranted level of distrust in government data and intelligence. That distrust has implications for public health and national security. A March 2021 assessment by the U.S. IC determined the following:

> Russian President Putin authorized, and a range of Russian government organizations conducted, influence operations aimed at denigrating President Biden's candidacy and the Democratic Party, supporting former President Trump, undermining public confidence in the electoral process, and exacerbating sociopolitical divisions in the US....A key element of Moscow's strategy

this [2020] election cycle was its use of proxies linked to Russian intelligence to push influence narratives—including misleading or unsubstantiated allegations against President Biden—to US media organizations, US officials, and prominent US individuals, including some close to former President Trump and his administration.... The primary effort the IC uncovered revolved around a narrative—that Russian actors began spreading as early as 2014—alleging corrupt ties between President Biden, his family, and other US officials and Ukraine. Russian intelligence services relied on Ukraine-linked proxies and these proxies' networks—including their US contacts—to spread this narrative to give Moscow plausible deniability of their involvement.

In a similar example, a Russian disinformation campaign—amplified by American alt-right media—convinced a large number of Texans that a U.S. military exercise was an attempt by the Obama administration to implement martial law.

As these external threats are only likely to grow in frequency, sophistication, and efficacy, leaders must be that much more vigilant (with reasonable consideration to the First Amendment) when they see the same tactics used by domestic actors. Homegrown distrust will result in an electorate that feels (and likely is) less informed. "If a nation expects to be ignorant and free, in a state of civilization, it expects what never was and never will be," Thomas Jefferson wrote. "No nation is permitted to live in ignorance with impunity." Disinformation combined with ignorance results in beliefs that should never have been as widespread as they were. One example is the notion that Saddam Hussein was in some way responsible for the September 11, 2001, al-Qaeda attacks in the United States. That narrative played a part in fueling domestic support for the 2003 U.S. invasion of Iraq.

Perhaps more concerning than a head of state spreading his own conspiracy theories is that person knowingly or unknowingly spreading conspiracy theories created with the help of a foreign adversary. President Trump developed a fondness for the One America News Network (OANN), which tended to air stories favorable to the president while also pushing outlandish conspiracy theories. As of 2019, it had on its payroll a journalist who simultaneously worked for Sputnik, a Kremlin-funded news service. The first post below demonstrates how spreading conspiracy theories might compromise the trust and cooperation of one of America's most dependable partners.

> @realDonaldTrump
> "Former CIA analyst Larry Johnson accuses United Kingdom Intelligence of helping Obama Administration Spy on the 2016 Trump Presidential Campaign."
> @OANN WOW! It is now just a question of time before the truth comes out, and when it does, it will be a beauty!
> 4:04 AM - Apr 24, 2019

> @realDonaldTrump
> .@FoxNews is not watchable during weekend afternoons. It is worse than Fake News @CNN. I strongly suggest turning your dial to @OANN. They do a really "Fair & Balanced" job!
> 1:31 PM - Aug 16, 2020

President Trump's trafficking in B.S. The following claims by President Trump were made during a *single* White House press briefing in August 2020: The president contradicted the conclusions of the U.S. intelligence community by claiming that Russia was not happy with his 2016 electoral victory. He claimed the existence of widespread fraud associated with mail-in voting and also claimed that there had been hundreds or even thousands of fraudulent ballots in a recent New York election. He then claimed that the Obama campaign had been caught red-handed spying on the Trump campaign with the help of the country's intelligence agencies and further suggested that the aforementioned "crime" was likely treason.

In *How Fascism Works*, Jason Stanley described how Trump employed his disinformation tactics during television interviews. "He's breaking down factuality; like the goal is to break down any kind of connection to reality and create this us/them narrative...by Tweeting really out-there conspiracy theories...he's trying to introduce into the public discourse stories that detach us from reality." Trump explained on more than one occasion that he posted these types of tweets in order to simply "put it out there." Intentionally propagating disinformation so that others might "decide for themselves" is inexcusable. As Savannah Guthrie, the moderator of an October 2020 NBC town hall event in Florida featuring President Trump put it, "You're the President. You're not like, someone's crazy uncle who can just retweet whatever."

In the following posts, President Trump attempted to shamelessly refute his own proclivity for spreading nonsense.

@realDonaldTrump

Mueller should have never been appointed, although **he did prove that I must be the most honest man in America!**

6:54 AM - Jun 4, 2020

@realDonaldTrump

"Trump could be the most honest president in modern history. When you look at the real barometer of presidential truthfulness, which is promise keeping, he is probably the most honest president in American history. He's done exactly what he said he would do." Marc Thiessen, WPost

4:30 AM - Oct 17, 2018

The president certainly could have been the most honest president in modern history if he had not fallen about thirty thousand false or misleading statements short of that goal.

President Trump used innuendo in pushing a conspiracy theory about a former congressional staffer who died of a medical condition. The president suggested that former congressman Joe Scarborough might have been responsible for her death. The widower accused the president of perverting his late wife's memory for perceived political gain and (unsuccessfully) implored Twitter's CEO to remove a series of posts that included the following:

@realDonaldTrump

A blow to her head? Body found under his desk? Left Congress suddenly? Big topic of discussion in Florida...and, he's a Nut Job (with bad ratings). Keep digging, use forensic geniuses!

8:05 PM - May 23, 2020

@realDonaldTrump
A lot of interest in this story about Psycho Joe Scarborough. So a young marathon runner just happened to faint in his office, hit her head on his desk, & die? I would think there is a lot more to this story than that? An affair? What about the so-called investigator? Read story!
10:29 AM - May 24, 2020

Almost thirty years earlier, Trump had played a leading role in pushing the narrative that five Black and Latino youths, known as the Central Park Five, deserved the death penalty for allegedly assaulting a woman. They served six to seven years in prison in the early 1990s before eventually being completely exonerated. Donald Trump was also a leading proponent of the myth that President Barack Obama was born in Kenya. Trump championed this conspiracy theory, referred to as the birther movement, while Obama was president. The dangerous implication of this conspiracy theory, as Anne Applebaum has explained, is that the government and media would have been necessarily guilty of concealing this "truth" from the American public, further implying that the entire system is "rotten."

In a redux of the birther conspiracy theory, President Trump in August 2020 suggested that Kamala Harris—who had just been selected as Joe Biden's running mate—might not be eligible to serve as vice president. While her parents were immigrants, Harris was born in California. When asked about it during a White House press conference, President Trump managed to incorporate into his answer many of the elements necessary to give a conspiracy theory credibility (Trump's comments are italicized):

First, one repeats something false without taking owner-ship of the claim. *So I just heard that. I heard it today that she doesn't meet the requirements.* Then one claims igno-rance regarding the veracity of the claim. *I have no idea if that's right.* Then one lends credibility to the original conspiracy theory while sowing doubt about whether Harris was properly vetted. *I would have assumed that the Democrats would have checked that out before she gets chosen to run for vice president.* Then one repeats the basic untruth while ascribing it to a vague "they." *They're saying that she doesn't qualify because she wasn't born in this country.* Finally, one touts the source's bona fides by describing the author as a *highly qualified, very talented lawyer.*

In the following example, President Trump again employed innuendo.

@realDonaldTrump
Buffalo protester shoved by Police could be an ANTIFA provocateur. 75 year old Martin Gugino was pushed away after appearing to scan police communica-tions in order to black out the equipment. @OANN I watched, he fell harder than was pushed. Was aiming scanner. Could be a set up?
8:34 AM · Jun 9, 2020

The seventy-five-year-old man's head impacted the ground with enough force to cause blood from his right ear to immediately start pooling on the sidewalk. When White House Press Secretary Kayleigh McEnany was asked by a reporter if the president regretted posting a baseless conspiracy theory about the man, she responded by saying, "The President was asking questions about an interaction in a video clip he saw, and the President has a right to ask those questions." When pressed, she added, "The President did have facts before he tweeted out that undergirded his questions." The president of the United States has all the resources at his disposal to get to the bottom of an incident like this. Public conjecture of this nature is inexcusable.

A particularly pernicious conspiracy theory propagated by President Trump is his assertion that the United States has a widespread election fraud problem. It does not. Instances of voter fraud in proportion to the millions of ballots cast in every election are exceptionally rare. Trump's own Presidential Advisory Commission on Election Integrity (established in May 2017) was disbanded within eight months of its creation, citing no proof of widespread fraud. When Trump lost the popular vote in 2016 by almost three million votes, he resorted to amplifying unsubstantiated claims.

@realDonaldTrump
Look forward to seeing final results of VoteStand.
Gregg Phillips and crew say at least 3,000,000 votes were illegal. We must do better!
5:12 AM - Jan 27, 2017

Combating disinformation. Conspiracy theories thrive when leaders are unwilling to defend the truth. When asked about the QAnon conspiracists who believe that Trump will save the country from the so-called deep state and a group of Satan-worshipping pedophiles who run a global child sex trafficking operation, President Trump failed to disavow them. He instead suggested that he had heard that "these are people that love our country...so I don't know really anything about it other than they do supposedly like me." When asked again in October 2020 at an election town hall event if he was willing to "just once and for all...disavow QAnon in its entirety," the president responded by saying, "I know nothing about QAnon. I know very little. You told me, but what you tell me, doesn't necessarily make it fact. I hate to say that. I know nothing about it. I do know they are very much against pedophilia. They fight it very hard. But I know nothing about it."

Republicans in Congress removed their colleague Marjorie Taylor Greene (R-GA) from her committees in early 2021 after she had publicly espoused QAnon conspiracy theories. Greene tried to excuse her QAnon-inspired statements by suggesting that she was "allowed to believe things that weren't true." She had been one of two QAnon believers elected to Congress in 2020.

Ashli Babbitt, an Air Force veteran and QAnon believer inspired by President Trump's disinformation, was shot and killed while trying to force her way into the Speaker's Lobby in the U.S. Capitol on January 6.

A national survey conducted in March 2021 suggested that 15 percent of American adults agreed with the main premise of QAnon. Twenty percent agreed that "there is a storm coming soon that will sweep away the elites in power and restore the rightful leaders." Fifteen percent agreed that "because things have gotten so far off track, true American patriots may have to resort to violence in order to save our country." The FBI warned in June 2021 that QAnon followers might resort to violence due to frustration resulting from their outlandish predictions not materializing (including Donald Trump's imminent restoration to the presidency). QAnon theories even gained traction among the Germans who were arrested in late 2022 for plotting to violently end Germany's democratic constitutional state.

A 2008 political rally provided a lesson in combating disinformation in real time when Republican presidential nominee Senator John McCain (R-AZ) chose truth over political opportunism. A woman approached McCain and explained that she could not trust Barack Obama because she had read that he was Arab (likely implying that he was also Muslim). McCain began shaking his head, took the microphone, and said the following about his political opponent:

> No ma'am. No ma'am. He's a decent family man, a citizen that I just happen to have disagreements with on fundamental issues, and that's what this campaign is all about. He's not. Thank you.

In another exchange minutes later, McCain—despite vocal opposition from some in the audience—addressed a supporter's fear of a potential Obama presidency:

> First of all, I want to be president of the United States and obviously I do not want Senator Obama to be. But I have to tell you—I have to tell you he is a decent person and a person that you do not have to be scared [of] as president of the United States. [Jeers from the crowd.] Now look—if I didn't think I'd be one heck of a better president, I wouldn't be running, okay, and that's the point.

Just prior to his death ten years later, McCain asked former president Obama if he would deliver remarks at his memorial service at the Washington National Cathedral. Reflecting on McCain's character, Obama said the following during the service:

> John believed in honest argument and hearing our views. He understood that if we get in the habit of bending the truth to suit political expediency or party orthodoxy, our democracy will not work....So much of our politics, our public life, our public discourse can seem small and mean and petty. Trafficking in bombastic manufactured outrage, it's politics that pretends to be brave and tough, but in fact is born of fear. John called on us to be bigger than that. He called on us to be better than that.

In society at large, critical thinking and healthy skepticism can combat disinformation. I defer again to author Jonathan Glover for a discussion on these tools:

> Rational people check their beliefs and ways of thinking against those of others. While some people have a marvelous skepticism and independence, most of us find our thoughts drawn by a kind of gravitational pull towards the larger mass of belief around us. This can be resisted, but the larger the mass the more strength resistance requires.
>
> The most effective opposition to the pull of Belief comes from a tradition and culture of criticism.

Glover reminds us that in early twentieth-century Germany, a culture of respect for authority that was stronger than a culture of criticism or skepticism contributed to the dominance of antisemitism, racial hygiene, and social Darwinism. In Glover's words, I am reminded of something I heard at age seventeen from my Presbyterian pastor. He often stressed to his confirmation class students that *what* you believe is less important than *why* you believe it. He was making the point that even religious beliefs should be informed by reason and critical thinking. Thomas Jefferson made the same point, explaining, "He who knows nothing is nearer the truth than he whose mind is filled with falsehoods and errors. It is always better to have no ideas than false ones; to believe nothing than to believe what is wrong." In that spirit, a better informed and more critically thinking electorate will be less susceptible to the types of disinformation presented in this chapter. Democracy relies on an informed electorate and leaders who are trusted messengers.

CHAPTER 25

Creating Distrust:
The 2020 Election
Disinformation Campaign

The spirit of 1776 is not dead. It has only been slumbering.
The body of the American people is substantially republican.
But their virtuous feelings have been played on by some fact
with more fiction; they have been the dupes of artful maneuvers,
and made for a moment to be willing instruments
in forging chains for themselves. But time and truth
have dissipated the delusion, and opened their eyes.

—THOMAS JEFFERSON

President Trump's crusade to delegitimize the 2020 election (and American democracy) began in earnest when polling in the summer of 2020 suggested he might lose to former vice president Joe Biden. His efforts occurred preelection, as ballots were being cast; postelection; and for several years after leaving office. As Trump's

371

August 2023 federal indictment alleged, his schemes or conspiracies to overturn the 2020 election were "built on the widespread mistrust the Defendant was creating through pervasive and destabilizing lies about election fraud."

By Trump's own account, the cast of characters and organizations who deprived him of victory through their alleged malice and corruption included the following: corrupt voters, rigged voting machines, the Democratic party, state and local election officials from both parties, state and federal courts (including federal judges he had appointed), the DOJ and FBI, and, finally, large technology companies. They had to be complicit, because as he had stated publicly and repeatedly between July and November 2020, "the only way they can take this election away from us is if this is a rigged election."

Preelection tactics. President Trump's preelection strategy was clear: cast the election as illegitimate and fraudulent in the event he was not victorious in November. Claims of *potential* fraud would serve to bolster and somehow give credence to equally unhinged claims made both during and after the election. A potential loss attributed to widespread fraud would necessarily justify "retaliatory" abuses of power.

In the midst of the 2020 COVID-19 pandemic (before vaccines were available), public health officials became concerned about the lack of social distancing with respect to in-person voting. In response, some states initiated efforts to expand mail-in voting (used since the Civil War and available to all voters in some states). President Trump wasted no time in sowing unjustified distrust in this means of voting by forecasting fraud on a massive scale. As with in-person voting, fraud associated with voting by mail (or absentee ballots) is relatively rare in the United States, and there are numerous safeguards that allow for the detection of fraudulently produced ballots. Ballots sent by mail are more likely to be undercounted because of the strict signature matching requirements in many states (in addition to the threat of heavy penalties associated with this type of voter fraud).

Many of the Trump administration officials who diligently echoed Trump's concerns about voting by mail had themselves voted by mail. The president routinely did so in his home state of Florida. His disinformation sought to unnecessarily curtail what is probably the most sacred democratic right and the most fundamental civic obligation. It was also an example of what is known as participatory disinformation, in which the target audience is primed, in this case, for concern about potential fraud.

@realDonaldTrump

Mail in ballots substantially increases the risk of crime and VOTER FRAUD!

8:29 PM - Apr 11, 2020

@realDonaldTrump

The United States cannot have all Mail In Ballots. It will be the greatest Rigged Election in history. People grab them from mailboxes, print thousands of forgeries and "force" people to sign. Also, forge names. Some absentee OK, when necessary. Trying to use Covid for this Scam!

10:08 AM - May 24, 2020

Similar works of literary desperation resulted in Twitter attaching its first-ever fact-check link to the bottom of a Trump tweet, encouraging readers to "Get the facts about mail-in ballots." After signing a retaliatory executive order two days later, the president was asked if he would try to shut down Twitter. "If it were able to be legally shut down, I'd do it," he responded.

@realDonaldTrump
.@Twitter is now interfering in the 2020 Presidential Election. They are saying my statement on Mail-In Ballots, which will lead to massive corruption and fraud, is incorrect, based on fact-checking by Fake News CNN and the Amazon Washington Post.... Twitter is completely stifling FREE SPEECH, and I, as President, will not allow it to happen!
7:40 PM - May 26, 2020

@realDonaldTrump
MAIL-IN VOTING WILL LEAD TO MASSIVE FRAUD AND ABUSE. IT WILL ALSO LEAD TO THE END OF OUR GREAT REPUBLICAN PARTY. WE CAN NEVER LET THIS TRAGEDY BEFALL OUR NATION. BIG MAIL-IN VICTORY IN TEXAS COURT TODAY. CONGRATS!!!
9:00 PM - May 28, 2020

@realDonaldTrump
RIGGED 2020 ELECTION: MILLIONS OF MAIL-IN BALLOTS WILL BE PRINTED BY FOREIGN COUNTRIES, AND OTHERS. IT WILL BE THE SCANDAL OF OUR TIMES!
7:16 AM - Jun 22, 2020

Several months before the November election, campaign manager Bill Stepien and House Minority Leader Kevin McCarthy advised President Trump to encourage his supporters to vote by mail. The president had already decided otherwise. He instead suggested delaying the election, an idea without legal merit that even his Republican allies quickly dismissed.

> @realDonaldTrump
> With Universal Mail-In Voting (not Absentee Voting, which is good), 2020 will be the most INACCURATE & FRAUDULENT Election in history. It will be a great embarrassment to the USA. **Delay the Election** until people can properly, securely and safely vote???
> 8:46 AM - Jul 30, 2020

Another tactic employed by the president was to cast doubt on the results if ballot counting continued beyond Election Day. This occurs regularly in American elections and was essentially guaranteed in 2020 due to the combination of record projected voter turnout and the extent to which mail-in ballots would be used. In some of the critical swing states that Trump would later contest, poll workers were legally prohibited from processing and counting mail-in ballots until Election Day (regardless of when they were received). The president would exploit these rules to demand that certain states (where Trump was initially ahead) stop counting votes after Election Day.

> @realDonaldTrump
> Must know Election results on the night of the Election, not days, months, or even years later!
> 4:22 PM - Jul 30, 2020

In September 2020, the FBI and CISA released a joint public service announcement about the threat of disinformation surrounding the results of the upcoming elections. In the context of increased mail-in voting, it acknowledged that vote counting could take longer than usual and warned about how this might be exploited.

> Foreign actors and cybercriminals could exploit the time required to certify and announce elections' results by disseminating disinformation that includes reports of voter suppression, cyberattacks targeting election infrastructure, voter or ballot fraud, and other problems intended to convince the public of the elections' illegitimacy.

A Department of Homeland Security bulletin warned in September that "Russia is likely to continue amplifying criticisms of vote-by-mail and shifting voting processes amidst the COVID–19 pandemic to undermine public trust in the electoral process." During a Senate hearing, FBI Director Christopher Wray was asked if voting by mail is secure. Wray responded, "We have not seen, historically, any kind of coordinated national voter fraud effort in a major election, whether it's by mail or otherwise."

@realDonaldTrump

The Ballots being returned to States cannot be accurately counted. Many things are already going very wrong!

10:21 AM - Sep 28, 2020

President Trump also targeted the opposition party and the media.

> @realDonaldTrump
> These Radical Left, Do Nothing Democrats,
> are doing great harm to our Country. They are
> lying & cheating like never before in our Country's
> history in order to destabilize the United States
> of America & it's upcoming 2020 Election.
> They & the Fake News Media are Dangerous
> & Bad!
> 7:07 PM - Sep 29, 2019

> @realDonaldTrump
> The Election should end on November 3rd.,
> not weeks later!
> 5:48 PM - Oct 30, 2020

Meanwhile, the Russian government was also amplifying election-related disinformation in its own campaign to undermine Americans' faith in their democracy. A U.S. IC assessment would later find that Russia's disinformation engine used President Trump's election commentary to achieve its goals.

Tactics circa Election Day. On the eve of the November 3 election, the president's criticism of an election-related Supreme Court decision sought to further undermine the election results. He was also predicting and potentially inciting violence.

@realDonaldTrump

The Supreme Court decision on voting in Pennsylvania is a VERY dangerous one. It will allow rampant and unchecked cheating and will undermine our entire systems of laws. It will also induce violence in the streets. Something must be done!

8:02 PM - Nov 2, 2020

As Election Day came and went, President Trump continued to cast doubt on the integrity of mail-in ballots when his early lead in key swing states began to evaporate. That lead had generally come courtesy of the ballots counted first—those cast in person on Election Day or during early voting. The subsequent counting of ballots sent by mail—often from large urban areas that leaned heavily Democratic—would begin decimating Trump's early leads. This post–Election Day shift in momentum had been anticipated months earlier and was all the more foreseeable because the president had discouraged many of his supporters from voting by mail. A seemingly incredulous Trump responded with feigned ignorance.

@realDonaldTrump

We are up BIG, but they are trying to STEAL the Election. We will never let them do it. Votes cannot be cast after the Polls are closed!

12:49 AM - Nov 4, 2020

In fact, state laws generally permit voters to vote after the polls close if they were in line prior to closing time.

@realDonaldTrump

How come every time they count Mail-In ballot
dumps they are so devastating in their
percentage and power of destruction?

10:17 AM - Nov 4, 2020

@realDonaldTrump

They are finding Biden votes all over the place
— in Pennsylvania, Wisconsin, and Michigan.
So bad for our Country!

11:55 AM - Nov 4, 2020

@realDonaldTrump

They are working hard to make up 500,000
 vote advantage in Pennsylvania disappear
— ASAP. Likewise, Michigan and others!

12:01 PM - Nov 4, 2020

@realDonaldTrump

Wow! It looks like Michigan has now found
the ballots necessary to keep a wonderful
young man, John James, out of the
U.S. Senate. What a terrible thing
is happening!

1:43 PM - Nov 4, 2020

The president's other tactics included claiming victory before all of
the ballots were counted and ostensibly mobilizing his supporters to
prevent an alleged electoral injustice.

@realDonaldTrump

We have claimed, for Electoral Vote purposes, the Commonwealth of Pennsylvania (which won't allow legal observers) the State of Georgia, and the State of North Carolina, each one of which has a BIG Trump lead. Additionally, we hereby claim the State of Michigan if, in fact,.....

4:56 PM - Nov 4, 2020

@realDonaldTrump

STOP THE FRAUD!

12:21 PM - Nov 5, 2020

Postelection. Immediately following the 2008 presidential election in which Barack Obama defeated John McCain, outgoing Republican president George W. Bush declared, "The American people can have confidence that this election was fundamentally fair, its integrity will be upheld, and its outcome is clear." By November 7, 2020, there was practically universal recognition from major media organizations that Biden had won the election. Despite this, President Trump had no intention of conceding. In a series of speeches, interviews, and posts, the president floated additional conspiracy theories suggesting the complicity of DOJ and FBI officials and the possibility that votes were somehow being counted outside of the United States.

Al Schmidt, a Republican City of Philadelphia commissioner, investigated and debunked claims of election fraud in his city. He had already received general threats before the president posted this:

@realDonaldTrump
A guy named Al Schmidt, a Philadelphia Commissioner
and so-called Republican (RINO), is being used big time by
the Fake News Media to explain how honest things were
with respect to the Election in Philadelphia. He refuses to
look at a mountain of corruption & dishonesty. We win!
9:03 AM - Nov 11, 2020

After the president mentioned him by name, the threats became much more specific and graphic. They included the names of his family members, their ages, their address, and pictures of their home.

On November 12, CISA, which is also charged with securing election infrastructure, characterized the election as "the most secure in American history" and reported that "there is no evidence that any voting system deleted or lost votes, changed votes, or was in any way compromised." The agency had also begun refuting baseless election-related conspiracy theories by fact-checking them on its website—including conspiracy theories floated by President Trump and his surrogates. The president fired CISA Director Chris Krebs five days later.

@realDonaldTrump
The recent statement by Chris Krebs on the security of
the 2020 Election was highly inaccurate, in that there
were massive improprieties and fraud - including dead
people voting, Poll Watchers not allowed into polling locations, "glitches" in the voting machines which changed...
...votes from Trump to Biden, late voting,
and many more. Therefore, effective immediately,
Chris Krebs has been terminated as Director of the
Cybersecurity and Infrastructure Security Agency.
7:07 PM – Nov 17, 2020

In mid-November, President Trump replaced the head of his campaign's legal team, Justin Clark, with Rudy Giuliani. In the former New York City mayor, Trump found someone willing to perpetuate his disingenuous fraud claims.

@realDonaldTrump

I look forward to Mayor Giuliani spearheading the legal effort to defend OUR RIGHT to FREE and FAIR ELECTIONS! Rudy Giuliani, Joseph diGenova, Victoria Toensing, Sidney Powell, and Jenna Ellis, a truly great team, added to our other wonderful lawyers and representatives!

10:11 PM - Nov 14, 2020

The Trump team's litigation efforts failed decisively across multiple states and legal jurisdictions. The president had appointed eleven of the judges who ruled against his legal team. United States District Court judge Linda Parker, who heard an election fraud suit brought in Michigan, determined that they had "filed this lawsuit in bad faith and for an improper purpose....And this case was never about fraud—it was about undermining the People's faith in our democracy and debasing the judicial process to do so." Judge Parker also concluded that Trump's attorneys had been "deceiving a federal court and the American people into believing that rights were infringed, without regard to whether any laws or rights were in fact violated....The attorneys who filed the instant lawsuit abused the well-established rules applicable to the litigation process by proffering claims not backed by law; proffering claims not backed by evidence (but instead, speculation, conjecture, and unwarranted suspicion)."

Sidney Powell was among the nine attorneys sanctioned in the Michigan case in order to, as Judge Parker explained, "deter the filing of future frivolous lawsuits designed primarily to spread the narrative that our election processes are rigged and our democratic institutions cannot be trusted." A comprehensive report released in mid-2021 by the Republican-led Michigan Senate Oversight Committee "found no evidence of widespread or systematic fraud in Michigan's prosecution of the 2020 election." In 2021, Rudy Giuliani's licenses to practice law in New York and Washington, D.C., were suspended. The New York court concluded the following in its detailed thirty-three-page decision:

> There is uncontroverted evidence that respondent communicated demonstrably false and misleading statements to courts, lawmakers and the public at large in his capacity as lawyer for former President Donald J. Trump and the Trump campaign in connection with Trump's failed effort at reelection in 2020. These false statements were made to improperly bolster respondent's narrative that due to widespread voter fraud, victory in the 2020 United States presidential election was stolen from his client. We conclude that respondent's conduct immediately threatens the public interest.

In July 2024, Giuliani was disbarred by the Supreme Court of the State of New York. Jenna Ellis was eventually forced to acknowledge during a March 2023 Colorado State Bar Association disciplinary procedure that she had knowingly misrepresented the facts in her public claims about election fraud. Giuliani and Powell would later appear as unnamed, unindicted coconspirators in the federal indictment related to Trump's efforts to overturn the 2020 election.

The president also used disinformation to pressure Georgia governor Brian Kemp.

@realDonaldTrump
Thousands of uncounted votes discovered in Georgia counties. When the much more important signature match takes place, the State will flip Republican, and very quickly. Get it done! @BrianKempGA
8:46 AM - Nov 19, 2020

@realDonaldTrump
Why is Joe Biden so quickly forming a Cabinet when my investigators have found hundreds of thousands of fraudulent votes, enough to "flip" at least four States, which in turn is more than enough to win the Election? Hopefully the Courts and/or Legislatures will have.... the COURAGE to do what has to be done to maintain the integrity of our Elections, and the United States of America itself. THE WORLD IS WATCHING!!!
8:18 PM - Nov 21, 2020

Brad Raffensperger, Georgia's Republican secretary of state, began receiving death threats after the president disparaged him and other state election officials while calling into question the integrity of that state's election. On November 23, Attorney General Barr explained to President Trump that the Justice Department had looked into the fraud claims and had determined that they were unfounded. Referring to Raffensperger three days later, President

Trump poured fuel on the fire in a speech from the White House: "This was a massive fraud. It should never take place in this country. We're like a third-world country....I understand the Secretary of State who is really—he's an enemy of the people." The president made similar claims about Pennsylvania's election.

@realDonaldTrump

The 1,126,940 votes were created out of thin air. I won Pennsylvania by a lot, perhaps more than anyone will ever know. The Pennsylvania votes were RIGGED. All other swing states also. The world is watching!

12:09 AM - Nov 28, 2020

On December 1, William Barr told the Associated Press, "To date, we have not seen fraud on a scale that could have effected a different outcome in the election." Based on the sworn testimony of a White House staffer, seeing Barr's statement on television caused the president to throw his lunch across the room. The FBI director would later concur with Barr's assessment during sworn testimony to the Senate. Barr debunked the various fraud claims concerning Pennsylvania and told the president that he did not agree with the idea of saying that the election was stolen. He further explained that the claims of fraud brought to Trump by his informal advisors were "bullshit." Trump had told his advisors in private that the voting machine claims were unsupported and that Sydney Powell's claims sounded "crazy." Barr had noticed that the president seemed to have stopped listening to him and the other cabinet secretaries postelection. The attorney general also told the president that there was "zero basis for the allegations" regarding Dominion voting machines, claims Barr characterized as "crazy stuff" and "a grave disservice to the country." President Trump nonetheless made the following comments from the White House the next day:

> We have a company that's very suspect. Its name is Dominion. With the turn of a dial, with the change of a chip, you can press a button for Trump and the vote goes to Biden. What kind of a system is this?

The president posted or reposted conspiracy theories about Dominion nearly three dozen times between mid-November and early January. In the context of the Dominion allegations, Chris Krebs would later suggest the following: "The biggest vulnerability in democracy is the people. It's the brain. It's the perception hack." That is, misinformation and disinformation pose a greater threat than the potential manipulation of voting machines. The president also claimed that in one state there were more votes than voters, something Barr had told him the day before was wrong and easily verifiable. Similar claims were made about so-called vote dumps, which his top advisors had told him were nonsense. Deputy White House Counsel Patrick Philbin informed Trump that "there is no world, there is no option in which you do not leave the White House [o]n January 20th."

On December 3, Rudy Giuliani made false claims regarding election fraud to the Judiciary Subcommittee of the Georgia State Senate. (Because those claims were made to public officials, a Georgia grand jury later charged Giuliani with making false statements and writings.)

@realDonaldTrump

Wow! Blockbuster testimony taking place right now in Georgia. Ballot stuffing by Dems when Republicans were forced to leave the large counting room. Plenty more coming, but this alone leads to an easy win of the State!

2:01 PM - Dec 3, 2020

Just days later, over 1,500 former prosecutors signed a letter condemning President Trump's legal team and calling on the American Bar Association to investigate the team for its filing of frivolous election-related lawsuits.

@realDonaldTrump

How do states and politicians confirm an election where corruption and irregularities are documented throughout? A Swing State hustle!

10:35 AM - Dec 13, 2020

On December 14, President Trump shared with Attorney General Barr a cybersecurity firm's report on Dominion voting machines. After reviewing the report, Barr characterized the president as "detached from reality if he really believes this stuff." The damage to public confidence in American elections caused by Trump's disinformation was reflected in one of his own posts.

@realDonaldTrump

Poll: 92% of Republican Voters think the election was rigged!

11:54 PM - Dec 15, 2020

(Fox News agreed in April 2023 to pay Dominion Voting Systems $787.5 million to settle a defamation lawsuit over falsehoods that the network's hosts knowingly promoted regarding Dominion machines in the 2020 election.)

On December 21, 2020, Attorney General Barr announced that there would be no need to appoint a special counsel to investigate election fraud. The attorney general, who had objected to the president's peddling of conspiracy theories and his repeated claims of a stolen election, had submitted his resignation a week earlier. Barr finally left the Justice Department on December 23.

> @realDonaldTrump
> After seeing the massive Voter Fraud in the 2020 Presidential Election, I disagree with anyone that thinks a strong, fast, and fair Special Counsel is not needed, IMMEDIATELY. This was the most corrupt election in the history of our Country, and it must be closely examined!
> 6:16 PM - Dec 23, 2020

Trump's chief of staff, Mark Meadows, personally observed and reported to the president that the state election officials in Cobb County, Georgia, performing the signature verification process were conducting themselves "in an exemplary fashion" and would find fraud if it existed. The president posted the following the next day.

> @realDonaldTrump
> They are slow walking the signature verification in Georgia. They don't want results to get out prior to January 6th. They know what they are trying so hard to hide. Terrible people! @BrianKempGA
> 12:08 PM - Dec 23, 2020

The following post encapsulates how President Trump created distrust through disinformation by soliciting coconspirators to overturn the election, alleging several types of unsubstantiated voter and electoral process fraud, inferring the negligence and perhaps complicity of federal law enforcement agencies, comparing American democracy to the most corrupt governments in the developing world, attacking the media and alleging an infringement on First Amendment rights, and, finally, by setting the stage for disappointment by assuring his supporters that the election would eventually be overturned.

@realDonaldTrump
Time for Republican Senators to step up and fight for the Presidency, like the Democrats would do if they had actually won. The proof is irrefutable! Massive late night mail-in ballot drops in swing states, stuffing the ballot boxes (on video), double voters, dead voters,....fake signatures, illegal immigrant voters, banned Republican vote watchers, MORE VOTES THAN ACTUAL VOTERS (check out Detroit & Philadelphia), and much more. The numbers are far greater than what is necessary to win the individual swing states, and cannot even be contested....Courts are bad, the FBI and "Justice" didn't do their job, and the United States Election System looks like that of a third world country. Freedom of the press has been gone for a long time, it is Fake News, and now we have Big Tech (with Section 230) to deal with....But when it is all over, and this period of time becomes just another ugly chapter in our Country's history, WE WILL WIN!!!
6:23 PM - Dec 26, 2020

On almost every day between December 23 and January 3, President Trump either called or met with Acting Attorney General Jeffrey Rosen to address his dissatisfaction with DOJ investigations into claims of election fraud. On December 27, for example, Rosen and his deputy, Richard Donoghue, spoke with the president by phone for over ninety minutes. The two men debunked all of the president's fraud allegations based on the dozens of investigations and hundreds of interviews conducted by the DOJ. The evidence did not support the allegations, and Rosen and Donoghue had told the president this repeatedly. Donoghue even walked the president through the details of the specific allegations concerning Georgia, Pennsylvania, Michigan, and Nevada. The president's White House legal team had also told him that the information he was receiving was not sufficiently credible for litigation.

> @realDonaldTrump
> "Breaking News: In Pennsylvania there were 205,000 more votes than there were voters. This alone flips the state to President Trump."
> 4:00 PM - Dec 28, 2020

On December 29, President Trump falsely told Vice President Pence that the "Justice Department [was] finding major infractions."

> @realDonaldTrump
> We now have far more votes than needed to flip Georgia in the Presidential race. Massive VOTER FRAUD took place. Thank you to the Georgia Legislature for today's revealing meeting!
> 4:51 PM - Dec 30, 2020

@realDonaldTrump

Why haven't they done signature verification in Fulton
County, Georgia. Why haven't they deducted all of
the dead people who "voted", illegals who voted,
non Georgia residents who voted, and tens of thousands of others who voted illegally, from the final vote
tally?....Just a small portion of these votes give US a
big and conclusive win in Georgia. Have they illegally
destroyed ballots in Fulton County? After many weeks,
we don't yet even have a judge to hear this large
scale voter fraud case. The only judge seems to be
Stacey's sister!

11:20 AM - Jan 2, 2021

Regarding the previous post, Attorney General Barr and his successor had both explained to the president that there was no evidence of malfeasance or fraud in the alleged Fulton County episode. Georgia's secretary of state would later conclude that only four votes in his state could be tied to deceased individuals. Furthermore, Georgia conducted three recounts after Election Day, including machine and hand recounts. On January 2, the Trump campaign's general counsel, Matthew Morgan, reiterated that any potential election fraud was "not sufficient to be outcome determinative."

Consequences. On January 4, Georgia's voting systems manager, Gabriel Sterling, presented a public point-by-point rebuttal of many of the president's election fraud claims. A month earlier, he had railed about the death threats election workers were receiving from Trump supporters:

It has to stop. Mr. President, you have not condemned these actions or this language. Senators, you have not condemned this language or these actions. This has to stop. We need you to step up. And if you're going to take a position of leadership, show some...and all of you who have not said a damned word are complicit in this... death threats, physical threats, intimidation—it's too much. It's not right....Every American, every Georgian, Democrat and Republican alike, should have that same level of anger. Mr. President...I get it, and you have the rights to go through the courts. What you don't have the ability to do—and you need to step up and say this— is stop inspiring people to commit potential acts of violence. Someone's going to get hurt. Someone's going to get shot. Someone's going to get killed. And it's not right....All of this is wrong.

Election officials and their staffs in several states received explicit and disturbing death threats, faced protests outside of their homes, and were followed in their cars. Governor Brian Kemp publicly implored fellow Trump supporters to stop harassing his wife and children.

Threats were even made against low- and mid-level election workers. President Trump mentioned the name of one Georgia election worker, Ruby Freeman, numerous times in his infamous January 5 phone call to Secretary of State Raffensperger. He referred to her as a "professional vote scammer and hustler" in the context of the alleged "suitcase" incident at State Farm Arena that Richard Donoghue and others at the DOJ had already debunked for the president. Trump's senior campaign advisor had described these and other claims in an email as "all just conspiracy shit beamed down from the mothership." In a public hearing before a committee of the Georgia House of Representatives in early December, Rudy Giuliani had accused Freeman and her daughter of "quite obviously surreptitiously passing around USB ports, as if they're vials of heroin or cocaine," further suggesting that they were criminals whose "places of work, their homes, should have been searched for evidence of ballots, for evidence of USB ports, for evidence of voter fraud." Several individuals (eventually charged in August 2023 by a Georgia grand jury) working on behalf of the president's reelection interests attempted to coerce Freeman into providing false testimony and confessing to election crimes that she did not commit. After their contact information was published, Freeman and her daughter received hundreds of threats from Trump supporters, some of whom showed up at their home. In early January, they left their home for weeks on the advice of the FBI. In December 2023, a federal judge presiding over a civil trial ruled that Guiliani had defamed Freeman and her daughter. The jury ordered Guiliani to pay them $148 million in damages.

American democracy relies on the work of local election officials, their staffs, and the volunteers who step forward each election cycle. A potentially devastating and long-term consequence of the aforementioned threats was the exodus of experienced election workers in numerous states, who for their own safety or peace of mind decided to quit or retire early. Adding insult to injury, by mid-2021, adherents of the president's big lie were beginning to replace the election workers who had left their positions. By the end of 2021, Reuters had documented over 850 threatening and hostile messages related to the 2020 election across sixteen states.

In a display of perverse logic, Senator Ted Cruz (R-TX)—declaring that American democracy was in crisis—urged his colleagues on the floor of the Senate on January 6 to support objections to the certification of Electoral College votes in some states based on the following arguments:

> Recent polling shows that 39 percent of Americans believe the election that just occurred "was rigged." You may not agree with that assessment. But it is nonetheless a reality for nearly half the country....Even if you do not share that conviction, it is the responsibility, I believe of this office to acknowledge that as a profound threat to this country and to the legitimacy of any administrations that will come in the future....I want to speak to the Republicans who are considering voting against these objections. I understand your concerns, but I urge you to pause and think, what does it say to the nearly half the country that believes this election was rigged if we vote not even to consider the claims of illegality and fraud in this election?

Senator Cruz and some of his Senate colleagues were themselves responsible for pushing the very conspiracy theories and untruths that produced the distrust he cites above. As one of his Senate colleagues would declare moments later, the way to dispel bogus claims of election fraud is simply to tell the American people the truth. The election-related disinformation that created so much distrust in 2020 would form the basis of similar conspiracy theories circulating online during the 2022 midterm elections. In just one example, a Republican-led county commission in New Mexico refused to certify election results based on familiar, unsubstantiated concerns about Dominion voting machines.

As the world would better understand by the end of January 6, creating unwarranted distrust in the legitimacy of free and fair elections risks the incitement of violence and may result in long-term harm to a democracy and its key institutions. Senator Gary Peters (D-MI) had addressed those threats three weeks earlier:

> When you look at other democracies around the world and the ones that have stumbled, the ones that have gone into authoritarian regimes and have seen that democracy disintegrate, one of the tactics used by authoritarians is to delegitimize elections....You delegitimize the judiciary. You delegitimize the press, the elections. That is out of the playbook. And when you have a president of the United States putting out this information and sowing discord and distrust, it's very difficult to maintain democracy. That's why it's so dangerous. And to me what is dangerous is not just that the president is saying it but you have so many elected Republicans that are also saying it....and yet they continue to stoke distrust and misinformation just to further their own partisan political gains. And they're doing it at the expense of this country's democracy. It is an incredibly dangerous game that they're playing. It can have very dangerous ramifications....the only way we govern this country is if we

come together and accept the results of an election.

Within two months after the election, the Trump campaign—along with the Republican National Committee and other fund-raising entities—raised over $250 million ($100 million within one week of the election) by exploiting unsubstantiated election fraud claims. The millions of fundraising emails sent to would-be donors through January 6 suggested that Vice President Biden would be an "illegitimate president" if he took office. They also claimed that donors would be supporting an "Election Defense Fund." No such fund existed. Most of the money went instead to the newly created Save America political action committee.

In *On Tyranny: Twenty Lessons from the Twentieth Century*, Timothy Snyder described the "sudden disaster that requires the end of checks and balances, the dissolution of opposition parties, the suspension of freedom of expression, the right to a fair trial." After declaring in 2022 his candidacy for the 2024 presidential election, the former president used his bogus claims of widespread election fraud to justify the termination of constitutional provisions: "A Massive Fraud of this type and magnitude allows for the termination of all rules, regulations, and articles, even those found in the Constitution."

The basis of our political systems is the right of the people
to make and to alter their constitutions of government.
But the Constitution which at any time exists, until changed
by an explicit and authentic act of the whole people,
is sacredly obligatory upon all.
—GEORGE WASHINGTON

CHAPTER 26

Fomenting
Fear

★ ★ ★

As Jon Meacham wrote in *The Soul of America*, "Our fate is contingent upon which element—that of hope or that of fear—emerges triumphant." A leader's reason, temperament, and tone can liberate people from irrational fears brought on by ignorance and prejudice. Furthermore, when peoples' fears are induced by genuinely troubling circumstances, leaders can respond with what lies between indifference and panic—rational hope.

Abraham Lincoln warned about the limitations of passion and how it could threaten liberty. His antidote was "cold, calculating, unimpassioned reason." Appeals to reason, openness, and understanding—which require more time and effort—are often overcome by fear. This is especially true when an impending fear of loss is induced by or combined with ignorance and prejudice. At their worst, leaders will exploit these largely irrational fears to incite distrust, division, and violence.

Exploiting fear. Fearmongers and hatemongers either exploit an existing fear of loss or manufacture a pretense to create new fears. As with those who resort to violence because they have no legitimate means or power to influence others, the fearmonger uses fear to intimidate, coerce, and divide—often with the goal of expanding or consolidating power at the expense of another person or specific group of people. Fear is also used to motivate or inspire someone to behave or act in a manner that ostensibly benefits that person, while instead advancing the interests of the fearmonger. Those who exploit fear understand that in times of crisis and uncertainty, their targets are more susceptible to the lies and conspiracy theories that can exacerbate a fear of loss. It is under these circumstances that people are also more susceptible to radicalization.

Donald Trump did not need a crisis to justify his exploitation of fear. His ascent to the presidency began when he opportunistically exploited racist sentiments to cast doubt on the legitimacy of Barack Obama's presidency by suggesting that he had not been born in the United States. His fearmongering continued with his characterization of Mexicans on the day he announced his candidacy for president. During the 2020 election cycle, he stoked unfounded fears of widespread election fraud. Building on that distrust, his son Donald Trump Jr. encouraged Trump supporters to gather at polling places as part of the "Army for Trump's election security operation," an action that would likely intimidate voters.

In the following posts, President Trump's rhetoric misrepresented existing and proposed fair housing and zoning regulations while also overtly exploiting anxieties at the intersection of race and prosperity.

@realDonaldTrump

The Suburban Housewives of America must read this
article. Biden will destroy your neighborhood and your
American Dream. I will preserve it, and make it even better!

2:46 PM - Jul 23, 2020

@realDonaldTrump

Biden supports Cory Booker's Bill that will force low
income housing in the Suburbs, which will lower property values and bring crime to your neighborhoods. If
Dems win, GOODBYE SUBURBS!

7:38 PM - Oct 7, 2020

Mark Twain suggested that "travel is fatal to prejudice, bigotry,
and narrow-mindedness, and many of our people need it sorely on these
accounts." President Trump was not shy about exploiting the bigotry
and racial anxieties that existed within his base with respect to America's
ongoing demographic shift. While there are legitimate concerns about
illegal migration, President Trump exaggerated the relative security threat
of undocumented immigrants (as compared to documented immigrants
or American citizens) by intentionally highlighting individual murder
cases. He also promoted an irrational fear of migrants by characterizing
the humanitarian crisis at the southern border as an "invasion."

@realDonaldTrump

Humanitarian Crisis at our Southern Border. I just got
back and it is a far worse situation than almost anyone
would understand, **an invasion!** I have been there
numerous times - The Democrats, Cryin' Chuck and
Nancy don't know how bad and dangerous it is for our
ENTIRE COUNTRY....

8:04 AM - Jan 11, 2019

During a seven-month period in 2019, over 2,100 Trump campaign ads on Facebook used the term *invasion* to describe migrants at the southern border.

A 2020 FBI report indicated that hate crimes rose by nearly 20 percent during President Trump's tenure. Pundits appropriately questioned whether the president understood the lethality of his rhetoric and suggested that he choose his words more carefully. It is more likely that Trump *was* deliberate in his choice of words when engaging in fearmongering. His rhetoric may have reinforced the sentiments of people like the gunman, linked to white-nationalist and anti-immigrant ideology, who in August 2019 intentionally targeted people he referred to as "Mexicans" in an El Paso Walmart. A majority of the twenty-three killed in his rampage were American citizens. The gunman's manifesto referred to the "Hispanic invasion of Texas." In the aftermath of the El Paso and Dayton mass shootings, the Trump White House released a message that stated in part, "We must recognize that the internet has provided a dangerous avenue to radicalize disturbed minds and perform demented acts.... The perils of the internet and social media cannot be ignored, and they will not be ignored."

The president also promoted unfounded fears of radical Islamic terrorists flowing across America's southern border.

@realDonaldTrump
Border rancher: "We've found prayer rugs out here.
It's unreal." Washington Examiner People coming
across the Southern Border from many countries,
some of which would be a big surprise.
5:22 AM - Jan 18, 2019

He also grossly overstated the terrorist risk of refugees fleeing war-torn majority-Muslim countries—especially given the extensive vetting process used to admit refugees to the United States. His fearmongering mirrored the intersection of American antisemitism and the exaggerated fear of spies that kept America from admitting more Jewish refugees during the Second World War. When a federal judge temporarily blocked the Trump administration's Muslim travel ban, the president was quick to exploit security-related fears.

> @realDonaldTrump
> Because the ban was lifted by a judge, many very bad and dangerous people may be pouring into our country. A terrible decision
> 1:44 PM - Feb 4, 2017

Fear as a political weapon. During a 2020 campaign rally, President Trump told his audience that he had to "fight to protect me and to protect you. Because once I'm not here, there's nobody else to protect you." That message and countless others like it communicated to his supporters that he was uniquely capable of guaranteeing their security and prosperity. He was in effect indispensable. During another campaign speech, the president said the following about Joe Biden, a man known to publicly profess his Catholic faith.

> He's going to do things that nobody ever, would ever think even possible, because he's following the radical left agenda. Take away your guns. Destroy your Second

Amendment. No religion, no anything. Hurt the Bible. Hurt God. He's against God. He's against guns. He's against energy, our kind of energy.

The threat of gun confiscation and economic disaster were common themes for Trump during the campaign.

@realDonaldTrump
Just like Radical Left New York is trying to destroy the NRA, if Biden becomes President your GREAT SECOND AMENDMENT doesn't have a chance. Your guns will be taken away, immediately and without notice. No police, no guns!
2:07 PM - Aug 6, 2020

@realDonaldTrump
Joe Biden and the Radical Left want to Abolish Police, Abolish ICE, Abolish Bail, Abolish Suburbs, Abolish the 2nd Amendment – and Abolish the American Way of Life. No one will be SAFE in Joe Biden's America!
11:51 AM - Jul 15, 2020

The president's misleading or patently false projections of loss could justifiably be compared to political posters printed for President Abraham Lincoln's 1864 opponent, George McClellan. The posters' fearmongering suggested (with Trump's fondness for all caps) that a reelected Lincoln would "bring on NEGRO EQUALITY, more DEBT, HARDER TIMES, another DRAFT! UNIVERSAL ANARCHY, and ULTIMATE RUIN."

@realDonaldTrump

....would destroy our American cities, and worse, if
Sleepy Joe Biden, the puppet of the Left, ever won.
Markets would crash and cities would burn. Our
Country would suffer like never before. We will beat
the Virus, soon, and go on to the Golden Age - better
than ever before!

10:58 PM - Jul 27, 2020

In similar posts, the president suggested that his political opponents
would destroy Medicare and Social Security and "indoctrinate your
children with poisonous anti-American lies."

The fearmongering in the following posts was ostensibly
related to restrictions on public gatherings enacted by states (versus
the federal government) during the COVID-19 pandemic.

@realDonaldTrump

DEMS WANT TO SHUT YOUR CHURCHES DOWN,
PERMANENTLY. HOPE YOU SEE WHAT IS HAPPENING.
VOTE NOW!

8:49 AM - Oct 7, 2020

@realDonaldTrump

Joe Biden is promising to delay the vaccine and turn
America into a prison state—locking you in your home
while letting far-left rioters roam free. The Biden
Lockdown will mean no school, no graduations, no
weddings, no Thanksgiving, no Christmas, no Fourth
of July, and...no future for America's youth. A vote for
Biden is a vote for Lockdowns, Layoffs and Misery.

Get out and VOTE tomorrow!
4:33 PM - Nov 2, 2020

In this final example taken from an October 2020 campaign rally at The Villages, Florida, the president's fearmongering employed ideological embellishment and, more concerningly, misogyny.

> Kamala [mispronounced] will not be your first female president....That's not the way it's supposed to be. We're not supposed to have a socialist. Look, we're not going to be a socialist nation. We're not going to have a socialist president, **especially a female socialist president**. We're not going to have it. We're not going to put up with it. It's not going to happen.

Autocracies are typically imposed through fear of one's fellow citizens. In contrast, maintaining a democracy requires that people have some degree of faith in each other in order to achieve consensus. In a democracy, the combination of decreased faith and increased fear boosts the likelihood of radicalization and violence. In that respect, public leaders play a crucial role in maintaining that all-important level of trust between citizens, along with a similar degree of trust in the public institutions that serve them.

Part 6

★ ★ ★

LEADERSHIP
AND THE
ETHICALLY CHALLENGED

CHAPTER 27

Ethics in Public Leadership

Labor to keep alive in your breast that little spark of celestial fire called conscience.

—Sixteenth-century French maxim

In the executive branch of the American government, everyone (arguably the president too) takes orders or receives direction from someone. Those giving the orders and making decisions that impact others must do so ethically and consistent with the law. This is especially relevant in the armed forces, where orders are more likely to put people into harm's way. In 1860, Abraham Lincoln stated, "Let us have faith that right makes might, and, in that faith, let us, to the end, dare to do our duty as we understand it." Leaders must be counted on to do what's right.

Right matters. As mentioned earlier, in October 2019, Army lieutenant colonel Alexander Vindman testified before Congress concerning the conduct of his commander in chief, President Trump. He did so despite the Trump administration's direction that he and others in the executive branch defy lawful congressional subpoenas. Vindman had assured his Soviet-born father that his public testimony would not put him at risk, because in America, "right matters." Just a few months later, during closing arguments in the first impeachment trial of President Trump, the lead House impeachment manager addressed the importance of "right" and "truth." He did so in the context of Vindman's assertion that "right matters," and because several U.S. senators had publicly declared their intentions to ignore their oaths by not conducting themselves as impartial jurors during the impeachment trial.

> If right doesn't matter, it doesn't matter how good the Constitution is. It doesn't matter how brilliant the framers were. It doesn't matter how good or bad our advocacy in this trial is. It doesn't matter how well-written the oath of impartiality is. If right doesn't matter, we're lost. If the truth doesn't matter, we're lost. The framers couldn't protect us from ourselves, if right and truth don't matter....But here, right is supposed to matter. It's what's made us the greatest nation on earth. No constitution can protect us if right doesn't matter anymore.... Because right matters and the truth matters. Otherwise, we are lost.

Franklin D. Roosevelt characterized the nature of presidential leadership as follows: "The presidency is not merely an administrative office. That's the least of it. It is more than an engineering job, efficient or inefficient. It is preeminently a place of moral leadership." While it is essential to have moral leadership at the highest levels, moral leadership is needed at *every* echelon of public service. The real-world consequences of a leader's decisions, policy choices, and personal example are inextricably linked to that person's character and principles. As former NATO supreme allied commander Admiral James Stavridis put it, the big door of leadership swings on the small hinge of character. Public leaders must possess a strong set of personal principles—that clear sense of right and wrong that informs one's actions despite momentary temptations or adverse personal circumstances.

The importance of character in organizational leadership is often underappreciated until absent. When leaders gradually dumb down ethical standards, it becomes more difficult for others to ascertain or appreciate when traditional norms and even clear-cut ethical standards are being violated. The lower a leader's standards, the more likely they will be to tolerate inappropriate conduct from subordinates. To avoid looking hypocritical, leaders who are ethically compromised may feel less compelled to enforce standards. The ethical violations that will inevitably follow may threaten the safety and well-being of employees, degrade unit morale (an organizational force multiplier), and compromise mission effectiveness.

Former FBI director and special counsel Robert Mueller testified to Congress after concluding the investigation into Russian interference in the 2016 election. The following exchange with Representative Adam Schiff highlights the inherent dangers of personal compromise (Mueller's responses are in italics):

I gather that you believe that knowingly accepting foreign

assistance during a presidential campaign is an unethical thing to do. *And a crime, given certain circumstances.*

And to the degree that it undermines our democracy and our institutions, we could agree that it's also unpatriotic. *True.*

And wrong. *True.*

The standard of behavior for a presidential candidate or any candidate, for that matter, shouldn't be merely whether something is criminal. They should be held to a higher standard, you would agree?…We should hold our elected officials to a standard higher than mere avoidance of criminality, shouldn't we? *Absolutely.…*

The need to act in an ethical manner is not just a moral one, but when people act unethically, it also exposes them to compromise. Particularly in dealing with foreign powers. Is that true? *True.*

Because when someone acts unethically in connection with a foreign partner, that foreign partner can later expose their wrongdoing and extort them. *True.*

And that unethical conduct can be of a financial nature if you have a financial motive or an illicit business dealing. Am I right? *Yes.*

But it can also just involve deception if you are lying about something that can be exposed, then you can be blackmailed. *Also true.*

In the case of Michael Flynn, he was secretly doing business with Turkey, correct? *Yes.*

And that could open him up to compromise, that financial relationship. *I presume.*

He also lied about his discussions with the Russian ambassador, and since the Russians were on the other side of that conversation, they could have exposed that, could they not? *Yes.*

On a macro level, ethical violations erode the trust between a nation's citizens and its public institutions. Thomas Jefferson wrote about this correlative relationship between individual character and the nation at large: "A character of good faith is of as much value to a nation as to an individual. A nation, as a society, forms a moral person, and every member of it is personally responsible for his society." Leaders are often a reflection of the society they represent, for better or worse.

A leader's unethical conduct also affects subordinates. It creates an atmosphere of consternation, makes professional relationships awkward, and negatively impacts subordinate job performance. This is especially true when abuses of authority result in momentous violations of trust, as with sexual harassment or assault. These types of violations may result in lingering organizational trust issues that transcend the original offender. Additionally, leaders who repeatedly direct their followers to commit unethical or illegal acts risk creating an environment where talented employees quit out of principle. Alternatively, they may become conditioned to ignore certain orders in order to avoid the retribution that would likely follow a principled challenge.

An organization that does not set and enforce ethical standards will descend into chaos. One's credibility as a leader, along with organizational success, depends on one's ability to make ethically sound decisions while encouraging and expecting others to do the same. Do not assume that all subordinates understand the difference between ethical and unethical actions.

Developing ethical leaders. People join governmental organizations from disparate personal backgrounds with respect to upbringing and ethics education. The values with which they identify may be widely shared or uniquely personal, and they may have varying capacities to honor those values. Early childhood and adolescent influences include family, educators, clergy, peers, public figures, literature, music, and other expressions of art and popular culture. With respect to pop culture, I was happy to observe while watching reruns of what was my favorite show at age six—*The Six Million Dollar Man*—that my fictional childhood hero was honest, decent, empathetic, respectful of others, loyal, conscientious, and only occasionally insubordinate.

The tendency early in life to succumb to peer pressure and to satisfy the expectations of others—for better and worse—can problematically carry on well into adulthood. Despite potentially questionable early influences with respect to role-modeling and character development, a person can still learn to consistently act in concert with their stated values and those of their organization.

There is an enormous difference between how unelected public servants and elected officials are selected for positions of leadership. Those who attain positions of leadership in government organizations (civil service or the military) have been trained to respect organizational values and have generally been chosen from within their ranks based on a proven track record of competence and ethical behavior. They are also more likely to have been held accountable by their organizations. The U.S. military, in particular, has a uniform culture with respect to values and, consequently, a lower tolerance for ethical ambiguity. Someone like Donald Trump would have been weeded out early in a military or civil service career (if even allowed to start one) and would have likely not attained any meaningful position of leadership. While not true for all elected leaders, too many are nonetheless voted into office without an adequate foundation in ethics (or with personality issues, such as psychopathic or narcissistic tendencies, making them more charming and persuasive but also more likely to engage in unethical behavior). When they then fail to meet their ethical obligations, accountability is often lacking. Despite the aforementioned differences, both unelected and elected leaders must be expected to adhere to standards of ethical behavior.

However strong one's personal leadership example may be, one should not discount the effect of organizational culture on individual behavior. Organizational culture is created in complex environments requiring nuance and judgment. Employees are more likely to adhere to an organization's professional code of ethics when leadership nurtures an ethical culture. This requires promoting leadership development through the consistent reinforcement of ethical values and the promotion of equitable accountability. It also requires providing channels for dissent and whistleblowing in an environment free of retribution. Leaders must incentivize people to do the right thing.

A case where a leader failed to set the example involves President Trump's secretary of state, Mike Pompeo. The secretary had warned his employees via memo that they were legally restricted from participating in certain partisan political activities, such as overtly expressing preferences for the upcoming 2020 presidential election. Nonetheless, Pompeo delivered a speech for the 2020 Republican National Convention that endorsed Donald Trump. Pompeo ignored his own directives and potentially violated the Hatch Act, which limits the political activities of many federal employees. Leaders serving in the Defense and State Departments, in particular, are expected to represent the United States abroad in a nonpartisan manner.

It is important for leaders to be able to differentiate mistakes or bad decisions from deliberate ethical lapses. The latter might include corrupt acts or abuses of power, topics addressed further in chapter 29. Another category is what legal commentators refer to as "awful, lawful acts," which tend to also result from poor ethical judgment. Though these unethical acts are technically legal, their effects can still threaten the effectiveness of an organization and the well-being of its beneficiaries. One such example is the use of deadly (excessive) force by police officers when a nonlethal means of self-defense would have sufficed.

As featured in the *Air and Space Power Journal*, the U.S. Air Force's Air University was as of 2019 using a quality enhancement plan known as "Leadership and Ethics across the Continuum of Learning." The plan sought to address growing ethical dilemmas in the military with an approach that more deliberately developed ethical leaders.

Though it was being developed for the Air Force, it has practical implications for any public organization. Some of its key features include:

- Viewing ethical leadership as central to and not separate from overall leadership development

- Focusing on follower internalization of norms and behaviors through relationships

- Development at the individual level allowing people to identify and reflect on their internal beliefs while connecting individual ethical values to organizational values so that the two might be aligned

- Developing and exercising the traits and skills of strategic-level ethical leadership starting at the beginning of a career versus waiting until one reaches the upper echelons of an organization; training material would become more sophisticated as one's career progressed

Delaying intentional ethical development increases the possibility that unchecked ethical compromises that occur early in a career will set the foundation for later lapses when the stakes are much higher. Public organizations without a preponderance of ethical leadership will contribute to a society drifting aimlessly among the wreckage of its damaged institutions, its diminished liberties, and its betrayed citizens.

Become an honest and useful man to those among whom we live.
Above all things be good, because without that we can neither
be valued by others nor set any value on ourselves.
—Thomas Jefferson

CHAPTER 28

Principled Loyalty

Profiles in Courage and Cowardice

★ ★ ★

Loyalty can be defined as "an unswerving allegiance" expressed as "faithfulness to a private person to whom faithfulness is due." Marriage is one example of a well-defined and principled rationale for loyalty. Loyalty can also be "faithfulness to a cause, ideal, custom, or institution." A third definition of loyalty involves being "faithful in allegiance to one's lawful sovereign or government." Inherent in all of these definitions is the concept of principle, even if that principle—which informs to whom or to what faithfulness is due—is sometimes justified by subjective personal convictions. Unprincipled loyalty is not a virtue.

Loyalty to a cause or institution generally requires that one's personal convictions align with the values of that cause or institution. Former military officer and Secretary of Transportation Pete Buttigieg articulated this notion of principled and selfless loyalty:

When you put your life on the line for this country, you do it not because it's the country you live in, but because it's a country you believe in. I believe in this country, because America uniquely holds the promise of a place where everyone can belong.

Thomas Jefferson wrote about a similar notion of unselfish loyalty expressed as principled patriotism:

The man who loves his country on its own account, and not merely for its trappings of interest or power, can never be divorced from it, can never refuse to come forward when he finds that she is engaged in dangers which he has the means of warding off.

In both fictional dramas and actual events, we are routinely presented with romanticized, unprincipled expressions of loyalty. Arbitrary and unprincipled loyalty is justified for a host of reasons, often self-serving. The romanticized notions of loyalty for loyalty's sake, or loyalty associated with misguided reciprocity, have no place in a society based on laws and principles such as "the common good."

Self-interest should not be a primary motive for loyalty. Even a criminal enterprise may value the loyalty of members to its cause, however self-serving that cause might be. Former president Jimmy Carter described the "natural human inclination to encapsulate ourselves in a superior fashion with people who are just like us—and to assume that we are fulfilling the mandate of our lives if we just confine our love to our own family or to people who are similar and compatible." He explained how this inclination is a barrier that prevents us from reaching out to others.

We can likewise break through the barrier of unprincipled, self-serving loyalty in order to practice a more expansive and principled loyalty, choosing to put oneself at risk to save a stranger or to support the rights of the oppressed, or risking one's life to defend one's fellow citizens and their constitutional freedoms.

Loyalty is too often motivated by arbitrary or unprincipled rationales. "To whom faithfulness is due" should ideally be linked to some virtuous standard or code of conduct. If one commits an unlawful act for someone out of perceived reciprocity, it is hardly an act of principled loyalty. The person requesting or demanding your "loyalty" has forfeited their right to your faithfulness because the unlawful nature of the act is disloyal to you and your interests (and to the common good). In this context, to abandon principle to embrace "loyalty at any cost" just amounts to conspiracy to commit wrongdoing, or perhaps conspiracy to obstruct justice. Nonetheless, people routinely lower their standards and fall for this "loyalty" trap with family, friends, and colleagues who have already violated or seek to violate societal or organizational standards.

Policing is one of several professions where people practice unprincipled and unwarranted loyalty when they fail to hold their colleagues accountable. One rationale for this special dispensation may be the physical danger shared by those serving in law enforcement. Nonetheless, when an officer intentionally violates an organization's norms, that person does not deserve the defense of their colleagues. The person who has been disloyal to organizational standards has also betrayed their coworkers. You are not "selling out one of your own" when you report serious misconduct. In fact, there is often more risk (with respect to one's professional standing) than gain for the person reporting misconduct. But in doing so, you remain loyal to your superiors, your peers, your subordinates, and the ethics and laws you have pledged to uphold.

Rutger Bregman, the author of *Humankind: A Hopeful History*, stated, "If you look at history, so often we do the most horrible things in the name of comradeship and of loyalty because we don't want to let down our own group." Following the 2020 police murder of George Floyd, police departments across the country put a renewed emphasis on bystander intervention training. The training promoted the notion that officers who prevented their peers from engaging in misconduct were being loyal to those colleagues and their shared institutional values.

Loyalty tests. There was significant reporting in early 2020 that the Trump White House sought to identify and remove or sideline government employees deemed insufficiently "loyal" to the president. Those targeted likely included officials who had contradicted the president with facts and evidence or who had made principled decisions—guided by the law—that nonetheless put them out of favor. An extreme example of this loyalty test phenomenon existed in the Soviet Union under Joseph Stalin. Children were encouraged to inform on family members deemed insufficiently loyal to their leader. Approximately eighty years later, Russia's parliament passed a law criminalizing dissent associated with Russia's 2022 invasion of Ukraine. President Putin and other government entities encouraged Russians to report on fellow citizens who opposed the war. Misled by official disinformation, children at two Russian schools recorded and reported the anti-war sentiments of their teachers.

While it may be reasonable in government to have, in certain key positions, individuals whose partisan ideologies mirror those of their bosses, partisan or political litmus or loyalty tests generally have no place in public service. Likewise, devotion to a particular person is never a prerequisite for service in a democracy and cannot supersede loyalty to the Constitution. One of the consequences of these types of loyalty tests is that the rank and file in government agencies may be afraid to voice their opinions for fear of being branded disloyal or insufficiently devoted. This dynamic can stymie the kind of vigorous debate that generates better policy solutions. Loyalty tests can also result in hiring that prioritizes perceived loyalty over needed competence. Most career civil servants are not replaceable by so-called loyalists who come along every election cycle.

> @realDonaldTrump
> It would be really great if the people within the Trump Administration, all well-meaning and good (I hope!), could stop hiring Never Trumpers, who are worse than the Do Nothing Democrats. Nothing good will ever come from them!
> 3:01 PM - Oct 23, 2019

As an Air Force general once reminded my colleagues and me, people in an organization can be genuinely disloyal. He explained to us in no uncertain terms that he was aware of and would not tolerate those who were intentionally working to undermine the organization and its leadership. He was not trying to silence dissent, and perhaps unlike what was happening in the Trump administration, he was not conflating policy differences with bad motives. He was referring specifically to people who were, based on their personal views, attempting to undermine legitimate, leadership-adopted organizational objectives.

To further explore the relationship between principled loyalty and leadership in the context of actual events, the remainder of this chapter will focus on the following four topics: (1) inappropriate loyalty to a superior, (2) leaders who expect inappropriate loyalty, (3) inappropriate loyalty to subordinates, and (4) examples of principled loyalty.

Inappropriate loyalty to a superior. Some leaders abandon principle and engage in inappropriate loyalty to a superior. Their misguided loyalty can start with the seemingly benign act of remaining silent when they should actually challenge a superior's dishonesty.

> *To sin by silence, when we should protest,*
> *makes cowards out of men.*
> —ELLA WHEELER WILCOX

There are countless (mostly self-serving) reasons why someone might not challenge an unethical leader. Fear of reprisal is one. Some may justify their inappropriate loyalty with the old saying "If you can't beat 'em, join 'em." More subtle motivations include the need to conform or be an "insider," the allure of power, and the emotional gratification derived from displays of "loyalty" and pleasing others.

When confronted with the need to question a superior's actions, motives, or ethics, the personal need to respect and please that superior can result in understandable tension and conflicting emotions. It can also contribute to a lack of objectivity concerning that person's performance and conduct. Worse yet, it can result in the kinds of personal compromises that lead to inappropriately defending that person, if not committing wrongdoing on that person's behalf. When a person in a prominent or influential position asks someone for an inappropriate personal favor, human nature can tend toward excessive deference and unprincipled loyalty in response to the confidence imparted by the requester. It can be difficult to resist a charismatic superior who, on balance, is competent and treats people fairly.

As described by Jonathan Glover, the studies conducted by Stanley Milgram in the 1960s on the human disposition to obey suggest a "widespread human tendency to give uncritical obedience to authority, even when the orders are appalling." While obedience to authority and conformity are necessary to some degree in society at large and in public institutions, Glover warned that the pressures to obey and conform can reinforce each other. When there is less pressure from peers or superiors to conform, there is a greater likelihood that someone will appropriately disobey unlawful orders (also known as disciplined disobedience). Those giving excessive obedience to any one superior have likely put all of their faith in that leader, failing to understand the limits of any one person's leadership.

The most straightforward motive for misguided loyalty is tangible personal gain. That was likely Michael Cohen's motive during the many years in which Donald Trump benefited from his inappropriate loyalty. As Cohen's personal legal woes intensified, his loyalty to the president initially held fast, as documented in the Mueller report:

Cohen said that…he believed he had the support of the White House if he continued to toe the party line, and he determined to stay on message and be a part of the team. At the time, Cohen understood that his legal fees were still being paid by the Trump Organization, which he said was important to him. Cohen believed he needed the power of the President to take care of him, so he needed to defend the President and stay on message.…Cohen understood based on…conversations about pardons with the President's personal counsel that as long as he stayed on message, he would be taken care of by the President, either through a pardon or through the investigation being shut down.

Cohen's inappropriate loyalty eventually ceased after the FBI surfaced incriminating evidence and served warrants to his home and offices. He chose to cooperate with prosecutors and pleaded guilty to eight offenses, including a campaign finance violation committed at the direction of—and for the benefit of—Donald Trump and the Trump Organization. (Trump was eventually indicted in March 2023 for falsifying business records in order to conceal an illegal conspiracy to influence the 2016 presidential election. On May 30, 2024, Trump became the first former president to be convicted of a felony when a jury of his peers in a Manhattan courthouse found him guilty on all thirty-four counts.) While personal gain certainly motivated Cohen's eventual cooperation, it would seem that the trajectory of Michael Cohen's life improved once he chose personal accountability, truth, and justice over misguided loyalty. The book Cohen later authored about his time working for Trump was aptly titled *Disloyal*.

At the conclusion of President Trump's second impeachment trial—for which he was charged with inciting the January 6, 2021, attack on the U.S. Capitol—seven Republican senators joined fifty Democrats and Independents in voting to convict the president. They were nonetheless short of the necessary two-thirds (sixty-seven) needed to convict and potentially disqualify Trump from ever again holding public office. Among the Republicans voting to convict were Richard Burr (R-NC) and Pat Toomey (R-PA). After being censured by his own party in North Carolina, Senator Burr said the following: "My party's leadership has chosen loyalty to one man over the core principles of the Republican Party and the founders of our great nation." In response to Senator Toomey's vote, a Republican official in Pennsylvania stated, "We did not send him there to vote his conscience. We did not send him there to do the right thing, or whatever he said he was doing. We sent him there to represent us." At stake when we practice unprincipled loyalty to a superior or national leader is the integrity and capacity of the very institutions on which we depend for liberty, security, and economic prosperity.

Leaders who expect inappropriate loyalty. Two days prior to President Trump's scheduled commencement address at the United States Military Academy, a group of West Point alumni that would eventually exceed one thousand in number and represent every graduating class from 1966 to 2019 published a letter for the Class of 2020. The letter primarily addressed the recent politicization of the military while also touching on the issue of loyalty:

> Your commitment to your oath will be tested throughout
> your career. Your loyalty will be questioned, and some

will attempt to use it against you. Loyalty is the most abused attribute of leadership. Weak or self-serving leaders will emphasize loyalty over duty under the guise of "good order and discipline."

In late January 2017, FBI Director James Comey received a firsthand lesson in expected inappropriate loyalty from recently inaugurated President Trump. As memorialized in the Mueller report, the president invited Director Comey to the White House for what would be—unbeknownst to Comey, and against the advice of the president's top advisors—a dinner for two:

> Comey said that when he arrived for the dinner that evening, he was surprised and concerned to see that no one else had been invited....The President repeatedly brought up Comey's future, asking whether he wanted to stay on as FBI director. Because the President had previously said he wanted Comey to stay on as FBI director, Comey interpreted the President's comments as an effort to create a patronage relationship by having Comey ask for his job....At one point during the dinner the President stated, "I need loyalty, I expect loyalty." Comey did not respond and the conversation moved on to other topics, but the President returned to the subject of Comey's job at the end of the dinner and repeated, "I need loyalty." Comey responded, "You will always get honesty from me." The President said, "That's what I want, honest loyalty." Comey said, "You will get that from me."

In an effort to remove the *public* from *public servant*, the president ultimately wanted an FBI director who would be loyal to his personal interests in lieu of Comey's well-defined obligations to the FBI and the Constitution.

The president similarly expected inappropriate loyalty during his first impeachment trial, finding it incomprehensible that a U.S. senator could still act out of principle following a history of mutual cooperation. The president's transactional perspective demanded "loyalty" from anyone he considered to be in his debt.

> @realDonaldTrump
> Unlike Senator Manchin, Big Jim Justice was very loyal to your favorite President during Pelosi's Impeachment Scam. Big Jim is doing a tremendous job for West Virginia. Vote for Big Jim! #MAGA
> 3:10 PM - Jun 7, 2020

The following passage from the Mueller report provides insight into the inappropriate loyalty President Trump expected from indicted associates Michael Flynn and Paul Manafort:

> After Flynn withdrew from a joint defense agreement with the President and began cooperating with the government, the President's personal counsel left a message with Flynn's attorneys reminding them of the President's warm feelings towards Flynn, which he said "still remains," and asking for a "heads up" if Flynn knew "information that implicates the President." When Flynn's counsel reiterated that Flynn could no longer

share information pursuant to a joint defense agreement, the President's personal counsel said he would make sure that the President knew that Flynn's actions reflected "hostility" towards the President. During Manafort's prosecution and when the jury in his criminal trial was deliberating, the President praised Manafort in public, said that Manafort was being treated unfairly, and declined to rule out a pardon. After Manafort was convicted, the President called Manafort "a brave man" for refusing to "break" and said that "flipping" [cooperating] "almost ought to be outlawed."

In a similar turn of events in the spring of 2022, Cassidy Hutchinson, former assistant to Chief of Staff Mark Meadows, was preparing to testify before the congressional committee investigating the January 6 attack on the U.S. Capitol. Multiple people associated with former president Trump phoned her regarding her upcoming testimony. In one phone call, Hutchinson was told that "Mark [Meadows] wants me to let you know that he knows you're loyal and he knows you'll do the right thing tomorrow and that you're going to protect him and the boss," an apparent reference to former president Trump. "You know, he knows that we're all on the same team and we're all a family." Hutchinson was told to protect who she needed to protect in order to stay in good graces in Trump world. She was also reminded that the former president reads transcripts.

Attorney General Jeff Sessions's principled loyalty problem. When the DOJ appointed Robert Mueller to take over the investigation into Russian interference in the 2016 election, President Trump had hoped to leverage his attorney general to shield himself from potential legal exposure. Because of Sessions's involvement in Trump's 2016 presidential campaign, Sessions was forced to consider recusing himself from the investigation over which he would normally have a supervisory role. In the lead-up to his decision to recuse in March 2017, White House advisors (on behalf of the president) had been pressuring Sessions not to recuse. He recused himself after career ethics officials at DOJ advised Sessions that his previous role in the campaign created a conflict of interest. The pressure on Sessions continued post-decision, as documented in the Mueller report:

> Sessions believed the decision to recuse was not a close call, given the applicable language in the Code of Federal Regulations (CFR), which Sessions considered to be clear and decisive....Sessions got the impression, based on calls he received from White House officials, that the President was very upset with him and did not think he had done his duty as Attorney General.... [Hope] Hicks recalled that the President viewed Sessions's recusal from the Russia investigation as an act of disloyalty....
>
> In early summer 2017, the President called Sessions at home and again asked him to reverse his recusal... Sessions did not reverse his recusal....In December 2017, shortly after Flynn pleaded guilty pursuant to a cooperation agreement, the President met with Sessions in the Oval Office and suggested, according to notes taken by a

senior advisor, that if Sessions unrecused and took back supervision of the Russia investigation, he would be a "hero,"…He did not unrecuse.

In the following post, the president suggested that Sessions's inability to personally influence the Russia investigation (ostensibly for Trump's benefit) was in effect a disqualifying criterion for his selection as attorney general.

> @realDonaldTrump
> ....chief law enforcement officer, and they told me later, 'oh by the way I'm not going to be able to particpate in the most important case in the office, I would be frustrated too...and that's how I read that - Senator Sessions, why didn't you tell me before I picked you.....
> 5:47 AM - May 30, 2018

> @realDonaldTrump
> "The recusal of Jeff Sessions was an unforced betrayal of the President of the United States."
> JOE DIGENOVA, former U.S. Attorney.
> 8:21 PM - May 30, 2018

Sessions had appropriately refused President Trump's demands for inappropriate loyalty, which arguably cost him his job in November 2018. It also resulted in the president's opposition to his 2020 Senate bid. When Sessions failed to regain his former Senate seat, Trump stated, "I made a bad decision...one bad decision. Jeff

Sessions. And now I feel good because he lost overwhelmingly in the great state of Alabama."

@realDonaldTrump
This is what happens to someone **who loyally gets appointed** Attorney General of the United States & then doesn't have the wisdom or courage to stare down & end the phony Russia Witch Hunt. Recuses himself on FIRST DAY in office, and the Mueller Scam begins!
7:31 AM · Mar 4, 2020

> *Associate yourself with men of good quality*
> *if you esteem your own reputation;*
> *for 'tis better to be alone than in bad company.*
> —Sixteenth-century French maxim

Inappropriate loyalty to subordinates. Acts of loyalty, even the inappropriate variety, are often rewarded with a psychological and emotional payoff from the appreciation of those to whom "loyalty" is shown. This may explain why some leaders take the path of least resistance, remaining inappropriately loyal to subordinates who have clearly engaged in wrongdoing.

There is a difference between helping people with ethical issues and enabling them. As members of the clergy like to say, we can hate the sin (enforce standards and provide accountability) but love the sinner (be empathetic and willing to rehabilitate the offender). Leaders cannot afford to selectively enforce standards. In doing so, they are being disloyal to the vast majority of

subordinates who maintain ethical and professional standards—
subordinates who are also likely aware of their colleagues' ethical
lapses.

Thomas Jefferson expressed this notion of dispassionate justice
in his description of George Washington: "His integrity was most
pure, his justice the most inflexible I have ever known, no motives of
interest or consanguinity, of friendship or hatred, being able to bias
his decision." In contrast, President Trump on numerous occasions
engaged in unprincipled loyalty by defending associates and subordinates who had clearly run afoul of the law. He may have even seen
himself in those he defended when making statements like, "I feel
badly for him." One rationale for inappropriately supporting an ethically challenged subordinate is that subordinate's ability to compromise his complicit superior.

The saga involving Trump associate Roger Stone (who was
not technically a subordinate) vividly demonstrates the cycle of
providing and rewarding unprincipled loyalty. Stone engaged, on
Trump's behalf, in questionable acts during the 2016 election. Stone
then lied to Congress about his actions in order to protect himself
and the president.

@realDonaldTrump
"I will never testify against Trump." This statement
was recently made by Roger Stone, essentially stating
that he will not be forced by a rogue and out of
control prosecutor to make up lies and stories about
"President Trump." Nice to know that some people
still have "guts!"
7:48 AM - Dec 3, 2018

The president publicly encouraged, expected, and then rewarded Stone's decision not to cooperate with prosecutors by influencing (through his attorney general) the length of Stone's prison sentence. Trump then commuted Stone's already curtailed prison sentence, ensuring Stone would serve zero prison time. The president ultimately pardoned Stone, all but guaranteeing that Stone would return Trump's "loyalty" by not incriminating him.

Examples of principled loyalty. A leader who is new to an organization deserves loyalty not for charisma or likability but simply by virtue of position and authority. Public servants must exhibit loyalty to promote the success of their leaders and their organizations. That said, a leader to whom loyalty is expected must also *earn* that loyalty (*to whom faithfulness is due*) through consistently ethical behavior and faithful adherence to the organization's values.

Every leader has a boss. The president of the United States has a boss—the American people. How a leader relates to his or her boss sets the example for principled followership throughout the chain of command.

Loyalty to a superior does not require that one agree with that leader's policies or objectives. Likewise, the extent of a superior's competence (unless detrimental to the mission) is not a necessary prerequisite for appropriate loyalty. Subordinates will occasionally challenge their superiors' proposals, assumptions, and decisions. That criticism should be delivered respectfully and in an appropriate setting. Professional loyalty also requires one to support the boss's eventual decision (provided it is ethical and legal) to avoid undermining authority. The ultimate test of loyalty may be following lawful orders with which one disagrees.

When presented with evidence that a superior has engaged in misconduct, appropriate and principled loyalty demands, first and foremost, loyalty to organizational standards and the Constitution. This puts one at odds with one's superior and potentially also with inappropriately sympathetic peers and subordinates. In reaction, some people compromise their own integrity by ignoring or deferring a necessary response to observed misconduct. Some rationalize waiting for a more serious transgression. It takes moral courage to reject the path of least resistance and instead take a stand for what is right. Potential consequences for doing the right thing might be considered, as civil rights icon John Lewis put it, "Good trouble, necessary trouble." In his eulogy for Lewis, former president Obama spoke to his persistent personal courage:

> What a revolutionary notion, this idea that any of us ordinary people, a young kid from Troy, can stand up to the powers and principalities and say, "No, this isn't right, this isn't true, this isn't just. We can do better."

While it may be appropriate to resign or retire in protest due to fundamental disagreements with a superior on legitimate and legal policies, those actions alone are insufficient when confronted with malfeasance. Principled loyalty requires blowing the whistle. One can have genuine affection for a superior and still hold them accountable. It may just make the job of reporting the misconduct more difficult, though not impossible. It is akin to the leader who "loves" his or her people but still recognizes the need to penalize unacceptable behavior.

President Trump attempted to influence and arguably tried

to sabotage the investigation into Russian interference in the 2016 election. His efforts, however, were largely unsuccessful because his subordinates generally chose principled loyalty over blind personal loyalty. The president, after learning that Special Counsel Robert Mueller was investigating him for obstructing the investigation, directed White House Counsel Don McGahn to have Mueller removed because of alleged conflicts of interest. The president's advisors had told him that such assertions were meritless and had already been considered by the DOJ. McGahn was on several occasions put in the unenviable position of choosing principled over inappropriate loyalty. McGahn held fast to what he knew was right, despite the potential consequences. The Mueller report also referenced others who pushed back against President Trump's inappropriate requests:

> Comey did not end the investigation of [Michael] Flynn, which ultimately resulted in Flynn's prosecution and conviction for lying to the FBI....[Corey] Lewandowski and [Rick] Dearborn did not deliver the President's message to Sessions that he should confine the Russia investigation to future election meddling only.

A similar dynamic unfolded immediately after the 2020 presidential election. Key DOJ leaders refused to go along with a plan to replace Acting Attorney General Jeffrey Rosen with someone sympathetic to the president's aim of using the DOJ to overturn the election (an affair covered in greater detail in the next chapter).

CHAPTER 29

Abuse of
Authority

★ ★ ★

I f you really want to test someone's character, give them power. Words to that effect were spoken in admiration of Abraham Lincoln a few decades after his death. Former first lady Michelle Obama similarly suggested that high office does not develop or change a person's character, it simply reveals it.

As articulated by retired U.S. Army general Clay T. Buckingham, when authority is used strictly in the conduct of one's official duties, it is being used legitimately and ethically. If one fails to use one's given authorities to fulfill assigned responsibilities, then one's negligence is itself unethical. Renowned U.S. Air Force general Wilbur L. Creech reportedly told his wing commanders that there were only four things for which they would be immediately dismissed: lapses in personal integrity, ruling through fear, losing one's temper in public, and abuse of office.

An increase in power and responsibility is normally accompanied by additional privileges and a greater capacity to influence.

More power also increases opportunities to abuse one's authority, as Justice Jackson explained in her dissent of the Supreme Court's July 2024 majority decision providing presidential immunity for official acts: "It is when the President commits crimes using his unparalleled official powers that the risks of abuse and autocracy will be most dire."

Abuse of authority is defined in American law as an arbitrary and capricious exercise of authority that is inconsistent with the mission of the executive agency concerned. Similarly, abuse of power can be the misuse of a position of power to take advantage of individuals, organizations, or governments. One can abuse one's authority by committing acts that are inherently illegal or by engaging in official acts with corrupt motives (motives forbidden by law) that provide improper personal or political benefit.

The framers of the American Constitution were concerned with the inherent power of officials to conceal corrupt or illegitimate objectives behind seemingly legitimate official acts. President Nixon's choices, unearthed by the Watergate scandal, are often cited as examples of this behavior. These corrupt departures from established institutional and leadership norms—these violations of public trust—can damage an entire organization when the perpetrator is at the helm.

Examples of criminal abuses of authority include bribery, accepting or soliciting foreign assistance in elections, and obstruction of justice. Obstruction of justice is not a mere process crime, as some of President Trump's defenders have claimed. As Special Counsel Robert Mueller explained in testimony to Congress, it "strikes at the core of the government's effort to find the truth and to hold wrongdoers accountable." The American system of justice relies on the illumination of truth through legal means. Examples of obstruction include the following: lying to investigators, destroying documents and other evidence, interfering in investigations by threatening or falsely accusing investigators or prosecutors, engaging in witness tampering or intimidation, dangling pardons, pressuring officials who have appropriately recused themselves from investigations to unrecuse, and directing subordinates to be uncooperative in legitimate investigations.

The potential to abuse one's authority grows not just with increased power but also with the view that certain constraints on conduct no longer apply when serving in more senior capacities. The notion that "the best way to uphold the law is to be above it" makes for good political satire, and some leaders actually rationalize that accountability is needed only for their subordinates. This of course violates the rule of law principle: no one is above the law. Similarly, some leaders may believe that their wisdom has grown in proportion to their increased authority, reducing or negating the need for input or advice. In the aviation world, this contributes to what is known as the halo effect, where subordinate crew members provide more senior pilots—and especially those who already have an aversion to crew input—excessive deference. All of these attitudes grow more dangerous when the protection of corrupt senior officials becomes institutionalized.

The framers of the Constitution also understood that elected officials—the president of the United States in particular—could potentially use their constitutional powers to harm institutions while furthering their personal or political interests. The House Judiciary Committee's 2019 report titled *Constitutional Grounds for Presidential Impeachment* reminded us of a well-known historical truth: "When corrupt motives take root, they drive an endless thirst for power and contempt for checks and balances. It is then only the smallest of steps toward acts of oppression and assaults on free and fair elections." The Constitution's authors warned that corruption and abuse of authority could erode our government from within. Not necessarily because of one person's corruption, but because as British historian and statesman James Bryce warned in *The American Commonwealth*, "A bold president who knew himself to be supported by a majority in the country, might be tempted to override the law, and deprive the minority of the protection which the law affords it. He might be a tyrant, not against the masses, but with the masses."

Financial greed is a powerful motive when the benefit is personal. During the 2017 sentencing of Trump campaign advisor Rick Gates, Judge Amy Berman Jackson disabused the notion, expressed in a request for leniency, that Gates's greed was a necessary consequence of politics:

> One of the letter writers said that he got caught up in D.C. political drama. But I reject that. It's perfectly possible to conduct yourself with ethics, integrity, and no hint of scandal, even in politics, even in D.C., even in Ukraine. Politics don't corrupt people, people corrupt politics. And what Gates got caught up in was Paul Manafort and the plain old-fashioned greed that was entirely independent of politics.

A particularly egregious abuse of power and exercise of undue influence is the improper use of one's authority over investigative functions or law enforcement agencies. President Trump seemed to relish suggesting or threatening the criminal investigation and prosecution of contemporary and former government employees. Such actions disregard due process and the traditional independence of the Justice Department.

> @realDonaldTrump
> Pocahontas just stated that the Democrats, lead
> by the legendary Crooked Hillary Clinton, rigged the
> Primaries! **Lets go FBI & Justice.**
> 4:55 AM - Nov 3, 2017

While the president of the United States does have broad powers regarding investigations and means of upholding the law, it is not in the liberal tradition for elected officials to spuriously call for investigations into their political foes. That has historically been a tool favored by autocrats.

> @realDonaldTrump
> **I hereby demand a second investigation, after**
> **Schumer, of Pelosi** for her close ties to Russia, and
> lying about it.
> 1:02 PM - Mar 3, 2017

The framers of the Constitution had a distrust of the king's ability to attack political dissidents, and that fear is reflected in the Fourth Amendment's protections against unreasonable search and seizure.

Trump's Ukraine saga. In late 2019, Representative Adam Schiff (perhaps questionably) provided a dramatic summary of sorts of President Trump's infamous July 2019 phone call with Ukrainian president Zelenskyy. The president then accused Schiff of attempting to pass it off as the actual White House–released readout of the call. Schiff had characterized his summary before reading it, comparing Trump's message to that of "a classic organized crime shakedown." "Shorn of its rambling character and in not so many words, this is the essence of what the president communicates," said Schiff. After summarizing Trump's side of the conversation, Schiff added that the summary was "in sum and character what the president was trying to communicate." It was fairly obvious to those watching the congressional hearing that Schiff was not quoting the actual readout. Nonetheless, his characterization of the more troubling portions of Trump's message to Zelenskyy were fairly accurate.

> @realDonaldTrump
> Rep. Adam Schiff illegally made up a FAKE & terrible statement, pretended it to be mine as the most important part of my call to the Ukrainian President, and read it aloud to Congress and the American people. It bore NO relationship to what I said on the call. **Arrest for Treason?**
> 8:12 AM - Sep 30, 2019

The president may have also believed that abusing his authority in plain view of his subordinates and later releasing a readout of the phone call would excuse the actions for which he would eventually be impeached.

@realDonaldTrump
All the Do Nothing Democrats are focused on is Impeaching the President for having a very good conversation with the Ukrainian President. **I knew that many people were listening, even have a transcript.** They have been at this "stuff" from the day I got elected. Bad for Country!
10:26 AM - Oct 2, 2019

The Ukraine saga provides an example of President Trump using an ostensibly legitimate authority (the implementation of foreign policy) for corrupt purposes. A summary of his abuse of authority was provided by Senator Mitt Romney on the day he and his fellow senators voted on the articles in Trump's first impeachment trial:

> The President asked a foreign government to investigate his political rival. The President withheld vital military funds from that government to press it to do so. The President delayed funds for an American ally at war with Russian invaders. The President's purpose was personal and political. Accordingly, the President is guilty of an appalling abuse of public trust. What he did was not "perfect"—No, it was a flagrant assault on our electoral rights, our national security interests, and our fundamental values. Corrupting an election to keep oneself in office is perhaps the most abusive and destructive violation of one's oath of office that I can imagine.

Though all of Senator Romney's Republican colleagues in the Senate voted to acquit the president on the charge of "abuse of power," many of those same senators nonetheless conceded that Trump had directed American foreign policy for personal political gain. Harvard Law School professor Noah Feldman, who testified in the impeachment hearings, described the president's actions as a corrupt abuse of the power of the presidency. Feldman further noted that the president's conduct embodied the framers' central worry— that a sitting president would "spare no efforts or means whatever to get himself re-elected." The president's scheme also emboldened an adversary (Russia), diminished his government's credibility with allies, and likely undermined American efforts to combat corruption and promote the rule of law.

Attempts to corrupt the Justice Department. Soon after the 2020 election, the head of the DOJ's Civil Division, Jeffrey Clark, drafted a letter for his superiors that was to be sent to the leadership of the Georgia state legislature. Other versions of the letter were intended for other states. The draft letter for Georgia contained knowingly false claims about the election and the Justice Department:

> At this time we have identified significant concerns that may have impacted the outcome of the election in multiple States, including the State of Georgia....
>
> In light of these developments, the Department recommends that the Georgia General Assembly should convene in special session....Time is of the essence, as the U.S. Constitution tasks Congress with convening

in joint session to count Electoral College certificates…
consider objections to any of those certificates, and decide
between any competing slates of elector certificates…on
January 6, 2021, with the Vice President presiding over
the session as President of the Senate.

The intended effect of the letter was to have the Georgia state legislature consider approving a new slate of electors to replace the legitimate electors already representing Joe Biden's win in the state. Clark forwarded the letter to Acting Attorney General Jeffrey Rosen and Acting Deputy Attorney General Richard Donoghue. Both men refused to sign the letter, understanding that it would falsely give the impression that President Trump's election fraud allegations were factual.

On December 27, the president called Rosen. Toward the end of the call, the president told him, "People tell me Jeff Clark is great" and "People want me to replace the DOJ leadership." The installation of Clark as acting attorney general would likely have assured the release of Clark's letter.

In a December 28 email to Clark, Donoghue suggested that the release of Clark's letter would be "a grave step for the Department to take and could have tremendous Constitutional, political and social ramifications for the country." Donoghue understood that it was not the DOJ's role to suggest or dictate how state legislatures select their electors. More importantly, Donoghue knew, based on DOJ investigations conducted since the election, that the letter's premise was contrary to the facts.

On December 31—just three weeks before President Trump was to leave office and only a week before Congress would count the Electoral College votes—senior DOJ leaders met with the president at the White House. Donoghue recalled that the president suggested that the DOJ seize voting machines. Toward the end of the meeting, the president told Rosen and Donoghue that he had been advised to "get rid of" both of them. As he had told the president just days earlier, Donoghue reiterated, "Mr. President, you should have the leadership that you want. But understand, the United States Justice Department functions on facts, evidence, and law, and those are not going to change. So you can have whatever leadership you want, but the department's position is not going to change."

On January 2, Clark informed Rosen that he would turn down the president's offer to install him as acting attorney general if Rosen and Donoghue agreed to sign the Georgia letter. This was essentially the president threatening to fire Rosen if he did not sign the letter that he and Donoghue believed had the potential to spark a constitutional crisis.

On January 3—three days before the attack on the U.S. Capitol—senior DOJ officials, including Rosen, Donoghue, Clark, and Steven Engel, joined President Trump in the Oval Office. By this time, several DOJ leaders (including recently resigned attorney general William Barr) had made clear to the president for weeks that there was no evidence of widespread fraud in the election. At the start of what would become a two-and-a-half-hour meeting, the president told Rosen, "One thing we know is you, Rosen, you aren't going to do anything. You don't even agree with the claims of election fraud, and this other guy [Clark] at least might do something." Rosen responded:

Mr. President, you're right that I'm not going to allow the Justice Department to do anything to try to overturn the election. That's true. But the reason for that is because that's what's consistent with the facts and the law, and that's what's required under the Constitution. So, that's the right answer and a good thing for the country, and therefore I submit it's the right thing for you, Mr. President.

Later in the meeting, the president asked what he had to lose if he were to replace Rosen with Clark. Donoghue told the president that he would resign immediately. The president then turned to Engel and said, "Steve, you wouldn't resign, would you?" Engel assured the president that he would indeed resign, and Donoghue then added that the entire DOJ leadership would resign within hours, with the potential of U.S. attorneys across the country doing the same (resulting in potentially hundreds of resignations). Engel then explained to the president, "The story is not going to be that the Department of Justice has found massive corruption that would have changed the result of the election. It's going to be the disaster of Jeff Clark." Donoghue had earlier explained to the president that Clark was very much unqualified to be attorney general. White House Counsel Pat Cipollone then described the Clark letter as a murder-suicide pact.

By the end of the meeting, the president had been persuaded not to replace Rosen with Clark. Trump's final remarks to Clark suggest that he relented because the plan would not work, and not because it was inappropriate and likely illegal.

I appreciate your willingness to do it. I appreciate you being willing to suffer the abuse. But the reality is, you're not going to get anything done. These guys are going to quit. Everyone else is going to resign. It's going to be a disaster. The bureaucracy will eat you alive. And no matter how much you want to get things done in the next few weeks, you won't be able to get it done, and it's not going to be worth the breakage.

Trump's eventual August 2023 federal indictment revealed (without naming him) that Jeff Clark was an unindicted coconspirator. For his role in the scheme to have the Justice Department transmit a letter with false election fraud claims to multiple states including Georgia, a Georgia grand jury in August 2023 charged Clark with criminal attempt to commit false statements and writings.

Policing abuse of authority. Though public servants are expected to be law abiding and of good character, various mechanisms for policing abuses of authority are clearly necessary. They include forms of oversight authorized by the separation-of-powers doctrine (congressional oversight and investigations), executive department inspector general programs, law enforcement investigations, whistleblower programs, and similar robust avenues for ethical dissent that reward those of honorable character. Outside of government, investigative journalism plays an important role in bringing abuses to light. A robust press also mitigates the risk posed to the careers of public servants who would otherwise independently expose serious wrongdoing. As demonstrated by the principled DOJ leaders in the Jeff Clark / President Trump fiasco, public servants can also appeal to the best interests of superiors on the verge of abusing authority.

A troubling phenomenon is the public leader who does not believe in reasonable and legal oversight, though such oversight (such as congressional requests for information) can sometimes be burdensome for government agencies. When a journalist asked President Trump if he intended to block Ambassador Yovanovitch from testifying during the 2019 congressional impeachment hearings, Trump stated, "You know, I don't think people should be allowed. You have to run a country. I don't think you should be allowed to do that." He may have been loosely alluding to the principle of executive privilege, but his aversion to legitimate oversight was evident. Former acting attorney general Sally Yates summarized President Trump's attempts to undermine the institutions that provide accountability:

> His constant attacks on the FBI, the free press, inspectors general, federal judges—they all have one purpose: to remove any check on his abuse of power. Put simply, he treats our country like it's his family business, this time bankrupting our nation's moral authority at home and abroad. But our country doesn't belong to him. It belongs to all of us.

Exposing institutional corruption becomes even more challenging when employees supporting a corrupt leader wrongly believe that their actions are somehow benefiting the institution.

As a leader in public service, you must maintain a degree of vigilance with respect to the propriety of your actions, those of your subordinates, and even those of your peers and superiors. You must maintain a level of self-awareness that allows you to evaluate if you are using your authority for the legitimate purpose of fulfilling your official responsibilities. Furthermore, your duty to act when confronted with abuses remains whether or not you are in a recognized position of leadership. That is, protecting the integrity of an organization and its mission does not require one to have a particular title. As the expression goes, you lead not with the example of your power but with the power of your example. The citizens you serve are counting on you to properly use your authorities to further their interests.

CHAPTER 30

The Spectrum of
Undue Influence

★ ★ ★

Leadership inherently provides opportunities to influence outcomes related to organizational processes, policy choices, and personnel matters. Consequently, leaders must learn to recognize when improper motives—including their own—might lead to undue influence that yields unwarranted and undesirable outcomes.

Undue influence in the workplace is the use of one's position and authority to inappropriately influence a process, an outcome, or the behavior of another person. Exerting undue influence is often an abuse of authority. On the more benign end of the spectrum of undue influence lies micromanagement. On the opposite end is undue influence that rises to the level of criminality. Between these bookends are preferential and prejudicial treatment, along with a manifestation of inappropriate spheres of influence—impeding specified authority.

Micromanagement and obtrusiveness. Micromanagement is easily recognizable and universally loathed. Supervisors who unnecessarily insert themselves into the work of their subordinates create more than just an annoyance. During my service as an Air Force officer, it was increased responsibility that provided me the greatest motivation. Micromanagement has the opposite effect. It undermines a person's authority and communicates a lack of faith in that person's ability to independently discharge their duties.

There is a difference between routine oversight and micromanagement. Leaders need to understand where that line exists in order to avoid stifling initiative and confidence. When supervising a subordinate who possesses specialized skills, it is reasonable to request more information or explanation because of your relative ignorance (and doing so also conveys an interest in their work). When one truly understands the responsibilities and abilities of one's subordinates, it becomes easier to "stay out of their business."

Obtrusiveness—imposing one's personal ideas, values, or beliefs on someone—is another form of undue influence. Proselytism (pushing one's religious beliefs) in the conduct of one's official duties is inappropriate. In addition to unwelcome pressure, it can create a culture of favoritism and, consequently, resentment. It may be appropriate to share one's personal beliefs in certain settings, but there should never be a perception that adopting or practicing the boss's personal beliefs puts one in better stead. A 2010 survey conducted at the United States Air Force Academy found that 41 percent of non-Christian cadets claimed to have faced unwanted proselytizing. The perpetrators were often superiors who had no official religious function.

In contrast, the U.S. military's chaplain corps attends to the spiritual needs of those practicing a variety of faiths. While military clergy normally minister to those practicing the same religion or belonging to the same denomination, they are sometimes charged with providing spiritual and counseling support irrespective of the recipient's religious beliefs (or lack thereof). This is especially true where a diversity of religious services might be lacking, such as in an overseas deployed location. When providing spiritual comfort to people of other faiths, these chaplains understand that it is not appropriate to proselytize. Similarly, I find it inappropriate when chaplains giving invocations at nonreligious functions (such as promotion ceremonies or sporting events) end their prayers by explicitly invoking the specific name of the deity associated with their particular faith. The concern here is not so much proselytizing as it is inclusiveness. At nonreligious government functions, an invocation should be sufficiently generic to allow for people of all faiths to participate comfortably. One's respect for the beliefs of others can also be a powerful way to unobtrusively communicate the values of one's own faith.

Preferential and prejudicial treatment. Personnel placement, evaluation, advancement, and retention are just a few of the areas in which a supervisor can slip into preferential or prejudicial behaviors. These behaviors can violate the federal civil service's Merit System Principles (MSPs), for example. They may also constitute prohibited personnel practices. Regarding personnel actions, deviations from established processes and procedural norms will result in resentment and an environment where subordinates have little faith in the fairness and objectivity of their leaders. Agencies and individuals who violate related federal laws may be subject to disciplinary action and fines. Research conducted by the U.S. Merit Systems Protection Board suggests that an actual or perceived failure to abide by the MSPs can lead to decreased individual and organizational performance, an increase in Equal Employment Opportunity complaints, and decreased retention.

Public leaders at every level must avoid even the appearance of favoritism. The most senior officers in the military, for example, have enormous influence over the careers of thousands of subordinates and can even influence jurisprudence and criminal investigations. One motive for providing preferential treatment is ego. Some engage in preferential treatment to feed a psychological and emotional need to feel more powerful, useful, and appreciated. While these motivations may also manifest themselves in the various contexts of our personal lives, they should be quashed in the workplace lest they result in undue influence.

Prejudicial treatment—treating subordinates unfairly, as defined by agency guidelines—is also a form of undue influence and an abuse of authority. Motives may include personal animus (expressed as reprisal) and bias unrelated to a person's actual performance or conduct. Excessive deference, or what is sometimes referred to in the military as "different spanks for different ranks," is another such manifestation that arguably involves both preferential and prejudicial treatment. Leaders must be conscious of their own biases as well as existing institutional biases to ensure that subordinates are treated fairly.

The sentencing of Roger Stone. President Trump's longtime friend and confidant Roger Stone was found guilty by a jury of his peers of obstructing a congressional investigation, making false statements to Congress, and witness tampering. The presiding judge in Stone's case emphasized that his obstructive crimes were committed as a means of covering up for President Trump. DOJ prosecutors in the case initially recommended a sentence of roughly seven to nine years. What followed was undue and preferential intervention by the president and DOJ leaders. The assistant U.S. attorney in the case, Aaron Zelinsky, stated in his testimony to Congress that during his career, he had "never seen political influence play any role in prosecutorial decision-making. With one exception: *United States v. Roger Stone.*" Zelinsky described how DOJ officials had exerted significant pressure on line prosecutors to ignore appropriate sentencing guidelines, in the process "distort[ing] the events that transpired in his trial and the criminal conduct that gave rise to his conviction." He had heard repeatedly from colleagues that Stone was being treated differently from any other defendant because of his relationship to the president and because the U.S. attorney handling the case was "afraid of the President."

Rather than succumbing to what he felt was the result of "wrongful political pressure," and in order not to undermine fundamental DOJ principles, Zelinsky and his three colleagues withdrew from the case. Continuing a pattern of interfering in the criminal investigations of political allies and foes, President Trump wasted no time in publicly weighing in on the original sentencing recommendation.

@realDonaldTrump

This is a horrible and very unfair situation. The real crimes were on the other side, as nothing happens to them. Cannot allow this miscarriage of justice!

1:48 AM - Feb 11, 2020

Later that same day, the DOJ filed a memorandum seeking a substantially lower sentence. The new filing resembled the president's "horrible and very unfair" characterization, describing the original sentence as "excessive and unwarranted."

@realDonaldTrump

Who are the four prosecutors (Mueller people?) who cut and ran after being exposed for recommending a ridiculous 9 year prison sentence to a man that got caught up in an investigation that was illegal, the Mueller Scam, and shouldn't ever even have started? 13 Angry Democrats?

9:45 PM - Feb 11, 2020

@realDonaldTrump

Two months in jail for a Swamp Creature, yet 9 years recommended for Roger Stone (who was not even working for the Trump Campaign). Gee, that sounds very fair! Rogue prosecutors maybe? The Swamp! @ foxandfriends @TuckerCarlson

7:06 AM - Feb 12, 2020

President Trump publicly recognized his attorney general's intervention while leveling unfounded accusations about a decorated veteran and distinguished career public servant, former FBI director Robert Mueller, whose reputation for integrity is widely recognized on both sides of the political divide.

> @realDonaldTrump
> Congratulations to Attorney General Bill Barr for taking charge of a case that was totally out of control and perhaps should not have even been brought. Evidence now clearly shows that the Mueller Scam was improperly brought & tainted. Even Bob Mueller lied to Congress!
> 6:53 AM - Feb 12, 2020

The judge presiding over Stone's trial and sentencing determined that the "government's initial memorandum was well researched and supported. It was true to the record. It was in accordance with the law and with DOJ policy, and it was submitted with the same level of evenhanded judgment and professionalism they exhibited throughout the trial." The judge also commented on the inappropriate nature of the president's public statements:

> This case also exemplifies why it is that this system, for good reason, demands that the responsibility falls to someone neutral. Someone whose job may involve issuing opinions in favor of and against the same administration in the same week, and not someone who has a longstanding friendship with the defendant. Not someone whose political career was aided by the defendant. And surely not someone who has personal involvement in the events underlying the case.

The Court cannot be influenced by those comments. They were entirely inappropriate, but I will not hold them against the defendant either.

Stone received a reduced sentence of forty months in prison. A letter signed by over 2,600 former DOJ officials condemned what they deemed "interference in the fair administration of justice" by Attorney General William Barr. They explained that the rule of law depends on the evenhanded administration of justice and that the department's legal decisions must be "impartial and insulated from political influence." They defended the actions of the prosecutors who "stood up for the Department's independence by withdrawing from the Stone case and/or resigning from the Department." They called on all current DOJ officials to report future abuses to the inspector general and other watchdog agencies and to refuse to carry out directives that are inconsistent with their oaths of office. The former DOJ officials also called for the other branches of government to "protect from retaliation those employees who uphold their oaths in the face of unlawful directives."

President Trump commuted Stone's sentence in July 2020, just days before he was to report to prison. A related White House statement referred to an "unjust sentence" and painted Stone as a "victim of the Russia Hoax." It also suggested that Stone would have not been facing time in prison had it not been for the "absolutely baseless" Special Counsel investigation (authorized by Trump's own DOJ). More accurately, Stone would not have been facing prison time if he had not committed and been convicted of several crimes. A November 2020 Senate report would later describe how the 2016 Trump campaign—through Roger Stone—sought to obtain advance information on the WikiLeaks release of emails stolen by Russian hackers for the purpose of compromising Hillary Clinton's presidential bid. This episode of undue influence concluded with President Trump's pardon of Stone in December 2020.

Impeding specified authority. Some authorities are intentionally delegated to distinct functions or persons for a variety of reasons, including relevant expertise and operational necessity. Inappropriate interference in delegated specified authorities can result in outcomes ranging from undesirable to catastrophic.

One such example involves the intentional limits placed on military commanders during the course of an Air Force mishap investigation. The Safety Investigation Board aims to prevent future mishaps by determining causal factors and implementing associated recommendations. While determining causal factors, the SIB is shielded from command influence that may be motivated by a desire to spare certain leaders embarrassment. The specified authorities that give the SIB its independence promote a more objective report, one more likely to prevent similar mishaps.

There were numerous instances in which President Trump chose not to respect the specified authorities of individuals or agencies within the executive branch or, in some cases, another branch of government. The following passage from the *Trump-Ukraine Impeachment Inquiry Report* characterizes the president's obstructive acts and his incursion on congressional authorities:

> In so doing, and despite the fact that the Constitution vests in the House of Representatives the "sole Power of Impeachment," the President sought to arrogate

to himself the right to determine the propriety, scope, and nature of an impeachment inquiry into his own misconduct, and the right to deny any and all information to the Congress in the conduct of its constitutional responsibilities.

President Trump had a habit of intentionally using "acting" inspectors general in executive branch departments in lieu of full-fledged IGs who were constitutionally vetted by Congress. This practice allowed the president to terminate IGs without providing the normally required notification and justification to Congress. It also facilitated Trump's inappropriate influence over these traditionally independent and nonpartisan officials who are normally primarily accountable to their executive branch agency heads and to Congress.

Respecting specified authority—examples from military aviation. As alluded to in an earlier chapter, aircraft commander authority in the military is delegated in such a way that the aircraft commander's discretion, with very few exceptions, is final. The fact that another member of the crew or a passenger is senior in rank is immaterial when one is designated on the flight orders as the aircraft commander. Roughly speaking, the senior officer may be in charge on the ground, but not in flight. Aircraft commander authority promotes safe mission accomplishment through clearly defined responsibilities, accountability, and singular decision-making. Consequently, it is problematic when that authority is challenged (crewmembers are expected to provide input, however, especially where safety is concerned).

While flying helicopters in metro Washington, D.C., I

occasionally provided flight instruction to general officers whose experience had been largely or entirely limited to fixed-wing aircraft. To their credit, these generals clearly understood that the instructor was in command of those flights. Similarly, while serving as my copilot on a distinguished visitor (DV, a.k.a. VIP) transport mission across metro Tokyo, my squadron commander began proposing a new course of action. I took his suggestion as routine crew input, and yet he immediately and with humility acknowledged that his suggestion might have been interpreted as an order that could potentially challenge my authority. I assured him that I had not taken his suggestion that way.

Criminal influence. As mentioned earlier, undue influence occasionally rises to the level of unlawful or potentially unlawful acts. Volume 2 of the voluminous Mueller report cites ten separate instances of likely obstruction of justice committed by Donald Trump and his colleagues during his time as presidential candidate, president-elect, and, finally, president. Not all of the instances of obstruction (during his time as president) involved the use of his constitutionally given authorities. Nonetheless, the conduct would be equally improper whether "effectuated through direct efforts to produce false testimony or suppress the truth, or through actual, threatened, or promised use of official powers to achieve the same result." As further described in the report, there were several factors that affected the obstruction analysis in this investigation:

> The President's position as the head of the Executive
> Branch provided him with unique and powerful means
> of influencing official proceedings, subordinate officers,

and potential witnesses—all of which is relevant to a potential obstruction-of-justice analysis....Unlike cases in which a subject engages in obstruction of justice to cover up a crime, the evidence we obtained did not establish that the President was involved in an underlying crime related to Russian election interference. Although the obstruction statutes do not require proof of such a crime, the absence of that evidence affects the analysis of the President's intent and requires consideration of other possible motives for his conduct.... Obstruction of justice can be motivated by a desire to protect non-criminal personal interests, to protect against investigations where underlying criminal liability falls into a gray area, or to avoid personal embarrassment. The injury to the integrity of the justice system is the same regardless of whether a person committed an underlying wrong.

The following summarizes President Trump's obstructive acts:

Our investigation found multiple acts by the President that were capable of exerting undue influence over law enforcement investigations, including the Russian-interference and obstruction investigations. The incidents were often carried out through one-on-one meetings in which the President sought to use his official power outside of usual channels. These actions ranged from efforts to remove the Special Counsel and to reverse the effect of the Attorney General's recusal; to the attempted use of official power to limit the scope of the investigation; to direct and indirect contacts with witnesses with the potential to influence their testimony.

The report also speculated on the president's possible personal motives:

These include concerns that continued investigation would call into question the legitimacy of his election and potential uncertainty about whether certain events—such as advance notice of WikiLeaks's release of hacked information or the June 9, 2016 meeting between senior campaign officials and Russians—could be seen as criminal activity by the President, his campaign, or his family.

The President also engaged in public attacks on the investigation, often referring to it as a hoax while personally attacking Special Counsel Robert Mueller. He publicly attacked potential witnesses who could offer adverse information and praised those seemingly not willing to cooperate. Those actions potentially constitute two types of obstructive crimes: witness intimidation and the dangling of pardons. The Mueller report described in detail how "the President's conduct towards Michael Cohen, a former Trump Organization executive, changed from praise for Cohen when he falsely minimized the President's involvement in the Trump Tower Moscow project, to castigation of Cohen when he became a cooperating witness."

@realDonaldTrump

"Michael Cohen asks judge for no Prison Time." You mean he can do all of the **TERRIBLE, unrelated to Trump, things** having to do with fraud, big loans, Taxis, etc., and not serve a long prison term? He makes up stories to get a GREAT & ALREADY reduced deal for himself, and get.....

7:24 AM - Dec 3, 2018

....his wife and father-in-law (who has the money?) off Scott Free. He lied for this outcome and should, in my opinion, serve a full and complete sentence.

7:29 AM - Dec 3, 2018

What the president failed to mention in the previous post, which was likely intended to dissuade other "rats" (as he publicly referred to Cohen) from cooperating with the government, is the "terrible" things Cohen did that were in fact related to Trump (and resulted in Trump's 2023 indictment by a Manhattan grand jury along with his 2024 conviction).

The Mueller report also provided evidence that "the President's effort to have [Attorney General] Sessions limit the scope of the Special Counsel's investigation to future election interference was intended to prevent further investigative scrutiny of the President's and his campaign's conduct." Trump also wanted the scope limited because of "reports that the President was being investigated for potential obstruction of justice." Mueller's investigators inferred that the president also "believed that an unrecused Attorney General would play a protective role and could shield the President from the ongoing Russia investigation." The report went on to state that "the President's efforts to influence the investigation were mostly unsuccessful, but that is largely because the persons who surrounded the President declined to carry out orders or accede to his requests." Though DOJ policy prevents federal prosecutors from indicting a sitting president, over one thousand former federal prosecutors signed a letter stating that President Trump's actions, as described in the Mueller report, would have otherwise resulted in multiple felony charges for obstruction of justice.

Only nine months later, the subsequent *Trump-Ukraine Impeachment Inquiry Report* described incidents of witness intimidation related to Congressional testimony:

> President Trump engaged in a brazen effort to publicly attack and intimidate witnesses who came forward to comply with duly authorized subpoenas and testify about his conduct, raising grave concerns about potential violations of the federal obstruction statute and other criminal laws intended to protect witnesses appearing before Congressional proceedings. President Trump issued threats, openly discussed possible retaliation, made insinuations about witnesses' character and patriotism, and subjected them to mockery and derision. The President's attacks were broadcast to millions of Americans—including witnesses' families, friends, and coworkers—and his actions drew criticism from across the political spectrum, including from his own Republican supporters.

It is a federal crime to intimidate or seek to intimidate any witness appearing before Congress. This statute applies to all citizens, including federal officials. Violations of this law can carry a criminal sentence of up to 20 years in prison.

This campaign of intimidation risks discouraging witnesses from coming forward voluntarily, complying with mandatory subpoenas for documents and testimony, and disclosing evidence that may support consideration of articles of impeachment.

As previously detailed in chapter 12, the president threatened and intimidated prospective and actual witnesses in an effort to "prevent, delay, or influence the testimony of those witnesses." He occasionally did so via Twitter.

> @realDonaldTrump
> Where's the Whistleblower?
> 8:40 AM - Oct 23, 2019

> @realDonaldTrump
> The Whistleblower must come forward to explain
> why his account of the phone call with the Ukrainian
> President was so inaccurate (fraudulent?).
> Why did the Whistleblower deal with corrupt
> politician Shifty Adam Schiff and/
> or his committee?
> 7:16 PM - Nov 1, 2019

In building the case for President Trump's first (Ukraine-related) impeachment, the report makes clear that the president cannot act with the corrupt intent of shielding himself from criminal punishment, avoiding financial liability, or preventing personal embarrassment. The law must be applied equally. What makes all of the aforementioned likely acts of obstruction perhaps more unique is their public nature, and how some have suggested the acts are consequently more benign. Mueller addressed that idea in his Russia investigation report:

> While it may be more difficult to establish that public-facing acts were motivated by a corrupt intent, the President's power to influence actions, persons, and events is enhanced by his unique ability to attract attention through use of mass communications. And no principle of law excludes public acts from the scope of obstruction statutes. If the likely effect of the acts is to intimidate witnesses or alter their testimony, the justice system's integrity is equally threatened.

Abusing executive clemency—dangling pardons. In the wake of a series of pardons issued by President Trump during his final weeks in office, presidential historian Michael Beschloss made the following observation:

> The founders really let us down. They added this pardon power. The idea was that a president would give pardons to the people for reasons of mercy or maybe to correct a mistake in the judicial process. What they didn't protect us against was something that one delegate to

the Constitutional Convention, George Mason, worried about—which was, what if you have a president who pardons people who may be involved in crimes that the president is involved in?

President Trump did not pardon all of those convicted as a result of the Mueller probe. He pardoned only the five former associates and subordinates who had refused to cooperate and who lied to obstruct the investigation. Regarding George Mason's concerns, Trump's pardons might have served as dangerous precedents for future presidents seeking to avoid legal exposure by dangling and eventually granting pardons. Unfortunately, however, the July 2024 Supreme Court decision on presidential immunity all but assured that presidents can use their pardon powers corruptly and with impunity.

Michael Flynn. In late 2017, Flynn pleaded guilty to providing false statements to the FBI about his interactions with Russian ambassador Kislyak and to providing false information and omissions on his registration with the DOJ regarding his work on behalf of Turkey. His dishonesty was especially concerning because as U.S. national security advisor, he was effectively compromised given that the Russians were aware of the substance of his conversations with their chief diplomat in Washington, D.C.

@realDonaldTrump

I had to fire General Flynn because he lied to the Vice President and the FBI. He has pled guilty to those lies. It is a shame because his actions during the transition were lawful. There was nothing to hide!

9:14 AM - Dec 2, 2017

The Mueller report provided insights into how the president handled Flynn's firing.

> On February 13, 2017, [White House Chief of Staff Reince] Priebus told Flynn he had to resign. Flynn said he wanted to say goodbye to the President, so Priebus brought him to the Oval Office. Priebus recalled that the President hugged Flynn, shook his hand, and said, "We'll give you a good recommendation. You're a good guy. We'll take care of you."

The report also showed how in a separate meeting, President Trump attempted to influence the FBI's handling of the Flynn case:

> According to Comey's account of the meeting, once they were alone, the President began the conversation by saying, "I want to talk about Mike Flynn." The President stated that Flynn had not done anything wrong in speaking with the Russians, but had to be terminated because he had misled the Vice President. The conversation turned to the topic of leaks of classified information, but the President returned to Flynn, saying, "he is a good guy and has been through a lot." The President stated, "I hope you can see your way clear to letting this go, to letting Flynn go. He is a good guy. I hope you can let this go." Comey agreed that Flynn "is a good guy," but did not commit to ending the investigation of Flynn. Comey testified under oath that he took the President's statement "as a direction" because of the President's position

and the circumstances of the one-on-one meeting.

The president's support for Flynn continued long after he had pleaded guilty.

> @realDonaldTrump
>
> What happened to General Michael Flynn, a war hero, should never be allowed to happen to a citizen of the United States again!
>
> 7:47 AM - Apr 30, 2020

By the spring of 2020, Flynn was still awaiting sentencing. He had initially been cooperating with the government's Russia investigation but then took a more combative approach after replacing his legal team. In early May 2020, Attorney General William Barr's DOJ filed a motion to have Flynn's case dismissed.

> @realDonaldTrump
>
> Yesterday was a BIG day for Justice in the USA. Congratulations to General Flynn, and many others. I do believe there is MUCH more to come! Dirty Cops and Crooked Politicians do not go well together!
>
> 7:18 AM - May 8, 2020

Barr denied that he was doing the president's bidding and stated that the FBI "did not have a basis for a counterintelligence investigation against Flynn" when they interviewed Flynn in 2017. He was suggesting that Flynn's lies were not materially relevant to the Russia election interference investigation, an argument that presiding judge

Emmet Sullivan characterized as a "newly minted definition of materiality." Dropping the charges against someone who had already twice pleaded guilty was essentially unheard of and pointed to favoritism and politization of the DOJ. Within three days, nearly two thousand former DOJ and FBI officials—including someone who had briefly served as acting attorney general—signed an open letter highly critical of Barr's decision. Meanwhile, the president's public support of Flynn persisted.

@realDonaldTrump
Be sure to watch, "Witch Hunt, the Flynn Vindication" hosted by the very knowledgeable @GreggJarrett on@ FoxNews tonight at 8:00 P.M. This is yet another part of the greatest Criminal Hoax in American History!
6:51 PM - May 24, 2020

@realDonaldTrump
Great! Appeals Court Upholds Justice Department's Request To Drop Criminal Case Against General Michael Flynn!
10:40 AM - Jun 24, 2020

@realDonaldTrump
Is James Comey and his band of Dirty Cops going to apologize to General Michael Flynn (and many others) for what they have done to ruin his life? What about Robert Mueller and his Angry Democrat Cronies - Are they going to say, SO SORRY? And what about Obama & Biden?
12:58 PM - Jun 24, 2020

As the legal controversy continued to play out in the courts, Judge Sullivan requested that another judge review the DOJ's motion to dismiss Flynn's case. Retired judge John Gleeson's eighty-two-page amicus brief was not kind to Barr's DOJ:

> The Department of Justice has a solemn responsibility to prosecute this case—like every other case—without fear or favor and, to quote the Department's motto, solely "on behalf of justice." It has abdicated that responsibility through a gross abuse of prosecutorial power, attempting to provide special treatment to a favored friend and political ally of the President of the United States…and in doing so has undermined the public's confidence in the rule of law.

Trump's attempts to unduly influence the Flynn case had seemingly morphed into inappropriate and perhaps unprecedented institutional intervention on Flynn's behalf.

In late November 2020, President Trump pardoned a Thanksgiving turkey named Corn. He also pardoned Michael Flynn. The former did not need a pardon, and the latter was not deserving of one.

> @realDonaldTrump
> It is my Great Honor to announce that General Michael T. Flynn has been granted a Full Pardon. Congratulations to @GenFlynn and his wonderful family, I know you will now have a truly fantastic Thanksgiving!
> 4:08 PM - Nov 25, 2020

@realDonaldTrump
Have a great life General Flynn!
7:34 PM - Nov 25, 2020

A related statement from the Trump White House suggested that Flynn did not require a pardon and that the original prosecution was "an injustice against an innocent man." Ironically, it went on to state that "it should also serve as a reminder to all of us that we must remain vigilant over those in whom we place our trust and confidence." When Judge Sullivan finally dropped the charges following the pardon, he also reminded the public that acceptance of a pardon implies an admission of guilt.

Two years later, while being deposed by the House committee investigating the January 6, 2021, attack on the U.S. Capitol, Michael Flynn was asked if he believed "in the peaceful transition of power in the United States of America." Flynn had urged President Trump to declare martial law and seize voting machines after the 2020 election. Consistent with most of the answers he gave that day, Flynn invoked his Fifth Amendment privilege to avoid self-incrimination.

Paul Manafort. The Mueller investigation concluded that evidence supported the inference that President Trump "intended Manafort to believe that he could receive a pardon, which would make cooperation with the government as a means of obtaining a lesser sentence unnecessary." The report detailed some of Trump's public support for his former campaign manager, as demonstrated in the following statement:

I think the whole Manafort trial is very sad when you

WHAT HANGS IN THE BALANCE

look at what's going on there. I think it's a very sad day for our country. He worked for me for a very short period of time. But you know what, he happens to be a very good person. And I think it's very sad what they've done to Paul Manafort.

The investigation also shed light on Trump's consideration of a pardon prior to Manafort's conviction.

> [Rudy] Giuliani told the Washington Post that the President had asked his lawyers for advice on the possibility of a pardon for Manafort and other aides, and had been counseled against considering a pardon until the investigation concluded....In response to a question about whether he was considering a pardon for Manafort, the President said, "I have great respect for what he's done, in terms of what he's gone through..."

The president continued to show his support prior to Manafort's conviction by opining on the sentence Manafort would likely receive.

> @realDonaldTrump
> Wow, what a tough sentence for Paul Manafort, who has represented Ronald Reagan, Bob Dole and many other top political people and campaigns. Didn't know Manafort was the head of the Mob. What about Comey and Crooked Hillary and all of the others? Very unfair!
> 10:41 AM - Jun 15, 2018

Manafort was eventually convicted on five counts of tax fraud, two counts of bank fraud, and one count of failure to file a report of foreign bank and financial accounts. In the following post, the president incorrectly characterized the timing of Manafort's crimes, which were still ongoing at the time of prosecution.

> @realDonaldTrump
> I feel very badly for Paul Manafort and his wonderful family. "Justice" took a 12 year old tax case, among other things, applied tremendous pressure on him and, unlike Michael Cohen, he refused to "break" - make up stories in order to get a "deal." Such respect for a brave man!
> 6:21 AM - Aug 22, 2018

When the president finally officially pardoned Manafort in December 2020, the White House predictably released a statement suggesting that Manafort had endured years of unfair treatment and, despite his crimes, had been the victim of "perhaps the greatest witch hunt in American history."

President Trump granted well over one hundred pardons and commutations in the final weeks of his presidency. The beneficiaries of pardons included Steve Bannon, who had served in the capacities of CEO of Trump's 2016 campaign and White House chief strategist. Bannon was charged with conspiracy to commit mail fraud in an alleged scheme to defraud donors in a border wall fundraising campaign (he would in 2022 be convicted of two counts of contempt of Congress for failing to comply with a subpoena related to the January 6 investigation). The president pardoned Charles

Kushner, the father of Trump's son-in-law. He also pardoned four ex-military Blackwater contractors found guilty of perpetrating the 2007 Nisour Square massacre in Baghdad in which seventeen Iraqi civilians were killed. The president's pardons also included two former Republican congressmen considered loyalists—Duncan Hunter (R-CA) and Christopher Collins (R-NY). Their crimes included stealing and misusing campaign funds and conspiracy to commit securities fraud (insider trading), respectively. Receiving a commuted sentence was Philip Esformes, found guilty in the largest health-care fraud scheme ever charged by the DOJ ($1.3 billion in fraudulent Medicare claims).

CHAPTER 31

Undue Influence in the 2020 Election

★ ★ ★

President Trump's attempts to reverse the outcome of the 2020 presidential election covered the spectrum of undue influence: exerting influence outside of one's lane, impeding specified authority, and engaging in what was likely criminal behavior. He applied pressure at every level of government—from local election workers all the way up to the vice president.

The president repeatedly asked DOJ leadership to endorse his discredited claims that the election had been stolen and pressured them to assist his efforts to overturn the election results. As reported in the October 2021 Senate Judiciary Committee report on Trump's DOJ pressure campaign, "White House Chief of Staff Mark Meadows asked Acting Attorney General Rosen to initiate election fraud investigations on multiple occasions, violating long-standing restrictions on White House-DOJ communications about specific law-enforcement matters." During a December 27, 2020, phone call, President Trump said the following to Acting Attorney

General Rosen and Acting Deputy Attorney General Donoghue: "Just say the election was corrupt and leave the rest to me and the Republican Congressmen." As described in chapter 29, President Trump also considered replacing Rosen with someone more inclined to pressure lawmakers in several states into overturning their states' election results.

Though President Trump's second impeachment dealt primarily with his incitement of the attack on the Capitol, the sole impeachment article also cited his "prior efforts to subvert and obstruct certification of the results of the 2020 Presidential election." Those prior efforts included exerting pressure on Republican elected officials in Pennsylvania, Arizona, Michigan, and Georgia to overturn their election results and commit what would have likely been fraud. In Arizona, the president and Rudy Giuliani pressured Republican State House Speaker Russell "Rusty" Bowers during a phone call to consider using the legislature to replace electors for Biden with an alternate (illegitimate) slate of electors for President Trump (as detailed in the congressional report on the January 6 attack on the Capitol):

> Bowers explained to Giuliani: "You are asking me to do something against my oath, and I will not break my oath."
>
> President Trump and his supporters' intimidation tactics affected Bowers, too. Bowers' personal cell phone and home address were doxed, leading demonstrators to show up at his home and shout insults until police arrived. One protestor who showed up at his home was armed and believed to be a member of an

extremist militia. Another hired a truck with a defamatory and profane allegation that Bowers, a deeply religious man, was a pedophile, and drove it through Bowers' neighborhood.

During a second call from Trump to Bowers about appointing fraudulent electors, the latter said to the president, "I voted for you. I worked for you. I campaigned for you. I just won't do anything illegal for you."

Similar pressure was put on Michigan's Republican leaders:

President Trump focused on Republican Senate Majority Leader Mike Shirkey and Republican House Speaker Lee Chatfield. He invited them to the White House for a November 20, 2020, meeting during which President Trump and [Rudy] Giuliani, who joined by phone, went through a "litany" of false allegations about supposed fraud in Michigan's election. Chatfield recalled President Trump's more generic directive for the group to "have some backbone and do the right thing," which he understood to mean overturning the election by naming Michigan's Electoral College electors for President Trump. Shirkey told President Trump that he wouldn't do anything that would violate Michigan law, and after the meeting ended, issued a joint statement with Chatfield: "We have not yet been made aware of any information that would change the outcome of the election in Michigan and as legislative leaders, we will follow the law and follow the normal process regarding

Michigan's electors, just as we have said throughout this election."

When President Trump couldn't convince Shirkey and Chatfield to change the outcome of the election in Michigan during that meeting or in calls after, he or his team maliciously tweeted out Shirkey's personal cell phone number and a number for Chatfield that turned out to be wrong. Shirkey received nearly 4,000 text messages after that, and another private citizen reported being inundated with calls and texts intended for Chatfield.

In a November 17 phone call, President Trump and Republican National Committee chairwoman Ronna McDaniel urged two Republican members of the Wayne County Board of Canvassers not to certify the approximately 878,000 votes cast in their county.

In Georgia, the president focused his pressure campaign on Governor Brian Kemp, Speaker of the House of Representatives David Ralston, and Secretary of State Brad Raffensperger. He phoned both Kemp and Ralston in early December to request that they call a special session of the Georgia General Assembly for the purpose of appointing "alternate" slates of electors. On December 8, Trump phoned Raffensperger to pressure him to support an election lawsuit filed by another state's attorney general. Raffensperger told Trump that investigations of alleged election fraud in Georgia had not produced evidence to support those claims.

@realDonaldTrump

What a fool Governor @BrianKempGA of Georgia is. Could have been so easy, but now we have to do it the hard way. Demand this clown call a Special Session and open up signature verification, NOW. Otherwise, could be a bad day for two GREAT Senators on January 5th.

12:03 AM - Dec 14, 2020

@realDonaldTrump

I love the Great State of Georgia, but the people who run it, from the Governor, @BrianKempGA, to the Secretary of State, are a complete disaster and don't have a clue, or worse. Nobody can be this stupid. Just allow us to find the crime, and turn the state Republican....

11:44 PM - Dec 29, 2020

@realDonaldTrump

Hearings from Atlanta on the Georgia Election over-turn now being broadcast. Check it out. @OANN @ newsmax and many more. @BrianKempGA should resign from office. He is an obstructionist who refuses to admit that we won Georgia, BIG! Also won the other Swing States.

9:26 AM - Dec 30, 2020

President Trump's efforts in Georgia also included his January 2, 2021, hour-long phone call to Raffensperger and his staff. During the call, the president urged Raffensperger to "find" enough votes to overturn the presidential election results, indirectly threatening legal consequences if he failed to do so. After Trump subjected the secretary of state to a litany of bogus election fraud claims, Raffensperger detailed the extent to which his office had already entertained all the points of contention raised by various state and national lawmakers. He further explained that a hand re-tally of the ballots matched the original machine count. The president was defiant, explaining that he had probably won by "half a million" votes. "Well Mr. President," Raffensperger responded, "the challenge that you have is, the data you have is wrong." Raffensperger and his general counsel then refuted some of the president's specific claims. As the president persisted with various election fraud conspiracy theories, the following exchange occurred:

> *Raffensperger:* We believe that we do have an accurate election.

> *Trump:* No, no you don't. You don't have. Not even close. You're off by hundreds of thousands of votes....And you are going to find that they are—which is totally illegal, it is more illegal for you than it is for them because, you know what they did and you're not reporting it. That's a criminal, that's a criminal offense. And you can't let that happen. That's a big risk to you and to Ryan [Germany], your lawyer. And that's a big risk....So look. All I want to do is this. I just want to find 11,780 votes, which is one more than we have because we won the state....Oh, I don't know, look Brad...I have to find 12,000 votes and I have them times a lot. And therefore, I won the

state....So what are we going to do here folks? I only
need 11,000 votes. Fellas, I need 11,000 votes. Give me
a break.

Raffensperger's general counsel then assured Trump that the
Georgia election numbers were accurate. Trump responded in part,
"But, I'm just curious why wouldn't, why do you keep fighting this
thing? It just doesn't make sense....So tell me, Brad, what are we
going to do? We won the election and it's not fair to take it away
from us like this. And it's going to be very costly in many ways."
As Georgia's secretary of state again insisted that he had to stand by
the official vote tally that he and his staff believed to be correct, the
president once again objected:

> Why do you say that? I don't know. I mean, sure, we
> can play this game with the courts, but why do you
> say that?...You just say, you stick by, I mean I've been
> watching you, you know. You don't care about anything.
> "Your numbers are right." But your numbers aren't right.
> They're really wrong, and they're really wrong, Brad. And
> I know this phone call is going nowhere other than—
> other than ultimately, you know—Look, ultimately I
> win, okay? Because you guys are so wrong.

As the call wound down, President Trump continued to threaten
Raffensperger and his staff:

> Well, under the law you're not allowed to give faulty
> election results, okay? You're not allowed to do that.

And that's what you've done. This is a faulty election result....You have a big election coming up on Tuesday [U.S. Senate run-off]. And therefore, I think that it really is important that you meet tomorrow and work out on these numbers. Because I know, Brad, that if you think we're right, I think you're going to say, and I'm not looking to blame anybody. I'm just saying you know, and, you know, under new counts, and under uh, new views, of the election results, we won the election.

@realDonaldTrump
I spoke to Secretary of State Brad Raffensperger yesterday about Fulton County and voter fraud in Georgia. He was unwilling, or unable, to answer questions such as the "ballots under table" scam, ballot destruction, out of state "voters", dead voters, and more. He has no clue!
8:57 AM · Jan 3, 2021

Raffensperger had indeed addressed Trump's claims regarding the alleged shredding of "3,000 pounds of ballots." As for the alleged "ballots under table" scam, Atlanta's top federal prosecutor—U.S. Attorney Byung Jin Pak—had already investigated the allegation at Attorney General Barr's request and found nothing suspicious. DOJ officials had already made the president aware of these findings. Trump forced Pak's resignation and publicly accused him of being a "Never Trumper."

During his January 6 speech at the Ellipse, the president continued to disparage Georgia's elected officials:

In Georgia, your secretary of state who—I can't believe this guy's a Republican. He loves recording telephone conversations....I thought it was a great conversation personally....People love that conversation because it says what's going on. These people are crooked. They're 100 percent, in my opinion, one of the most corrupt, between your governor and your secretary of state.

When Raffensperger was later asked why he didn't just quit and walk away after receiving a flood of threats and after his daughter-in-law's house was broken into, he provided the following answer:

Because I knew that we had followed the law, we had followed the Constitution. And I think sometimes moments require you to stand up and just take the shots. You're doing your job. And that's all we did. We just followed the law, and we followed the Constitution, and at the end of the day, President Trump came up short. But I had to be faithful to the Constitution. And that's what I swore an oath to do.

A special purpose grand jury was impaneled from May to December 2022 in Fulton County to investigate the facts and circumstances related to possible attempts to disrupt the lawful administration of the 2020 presidential election in the state of Georgia. The grand jury heard extensive testimony on the subject of alleged fraud, including from persons claiming that such fraud took place. It found unanimously that no widespread fraud took place that could result in overturning the election.

In August 2023, a Georgia grand jury charged former president Trump; his chief of staff, Mark Meadows; and seventeen others, including Jeffrey Clark, Rudy Giuliani, Sidney Powell, Jenna Ellis, and John Eastman, with racketeering and a host of other crimes related to their conspiracy to overturn Georgia's presidential election and for the fake elector scheme more broadly. In response to the indictment, Raffensperger stated that "the most basic principles of a strong democracy are accountability and respect for the Constitution and rule of law. You either have it, or you don't."

Pressuring Vice President Pence. The vice president had already endured a days-long pressure campaign as he prepared to preside over the largely ceremonial role of counting Electoral College votes in the January 6 joint session of Congress. The president and his loyalists saw Pence as their last hope for overturning the election. When Pence phoned the president on December 25 to wish him a merry Christmas, the president requested that he reject the electoral votes on January 6. In response, Pence once again told him, "You know I don't think I have the authority to change the outcome." On January 1, the president berated Pence over the phone for opposing a lawsuit seeking to give Pence the authority to reject or return electoral votes. The vice president again told his boss that "there was no constitutional basis for such authority and that it was improper." Trump replied to Pence, "You're too honest." Two days later, the president again insisted to Pence that he had the absolute right to reject electoral votes and the ability to overturn the election. Pence reminded Trump that a federal appeals court had rejected the aforementioned lawsuit the previous day.

On January 4, Pence was summoned to the Oval Office, where

President Trump and John Eastman tried to convince him that he could either reject slates of electors from seven targeted states won by Joe Biden or send the certified electoral votes back to state legislatures for further deliberation. Neither option would have been legal. During a rally that evening in Dalton, Georgia, President Trump sought to increase public pressure on Pence by telling the crowd, "I hope Mike Pence comes through for us."

> @realDonaldTrump
> The Vice President has the power to reject fraudu-
> lently chosen electors.
> 11:06 AM · Jan 5, 2021

On January 5, the president again demanded to see Pence. They met alone, without staff present. When Pence once again refused to obstruct the upcoming certification, the president told him that he would have to publicly criticize him. Concerned for Pence's safety, Pence's chief of staff alerted the head of the vice president's Secret Service detail. That evening, the president disingenuously issued a statement stating that he and the vice president were "in total agreement that the Vice President has the power to act." The president's statement also made the following incorrect assertions:

> Our Vice President has several options under the U.S. Constitution. He can decertify the results or send them back to the states for change and certification. He can also decertify the illegal and corrupt results and send them to the House of Representatives for the one vote for one state tabulation.

On January 6, the president's pressure on Pence began long before daybreak.

> **@realDonaldTrump**
>
> **If Vice President @Mike_Pence comes through for us,** we will win the Presidency. Many States want to decertify the mistake they made in certifying incorrect & even fraudulent numbers in a process NOT approved by their State Legislatures (which it must be). **Mike can send it back!**
>
> 1:00 AM - Jan 6, 2021

> **@realDonaldTrump**
>
> States want to correct their votes, which they now know were based on irregularities and fraud, plus corrupt process never received legislative approval. **All Mike Pence has to do** is send them back to the States, AND WE WIN. **Do it Mike,** this is a time for extreme courage.
>
> 8:17 AM - Jan 6, 2021

The president then phoned Pence late that morning, reminding him that he allegedly had the legal authority to send the electoral votes back to their respective States. During the heated conversation, the president suggested that Pence was "not tough enough to make the call," further calling him a "wimp." He also told the vice president that he had made the wrong decision when he had in 2016 chosen Pence as his running mate. A few hours later during his speech at the Ellipse, the president went off script when targeting Pence:

Mike Pence is going to have to come through for us, and if he doesn't, that will be a, a sad day for our country because you're sworn to uphold our Constitution.... And if you're not, I'm going to be very disappointed in you. I will tell you right now. I'm not hearing good stories...."The Constitution doesn't allow me to send them back to the States." Well, I say, yes it does, because the Constitution says you have to protect our country and you have to protect our Constitution, and you can't vote on fraud. And fraud breaks up everything, doesn't it? When you catch somebody in a fraud, you're allowed to go by very different rules. So I hope Mike has the courage to do what he has to do. And I hope he doesn't listen to the RINOs [Republicans in name only] and the stupid people that he's listening to.

In response to Trump's pressure and in an effort to explain to Americans his responsibilities during the joint session of Congress that he was only minutes away from presiding over, Pence released a letter as the president was concluding his speech at the Ellipse. The vice president had described the letter to his staff by saying, "This may be the most important thing I ever say." It included the following excerpts:

It is my considered judgment that my oath to support and defend the Constitution constrains me from claiming unilateral authority to determine which electoral votes should be counted and which should not....I welcome the efforts of Senate and House members who have stepped forward to use their authority under the law to raise objections and present evidence.... Today it will be my duty to preside when the Congress convenes in Joint Session to count the votes of the Electoral College, and I will do so to the best of my ability. I ask only that Representatives and Senators who will assemble before me approach this moment with the same sense of duty and an open mind, setting politics and personal interests aside, and do our part to faithfully discharge our duties under the Constitution.

Vice President Pence held firm during the joint session of Congress, ensuring that objections to the vote count adhered to the process set forth in the Electoral Count Act. In so doing, he averted a likely constitutional crisis. Just over a year later, former vice president Pence said the following:

President Trump said I had the right to overturn the election. But President Trump is wrong. I had no right to overturn the election. The presidency belongs to the American people and the American people alone. And frankly, there's no idea more un-American than the notion that any one person could choose the American president.

CHAPTER 32

Deepening Division

D onald Trump was the first president in 152 years not to attend the inauguration of his successor. It was a vivid reminder of how Trump came to personify division fueled by fear and distrust. During the final three minutes of Trump's presidency, President-elect Biden implored Americans to seek unity by striving to better understand those with different views. It was President Trump's conspicuous absence that made the following segment of Biden's inaugural speech all the more poignant:

> Yet hear me clearly: Disagreement must not lead to disunion....I understand they [many Americans] worry about their jobs, about taking care of their families, about what comes next. I get it. But the answer is not to turn inward, to retreat into competing factions, distrusting those who don't look like you do, or worship the way you do, or don't get their news from the same

sources you do. We must end this uncivil war that pits red against blue, rural versus urban, conservative versus liberal. We can do this if we open our souls instead of hardening our hearts. If we show a little tolerance and humility. If we're willing to stand in the other person's shoes just for a moment. Because here is the thing about life: There is no accounting for what fate will deal you. There are some days when we need a hand. There are other days when we're called on to lend one. That is how we must be with one another. And, if we are this way, our country will be stronger, more prosperous, more ready for the future.

Tribalism. The tendency to differentiate people into groups of "us" and "them" may occasionally promote survival, but it more often just results in unwarranted discrimination and hostility. Leaders have long exploited fears related to race, nationality, religion, and ideology to perpetuate self-serving boundaries. Increased unity becomes more elusive when leaders opportunistically encourage tribalism and division. As with fear's power to inhibit reason, fear-based tribalism tends to encourage responses more emotional than logical.

Former president Obama once stated, "If you have to win a campaign by dividing people, you're not going to be able to govern them. You won't be able to unite them later." Promoting genuine unity was never President Trump's objective. His former secretary of defense and retired four-star general James Mattis described Trump as the first president in his lifetime who not only did not even pretend to try to unite Americans but intentionally sought to divide them. In an effort to gain and then maintain power, he exploited existing cultural fault lines while promoting racial and political stereotypes to bolster his base of support. As Trump's former attorney Michael Cohen explained in *Disloyal: A Memoir*, Trump identified issues he could exploit because of their divisiveness and their ability to elicit strong emotional reactions from likely supporters. He played on people's fears and prejudices with disinformation in order to create the us-versus-them dynamic.

Foreign adversaries seek to weaken democracies by exploiting their existing divisions. This threat increases when domestic leaders are already fanning the flames of tribalism. President Trump's former national security advisor, retired lieutenant general H. R. McMaster, explained to MSNBC the mechanics of Russia's goal of dividing and weakening the United States and Europe:

> The Russians have new tools available to them, and especially this cyber-enabled information warfare that they're waging against us...they want to divide us. They don't create those divisions, but they try to widen those divisions. And what they mainly focus on—and it's not just during an election period, it's a sustained effort—is on issues of race. And really a very distant second to that are issues of immigration and gun control. So wherever there are maybe extreme positions on either side of the political spectrum, they try to magnify the voices on those extremes and pit us against each other.

The largely discredited and mostly unsubstantiated Steele "dossier" was nonetheless credible regarding President Putin's aim of "cultivating and supporting" candidate Trump in order to "sow discord and disunity both within the U.S. itself, but more especially within the Transatlantic [NATO] alliance which was viewed as inimical to Russia's interests."

The exploitation and deepening of divisions in a democracy has consequences. A leader who celebrates division and encourages tribalism—especially with supporters who welcome this behavior—will exacerbate existing polarization, hyper-partisanship, and government gridlock. On the individual level, people may become less tolerant and respectful of those with different views. This creates a sort of ideological segregation that inhibits simple discourse, the mediation of differences, and the collaboration needed to defeat existential threats. This "encouraged" tribalism also makes it easier to brand others as "enemies" who allegedly threaten a nation's virtues. Worse yet, tribalism can narrow moral identity to the point that the abuse of others is tolerated, if not encouraged.

Countering tribalism and promoting unity. The National Geographic series *One Strange Rock* is a fascinating exploration of Earth from the perspective of astronauts who lived on the International Space Station. Their off-planet vantage point provided a rare glimpse of our planet's beauty and, more importantly, a unique appreciation of the interconnectedness of Earth's natural phenomena. That interconnectedness also puts into perspective our collective fates in the context of armed conflict and other existential threats like climate change.

A decades-long Harvard University study that traced people into old age determined that happy people avoid toxic tribalism. In 2020, then presidential candidate Joe Biden reminded Americans that they were facing too many crises, had too much work to do, and had too bright a future "to have it shipwrecked on the shoals of anger and hate and division." Several months earlier, Jon Meacham had put the themes of interconnectedness and unity into historical context:

> In his final Sunday sermon, days before his death, Martin Luther King Jr. said, "We are tied together in the single garment of destiny. This is the way God's universe is made. This is the way it is structured." A single garment of destiny. We the people cannot escape that reality, nor as Lincoln taught us, can you and I escape history....Extremism, nativism, isolationism, and a lack of economic opportunity for working people are all preventing us from realizing our nation's promise.... The Civil War led to segregation. The New Deal to right-wing reaction, Civil Rights to white backlash. Yet history, which will surely be our judge, can also be our guide. From Harriet Tubman to Alice Paul to John Lewis, from the beaches of Normandy to the rendering of the Iron Curtain—our story has soared when we've built bridges, not walls. When we've lent a hand, not when we've pointed fingers. When we've hoped, not feared.

A spirit of cooperation and common purpose is more attainable when elected leaders are guided more by principal and substantive policy outcomes and less by allegiances that rely heavily on narrow ideological or organizational (party) identities. In a January 2019 opinion piece, Senator Mitt Romney addressed the relationship between domestic political tribalism and America's traditional role on the world stage:

To reassume our leadership in world politics, we must repair failings in our politics at home. That project begins, of course, with the highest office once again acting to inspire and unite us. It includes political parties promoting policies that strengthen us rather than promote tribalism by exploiting fear and resentment.... The people of this great land will eschew the politics of anger and fear if they are summoned to the responsibility by leaders in homes, in churches, in schools, in businesses, [and] in government.

President Nelson Mandela understood the importance of breaking down the resentment inherent in tribal narratives in order to promote unity and break the cycle of revenge in newly democratic, post-apartheid South Africa. When he urged South Africans to "forget the past," most of them believed that he had. This had a double effect: it made whites trust Mandela more and it made them feel more generous toward the people they had so recently oppressed. In another simple and symbolic yet profound gesture of unity aimed at rewriting those tribal narratives, Mandela donned the jersey of the formerly all-white Springbok rugby team during their quest to win the 1995 Rugby World Cup (events memorialized in the film *Invictus*). Mandela may have been practicing what author Bob Johansen of Institute for the Future referred to as one of ten new leadership skills for an uncertain world—*constructive depolarizing*. It is the ability to bring people from divergent cultures toward constructive engagement.

In the world of sports, rabid allegiance to a particular team occasionally results in violence, reflecting the darker consequences of tribalism in domestic and geopolitics. There are examples, however, that stand as exceptions to this dynamic and suggest a willingness to transform the traditional relationship between identity and allegiance.

Using Formula 1 automobile racing as an example, there are certainly allegiances based on nationality. These include Ferrari and its adoring Italian "Tifosi" fan base, in addition to traditional national support for a country's drivers. But more often, individual support for a particular team or driver is independent of nationality, as evidenced by Ferrari's popularity worldwide and the affection fans pour on drivers from other countries. What this phenomenon demonstrates is the ability to identify with others for reasons other than nationalistic tribal identities. More importantly, these fans are—by and large—respectful of those who support other teams and drivers. This model demonstrates, albeit in a less consequential context, that people can choose their allegiances outside of traditionally rigid constructs and that they can express those allegiances while still respecting those with different preferences or loyalties.

CHAPTER 33

Inciting Violence:
The Attack on the Capitol

History has taught us that what begins
with words ends in far worse.

—REPRESENTATIVE LIZ CHENEY

The by-products of fear and distrust include resentment, anger, and hate. These in time lead to unrest and violence.

In early 2021, the assistant director of the FBI's Counter-terrorism Division noted that between 2015 and 2020, racially or ethnically motivated violent extremists were responsible for the most lethal domestic terrorism threat. Furthermore, 2019 was the most lethal year for domestic violent extremist attacks since the Oklahoma City bombing in 1995.

A leader's words can inspire. They can also incite. Divisive and racist rhetoric has the effect of normalizing extremist views and agendas. When leaders demonize immigrants, post content containing extremist conspiracy theories, or give tacit approval to groups that support white nationalism, they are inciting violence against minority communities and perceived political enemies.

The Michigan State Capitol plot. In March 2020, Michigan governor Gretchen Whitmer issued a series of executive orders that severely restricted personal and business activities in an effort to control the spread of COVID-19. President Trump responded, as he had with other states enacting similar measures, with an inflammatory two-word post.

@realDonaldTrump
LIBERATE MICHIGAN!
11:22 AM - Apr 17, 2020

On April 30, hundreds of protesters—including militia members armed with long guns—gathered inside the Michigan State Capitol and attempted to enter the legislative chamber where lawmakers were debating the potential extension of the governor's pandemic-related emergency powers.

@realDonaldTrump
The Governor of Michigan should give a little, and put out the fire. These are very good people, but they are angry. They want their lives back again, safely! See them, talk to them, make a deal.
8:42 AM - May 1, 2020

Some of the armed "very good people" referenced by the president had already begun conspiring to storm the Michigan State Capitol, overthrow the state government, and kidnap and possibly assassinate Governor Whitmer.

In October 2020, while the conspiracy was still in the planning and rehearsal phases, the FBI arrested thirteen militia members connected to the plot. On the day of the arrests, President Trump attacked Governor Whitmer for doing a "terrible job" with respect to her pandemic response but also praised federal law enforcement agencies for thwarting the terrorist plot. Though he did denounce "any extreme violence," the president did not directly condemn the far-right anti-government militia members. Two of the men were eventually convicted of kidnapping conspiracy and conspiracy to use a weapon of mass destruction. They received prison sentences of between sixteen and twenty years each. Five others were convicted of crimes that included providing support for terrorist acts and kidnapping conspiracy.

During an October 2020 Trump campaign rally in Michigan, the crowd—referring to Governor Whitmer—chanted "lock her up." The president responded with, "lock 'em all up." On the same day, Governor Whitmer and one of her staffers posted about the effects of Trump's rhetoric.

> @GovWhitmer
> This is exactly the rhetoric that has put me, my family, and other government officials' lives in danger while we try to save the lives of our fellow Americans. It needs to stop.
> 6:14 PM - Oct 17, 2020

@tori_saylor

I am the Governor's Deputy Digital Director. I see
everything that is said about and to her online. Every
single time the President does this at a rally, the
violent rhetoric towards her immediately escalates on
social media. It has to stop. It just has to.

6:18 PM - Oct 17, 2020

The April siege of the Michigan Capitol, along with the
FBI-thwarted militia plot, would to some extent foreshadow the
upcoming attack on the U.S. Capitol. Just days before the presidential election, President Trump could not have been more ironically
prophetic.

@realDonaldTrump

One of the most important issues is LAW & ORDER.
Biden stands with the rioters & looters - I stand with
the HEROES of law enforcement. If Biden wins, the
rioters in the streets will be running your federal
government. No city, no family, and no community will
be safe. VOTE #MAGA!

5:46 PM - Oct 30, 2020

The attack on the Capitol. The planned and coordinated
attack on the U.S. Capitol by a riotous and insurrectionist mob of
Americans on January 6, 2021, resulted in the greatest defilement
of the symbolic and physical heart of American constitutional
democracy in over two centuries. The Capitol was vandalized,
desecrated, and looted after the mob viciously attacked the police
officers who were guarding the building and protecting America's

elected representatives. To undo President Trump's loss, the rioters intended to subvert the Constitution by preventing the joint session of Congress's counting and certification of Electoral College votes and, consequently, the peaceful transfer of power.

The road to the violence of January 6 was paved with deception, fear, distrust, and division. Along the way, President Trump emboldened the long-held convictions of far-right extremists while failing to commit to a peaceful transfer of power. As his eventual August 2023 federal indictment suggested, "The Defendant had a right, like every American, to speak publicly about the election and even to claim, falsely, that there had been outcome-determinative fraud during the election and that he had won." Nonetheless, the irresponsibility of President Trump's yearslong assault on the truth played an outsize role in inciting the violence of January 6.

Presidential incitement. The president's yearslong disinformation campaign involving baseless claims of widespread election fraud arguably began with his suggestion that massive voter fraud in California contributed to his national popular vote deficit in the 2016 presidential contest. It continued with his suggestion that the investigation into Russian interference in the 2016 election was an attempt to somehow overturn his 2016 victory and that his first impeachment was an opposition party attempt to rig the 2020 election. As election season 2020 heated up, the president persevered.

@realDonaldTrump
We can't let the Fake News, and their partner, the Radical Left, Do Nothing Democrats, get away with stealing the Election. They tried that in 2016. How did that work out?
10:09 AM - Apr 30, 2020

@realDonaldTrump
Don't allow RIGGED ELECTIONS!
7:36 PM - May 1, 2020

Throughout the summer of 2020, Trump continued to claim that the election would be the most rigged in history. In his first debate with Joe Biden in September, he emboldened far-right extremists (and specifically the Proud Boys) when he told them to "stand back and stand by." Those words would be featured in the group's new logo, and as a Proud Boy would later testify, membership in the group probably tripled after the president's comment. The president generally denounced white supremacist groups the next day, but the damage had already been done.

Three weeks before the election, Senator Mitt Romney published a letter warning about the tone of political discourse in the United States:

> The rabid attacks kindle the conspiracy mongers and the haters who take the small and predictable step from intemperate word to dangerous action. The world is watching America with abject horror; more consequentially, our children are watching. Many Americans are frightened for our country—so divided, so angry, so mean, so violent. It is time to lower the heat. Leaders must tone it down. Leaders from the top and leaders of all stripes: parents, bosses, reporters, columnists, professors, union chiefs, everyone. The consequence of the crescendo of anger leads to a very bad place. No sane person can want that.

Just days before the November 3 election, journalist Ron Suskind wrote a prescient piece in the *New York Times*. He warned that a defeated Trump might still declare victory the day after the election, potentially inciting violence among his supporters. As predicted, the president claimed that he had won the election. On November 5, two days before the race was called by any major media outlet, Trump declared, "This is a case where they're trying to steal an election. They're trying to rig an election, and we can't let that happen." Trump's rhetoric encouraged his supporters to surround the homes of state election officials, some of whom received death threats. Georgia election official Gabriel Sterling criticized the president and Georgia Republicans for failing to denounce the threats of violence and warned that someone was likely to die if the inflammatory rhetoric did not stop.

Shortly after the election, the president reposted a video by actor Jon Voight, whose message about alleged injustices in the 2020 election included the following: "This is now our greatest fight since the Civil War: the battle of righteousness versus Satan. Yes, Satan, because these leftists are evil....Let us fight this fight as if it is our last fight on Earth."

A long and rambling airing of election grievances from President Trump on December 2 included the declaration, "You can't let another person steal that election from you. All over the country, people are together in holding up signs: 'Stop the steal.'...If we don't root out the fraud, the tremendous and horrible fraud that's taken place in our 2020 election, we don't have a country anymore." During a December 5 rally in Valdosta, Georgia, Trump suggested that he would be a "very gracious loser" if losing, while also declaring, "We're all victims. Everybody here, all these thousands of people here tonight, they're all victims, every one of you."

@realDonaldTrump

"People are upset, and they have a right to be.
Georgia not only supported Trump in 2016, but now.
This is the only State in the Deep South that went
for Biden? Have they lost their minds? This is going
to escalate dramatically. This is a very dangerous
moment in our history....
....The fact that our Country is being stolen. A coup is
taking place in front of our eyes, and the public can't
take this anymore." A Trump fan at Georgia Rally on
@OANN Bad!

9:33 AM - Dec 10, 2020

On December 12, Trump supporters gathered for the March for Trump rally in Washington, D.C., where members of the Proud Boys tore down Black Lives Matter signs posted in front of historically Black churches.

@realDonaldTrump

Wow! Thousands of people forming in Washington
(D.C.) for Stop the Steal. Didn't know about this, but
I'll be seeing them! #MAGA

9:59 AM - Dec 12, 2020

As state electors convened to vote for president on December 14, threats of violence and planned protests necessitated unusual security precautions at state houses in Michigan, Arizona, and Wisconsin. The next day, Republican Senate majority leader Mitch McConnell recognized Biden as the president-elect, stating, "The Electoral College has spoken. So today I want to congratulate President-elect Joe Biden."

@realDonaldTrump
Democrats would never put up with a Presidential
Election stolen by the Republicans!
6:10 PM - Dec 17, 2020

Having exhausted all legal avenues to challenge his election loss, President Trump on December 19 posted his consequential "will be wild!" tweet in which he invited his supporters to Washington, D.C.

@realDonaldTrump
Peter Navarro releases 36-page report alleging
election fraud 'more than sufficient' to swing victory
to Trump washex.am/3nwaBCe. A great report by
Peter. Statistically impossible to have lost the 2020
Election. **Big protest in D.C. on January 6th. Be
there, will be wild!**
1:42 AM - Dec 19, 2020

Trump's supporters understood the significance of January 6, the date on which the joint session of Congress would count the Electoral College votes previously certified by the states. Far-right extremist groups like the Proud Boys, believing the stolen election narrative, began their January 6 planning immediately. The leadership of the Proud Boys understood that their purpose for traveling to Washington, D.C., was to stop the certification of the Electoral College vote. To that end, they agreed that they were willing to use force against police or other government officials when eventually storming the Capitol.

Leaders of the Oath Keepers group saw Trump's post as a

"NATIONAL CALL TO ACTION FOR DC JAN 6TH." One leader communicated that President Trump "called us all to the Capitol and wants us to make it wild!!!...Gentlemen we are heading to DC pack your shit!!" The Three Percenters—Original anti-government militia group responded to the president's post by instructing "any member who can attend…to participate" because "the President of the United States has put out a general call for the patriots of this Nation to gather." Three Percenter groups from various other states put out similar messages. Many of these Trump supporters believed that it was their patriotic duty and civic responsibility to support the president on January 6.

More troubling was that these nonaligned groups began aligning after the president's December 19 post. Armed militias began collaborating online with white supremacy and conspiracy theory groups toward a common goal for January 6. Their new alliance was creating—in terrorism parlance—a blended ideology.

In another airing of grievances on December 22, President Trump stated, "We won this election by a magnificent landslide, and the people of the United States know it. All over, they're demonstrating, they're angry, they're fearful. We cannot allow a completely fraudulent election to stand."

@realDonaldTrump

If a Democrat Presidential Candidate had an Election Rigged & Stolen, with proof of such acts at a level never seen before, the Democrat Senators would consider it an act of war, and fight to the death. Mitch & the Republicans do NOTHING, just want to let it pass. NO FIGHT!

8:00 AM - Dec 26, 2020

@realDonaldTrump
See you in Washington, DC, on January 6th. Don't
miss it. Information to follow!
5:51 PM - Dec 27, 2020

@realDonaldTrump
JANUARY SIXTH, SEE YOU IN DC!
2:06 PM - Dec 30, 2020

@realDonaldTrump
The BIG Protest Rally in Washington, D.C., will take
place at 11.00 A.M. on January 6th. Locational
details to follow. StopTheSteal!
2:53 PM - Jan 1, 2021

@realDonaldTrump
Massive amounts of evidence will be presented on
the 6th. We won, BIG!
3:10 PM - Jan 1, 2021

On January 2, the FBI discovered a social media post that read, "This is not a rally and it's no longer a protest. This is a final stand...many are ready to die to take back #USA....And don't be surprised if we take #capital building." On the same day, White House Chief of Staff Mark Meadows told his assistant, Cassidy Hutchinson, that "things might get real, real bad on the sixth." By this time, White House staffers and key rally organizers were aware that the president intended to direct his supporters to proceed to the Capitol.

@realDonaldTrump

An attempt to steal a landslide win. Can't let it happen!

6:15 PM - Jan 2, 2021

@realDonaldTrump

"Georgia election data, just revealed, shows that over 17,000 votes illegally flipped from Trump to Biden." @OANN This alone (there are many other irregularities) is enough to easily "swing Georgia to Trump". #StopTheSteal @HawleyMO @SenTedCruz @ Jim_Jordan

9:20 AM - Jan 3, 2021

A Capitol Police intelligence memo released three days before the attack warned that "supporters of the current president see January 6, 2021, as the last opportunity to overturn the results of the presidential election....This sense of desperation and disappointment may lead to more of an incentive to become violent....Congress itself is the target on the 6th." Meanwhile, President Trump continued putting pressure on Republican members of Congress.

@realDonaldTrump

How can you certify an election when the numbers being certified are verifiably WRONG. You will see the real numbers tonight during my speech, but especially on JANUARY 6th. @SenTomCotton Republicans have pluses & minuses, but one thing is sure, THEY NEVER FORGET!

10:07 AM - Jan 4, 2021

@realDonaldTrump

The "Surrender Caucus" within the Republican Party will go down in infamy as weak and ineffective "guardians" of our Nation, who were willing to accept the certification of fraudulent presidential numbers!

10:45 AM - Jan 4, 2021

During a January 4 rally in Georgia, the president insisted, "There is no way we lost Georgia....You know, I've had two elections. I won both of them. It's amazing. And I actually did much better on the second one....They're not taking this White House. We're going to fight like hell." In the following, the president foreshadowed the desperation and violence that would be on display two days later:

> I hope Mike Pence comes through for us...If you don't fight to save your country with everything you have, you're not going to have a country left....We will not bend. We will not break. We will not yield. We will never give in. We will never give up. We will never back down. We will never, ever surrender.

Hope Hicks, a counselor to the president, was one of two White House staffers to suggest that the president preemptively and publicly state that January 6 must remain peaceful. The president ignored their advice.

On January 5, an FBI field office in Virginia warned law enforcement agencies about violence and "war" at the Capitol. The report quoted a far-right group's online thread that read, "Get violent…stop calling this a march, or rally, or a protest. Go there ready for war. We get our President or we die. NOTHING else will achieve this goal." Major media outlets brought attention to the January 6 threat based on posts in far-right internet forums. The FBI had also learned that the far-right Oath Keepers group was storing firearms (that were illegal in Washington, D.C.) in a nearby Virginia hotel. If needed, the weapons would be ferried into D.C. on January 6 for use by a "quick reaction force."

On the eve of the attack, President Trump continued to pressure members of Congress while promoting the big lie to his supporters.

> @realDonaldTrump
> Pleased to announce that @KLoeffler & @sendavid-perdue have just joined our great #StopTheSteal group of Senators. They will fight the ridiculous Electoral College Certification of Biden. How do you certify numbers that have now proven to be wrong and, in many cases, fraudulent!
> 9:50 AM - Jan 5, 2021

> @realDonaldTrump
> See you in D.C.
> 10:27 AM - Jan 5, 2021

The first of the following posts was in response to the president hearing, from the Oval Office, the pro-Trump "Stop the Steal" rally being held in nearby Freedom Plaza.

@realDonaldTrump

Washington is being inundated with people who don't want to see an election victory stolen by emboldened Radical Left Democrats. Our Country has had enough, they won't take it anymore! **We hear you (and love you) from the Oval Office.** MAKE AMERICA GREAT AGAIN!

5:05 PM - Jan 5, 2021

@realDonaldTrump

I hope the Democrats, and even more importantly, the weak and ineffective RINO section of the Republican Party, are looking at the thousands of people pouring into D.C. They won't stand for a landslide election victory to be stolen. @senatemajldr @JohnCornyn @ SenJohnThune

5:12 PM - Jan 5, 2021

@realDonaldTrump

I will be speaking at the SAVE AMERICA RALLY tomorrow on the Ellipse at 11AM Eastern. Arrive early — doors open at 7AM Eastern. BIG CROWDS!

5:43 PM - Jan 5, 2021

A Secret Service briefing mentioned online chatter focused on Vice President Pence's constitutional role in presiding over the January 6 joint session of Congress. After a phone call between President Trump and Steve Bannon, Bannon announced on his program that "all hell is going to break loose tomorrow."

January 6. President Trump began the day by insinuating that election fraud was occurring in Georgia's U.S. Senate run-off election and by insisting that he must stay in office.

@realDonaldTrump
Just happened to have found another 4000 ballots from Fulton County. Here we go!
12:08 AM - Jan 6, 2021

@realDonaldTrump
THE REPUBLICAN PARTY AND, MORE IMPORTANTLY, OUR COUNTRY, NEEDS THE PRESIDENCY MORE THAN EVER BEFORE - THE POWER OF THE VETO. STAY STRONG!
8:22 AM - Jan 6, 2021

@realDonaldTrump
They just happened to find 50,000 ballots late last night. The USA is embarrassed by fools. Our Election Process is worse than that of third world countries!
9:00 AM - Jan 6, 2021

The large crowds that began gathering on the morning of January 6—as later described by FBI Director Christopher Wray—could be categorized into three groups. The largest group was composed of mostly peaceful protesters who were not violating the law. The second group may have come for a peaceful protest but were "swept up in the emotion" and engaged in low-level criminal behavior like trespassing on the Capitol grounds. The third and smallest group breached the Capitol grounds, engaged in violence against law enforcement, and attempted to disrupt the constitutional responsibilities of Congress. Director Wray testified that the violence planned by this third group constituted domestic terrorism and was composed of normally disparate groups with different perspectives. They included white supremacists, antisemites, anti-government militias, Second Amendment rights protesters, radicalized adherents of QAnon, and die-hard Trump supporters who believed that they needed to "stop the steal."

These groups were united in the common cause of supporting their chosen leader. As Professor Cynthia Miller-Idriss of American University explained, they were mobilized by a sense of precarity whereby something to which they were allegedly entitled was going to be taken away if they did not fight to preserve it. They were being told that their democracy was a fraud because it had been hijacked by traitors.

As the morning of January 6 progressed, President Trump continued to exert pressure on his vice president by attributing to him magical, extra-constitutional powers. The Secret Service's intelligence division detected online chatter suggesting that the vice president was a "dead man walking" if he "[didn't] do the right thing." There was also chatter about storming the Capitol.

Some of Trump's supporters gathered at the Ellipse for the president's "Save America" rally speech were observed with firearms and an assortment of other weapons. About half of the approximately fifty-three thousand gathered refused to be screened in magnetometers. President Trump was angry that more of his supporters were not closer to the stage and wanted the magnetometers removed despite having been told that his supporters avoided them because they did not want their weapons confiscated, as many already had. The Secret

Service had confiscated 242 cannisters of pepper spray, 269 knives or blades, eighteen brass knuckles, eighteen tasers, six pieces of body armor, three gas masks, and thirty batons or blunt instruments. The president told an aide something to the effect of, "I don't care that they have weapons. They're not here to hurt me. Take the fucking mags away. Let my people in. They can march to the Capitol from here."

Before taking the stage for his speech, the president's surrogates peppered the crowd with inflammatory rhetoric. Congressman Mo Brooks (R-AL) excoriated Republican members of Congress who he expected would certify the Electoral College vote. His speech also included the following:

> Today is the day American patriots start taking down names and kicking ass. Now our ancestors sacrificed their blood, their sweat, their tears, their fortunes, and sometimes their lives to give us—their descendants—an America that is the greatest nation in world history. So I have a question for you. Are you willing to do the same? My answer is yes. Louder! Are you willing to do what it takes to fight for America? Louder! Will you fight for America?

President Trump took the stage at noon and spoke for about seventy minutes. Throughout the speech, he repeated known falsehoods about alleged election fraud in Wisconsin, Georgia, Arizona, Nevada, Michigan, and Pennsylvania. He suggested that the election was stolen and that the certification of Biden's electoral victory must be stopped and that Vice President Pence had the power to stop it:

All of us here today do not want to see our election victory stolen by emboldened radical-left Democrats, which is what they're doing. And stolen by the fake news media....We will never give up; we will never concede. It doesn't happen. You don't concede when there's theft involved. Our country has had enough. We will not take it anymore, and that's what this is all about. And to use a favorite term that all of you people really came up with: We will stop the steal [Audience chants: "Fight for Trump."]...Because if Mike Pence does the right thing, we win the election....We're gathered together in the heart of our nation's capital for one very, very basic and simple reason: To save our democracy....We want to go back and we want to get this right because we're going to have somebody in there that should not be in there and our country will be destroyed and we're not going to stand for that....You know, America is blessed with elections. All over the world they talk about our elections. You know what the world says about us now? They said, we don't have free and fair elections....And Mike Pence is going to have to come through for us, and if he doesn't, that will be a sad day for our country because you're sworn to uphold our Constitution. Now, it is up to Congress to confront this egregious assault on our democracy. And after this, we're going to walk down—and I'll be there with you—we're going to walk down...Because you'll never take back our country with weakness. You have to show strength and you have to be strong. We have come to demand that Congress do the right thing and only count the electors who have been lawfully slated.

In what was predominantly a call to arms to save a democracy allegedly under siege, the president made one reference to peaceful protest (inserted by his speechwriters) before continuing to promote the big lie:

> I know that everyone here will soon be marching over to the Capitol building to peacefully and patriotically make your voices heard....Our country has been under siege for a long time....We will not be intimidated into accepting the hoaxes and the lies that we've been forced to believe....You will have an illegitimate president. That's what you'll have. And we can't let that happen.... The radical left knows exactly what they're doing. They're ruthless, and it's time that somebody did something about it....We won in a landslide. This was a landslide. They said it's not American to challenge the election. This the most corrupt election in the history, maybe of the world.

Vice President Pence released his statement indicating that he would adhere to the Constitution during the imminent joint session of Congress. News spread among President Trump's supporters that Pence had "caved," that he would not be rejecting "fraudulent electoral votes," and that in so doing, he had betrayed the president. Some were heard chanting "Bring out Pence" and "Hang Mike Pence."

At 12:53 p.m., rioters at the Capitol (led by the Proud Boys) forced their way through barricades and began their assault on the Capitol Police. Many Trump supporters at the Ellipse began making their way to the Capitol before the end of the president's speech. At 1:05 p.m., the vice president, the House of Representatives, and the Senate convened to count the votes of the Electoral College. Around the same time, potentially lethal pipe bombs planted the night before were discovered at buildings adjacent to the Capitol. The president's speech was ending:

> This is not just a matter of domestic politics, this is a matter of national security....We must stop the steal and then we must ensure that such outrageous election fraud never happens again...If we allow this group of people to illegally take over our country, because it's illegal when the votes are illegal when the way they got there is illegal when the states that vote are given false and fraudulent information....As this enormous crowd shows, we have truth and justice on our side. We have a deep and enduring love for America in our hearts. We love our country. We have overwhelming pride in this great country and we have it deep in our souls. Together, we are determined to defend and preserve government of the people, by the people, and for the people....And we fight. We fight like hell. And if you don't fight like hell, you're not going to have a country anymore....So we're going to, we're going to walk down Pennsylvania Avenue. I love Pennsylvania Avenue. And we're going to the Capitol...So let's walk down Pennsylvania Avenue.

When the speech ended at 1:11 p.m., more Trump supporters made their way to the Capitol. Court documents would later show that many pro-Trump rioters believed that they were answering their president's call to action. The president returned to the White House at 1:15 p.m., where he was immediately informed that violence had broken out at the Capitol. The president nonetheless continued to insist that he be taken to the Capitol. His security personnel became alarmed about the possibility of increased violence should the president join his supporters and effectively shut down the proposed movement.

The rioters entered the Capitol at 2:13 p.m. The vice president, along with his wife and daughter, were ushered off the Senate floor. The Senate and House were declared in recess. Members of Congress halted their constitutional duties and were forced to flee the House and Senate chambers. Congressional staffers barricaded themselves in offices. Secret Service communications revealed that members of the vice president's security detail feared for their own lives. Around the same time, rioters in the Capitol were heard yelling, "Hang Mike Pence," "Find Pence," "Stop the steal," and "Fight for Trump." President Trump then incited additional outrage by attacking his vice president.

@realDonaldTrump

Mike Pence didn't have the courage to do what should have been done to protect our Country and our Constitution, giving States a chance to certify a corrected set of facts, not the fraudulent or inaccurate ones which they were asked to previously certify. USA demands the truth!

2:24 PM - Jan 6, 2021

Outside the Capitol building, Trump's supporters read the post over a bullhorn. At 2:25 p.m., the vice president was moved from his ceremonial office near the Senate chamber to a secure location in an underground loading dock within the Capitol complex. On his way there, he avoided the rioters by a mere forty feet. Shortly after the 2:24 p.m. post, Twitter employees became concerned when they began to see hashtags calling for Pence's execution. A Secret Service message reported, "POTUS [the president of the U.S.] just tweeted about Pence, probably not going to be good for Pence." They also noted that the post received twenty-four thousand likes within two minutes. Deputy National Security Advisor Matt Pottinger decided immediately to resign upon seeing the post. As later demonstrated by evidence presented to the congressional committee investigating the attack, the president's post precipitated an increased level of violence at the Capitol.

Trump's eventual 2023 federal indictment would allege that as the violence ensued, the president and his coconspirators "exploited the disruption [the attack] by redoubling efforts to levy false claims of election fraud and convince Members of Congress to further delay the certification based on those claims." President Trump's final social media post of the day effectively justified and glorified the crimes committed by his supporters.

@realDonaldTrump

These are the things and events that happen when a sacred landslide election victory is so unceremoniously & viciously stripped away from great patriots who have been badly & unfairly treated for so long. Go home with love & in peace. **Remember this day forever!**

6:01 PM - Jan 6, 2021

As the process of counting and recording the Electoral College votes resumed late into the evening of January 6, several Republican senators addressed their colleagues regarding the significance of the day's events and the ongoing process of certifying the Electoral College votes.

Senator Mitch McConnell:

> They tried to disrupt our democracy. They failed.... They failed to attempt to obstruct the Congress. This failed insurrection only underscores how crucial the task before us is for our republic. Our nation was founded precisely so that the free choice of the American people is what shapes our self-government and determines the destiny of our nation—not fear, not force, but the peaceful expression of the popular will.

Senator Mitt Romney:

> Now we gather due to a selfish man's injured pride and the outrage of supporters who he has deliberately misinformed for the past two months and stirred to action this very morning. What happened here today was an insurrection incited by the president of the United States. Those who choose to continue to support his dangerous gambit by objecting to the results of a legitimate democratic election will forever be seen as being complicit in an unprecedented attack against our democracy. Fairly or not, they'll be remembered for

their role in this shameful episode in American history. That will be their legacy....The best way we can show respect for the voters who are upset is by telling them the truth. [Twenty-two seconds of applause] That's the burden. That's the duty of leadership. The truth is that President-elect Biden won the election. President Trump lost. I've had that experience myself. It's no fun! Scores of courts, the president's own attorney general, state election officials—both Republican and Democrat— have reached that unequivocal decision. And in light of today's sad circumstances, I ask my colleagues—do we weigh our own political fortunes more heavily than we weigh the strength of our republic, the strength of our democracy, and the cause of freedom? What's the weight of personal acclaim compared to the weight of conscience? Leader McConnell said that the vote today is the most important in his thirty-six years of public service. Think of that...He said that not because the vote reveals something about the election. It's because this vote reveals something about us.

Among those condemning the attack and affirming the legitimacy of the 2020 election were the four living former U.S. presidents and several former Trump cabinet officials. At least sixteen Trump administration officials, including two cabinet secretaries, resigned after the attack. Trump's former secretary of defense, James Mattis, spoke to the culpability of the president and his acolytes:

Today's violent assault on our Capitol, an effort to subjugate American democracy by mob rule, was fomented by Mr. Trump. His use of the Presidency to destroy trust in our election and to poison our respect for fellow citizens has been enabled by pseudo political leaders whose names will live in infamy as profiles in cowardice. Our Constitution and our republic will overcome this stain and We the People will come together again in our never-ending effort to form a more perfect Union, while Mr. Trump will deservedly be left a man without a country.

As the joint session of Congress finally concluded at 3:42 a.m. on January 7, Chaplain of the Senate Barry Black included the following words in his closing prayer:

> These tragedies have reminded us that words matter and that the power of life and death is in the tongue. We have been warned that eternal vigilance continues to be freedom's price....You have strengthened our resolve to protect and defend the Constitution of the United States against all enemies, domestic as well as foreign. Use us to bring healing and unity to a hurting and divided nation and world. Thank you for what you have blessed our lawmakers to accomplish in spite of threats to liberty.

Asked six days after the attack about the appropriateness of his January 6 rhetoric, President Trump told reporters, "People thought that what I said was totally appropriate." The president was impeached by the House of Representatives three weeks later for "incitement of insurrection." Lead House Impeachment Manager Jamie Raskin (D-MD) remarked during the Senate trial that "January sixth was a culmination of the president's actions, not an aberration from them. The insurrection was the most violent and dangerous episode so far in Donald Trump's continuing pattern and practice of inciting violence—but I emphasize *so far*." House Impeachment Manager Joaquin Castro (D-TX) underscored the danger of Trump's rhetoric:

> The most combustible thing you can do in a democracy is convince people that an election doesn't count, that their voice and their vote don't count, and that it has all been stolen, especially if what you're saying are lies.... They had bought into his big lie. President Trump told his supporters over and over again, nearly every day, in dozens of tweets, speeches, and rallies, that their most precious right in our democracy—their voice, their vote—was being stripped away and they had to fight to stop that. And they believed him, and so they fought.

Moments after voting to find the president not guilty in the Senate trial, Senator Mitch McConnell nonetheless spoke to Trump's culpability:

> January sixth was a disgrace. American citizens attacked their own government. They used terrorism to try to stop a specific piece of domestic business they did not like.... They did this because they'd been fed wild false-hoods by the most powerful man on Earth because he

was angry he lost an election. Former president Trump's actions preceding the riot were a disgraceful, disgraceful dereliction of duty....There's no question—none—that President Trump is practically and morally responsible for provoking the events of the day. No question about it. The people who stormed this building believed they were acting on the wishes and instructions of their president. And having that belief was a foreseeable consequence of the growing crescendo of false statements, conspiracy theories, and reckless hyperbole which the defeated president kept shouting into the largest megaphone on planet Earth....The leader of the free world cannot spend weeks thundering that shadowy forces are stealing our country and then feign surprise when people believe him and do reckless things. Now sadly, many politicians sometimes make overheated comments or use metaphors...that unhinged listeners might take literally....That's different from what we saw. This was an intensified crescendo of conspiracy theories orchestrated by an outgoing president who seemed determined to either overturn the voters' decision or else torch our institutions on the way out.

Senator McConnell did not mention the supporting role of over 120 Republican members of Congress who sought to delegitimize the results of the election by championing the "stop the steal" movement and by supporting the frivolous Texas lawsuit aimed at overturning election results in Georgia, Michigan, Pennsylvania, and Wisconsin. An even larger number of congressional Republicans publicly signaled their intent—before the attack on the Capitol—to challenge the state-certified Electoral College votes from several states in which Trump had lost. Most of them continued to challenge the votes when the joint session of Congress resumed just hours after the attack.

During his final two weeks in office, President Trump continued to champion his big lie of a stolen election. Twitter suspended his account on January 8 "due to the risk of further incitement of violence." He was eventually banned or restricted by seventeen additional tech platforms that also sought to curtail his dissemination of disinformation. With his Twitter privileges restored in late 2022, the former president's first post on Twitter (by then rebranded as X) featured his August 2023 mugshot from Atlanta's Fulton County jail.

Consequences. During testimony provided to the Senate six weeks after the attack, the former chief of the Capitol Police characterized the nature of the assault: "We properly planned for a mass demonstration with possible violence. What we got was a military-style coordinated assault on my officers and a violent take-over of the Capitol building." Three people died as a direct result of the chaos on January 6, including one Capitol Police officer and two of President Trump's supporters. Within ten days of the attack, two additional police officers who had responded on January 6 committed suicide. Approximately 140 police officers sustained injuries that included cracked ribs, shattered spinal discs, and brain injuries. The casualty count could have easily been higher. In an attack visually reminiscent of the 1979 storming of the U.S. embassy in Tehran by militant Islamic students, the rioters fortunately failed to take hostages or kill lawmakers.

Almost four years earlier, President Trump had posted a somewhat ironically prophetic message related to the investigation into Russia's interference in America's 2016 election.

@realDonaldTrump
Russia must be laughing up their sleeves watching as the U.S. tears itself apart over a Democrat EXCUSE for losing the election.
1:34 PM - May 11, 2017

Following the attack on the Capitol, America's allies expressed shock and urged respect for the outcome of the election. As reported in a U.S. government joint threat assessment, the attack provided an opportunity for adversaries like Russia, China, and Iran to "amplify narratives in furtherance of their policy interest amid the presidential transition." Russia and China used the attack to question America's right to advocate for pro-democracy movements in Hong Kong and elsewhere around the world. As explained by President Trump's former deputy national security advisor Matt Pottinger, "It emboldened our enemies by helping [to] give them ammunition to feed a narrative that our system of government doesn't work, that the United States is in decline."

By January 2024, more than seven hundred individuals had pleaded guilty to a variety of offenses, and around 170 had been convicted at trial. The affidavits of various January 6 defendants suggested that given the opportunity, they would have killed Vice President Pence and Speaker of the House Pelosi (the latter of whom Trump had publicly accused of treason as early as 2019). For their roles in opposing by force the lawful transfer of presidential power, six members of the Oath Keepers and four members of the Proud Boys were convicted of seditious conspiracy and other crimes. The leaders of the Oath Keepers and Proud Boys, Stewart Rhodes and Enrique Tarrio, were sentenced to eighteen and twenty-two years in prison, respectively. The Trump-appointed judge who sentenced Tarrio found that his conduct constituted an official act of terrorism.

Normalizing political extremism. In a formal Republican National Committee (RNC) censure of the two Republicans who served on the House committee to investigate the attack on the Capitol, the RNC suggested that Representatives Liz Cheney and Adam Kinzinger (R-IL) were participating in a "persecution of ordinary citizens engaged in legitimate political discourse." Senator Mitch McConnell criticized the censure and the RNC's benign characterization of the rioters: "We saw it happen. It was a violent insurrection for the purpose of trying to prevent the peaceful transfer of power after a legitimately certified election, from one administration to the next. That's what it was." In his sentencing notes for one particular January 6 rioter, United States District Judge Royce C. Lamberth included the following:

> Those who think political ends justify violent means seek to replace persuasion with intimidation, the rule of law with "might makes right." Violence risks begetting a vicious cycle that could threaten cherished conventions and imperil our very institutions of government. In that sense, political violence rots republics. Therefore, January 6 must not become a precedent for further violence against political opponents or governmental institutions.

This is not normal. This cannot become normal. We as
a community, we as a society, we as a country cannot
condone the normalization of the January 6 Capitol riot.

As Representative Jamie Raskin warned during the January 6
committee hearings, "the problem of incitement to political violence
has only grown more serious in the internet age." In 2016, the
Capitol Police investigated 902 threats against lawmakers of both
political parties. That number jumped to almost four thousand in
2017. By 2021, the number had risen to 9,625—more than tenfold
the number in 2016.

One consequence of the Capitol attack was its enormous
recruiting potential for domestic extremist groups. The combination of surging recruitment and extremists newly emboldened by
the attack increases the likelihood of violence against elected officials, government facilities, minority groups, and journalists for years
to come. A January 2021 joint intelligence bulletin suggested that
"in-person engagement between DVEs [domestic violent extremists]
of differing ideological goals during the Capitol breach likely served
to foster connections, which may increase DVEs' willingness, capability, and motivation to attack and undermine a government they
view as illegitimate." As with those who turn to extremists when they
feel something has been wrongfully taken from them, the bulletin
also warned that the "shared false narrative of a 'stolen' election…
may lead some individuals to adopt the belief that there is no political
solution to address their grievances and violent action is necessary." A
survey conducted in June 2023 by the Chicago Project on Security
and Threats estimated that 7 percent of American adults (approximately eighteen million) agreed that "the use of force is justified to

restore Donald Trump to the presidency." The survey also noted that 17 percent, from across the political spectrum, supported the use of force to coerce members of Congress.

The January 6 attack may have also inspired the plot—foiled in 2022—to violently end Germany's democracy. Just days after Brazil's 2023 presidential inauguration, and almost two years to the day after the attack on the U.S. Capitol, supporters of defeated president Jair Bolsonaro attacked Brazil's Congress, Presidential Palace, and Supreme Court. Like Trump, Bolsonaro had claimed for months that he could lose only if the results were falsified. In early 2023, Republican candidate for state representative in New Mexico, Solomon Peña, was arrested for allegedly paying the men who fired shots at the homes of Democratic state legislators and county commissioners in Albuquerque. Peña had attended President Trump's January 6 rally at the Ellipse. He, too, blamed his own failed candidacy on election fraud.

Following Trump's four felony indictments in 2023, threats against law enforcement authorities and judges accelerated. The top prosecutors in each of the four cases required around-the-clock protection. The judge overseeing the case in Georgia added extra protections to safeguard the identities of prospective jurors. The FBI created a special unit to deal with the increased threats to its personnel and facilities.

On October 30, 2020, the chairman of the Joint Chiefs of Staff, General Mark Milley, phoned his Chinese counterpart who reportedly believed that the United States was planning to attack China. Almost three years later, Trump addressed the call by suggesting that Milley, still serving as the nation's senior military official, was a traitor who deserved the death penalty. Not to be outdone, Congressman

Paul Gosar (R-AZ) suggested, "In a better society...General Milley would be hung."

During a 2023 campaign speech on Veterans Day (later amplified on social media), the former president pledged to "root out the Communists, Marxists, Fascists, and the radical-left thugs that live like vermin within the confines of our country, that lie and steal and cheat on elections and will do anything possible...whether legally or illegally, to destroy America, and to destroy the American Dream."

Part 7

★ ★ ★

SERVICE
BEFORE SELF

CHAPTER 34

Leadership Is Not a Popularity Contest

At the conclusion of President Trump's second impeachment trial, the Senate majority leader characterized President George Washington's farewell address as "an amazing gift to the future generations, the knowledge that this country will always be greater than any one person, even our most renowned." Facing censure from Nebraska Republicans over his criticism of former president Trump's January 6 incitement, Senator Ben Sasse (R-NE) similarly reminded his Nebraska colleagues that "politics isn't about the weird worship of one dude."

A cult of personality relies heavily on charisma, divisive rhetoric, and corrupt patronage. The cult typically demonstrates a blind loyalty to its leader that preempts coherent ideology or legitimate accountability. It was perhaps in this context that President Trump hoped that his cult-like following would serve as a shield against future political accountability.

@realDonaldTrump

How do you impeach a president who has won
perhaps the greatest election of all time, done nothing
wrong (no Collusion with Russia, it was the Dems that
Colluded), had the most successful first two years of
any president, **and is the most popular Republican in
party history 93%?**

5:16 AM - Jan 4, 2019

For elected officials, the mere attainment of office does not indicate wisdom, integrity, or general leadership acumen. Though the process of getting elected or appointed to a position of public leadership is to varying degrees a popularity contest, the work of leading is about purpose and principle. It may be easier to lead when one is well liked or admired, though that should never be the primary objective. Rather, admiration and more importantly respect are the natural by-products of effective and ethical leadership.

Leadership and public opinion. Elected officials can work to meet the needs of and curry favor with constituents and subordinates without sacrificing standards, principles, and organizational imperatives. Working to get buy-in from constituencies for various policies and courses of action is necessary and is distinct from seeking popularity for its own sake. Though public opinion polls can measure policy preferences, poll results should not play a major role in informing complex policy decisions that require considerable deliberation and risk analysis. Hence the political adage that you cannot lead from the polls.

Job approval is often tied to respect, and the leader who is respected for sticking to principle versus pandering may yet garner the approval and support of constituents who do not necessarily support all of that leader's policies. This is especially true in times of crisis when leaders are required to make difficult choices.

Former deputy assistant secretary of state George Kent described Ambassador Marie Yovanovitch's efforts in Ukraine by saying, "You can't promote principled anticorruption action without pissing off corrupt people." Thomas Jefferson described principled leadership when he wrote, "Our part is to pursue with steadiness what is right, turning neither to the right nor left for the intrigues or popular delusions of the day, assured that the public approbation will in the end be with us." One must have the courage to make principled decisions despite inevitable criticism.

Abraham Lincoln once stated, "With public sentiment, nothing can fail; without it nothing can succeed." For President Trump, the statement "many people agree with me" often served to justify his pursuit of self-serving policies. It represented a mindset that conflates personal needs with organizational objectives. It prioritizes personal popularity over substantive discourse and genuine consensus-building.

In the following post, the president was right to question his initial assessment.

@realDonaldTrump

Great honor, I think? Mark Zuckerberg recently stated that "Donald J. Trump is Number 1 on Facebook. Number 2 is Prime Minister Modi of India." Actually, I am going to India in two weeks. Looking forward to it!

6:38 PM - Feb 14, 2020

President Trump also put a premium on television ratings, which is hardly a measure of leadership success.

> @realDonaldTrump
> I've had great "ratings" my whole life, there's nothing unusual about that for me. The White House News Conference ratings are "through the roof" (Monday Night Football, Bachelor Finale, @nytimes) **but I don't care about that.** I care about going around the Fake News to the PEOPLE!
> 6:57 AM - Apr 21, 2020

For a president who would have preferred a "Daily Ratings Brief" over his actual President's Daily Brief covering national security issues, his aforementioned "I don't care about that" comment rings hollow.

> @realDonaldTrump
> Wow, television ratings just out: 31 million people watched the Inauguration, 11 million more than the very good ratings from 4 years ago!
> 4:51 AM - Jan 22, 2017

> @realDonaldTrump
> Thank you for all of the nice compliments and reviews on the State of the Union speech. 45.6 million people watched, the highest number in history. @FoxNews beat every other Network, for the first time ever, with 11.7 million people tuning in. Delivered from the heart!
> 4:02 AM - Feb 1, 2018

@realDonaldTrump

Do not believe the Fake News Media. Oklahoma
speech had the highest Saturday television ratings
in @FoxNews history. @seanhannity dominated T.V.
with my interview on Thursday night, more than @CNN
& MSDNC COMBINED. These are the real polls, the
Silent Majority, not FAKE POLLS!

7:17 AM - Jun 27, 2020

Crowd size was perhaps one of the few measures of success
more important to the president than television viewership.

@realDonaldTrump

The crowds at my Rallies are far bigger than they have
ever been before, including the 2016 election. Never
an empty seat in these large venues, many thousands
of people watching screens outside. Enthusiasm
& Spirit is through the roof. SOMETHING BIG IS
HAPPENING - WATCH!

5:11 AM - Oct 15, 2018

Tragically, the numbers of people attending his rallies were seldom, if
ever, acknowledged to his satisfaction.

@realDonaldTrump

Hope the Fake News, which never discusses it, is
talking about the big crowds forming for my New
Hampshire Rally tonight. They won't!

8:14 AM - Feb 10, 2020

WHAT HANGS IN THE BALANCE

@realDonaldTrump
Great news! Tonight, we broke the all-time attendance
record previously held by Elton John at #SNHUArena
in Manchester, New Hampshire!
10:52 PM - Aug 15, 2019

I can only assume that Sir Elton John's congratulatory call to President
Trump also went unreported by the "Fake News Media." The president's inordinate need to post about crowd size and television ratings
distracted from the more pressing concerns of a national leader. His
focus on these matters also suggests a self-esteem-induced drive for
validation that is associated with certain personality disorders—the
topic of the next chapter.

CHAPTER 35

Personality Disorders

★ ★ ★

The leadership failures chronicled in this book feature behaviors associated with at least three major personality disorders. They include *narcissistic* personality disorder (NPD), *antisocial* personality disorder (ASPD), and *paranoid* personality disorder (PPD). These disorders make up three of the ten distinct personality disorders detailed in the American Psychiatric Association's *Diagnostic and Statistical Manual of Mental Disorders (DSM-5-TR™)*.

A professional diagnosis of a personality disorder requires evidence of long-term behavior patterns matching a designated number of criteria associated with that disorder (among other factors). The extent of an individual's "functional impairment" can be judged based on a person's behaviors and, perhaps more importantly, by the consequences of those behaviors. The public leadership examples provided in the following pages, as they relate to the stated criteria for each disorder, are *not* intended to form the basis of any diagnosis. They are presented merely as examples of behaviors that resemble the associated criteria.

Narcissistic Personality Disorder

Diagnostic Criteria F60.81

A pervasive pattern of grandiosity (in fantasy or behavior), need for admiration, and lack of empathy, beginning by early adulthood and present in a variety of contexts, as indicated by five (or more) of the following:

1. Has a grandiose sense of self-importance (e.g., exaggerates achievements and talents, expects to be recognized as superior without commensurate achievements).

2. Is preoccupied with fantasies of unlimited success, power, brilliance, beauty, or ideal love.

3. Believes that he or she is "special" and unique and can only be understood by, or should associate with, other special or high-status people (or institutions).

4. Requires excessive admiration.

5. Has a sense of entitlement (i.e., unreasonable expectations of especially favorable treatment or automatic compliance with his or her expectations).

6. Is interpersonally exploitative (i.e., takes advantage of others to achieve his or her own ends).

7. Lacks empathy: is unwilling to recognize or identify with the feelings and needs of others.

8. Is often envious of others or believes that others are envious of him or her.

9. Shows arrogant, haughty behaviors or attitudes.

Reprinted with permission from the Diagnostic and Statistical Manual of Mental Disorders, Fifth Edition, Text Revision (Copyright © 2022). American Psychiatric Association. All Rights Reserved.

Criterion 1*—Has a grandiose sense of self-importance (e.g., exagger-ates achievements and talents, expects to be recognized as superior without commensurate achievements).* With respect to an inflated sense of self-importance, President Trump routinely struggled to differentiate himself from the institution of the presidency, the entire executive branch, and even the nation as a whole. He described the accomplishments of federal agencies by declaring, "I did this." He responded to personal criticism with statements like, "They can't treat the U.S. that way." He branded whistleblowers as "traitors" and "enemies of the state." This lack of differentiation (and respect for boundaries) contributed to episodes of undue influence, reprisal, and other abuses of power.

A critical leadership attribute is possessing the self-awareness and rational introspection to understand one's strengths and compensate for one's weaknesses. Individuals with NPD *tend to overestimate their abilities,*[1] as summarized in Donald Trump's declaration, "I alone can fix it."

> @realDonaldTrump
> THE LONE WARRIOR!
> 10:49 AM - Jun 30, 2020

He also tended to exaggerate the fruits of his diplomatic efforts.

> @realDonaldTrump
> Just landed - a long trip, but **everybody can now feel much safer than the day I took office. There is no longer a Nuclear Threat from North Korea.** Meeting with Kim Jong Un was an interesting and very positive experi-ence. North Korea has great potential for the future!
> 2:56 AM - Jun 13, 2018

....
[1] American Psychiatric Association, *DSM-5-TR*™, 761.

Thomas Jefferson assessed his own momentous contributions to American democracy:

> Having been one of those who entered into public life at the commencement of an era the most extraordinary which the history of man has ever yet presented to his contemplation, I claim nothing more, for the part I have acted in it, than a common merit of having, with others, faithfully endeavored to do my duty in the several stations allotted me.
>
> I have been connected, as many fellow laborers were, with the great events which happened to mark the epoch of our lives. But these belong to no one in particular, all of us did our parts, and no one can claim the transactions to himself.

Humility permeates Jefferson's insightful and selfless reflection. In stark contrast, an inability to grasp the actual scope of one's accomplishments with respect to historically significant milestones and movements can result in delusions of grandeur.

> @realDonaldTrump
>
> **I have done more for WOMEN than just about any President in HISTORY!** As we celebrate the 100th Anniversary of women's voting rights, we should build a BEAUTIFUL STATUE in Washington D.C. to honor the many brave women who made this possible for our GREAT COUNTRY...
>
> 12:20 PM - Aug 14, 2020

The president was not afraid of appearing *boastful and pretentious.*[2]

@realDonaldTrump

....The best thing that ever happened to Puerto Rico is President Donald J. Trump. So many wonderful people, but with such bad Island leadership and with so much money wasted. Cannot continue to hurt our Farmers and States with these massive payments, and so little appreciation!

4:45 AM - Apr 2, 2019

@realDonaldTrump

Despite the tremendous success that I have had as President, including perhaps the greatest ECONOMY and most successful first two years of any President in history, they have stolen two years of my (our) Presidency (Collusion Delusion) that we will never be able to get back.....

8:05 PM - May 5, 2019

@realDonaldTrump

Just arrived in Colorado. Getting ready to deliver the commencement speech at the Air Force Academy graduation. **Very exciting - probably will be broadcast live on TV. They want good ratings!**

9:30 AM - May 30, 2019

....

[2] American Psychiatric Association, *DSM-5-TR™*, 761.

@realDonaldTrump
The Dow Jones Industrial just closed above 29,000!
You are so lucky to have me as your President With
Joe Hiden' it would crash
4:05 PM - Sep 2, 2020

Juneteenth is the oldest nationally celebrated commemoration of the ending of slavery in the United States (becoming a federal holiday in 2021). When a *Wall Street Journal* reporter in 2020 asked President Trump if he knew what Juneteenth was, he responded with the following:

> I did something good. I made it famous. I made Juneteenth very famous. It's actually an important event, an important time. But nobody had ever heard of it. Very few people have heard of it. Actually, a young African American Secret Service agent knew what it was. I had political people who had no idea. Did you ever hear of Juneteenth before?

Those with NPD *may blithely assume that others attribute the same value to their efforts and may be surprised when the praise they expect and feel they deserve is not forthcoming.*[3]

@realDonaldTrump
The Republicans are 5-0 in recent Congressional races, a point which the Fake News Media continuously fails to mention. **I backed and campaigned for all of the winners. They give me credit for one.** Hopefully, Rick Saccone will be another big win on Tuesday.
10:02 AM - Mar 11, 2018

....

[3] American Psychiatric Association, *DSM-5-TR*™, 761.

@realDonaldTrump

The Trump Administration has achieved more in the first 2 1/2 years of its existence than perhaps any administration in the history of our Country. **We get ZERO media credit for what we have done, and are doing,** but the people know, and that's all that is important!

10:55 AM - Sep 9, 2019

@realDonaldTrump

Great, Just Out! 51% Approval Rating in Rasmussen Poll. 95% in Republican Party. Stock Market up BIG today. **Will I ever be given credit** for the Markets and Economy? Next year will be BIG!

10:21 AM - Sep 14, 2020

Often implicit in the inflated judgments of their own accomplishments is an underestimation or devaluation of the contributions of others.[4]

@realDonaldTrump

Thank you Georgia! **They say that my endorsement last week of Brian Kemp,** in the Republican Primary for Governor **against a very worthy opponent, lifted him from 5 points down to a 70% to 30% victory!** Two very good and talented men in a great race, but congratulations to Brian!

5:16 PM - Jul 25, 2018

....

[4] American Psychiatric Association, *DSM-5-TR*™, 761.

***Criterion 2**—Is preoccupied with fantasies of unlimited success, power, brilliance, beauty, or ideal love.* A decades-long Harvard study that traced people into old age determined that happy people are not self-absorbed.

> @realDonaldTrump
> ...or a very nervous and skinny version of Pocahontas (1/1024th), **as your President, rather than what you have now, so great looking and smart, a true Stable Genius!** Sorry to say that even Social Media would be driven out of business along with, and finally, the Fake News Media!
> 8:52 AM - Jul 11, 2019

They may *compare themselves favorably with famous or privileged people.*[5]

> @realDonaldTrump
> .@newtgingrich just stated that there has been **no president since Abraham Lincoln** who has been treated worse or more unfairly by the media than your favorite President, me! At the same time there has been no president who has accomplished more in his first two years in office!
> 7:11 AM - Jan 19, 2019

> @realDonaldTrump
> **"This President has done more for African Americans**

....

[5] American Psychiatric Association, *DSM-5-TR™*, 761.

in this Country than any President since Lincoln."
@LouDobbs
8:16 PM - Feb 6, 2020

With respect to the last post, both Dobbs and Trump may have forgotten about the Civil Rights Acts of 1964 and 1968 and the Voting Rights Act of 1965, to name a few.

Criterion 3—Believes that he or she is "special" and unique and can only be understood by, or should associate with, other special or high-status people (or institutions).

@realDonaldTrump
Nobody could have done what I've done for
#PuertoRico with so little appreciation. So much work!
4:37 PM - Oct 8, 2017

The president's self-esteem may have been enhanced when he publicly associated himself with successful individuals and institutions.

@realDonaldTrump
Spoke to @TigerWoods to congratulate him on the great victory he had in yesterday's @TheMasters, & to inform him that because of his incredible Success & Comeback in Sports (Golf) and, more importantly, LIFE, I will be presenting him with the PRESIDENTIAL MEDAL OF FREEDOM!
10:35 AM - Apr 15, 2019

@realDonaldTrump

Has anyone noticed that the **top shows on @foxnews and cable ratings are those that are Fair (or great) to your favorite President, me!** Congratulations to @seanhannity for being the number one show on Cable Television!

10:24 AM - Aug 31, 2019

Characteristic of Criterion 3 is the tendency to *devalue the credentials of those who disappoint them.*[6]

@realDonaldTrump

John Bolton, one of the dumbest people I've met in government and sadly, I've met plenty, states often that I respected, and even trusted, Vladimir Putin of Russia more than those in our Intelligence Agencies. While of course that is not true, if the first people you met from....

...so called American Intelligence were Dirty Cops who have now proven to be sleazebags at the highest level like James Comey, proven liar James Clapper, & perhaps the lowest of them all, Wacko John Brennan who headed the CIA, you could perhaps understand my reluctance to embrace!

7:45 AM - Aug 11, 2020

***Criterion 4**—Requires excessive admiration.* Trump's apparently fragile self-esteem demanded heavy doses of validation and admiration.

....

[6] American Psychiatric Association, *DSM-5-TR*™, 762.

@realDonaldTrump
They do stories so big on Elizabeth "Pocahontas"
Warren's crowd sizes, adding many more people than
are actually there, **and yet my crowds, which are far
bigger, get no coverage at all.** Fake News!
6:04 PM - Aug 27, 2019

@realDonaldTrump
96% Approval Rating in the Republican Party. 50% in
new Rasmussen Poll (higher than Obama at this point
in time). Thank you!
8:22 AM - Aug 3, 2020

@realDonaldTrump
It is amazing that I can be at 51% with Zogby when
the Fake & Corrupt News is almost 100% against me.
Great job Mr. President!
5:49 PM - Aug 27, 2019

He was also preoccupied with how others regarded him, even
when the focus should have been on the devastation that
resulted from successive hurricanes, and those working at the
CIA, respectively.

@realDonaldTrump
A great day in Puerto Rico yesterday. While some
of the news coverage is Fake, most showed great
warmth and friendship.
3:25 AM - Oct 4, 2017

@realDonaldTrump
Had a great meeting at CIA Headquarters yesterday, **packed house**, paid great respect to Wall, **long standing ovations**, amazing people. **WIN!**
4:35 AM - Jan 22, 2017

In August 2019, mass shootings in Dayton, Ohio, and El Paso, Texas, claimed the lives of thirty-two people. During a press conference in El Paso, the president was asked about what he had seen during his visit to the two cities. His reply began with, "We had an amazing day. As you know, we left Ohio. And the love and the respect for the office of the presidency, it was—I wish you could have been in there to see it. I wish you could have been in there."

Former Iraqi president Saddam Hussein was known to publicly question his citizens about who was responsible for their economic well-being, only to turn the predictable answers into propaganda. For an insecure leader who does not have the "luxury" of coercing his constituents, it may become "necessary" to congratulate oneself or suggest that others provide that validation.

@realDonaldTrump
Also, congratulations to @OANN on the great job you are doing and the big ratings jump (**"thank you President Trump"**)!
3:56 AM - May 13, 2019

@realDonaldTrump
Another Vaccine just announced. This time by Moderna, 95% effective. For those great "historians", **please remember that these great discoveries**, which will end the China Plague, **all took place on my watch!**
9:19 AM - Nov 16, 2020

Criterion 5—*Has a sense of entitlement (i.e., unreasonable expectations of especially favorable treatment or automatic compliance with his or her expectations).*

@realDonaldTrump
Impeached for what, having created the greatest Economy in the history of our Country, building our strongest ever Military, Cutting Taxes too much?
11:53 PM - Oct 9, 2019

Immediately following the 2020 election, President Trump stated, "I don't get it. All these other Republicans, all over the country, they all win their races. And I'm the only guy that loses?" What he failed to understand was that many voters skipped the presidential race but still voted down-ballot in other races. This was the case in Georgia, for example, where the state's Republican secretary of state reported that approximately twenty-eight thousand Georgians declined to vote for president. This resulted in one Republican congressman in Georgia getting about thirty-three thousand more votes than President Trump.

Those with NPD *expect to be catered to and are puzzled or furious when this does not happen.*[7] President Trump expected that Attorney General Sessions would inappropriately shield him from the investigation into Russian election interference. Sessions's recusal resulted in presidential criticism that continued well beyond Session's time in the Trump administration.

....

[7] American Psychiatric Association, *DSM-5-TR*™, 762.

@realDonaldTrump

Jeff, you had your chance & you blew it. Recused yourself ON DAY ONE (you never told me of a problem),
and ran for the hills. You had no courage, & ruined
many lives. The dirty cops, & others, got caught by
better & stronger people than you. Hopefully this
slime will pay a big...

6:53 PM - May 23, 2020

Another feature of Criterion 5 is the tendency to *get irritated when others fail to assist "in their very important work."*[8]

@realDonaldTrump

Attorney General Jeff Sessions has taken a VERY
weak position on Hillary Clinton crimes (where are
E-mails & DNC server) & Intel leakers!

3:12 AM - Jul 25, 2017

Criterion 6—*Is interpersonally exploitative (i.e., takes advantage of others to achieve his or her own ends).* A feature of this criterion is the tendency *to form friendships or romantic relationships only if the other person seems likely to advance their purposes or otherwise enhance their self-esteem.*[9] In the president's professional relationships, this tendency was evident in his diplomatic flirtations with autocrats and authoritarians like Kim Jong Un, Recep Tayyip Erdoğan, and Vladimir Putin.

. . . .

[8] American Psychiatric Association, *DSM-5-TR*™, 762.

[9] American Psychiatric Association, *DSM-5-TR*™, 762.

Criterion 7—*Lacks empathy: is unwilling to recognize or identify with the feelings and needs of others.*

@realDonaldTrump
Anthony Scaramucci is a highly unstable "nut job" who was with other candidates in the primary who got shellacked, & then unfortunately wheedled his way into my campaign. I barely knew him until his 11 days of gross incompetence-made a fool of himself, bad on TV. Abused staff,...

....got fired. Wrote a very nice book about me just recently. Now the book is a lie? Said his wife was driving him crazy, "something big" was happening with her. Getting divorced. He was a mental wreck. We didn't want him around. Now Fake News puts him on like he was my buddy!
9:19 AM - Aug 19, 2019

Criterion 8—*Is often envious of others or believes that others are envious of him or her.*

@realDonaldTrump
The Democrats are just ANGRY that the vaccine and delivery are so far ahead of schedule. They hate what they are seeing. Saving lives should make them happy, not sad!
4:44 PM - Sep 17, 2020

They may begrudge others their successes or possessions, feeling that they better deserve those achievements, admiration, or privileges.[10]

> @realDonaldTrump
> Something how Dr. Fauci is revered by the LameStream Media as such a great professional, having done, they say, such an incredible job, yet he works for me and the Trump Administration, and I am in no way given any credit for my work. Gee, could this just be more Fake News?
> 10:11 AM - Jan 3, 2021

Criterion 9—*Shows arrogant, haughty behaviors or attitudes.*

> @realDonaldTrump
> The problem with banker Jamie Dimon running for President is that he doesn't have the aptitude or "smarts" & is a poor public speaker & nervous mess - otherwise he is wonderful. I've made a lot of bankers, and others, look much smarter than they are with my great economic policy!
> 4:22 AM - Sep 13, 2018

> @realDonaldTrump
> I have been very critical about the way the U.K. and Prime Minister Theresa May handled Brexit. **What a mess she and her representatives have created. I told her how it should be done**, but she decided to go another way. I do not know the Ambassador, but he is not liked or well....
> 11:31 AM - Jul 8, 2019

....
[10] American Psychiatric Association, *DSM-5-TR*™, 762.

@realDonaldTrump
Mini Mike Bloomberg just "quit" the race for President. **I could have told him long ago that he didn't have what it takes**, and he would have saved himself a billion dollars, the real cost. Now he will pour money into Sleepy Joe's campaign, hoping to save face. It won't work!
10:40 AM - Mar 4, 2020

Vulnerability in self-esteem makes individuals with narcissistic personality disorder very sensitive to criticism or defeat.[11]

@realDonaldTrump
To all of those who have asked, I will not be going to the Inauguration on January 20th.
10:44 AM - Jan 8, 2021

Antisocial Personality Disorder
Diagnostic Criteria F60.2
A. A pervasive pattern of disregard for and violation of the rights of others, occurring since age 15 years, as indicated by three (or more) of the following:

1. Failure to conform to social norms with respect to lawful behaviors, as indicated by repeatedly performing acts that are grounds for arrest.

2. Deceitfulness, as indicated by repeated lying, use of aliases, or conning others for personal profit or pleasure.

....
[11] American Psychiatric Association, *DSM-5-TR*™, 763.

3. Impulsivity or failure to plan ahead.

4. Irritability and aggressiveness, as indicated by repeated physical fights or assaults.

5. Reckless disregard for safety of self or others.

6. Consistent irresponsibility, as indicated by repeated failure to sustain consistent work behavior or honor financial obligations.

7. Lack of remorse, as indicated by being indifferent to or rationalizing having hurt, mistreated, or stolen from another.

B. The individual is at least age 18 years.

C. There is evidence of conduct disorder with onset before age 15 years.

D. The occurrence of antisocial behavior is not exclusively during the course of schizophrenia or bipolar disorder.

Reprinted with permission from the Diagnostic and Statistical Manual of Mental Disorders, Fifth Edition, Text Revision (Copyright © 2022). American Psychiatric Association. All Rights Reserved.

Criterion A1—*Failure to conform to social norms with respect to lawful behaviors, as indicated by repeatedly performing acts that are grounds for arrest,* as in President Trump's extra-constitutional attempts to hold on to power following the 2020 election.

@realDonaldTrump
#OVERTURN
10:34 AM - Dec 9, 2020

As President Trump departed the White House at the end of his term, he was personally involved with packing boxes that would be transported to his Mar-a-Lago Club and residence in Palm Beach, Florida. Many of the boxes contained classified documents, including top-secret documents further categorized as sensitive compartmented information and protected by special access programs. By definition, the unauthorized disclosure of top-secret information reasonably could be expected to cause exceptionally grave damage to the national security of the United States. Among the hundreds of classified documents was information regarding defense and weapons capabilities, America's nuclear programs, and potential vulnerabilities of the U.S. and its allies to attack. Some of the documents would later make their way to his Bedminster club and residence in New Jersey, where he on two occasions shared their contents with unauthorized personnel. Trump was not legally authorized to retain these documents, and his clubs/residences—which regularly hosted social events—were not authorized for their storage. While president, Trump had stated the following about the importance of protecting classified information:

> As the head of the executive branch and Commander in Chief, I have a unique, Constitutional responsibility to protect the Nation's classified information, including by controlling access to it....More broadly, the issue of [a former executive branch official's] security clearance raises larger questions about the practice of former officials maintaining access to our Nation's most sensitive secrets long after their time in Government has ended.... Any access granted to our Nation's secrets should be in furtherance of national, not personal, interests.

After repeated attempts by federal agencies to have the former president return *all* of the documents with classification markings (Trump's legal team had already returned some documents), a federal grand jury issued a subpoena in May 2022 to compel Trump to do the right thing. He did not, and he further claimed through his attorneys that he was no longer in possession of classified materials. A search conducted by the FBI pursuant to a court-issued warrant in August 2022 turned up an additional 102 documents with classification markings in the former president's Mar-a-Lago office and storage room. In June 2023, Donald Trump became the first president—current or former—to be *federally* indicted. He was charged with willful retention of national defense information, conspiracy to obstruct justice, scheme to conceal, false statements and representations, and various counts for corruptly concealing, altering, destroying, and mutilating a document, record, or other object. Trump pleaded not guilty to all forty counts. Two of the former president's subordinates were also charged.

Criterion A2—Deceitfulness, as indicated by repeated lying, use of aliases, or conning others for personal profit or pleasure.

@realDonaldTrump

No Collusion, **No Obstruction, Complete and Total EXONERATION.** KEEP AMERICA GREAT!

1:42 PM - Mar 24, 2019

@realDonaldTrump

I WON THE ELECTION!

11:55 PM - Nov 15, 2020

***Criterion A5**—Reckless disregard for safety of self or others.* One example is President Trump's insistence that he hold large (sometimes indoor) rallies before the availability of COVID-19 vaccines.

@realDonaldTrump
Heading to North Carolina soon. Really Big Crowd. We will have a great time!!!
11:10 AM - Oct 15, 2020

***Criterion A7**—Lack of remorse, as indicated by being indifferent to or rationalizing having hurt, mistreated, or stolen from another.*

@realDonaldTrump
"IT WAS A PERFECT CONVERSATION WITH UKRAINE PRESIDENT!"
9:25 AM - Sep 27, 2019

@realDonaldTrump
You can't Impeach someone who hasn't done anything wrong!
6:48 PM - Nov 1, 2019

An associated feature of APD is the tendency to *be excessively opinionated, self-assured, or cocky.*[12]

@realDonaldTrump
LONDON needs a new mayor ASAP. Khan is a disaster - will only get worse!
11:47 AM - Jun 15, 2019

....

[12] American Psychiatric Association, *DSM-5-TR*™, 750.

@realDonaldTrump

Being nice to Rocket Man hasn't worked in 25 years, why would it work now? Clinton failed, Bush failed, and Obama failed. **I won't fail.**

12:01 PM - Oct 1, 2017

@realDonaldTrump

Mini Mike Bloomberg's debate performance tonight was perhaps the worst in the history of debates, and there have been some really bad ones. He was stumbling, bumbling and grossly incompetent. If this doesn't knock him out of the race, nothing will. **Not so easy to do what I did!**

1:19 AM - Feb 20, 2020

Paranoid Personality Disorder

Diagnostic Criteria F60.0

A. A pervasive distrust and suspiciousness of others such that their motives are interpreted as malevolent, beginning by early adulthood and present in a variety of contexts, as indicated by four (or more) of the following:

1. Suspects, without sufficient basis, that others are exploiting, harming, or deceiving him or her.

2. Is preoccupied with unjustified doubts about the loyalty or trustworthiness of friends or associates.

3. Is reluctant to confide in others because of unwarranted fear that the information will be used maliciously against him or her.

4. Reads hidden demeaning or threatening meanings into benign remarks or events.

5. Persistently bears grudges (i.e., is unforgiving of insults, injuries, or slights).

6. Perceives attacks on his or her character or reputation that are not apparent to others and is quick to react angrily or to counterattack.

7. Has recurrent suspicions, without justification, regarding fidelity of spouse or sexual partner.

B. Does not occur exclusively during the course of schizophrenia, a bipolar disorder or depressive disorder with psychotic features, or another psychotic disorder and is not attributable to the physiological effects of another medical condition.

Note: If criteria are met prior to the onset of schizophrenia, add "premorbid," i.e., "paranoid personality disorder (premorbid)."
Reprinted with permission from the Diagnostic and Statistical Manual of Mental Disorders, Fifth Edition, Text Revision (Copyright © 2022). American Psychiatric Association. All Rights Reserved.

Criterion A1—*Suspects, without sufficient basis, that others are exploiting, harming, or deceiving him or her.*

@realDonaldTrump
The Radical Left Democrats, working with their partner, the Fake News Media, are trying to STEAL this Election. We won't let them!
10:37 AM - Nov 16, 2020

Criterion A5—Persistently bears grudges (i.e., is unforgiving of insults, injuries, or slights). In the following interview conducted by Jonathan Swan (Axios/HBO) in August 2020, President Trump was asked about the legacy of civil rights icon John Lewis:

Swan: John Lewis is lying in State in the U.S. Capitol. How do you think history will remember John Lewis?

Trump: I don't know. I really don't know. I don't know. I don't know John Lewis. He chose not to come to my inauguration. He chose, uh, I never met John Lewis actually, I don't believe.

Swan: Do you find him impressive?

Trump: I can't say one way or the other. I find a lot of people impressive. I find many people not impressive...

Swan: Do you find his story impressive?

Trump: He didn't come to my inauguration. He didn't come to my State of the Union speeches. And that's okay. That's his right. And again, nobody has done more for Black Americans than I have. He should have come. I think he made a big mistake by not showing up.

Swan: But taking your relationship with him out of it, do you find his story impressive, what he's done for this country?

Trump: He was a person that devoted a lot of energy and a lot of heart to civil rights. But there were many others also.

When another reporter asked President Trump if he planned to pay tribute to Lewis at the Capitol, Trump responded, "No. I won't be going. No."

Criterion A6—*Perceives attacks on his or her character or repu-tation that are not apparent to others and is quick to react angrily or to counterattack.* President Trump referred to a government study on hydroxychloroquine as "anti-Trump" because it did not support his personal assessment of the drug's effectiveness in preventing and treating COVID-19. In the following post, he suggested that personal animus may have motivated the Supreme Court's determi-nation that his administration's termination of the Deferred Action for Childhood Arrivals (DACA) program was done in an "arbitrary and capricious manner."

@realDonaldTrump
Do you get the impression that the Supreme Court doesn't like me?
11:10 AM - Jun 18, 2020

An associated feature of PPD is the *need to have a high degree of control over those around them.*[13] This behavior can result in various mani-festations of undue influence and demands for inappropriate loyalty.

....

[13] American Psychiatric Association, *DSM-5-TR™*, 739.

The essential feature of paranoid personality disorder is a pattern of pervasive distrust and suspiciousness of others such that their motives are interpreted as malevolent.[14] An example of this phenomenon was President-elect Trump's view that the purpose of the sanctions imposed on Russia by the Obama administration (in response to their interference in the 2016 election) was to embarrass him by delegitimizing his victory. Similarly, he accused his attorney general of "hating Trump" after Barr publicly stated that there was no evidence of widespread fraud in the 2020 election.

Those with PPD *are often attuned to issues of power and rank,*[15] as in Trump declaring, "When somebody is the president of the United States, the authority is total." *Attracted by simplistic formulations of the world, they are often wary of ambiguous situations,*[16] as when Trump declared that the coronavirus would "go away like things go away." Finally, *they may be perceived as "fanatics" and form tightly knit "cults" or groups with others who share their paranoid belief systems.*[17] The "Stop the Steal" movement and QAnon are two such examples.

The nexus of personality disorders and self-interest. The combination of a grandiose sense of self-importance, fantasies of unlimited power and brilliance, the belief that one is special or unique, and the "self-protective" instincts associated with paranoia may fuel a sense of entitlement that encourages the brazen pursuit of self-interest. The need for constant attention and admiration

....

[14] American Psychiatric Association, *DSM-5-TR*™, 738.

[15] American Psychiatric Association, *DSM-5-TR*™, 739.

[16] American Psychiatric Association, *DSM-5-TR*™, 739.

[17] American Psychiatric Association, *DSM-5-TR*™, 739.

might similarly fuel a desire for power and "success" at any cost. The pursuit of self-interest is further enabled by deceitfulness, an absence of empathy and remorse, and the tendency to be interpersonally (and institutionally) exploitative. The result is a person unconstrained by social norms and lawful behaviors. Self-interest becomes the primary consideration in decision-making.

> *The virtues are lost in self-interest as rivers are lost in the sea.*
> —FRANÇOIS DE LA ROCHEFOUCAULD

Thomas Jefferson wrote, "Take from man his selfish propensities, and he can have nothing to seduce him from the practice of virtue." The consequences of the aforementioned behavioral patterns are far more harmful than the seemingly benign dysfunction revealed in a collection of presidential posts. They can, for example, result in leaders conflating themselves with the institutions they are meant to serve and protect. Runaway self-interest fuels myriad abuses of power, including sexual harassment or assault and investigative and prosecutorial misconduct, to name a few. It results in people violating their oaths and failing to uphold core values and ethical norms. Excessive self-interest leaves in its wake the ruined careers of public servants who have dedicated their lives to something greater than—and often at the expense of—self-interest. Professional and diplomatic relationships—maintained through acts of unprincipled loyalty—are manipulated to serve personal interests at the expense of organizational interests. The abuses spurred by self-interest can diminish public trust in government and science. Self-interest can also pervert patriotism, undermine a free press, obstruct justice, threaten national security, and incite fear and violence.

President Trump's former secretary of defense Mark Esper said the following about his former boss: "He is an unprincipled person who, given his self-interest, should not be in the position of public service." Esper was but one of many former senior Trump administration officials to express that sentiment.

Other than his relatively poor handling of the COVID-19 pandemic and the actions that led to his two impeachments (his attempt to extort Ukraine and his efforts to overturn the 2020 election), the most problematic manifestation of President Trump's inability to separate personal and national interest was arguably the neglect he displayed in the aftermath of Russia's 2016 election interference. With Russia's preference for Trump in the 2016 election, the president's need for excessive admiration and approval made it next to impossible for him to acknowledge Russia's role and to combat future election meddling. His public comments undermined U.S. intelligence agencies and bolstered an adversary's ongoing efforts to destabilize the Western democratic order. Acknowledging the extent of Russia's efforts would have, in his view, questioned the legitimacy of his 2016 victory. The DOJ's investigation into Russian interference identified additional concerns that compromised the president's priorities:

> The evidence shows that the President was focused on the Russia investigation's implications for his presidency—and, specifically, on dispelling any suggestion that he was under investigation or had links to Russia.

President Trump's inability to separate personal interests from his solemn obligations as commander in chief continued until the waning days of his presidency. A Russian cyberattack discovered in late 2020 affected at least 250 systems within the federal government and the private sector (including several national security agencies). It was described as the most significant cyberespionage breach in U.S. history. President Trump was again hesitant to acknowledge the scope of the attack and the most likely perpetrator, as determined by his own cabinet officials.

> @realDonaldTrump
> The Cyber Hack is far greater in the Fake News Media than in actuality. I have been fully briefed and everything is well under control. Russia, Russia, Russia is the priority chant when anything happens because Lamestream is, for mostly financial reasons, petrified of....discussing the possibility that it may be China (it may!). There could also have been a hit on our ridiculous voting machines during the election, which is now obvious that I won big, making it an even more corrupted embarrassment for the USA. @DNI_Ratcliffe @SecPompeo
> 11:30 AM - Dec 19, 2020

The president's former national security advisor John Bolton described his former boss to the *New York Times Magazine* as follows:

> A complete aberration in the American system. We've had good and bad presidents, competent and incompetent presidents. But none of them was as centered on their own interest, as opposed to the national interest,

except Trump. And his concept of what the national interest was really changed from day to day and had a lot more to do with what his political fortunes were.

It was a combination of narcissistic, antisocial, and paranoid tendencies that led President Trump to sow distrust deceptively and exploitatively when undermining America's electoral processes and institutions. He falsely and persistently alleged that the 2020 presidential election was fraudulent—all for the purpose of maintaining power. Motivated by excessive self-interest, Trump attempted to use extra-constitutional means to overturn the results of a legitimate election and interfere with the peaceful transfer of power. As one U.S. senator explained after Trump's second impeachment, "This trial was about the final acts of a president who represents the very antitheses of our first president, and sought to place one man before the entire country—himself." The distrust Trump engendered may continue to unleash antidemocratic forces at home while potentially accelerating a fifteen-year global trend in democratic deterioration. At stake is the survival of a political system created to ensure popular sovereignty, equality, and individual rights.

CHAPTER 36

The Art of Exacerbating a Crisis: The COVID-19 Pandemic

★ ★ ★

In 2019, the Department of Health and Human Services (HHS) conducted a simulation (Crimson Contagion) to gauge the federal government's ability to contain a pandemic—specifically a novel influenza virus from China that would result in a predicted 110 million infections and 586,000 deaths in the United States. The simulation exposed inadequate and conflicting government policies, a strategic national stockpile with insufficient quantities of personal protective equipment (PPE), and an inadequate domestic manufacturing capacity. It revealed that America was not adequately postured for what would be the greatest public health crisis in a century: the COVID-19 pandemic.

A House Select Subcommittee report released almost three years after the start of the pandemic reiterated that America had been underprepared for such a crisis. Chronic underfunding, long-standing health disparities, and a failure to invest in preparedness were among the reasons. Dr. Anthony Fauci—serving as the director of the National Institute of Allergy and Infectious Diseases—suggested that the United States was not more successful in controlling the virus due to a variety of contributing factors. They included the absence of a uniform strategy (for testing and procuring medical equipment and PPE), a culture of resisting authority, an anti-science trend, and political divisiveness. The CDC admitted that its public guidance was confusing, further contributing to public distrust. As Dr. Deborah Birx, President Trump's White House coronavirus response coordinator, testified in 2022, public health guidance must be transparent about the evidence behind it. Finally, the divided nature of the American health system, among several layers of government and various private organizations, further complicated the response.

President Trump oversaw America's response to the pandemic from January 2020, when the first case was detected in the United States, to January 2021, when he left office. During that time, the virus killed over 450,000 Americans. Birx estimated that 130,000 of those deaths were preventable and that 30 to 40 percent of the deaths from early 2020 through mid-2022 were avoidable. The national death toll grew to over 840,000 by the end of 2021 and to one million by April 2022. In addition to the deaths, hundreds of thousands of other people—especially those over the age of seventy—suffered the effects of hospitalization, while countless others continue to suffer from the effects of long COVID.

President Trump was generally not responsible for the aforementioned systemic deficiencies. That said, when a significant and sudden event threatens an organization or the general public, senior public servants are expected to provide crisis leadership that is competent, ethical, empathetic, and selfless. The president's actions should not have contributed to the number of hospitalizations and deaths, as they most assuredly did. President Trump's response to the pandemic was characterized by narcissism and incompetence. His unquenchable thirst for recognition along with his exigency for a second term in the White House perverted his priorities and fueled reckless acts of self-interest. As demonstrated in the following pages, the president repeatedly downplayed the threat of the virus, engaged in wishful thinking, and trafficked in misinformation and inconsistent messaging. He also undermined the efforts of public health officials, along with state and local government leaders. The president's inflammatory language also contributed to discrimination and violence against Asian Americans.

Encouraging discrimination and violence. The COVID-19 pandemic originated in China, most likely from animal-to-human transmission or from an accidental leak from a laboratory in Wuhan. Despite intelligence reports questioning the transparency of the Chinese government at the outset of the pandemic, President Trump initially showered China's president with praise for his efforts to contain the virus.

During the first six weeks of the declared public health emergency, President Trump favored the commonly used term *coronavirus*. Beginning in mid-March, however, the president began referring to COVID-19 as "the Chinese virus." In a single day, he used the term in four posts in phrases such as "onslaught of the Chinese Virus" and "combat the Chinese Virus." As hate incidents against Asian Americans had already begun to rise nationwide, the president was compelled to address the issue.

@realDonaldTrump

It is very important that we totally protect our Asian American community in the United States, and all around the world. They are amazing people, and the spreading of the Virus....

....is NOT their fault in any way, shape, or form. They are working closely with us to get rid of it. WE WILL PREVAIL TOGETHER!

5:31 PM - Mar 23, 2020

On March 31, Representative Judy Chu (D-CA) spoke out about the surge of anti-Asian bigotry and hate crimes. She claimed that there had been at least one thousand hate crimes committed against Asian Americans in the previous five weeks and as many as one hundred hate crimes per day by late March. China's government certainly bore responsibility for the outbreak, for its lack of transparency, and for its initially slow response. Representative Chu was nonetheless compelled to express concern about the ongoing effect of Trump's "Chinese virus" rhetoric, which was also being amplified by conservative media outlets and even senior Trump administration officials.

@realDonaldTrump

All over the World the CoronaVirus, **a very bad "gift" from China**, marches on. Not good!

10:34 AM - May 28, 2020

In late June, the president held a rally in a Phoenix mega-church where he referred to COVID-19 as "the China flu," "Chinese flu," and "kung flu." As reports of anti-Asian verbal harassment and physical assaults continued to rise, many Asian Americans were reportedly afraid to return to normal life.

@realDonaldTrump

As I watch the Pandemic spread its ugly face all across the world, including the **tremendous damage it has done to the USA, I become more and more angry at China. People can see it, and I can feel it!**

6:52 PM - Jun 30, 2020

@realDonaldTrump

China has caused great damage to the United States and the rest of the World!

8:28 AM - Jul 6, 2020

The president likely exacerbated the harassment of Asian Americans by continuing to tie the virus's human and economic devastation to terms such as *China virus, Chinese virus, Wuhan virus,* and *China plague*—as he did in at least sixty-four posts, reposts, and in countless speeches and press conferences. Despite a general decline in hate crimes in the United States in 2020, attacks against Asian Americans during the same period rose by nearly 150 percent in sixteen of America's largest cities.

Narcissistic behavior. President Trump's narcissistic tendencies likely contributed to the wishful thinking that allowed him to recklessly downplay the threat of the virus and spread misinformation (topics addressed later in the chapter). The following examples showcase the president's narcissistic tendencies and overconfidence in his handling of the pandemic.

During a visit to the CDC in early March, the president was asked if he had considered not holding campaign rallies. Trump responded, "No, I haven't. Well, I'll tell you what. I haven't had any problems filling them. I mean, we just had one in North Carolina, South Carolina—all over the place. And we have tens of thousands of people standing outside the arena." When asked about the risk of having so many people close together, he responded, "It doesn't bother me at all and it doesn't bother them at all." When asked about the option of removing a group consisting mostly of Americans (some of whom had tested positive) from a cruise ship docked in California and putting them into quarantine, the president expressed concern about how that would raise the official number of cases on American soil.

> I would rather—because I like the numbers being where they are. I don't need to have the numbers double because of one ship. That wasn't our fault, and it wasn't the fault of the people on the ship, either. Okay? It wasn't their fault either. And they're mostly Americans, so I can live either way with it. I'd rather have them stay on, person-ally. But I fully understand if they want to take them off.

The president then proceeded to share with the press corps his acumen as an amateur virologist:

> I like this stuff. You know, my uncle was a great person. He was at MIT. He taught at MIT for, I think, like a record number of years. He was a great super genius. Dr. John Trump. I like this stuff. I really get it. People are

surprised that I understand it. Every one of these doctors said, "How do you know so much about this?" Maybe I have a natural ability. Maybe I should have done that instead of running for president....I understand that whole world. I love that world. I really do.

In mid-March, a reporter asked the president how he rated his response to the crisis on a scale of one to ten. "I'd rate it a ten. I think we've done a great job," Trump responded. Just a few days later during a Coronavirus Task Force briefing, President Trump was unable to compliment a subordinate without also praising himself. "The FDA commissioner, Stephen Hahn, who's with us, he's fantastic, and he has been working twenty-four hours a day....He's worked probably as hard or harder than anybody in the group, other than maybe Mike Pence or me."

@realDonaldTrump
"New York Governor Cuomo says President Trump has been "very helpful." @foxandfriends Thank you, every-body is working very hard!
7:27 AM - Mar 31, 2020

@realDonaldTrump
The Wall Street Journal always "forgets" to mention that the ratings for the White House Press Briefings are "through the roof" (Monday Night Football, Bachelor Finale, according to @nytimes) & is only way for me to escape the Fake News & get my views across. WSJ is Fake News!
3:35 PM - Apr 9, 2020

The president continued to seek validation, with the needle on his hubris gauge well into the red.

> @realDonaldTrump
>
> **Just like I was right on Ventilators** (our Country is now the "King of Ventilators", other countries are calling asking for help-we will!), **I am right on testing.** Governors must be able to step up and get the job done. We will be with you ALL THE WAY!
>
> 12:36 PM - Apr 19, 2020

> @realDonaldTrump
>
> 96% Approval Rating in the Republican Party. Thank you! This must also mean that, most importantly, we are doing a good (great) job in the handling of the Pandemic.
>
> 7:15 AM - Apr 21, 2020

In the thirty days preceding the following post, COVID-19 deaths in the United States were averaging two thousand per day.

> @realDonaldTrump
>
> We've done a GREAT job on Covid response, **making all Governors look good, some fantastic** (and that's OK), but the Lamestream Media doesn't want to go with that narrative, and the Do Nothing Dems talking point is to say only bad about "Trump". **I made everybody look good, but me!**
>
> 9:30 AM - May 16, 2020

@realDonaldTrump

**We made most Governors look very good, even
great,** by getting them the Ventilators, unlimited
Testing, and supplies, all of which they should have
had in their own stockpiles. **So they look great, and
I just keep rolling along, doing great things** and
getting Fake Lamestream News!
11:01 AM - May 26, 2020

In a July Fox News interview, Chris Wallace confronted the
president with several of his own instances of minimizing the threat
of the virus. Asked if those statements discredited him, Trump
responded, "It's going to disappear and I'll be right. I don't think
so....You know why? Because I've been right probably more than
anybody else."

In late July, President Trump raised—and not for the first
time—Fauci's approval rating:

So it's interesting. He's got a very good approval rating,
and I like that. It's good, because remember, he's working
for this administration. He's working with us, John. We
could have gotten other people. We could have gotten
somebody else. It didn't have to be Dr. Fauci. He's working
with our administration, and for the most part, we've done
pretty much what he and others, Dr. Birx and others, who
are terrific, recommended. He's got this high approval
rating. So why don't I have a high approval rating and
the administration with respect to the virus? We should
have a very high—because what we've done....So it sort

of is curious. A man works for us, with us very closely, Dr. Fauci and Dr. Birx also, highly thought of, and yet they're highly thought of, but nobody likes me. It can only be my personality.

@realDonaldTrump

With the exception of New York & a few other locations, we've done MUCH better than most other Countries in dealing with the China Virus. Many of these countries are now having a major second wave. **The Fake News is working overtime to make the USA (& me) look as bad as possible!**

7:46 AM - Aug 3, 2020

With his focus on the upcoming election, the president's narcissism fueled accusations that Democrat-led states were employing pandemic mitigation measures solely to hurt his electoral prospects.

@realDonaldTrump

The Democrats will open up their states on November 4th, the day after the Election. These shutdowns are ridiculous, and **only being done to hurt the economy** prior to the most important election, perhaps, in our history! #MAGA

8:43 AM - Sep 8, 2020

In early October, the president was admitted to Walter Reed National Military Medical Center where he was treated with drugs used for the most serious COVID cases—an experimental monoclonal antibody therapy and the steroid dexamethasone. Several days later, the president released a video in which he discussed vaccine development and his recent treatment:

> Hi. Perhaps you recognize me. It's your favorite president....We're going to have a great vaccine very, very shortly....Nobody else, nobody else would have been able to do it....For me, I walked in, I didn't feel good. A short twenty-four hours later I was feeling great.... So I think this was a blessing from God that I caught it. This was a blessing in disguise I caught it. I heard about this drug. I said, "Let me take it." It was my suggestion. I said, "Let me take it," and it was incredible the way it worked. Incredible. And I think if I didn't catch it, we'd be looking at that like a number of other drugs....So we're going to get you the drug.

@realDonaldTrump
"Donald Trump must get the credit for the vaccines. It is a miracle." @Varneyco
10:32 AM - Dec 11, 2020

Undermining public health officials and other public leaders. The House Select Subcommittee on the Coronavirus Pandemic that investigated the pandemic response identified challenges that included the following: distrust in public health expertise, harassment and threats against public health officials, and perceived interference with public health response activities at the CDC and FDA.

In late February 2020, the director of the CDC's National Center for Immunization and Respiratory Diseases, Dr. Nancy

Messonnier, participated in a CDC telebriefing in which she described community spread (transmission of the virus without a known source) occurring in several countries outside of the United States. She warned that community spread in the United States was inevitable. Messonnier also warned that disruptions to everyday life could be severe and that individuals, businesses, hospitals, communities, and schools should begin preparing for such an eventuality. The stock market reacted negatively to her comments, and President Trump was reportedly infuriated and threatened to fire her. As he had done before, the president continued his practice of discouraging subordinates from reporting information he deemed unfavorable to his presidency.

In the Coronavirus Task Force briefings, President Trump often overshadowed and sometimes contradicted his public health experts while consistently meandering into unrelated topics. Lacking the brevity and clarity required during a crisis, he often failed to deliver a credible and unifying message made more necessary by the lack of a clear focal point in the expansive public health bureaucracy. Following the lead of some conservative media outlets and unofficial outside advisors, President Trump began touting largely anecdotal evidence that hydroxychloroquine—an antimalarial drug with questionable efficacy in the treatment of COVID-19—was a safe and promising treatment. He suggested that he might take it himself as a prophylactic before asking rhetorically, "What do you have to lose?...But I've seen things that I sort of like, so what do I know? I'm not a doctor, I'm not a doctor, but I have common sense." When a reporter asked Fauci for his views on the drug, Trump intervened and suggested that Fauci had "answered that question fifteen times."

@realDonaldTrump
HYDROXYCHLOROQUINE & AZITHROMYCIN, taken
together, have a real chance to be one of the biggest
game changers in the history of medicine. The FDA
has moved mountains - Thank You! Hopefully they will
BOTH (H works better with A, International Journal of
Antimicrobial Agents).....
....be put in use IMMEDIATELY. PEOPLE ARE
DYING, MOVE FAST, and GOD BLESS EVERYONE! @
US_FDA @SteveFDA @CDCgov @DHSgov
10:13 AM - Mar 21, 2020

Three days later, a man in Arizona who had heard the president's suggestion died after he and his wife ingested the fish-tank additive chloroquine phosphate, one of the ingredients in hydroxychloroquine.

President Trump supported the decision to fire the commander of the aircraft carrier USS *Theodore Roosevelt*, who had sent a letter to his Navy superiors pleading for adequate land-based facilities for his crew amid a COVID outbreak aboard his ship. The letter subsequently leaked to the press, and the president suggested that "it was terrible what he did, to write a letter."

Continuing a broader pattern of removing and replacing executive branch independent watchdogs, President Trump removed, without cause, Glenn Fine, the acting inspector general at the Pentagon. Fine had been selected by a council of inspectors general to lead the Pandemic Response Accountability Committee that was overseeing $2 trillion in coronavirus relief funds passed by Congress. The president designated another IG to replace him.

An HHS IG report revealed that hospitals across the country

were reporting severe shortages of testing and other critical supplies, widespread shortages of PPE, difficulty maintaining adequate staffing, and a lack of adequate logistical support. President Trump responded by attacking the report's author.

> @realDonaldTrump
> Why didn't the I.G., who spent 8 years with the Obama Administration (Did she Report on the failed H1N1 Swine Flu debacle where 17,000 people died?), want to talk to the Admirals, Generals, V.P. & others in charge, before doing her report. Another Fake Dossier!
> 11:22 AM - Apr 7, 2020

In an April interview with Bob Woodward, Senior Advisor to the President (and Trump son-in-law) Jared Kushner described the president's push to quickly reopen the country as "getting the country back from the doctors....Trump is now back in charge. It's not the doctors."

The head of the Biomedical Advanced Research and Development Authority, Rick Bright, submitted a whistleblower complaint in which he claimed that he was retaliated against when he was removed from his position. Bright had raised concerns about the administration's general strategy to combat COVID-19 and, more specifically, his opposition to the widespread distribution of hydroxychloroquine.

In a likely episode of undue influence, recommendations in a CDC report for a South Dakota meatpacking plant experiencing a COVID-19 outbreak were edited in an apparently unprecedented manner. The rescinded report was replaced with language that made recommendations "discretionary," to be implemented "whenever possible" and "if feasible."

Despite polls showing broad support in early May for adherence to COVID-19 mitigation guidelines implemented by state and local officials, the president suggested that Americans would not stand for it. He went on to suggest that "the people of our country should think of themselves as warriors."

In mid-May, the president suggested that testing for the virus might be "frankly, overrated. Maybe it is overrated....And don't forget, we have more cases than anybody in the world. But why? Because we do more testing....When you test, you find something is wrong with people. If we didn't do any testing, we would have very few cases." The president also announced that he had been taking hydroxychloroquine as a prophylactic because "I think it's good—I've heard a lot of good stories." He also claimed that frontline workers had been using it, in addition to "a lot of doctors."

To avoid what might have appeared to be criticism of President Trump, White House officials and HHS political appointees insisted on changes to CDC weekly reports and public health recommendations to better align with President Trump's more optimistic messaging. Fauci later described this undue influence as "an aberrancy that I haven't seen in the almost forty years that I've been doing this. So, it's just one of those things that is chilling when you see it happen." He further described this dynamic as a "situation where science was distorted and/or rejected. And a lot of pressure was put on individuals and organizations to do things that were not directly related to what their best opinion would be, vis-a-vis the science...to do things that just are not compatible with the science. And I think the only way that happens is when you have leadership from the very top, and people surrounding the leadership, that essentially let that happen."

In early July, just two days after the United States surpassed three million confirmed cases, the Trump administration formally announced that America would withdraw from the World Health Organization (WHO) effective July 2021. Though reforms at the WHO were needed, both Republican and Democrat lawmakers criticized the move, warning that it could hamper global vaccine development and make it more difficult to stop viruses that originate in other countries. One lawmaker described the announcement as "an abdication of America's role as a global leader and it is the opposite of putting America first—it will put America at risk." The planned withdrawal was ultimately reversed by Trump's successor.

Continuing to undermine public health officials, President Trump reposted a former game show host's conspiracy theory claiming that the CDC, doctors, and the media were all lying about COVID-19 in an effort to hurt the economy and therefore Trump's chances for reelection. The president was conditioning people to distrust medical expertise at a time when they needed it most. Asked during an interview with CBS if he thought that spreading that kind of information was confusing for the public, Trump responded, "No. When I repost a tweet I'm just giving—I didn't make a comment. I did, I reposted a tweet that a lot of people feel—but all I'm doing is making a comment. I'm just putting somebody's voice out there. There are many voices. There are many people that think we shouldn't do this kind of testing because all we do—it's a trap."

In a peer-reviewed study of 177 countries published in *The Lancet* in early 2022, higher pre-pandemic trust in government and one's fellow citizens were the factors most clearly linked to better national outcomes during the COVID-19 pandemic. A high level of trust in science, institutions, and each other seemed to have helped Australians to suffer only one-tenth the COVID death rate experienced by Americans.

When during a television interview Birx described the virus as being extraordinarily widespread and warned those in rural areas that they were not immune to or protected from the virus, the president publicly chastised her.

@realDonaldTrump

So Crazy Nancy Pelosi said horrible things about Dr. Deborah Birx, going after her because she was too positive on the very good job we are doing on combatting the China Virus, including Vaccines & Therapeutics. **In order to counter Nancy, Deborah took the bait & hit us. Pathetic!**

9:44 AM - Aug 3, 2020

The president announced that Dr. Scott Atlas—a neuroradiologist with no expertise in infectious disease—would join the White House Coronavirus Task Force. Atlas had frequently appeared on Fox News in the months preceding his appointment, often praising the president's response to the pandemic. His presence to some extent sidelined the other voices on the task force and he became the president's go-to COVID-19 advisor. In her congressional testimony, Birx described how Atlas told the president, "No matter what we do, the outcome will be the same." Atlas further advised the president that testing was "very overrated" and that case identification was bad for the president's reelection.

In late August, the Big Ten football conference announced that its fall season was postponed "due to ongoing health and safety concerns related to the COVID-19 pandemic" and because there was "too much uncertainty regarding potential medical risks to allow our student-athletes to compete this fall."

> @realDonaldTrump
> Disgraceful that Big Ten is not playing football. Let them PLAY!
> 12:19 AM - Aug 29, 2020

In mid-September, President Trump defied Nevada's restriction on gatherings of fifty or more people when he held an indoor rally near Las Vegas.

All thirty-four editors of the traditionally nonpartisan *New England Journal of Medicine* issued a scathing editorial suggesting that America's leadership failures "have taken a crisis and turned it into a tragedy." The editorial cited the denigration of experts as one of several factors contributing to tens of thousands of excess deaths. It also criticized the evisceration and politicization of key federal public health agencies. It praised the government's heavy investment in vaccines but warned that politicization of the development process could lead to growing public distrust. "Our current leaders have undercut trust in science and in government....Anyone else who recklessly squandered lives and money in this way would be suffering legal consequences....When it comes to the response to the largest public health crisis of our time, our current political leaders have demonstrated that they are dangerously incompetent."

Amid renewed concern about undue influence in the push to

approve vaccines prior to Election Day, FDA Commissioner Stephen Hahn reassured Congress that "decisions to authorize or approve any such vaccine…will be made by the dedicated career staff at FDA, through our thorough review processes, and science will guide our decisions. FDA will not permit any pressure from anyone to change that." A Kaiser Family Foundation poll conducted in September had already indicated that 62 percent of Americans were concerned that political pressure from the Trump administration would cause the FDA to rush approval. Just days after Hahn's testimony, the president politicized the FDA's vaccine approval process and called out the FDA administrator.

> @realDonaldTrump
> New FDA Rules make it more difficult for them to speed up vaccines for approval before Election Day. **Just another political hit job! @SteveFDA**
> 9:09 PM - Oct 6, 2020

The president also took the time to skewer seventy-nine-year-old Fauci, who had in July thrown out the ceremonial first pitch for Major League Baseball.

> @realDonaldTrump
> Actually, Tony's pitching arm is far more accurate than his prognostications. "No problem, no masks". WHO no longer likes Lockdowns - just came out against. Trump was right. We saved 2,000,000 USA lives!!!
> 8:11 AM - Oct 13, 2020

@realDonaldTrump

Dr.Tony Fauci says we don't allow him to do television, and yet I saw him last night on @60Minutes, and he seems to get more airtime than anybody since the late, great, Bob Hope. All I ask of Tony is that he make better decisions. He said "no masks & let China in". Also, Bad arm!...P.S. Tony should stop wearing the Washington Nationals' Mask for two reasons. Number one, it is not up to the high standards that he should be exposing. Number two, it keeps reminding me that Tony threw out perhaps the worst first pitch in the history of Baseball!

2:08 PM - Oct 19, 2020

As daily case numbers were rising exponentially in early November, President Trump held a rally in Florida during which the crowd began a chant of "Fire Fauci." The president responded with, "Don't tell anybody, but let me wait till a little bit after the election. I appreciate the advice. I appreciate it…he's been wrong on a lot." As Fauci was not a political appointee, the president did not technically have the authority to fire him.

As case numbers and deaths were trending steeply upward in early November, President Trump was refusing to concede the election. The resulting delay of several weeks for the presidential transition meant that the incoming administration was denied access to key public health officials and data on programs such as Operation Warp Speed, the government's ongoing effort to accelerate vaccine development and distribution by funding the manufacturing of promising commercially developed vaccines undergoing clinical trials.

A month earlier, over one thousand current and former physicians, nurses, scientists, and other health professionals from the CDC's Epidemic Intelligence Service had published an open letter expressing concern about "the ominous politicization and silencing of the nation's health protection agency during the ongoing COVID-19 pandemic." They described the absence of national leadership on COVID-19 as "unprecedented and dangerous":

> In previous public health crises, CDC provided the best available information and straightforward recommendations directly to the public. It was widely respected for effectively synthesizing and applying scientific evidence from epidemiologists and biomedical researchers at CDC and worldwide. Its historic credibility was based on incomparable expertise and 70+ years of institutional memory. That focus and organization is hardly recognizable today.

The letter's signatories also claimed that states and territories had been left to "invent their own differing systems for defining, diagnosing and reporting cases of this highly contagious disease.... Such chaos is what CDC customarily avoided by its long history of collaboration with state and local health authorities in developing national systems for disease surveillance and coordinated control."

In what was likely continued undue influence in the following post, President Trump may have further contributed to future vaccine hesitancy.

@realDonaldTrump
While my pushing the money drenched but heavily bureaucratic @US_FDA saved five years in the approval of NUMEROUS great new vaccines, it is still a big, old, slow turtle. **Get the dam vaccines out NOW, Dr. Hahn @SteveFDA. Stop playing games** and start saving lives!!!
7:11 AM - Dec 11, 2020

@realDonaldTrump
FDA APPROVES PFIZER VACCINE FOR EMERGENCY USE!!!
12:38 AM - Dec 12, 2020

Vice President Pence, Speaker Pelosi, and Senate Majority Leader McConnell received the vaccine on live television. Dr. Fauci and President-elect Biden soon followed suit, while former presidents Bush, Clinton, and Obama volunteered to be publicly vaccinated when eligible. President Trump's first vaccine was delayed, likely due to the monoclonal antibody treatments he had received in October.

@realDonaldTrump
All-time Stock Market high. The Vaccine and the Vaccine rollout are getting the best of reviews. Moving along really well. Get those "shots" everyone! Also, stimulus talks looking very good.
9:52 AM - Dec 17, 2020

Despite encouraging the vaccine via social media, President Trump did not disclose that he had received the vaccine before

592

leaving office. Public reports of his vaccination did not surface until March 1, 2021. The president missed a golden opportunity, while still in office, to personally promote the safety and efficacy of the vaccines—especially to his supporters who were among the most vaccine-hesitant political demographic in the country.

Within six months of Trump's departure, the arrival of the far more transmissible Delta variant led to a surge of new cases, hospitalizations, and deaths. It was referred to as a pandemic of the unvaccinated. Data from the Washington State Department of Health showed that the unvaccinated and partially vaccinated accounted for over 81 percent of the state's COVID-19 deaths recorded between February and November 2021.

The recklessness of wishful thinking and downplaying the threat. As Birx stated in her June 2022 testimony to Congress regarding her time in the Trump administration, "Consistent and factual communication from the president to the country was lacking."

Reporting from multiple national media organizations suggested that in January 2020, Trump's presidential Daily Briefs began highlighting the potential domestic threat of the virus that was already circulating in China. On January 20, the CDC confirmed the first case of COVID-19 in the United States. The infected man had returned from Wuhan, China, five days earlier. While in Davos, Switzerland, the president was asked if he was worried about a pandemic. "No. Not at all. And we're—we have it totally under control. It's one person coming in from China, and we have it under control. It's going to be just fine." President Trump also expressed confidence in China's transparency while noting his "great relationship with President Xi."

On January 23, the WHO announced that human-to-human transmission was occurring to an unknown extent and warned that "all countries should be prepared for containment, including active surveillance, early detection, isolation and case management, contact tracing and prevention of onward spread" of the virus. Chinese authorities began locking down thirty million people across ten cities in Hubei province in an effort to contain the virus.

> @realDonaldTrump
> China has been working very hard to contain the Coronavirus. The United States greatly appreciates their efforts and transparency. **It will all work out well.** In particular, on behalf of the American People, I want to thank President Xi!
> 4:18 PM - Jan 24, 2020

On January 29, President Trump announced the formation of a White House Coronavirus Task Force. At this point it was clear that the virus was causing severe primary pneumonia, a condition necessitating intensive care unit (ICU) facilities and ventilators. On January 30, the WHO declared a "public health emergency of international concern." On the same day, President Trump reassured Americans, saying, "We think we have it very well under control" and "We think it's going to have a very good ending for us. So that I can assure you."

> @realDonaldTrump
> Working closely with China and others on Coronavirus outbreak. Only 5 people in U.S., all in good recovery.
> 5:04 PM - Jan 30, 2020

Evidence of asymptomatic transmission was confirmed by the end of the month, and the Trump administration declared a public health emergency on January 31.

By early February, the president fully understood that COVID's mortality rate was significantly higher than the flu. He suggested at a rally that "by April, you know, in theory, when it gets a little warmer, it miraculously goes away." The CDC director, Dr. Robert Redfield, was forced to contradict the president days later, suggesting that "this virus is probably with us beyond this season, beyond this year, and I think eventually the virus will find a foothold and we will get community-based transmission." Days later, the president stated, "I think it's going to work out fine. I think when we get into April, in the warmer weather, that has a very negative effect on that and that type of a virus. So let's see what happens, but I think it's going to work out fine."

In late February, the administration's most senior public health officials determined that Americans should be warned about the risk of the virus and that it was time to move from containment to mitigation efforts.

@realDonaldTrump

The Coronavirus is very much under control in the USA. We are in contact with everyone and all relevant countries. CDC & World Health have been working hard and very smart. **Stock Market starting to look very good to me!**

4:42 PM - Feb 24, 2020

@realDonaldTrump

Low Ratings Fake News MSDNC (Comcast) & @CNN are doing everything possible to make the Caronavirus look as bad as possible, including panicking markets, if possible. Likewise their incompetent Do Nothing Democrat comrades are all talk, no action. **USA in great shape!** @CDCgov.....

8:03 AM - Feb 26, 2020

During a February 26 press conference, the president stated the following regarding the number of COVID cases in the United States:

When you have fifteen people, and the fifteen within a couple of days is going to be down to close to zero, that's a pretty good job we've done....I think every aspect of our society should be prepared....We're going very substantially down, not up. But yeah, I think schools should be preparing, and you know, get ready just in case....But when I mentioned the flu, I said—actually, I asked the various doctors. I said, "Is this just like flu?" Because people die from the flu, and this is very unusual. And it is a little bit different, but in some ways, it's easier. And in some ways, it's a little bit tougher. But we have it so well under control. We really have done a very good job....We're testing everybody that we need to test and we're finding very little problem, very little problem....I think that there's a chance that it could get worse. There's a chance it could get fairly substantially worse, but nothing's inevitable.

Asked if he was concerned about the expected community spread of the virus, the president responded, "No, because we're ready for it. It is what it is. We're ready for it. We're really prepared." On the same day, the CDC confirmed the first case of community spread in the United States. The next day the president suggested, "It's going to disappear. One day it's like a miracle, it will disappear." He implied during a February 28 rally that Democrats were politicizing the coronavirus and that the politicization constituted their "new hoax." He also noted the absence of any coronavirus-related deaths in the United States. The first death was announced the very next day in the state of Washington (though it was later determined that the first U.S. COVID-related death occurred twenty-three days earlier in California).

In early March, Fauci warned that the virus had reached outbreak proportions in the United States and would likely reach pandemic proportions. Vice President Pence—now leading the nation's coronavirus response—announced that the country currently did not have enough tests to meet anticipated demand.

During a visit to the CDC, President Trump suggested that the mortality rate for those infected with the virus had likely been exaggerated, in part because people with mild cases were not being tested. He suggested that the rate was more likely below 1 percent, and "they said one-tenth of 1 percent in one case. But nobody really knows. We'll be able to find out." The president then downplayed issues with COVID test availability, incorrectly claiming, "Anybody that wants a test can get a test. That's what the bottom line is…and the tests are all perfect."

@realDonaldTrump

So last year 37,000 Americans died from the common Flu. It averages between 27,000 and 70,000 per year. Nothing is shut down, life & the economy go on. **At this moment there are 546 confirmed cases of CoronaVirus, with 22 deaths. Think about that!**

10:47 AM - Mar 9, 2020

As Birx would later testify, the president's comparisons to the flu and downplaying of the pandemic, at a time when high fatality rates had already been seen in China, other parts of Asia, and Europe, "created a sense among the American people that this was not going to be a serious pandemic." Birx further suggested that the lack of concise, consistent communication by President Trump and other leaders about the seriousness of the pandemic "resulted in inaction early on, I think, across our agencies."

During a March 10 visit to Capitol Hill, the president again engaged in wishful thinking. "And it will go away. Just stay calm. It will go away." On March 11, the WHO declared the coronavirus a pandemic. On the same day, Fauci informed Congress that the situation would get worse. He estimated the mortality rate to be about 1 percent, or ten times that of the common flu. He also stressed that mitigation was needed immediately, while case numbers were still low.

During a task force press conference, the president stated, "This is a very contagious virus. It's incredible, but it's something that we have a tremendous control of." The next day, he reiterated that the virus "is a very bad one. This is bad in the sense that it's so contagious. It's just so contagious, sort of a record-setting-type contagion."

@realDonaldTrump
We are going to WIN, sooner rather than later!
8:54 AM - Mar 19, 2020

After more than two hundred COVID-related deaths in the United States, a reporter asked President Trump what he would say to the millions of Americans who were scared. President Trump missed an opportunity to respond clearly and empathetically when he said, "I say that you're a terrible reporter. That's what I say. I think it's a very nasty question, and I think it's a very bad signal that you're putting out to the American people. The American people are looking for answers and they're looking for hope, and you're doing sensationalism."

On March 29, the president suggested that if left unchecked, the virus could kill as many as 2.2 million Americans. "If we can hold that down as we're saying, to 100,000 [deaths], it's a horrible number—maybe even less, but to 100,000, so we have between 100 and 200,000, we altogether have done a very good job." His efforts to engender distrust in mainstream media outlets encouraged many of his supporters to embrace conspiracy theories and foreign disinformation about COVID-19.

@realDonaldTrump
...The CBS News poll said 13 percent of Republicans trusted the news media for information about the virus." Michael M. Grynbaum @NYTimes
1:49 PM - Mar 29, 2020

@realDonaldTrump

Polls are showing tremendous disapproval of
Lamestream Media coverage of the Virus crisis. The
Fake News just hasn't figured that out yet!

12:53 PM - Mar 29, 2020

On March 31, the president delivered a more sober, albeit shortsighted assessment. "I want every American to be prepared for the hard days that lie ahead. We're going to go through a very tough two weeks. And then hopefully as the experts are predicting, as I think a lot of us are predicting—after having studied it so hard— you're going to start seeing some real light at the end of the tunnel. But this is going to be a very painful, very, very painful two weeks."

The uncontrolled spread of the virus resulted in state and local authorities imposing lockdowns (stay-at-home orders, curfews, restrictions on large gatherings, et cetera) to prevent the health-care system from becoming overwhelmed. Businesses deemed nonessential were temporarily closed.

In early April, the president was asked about his recent claims that cases would soon be at zero within a couple of days and that the virus would "go away." The president responded by describing his role as cheerleader in chief:

> Which I was right about. It will go away. Well, the cases really didn't build up for a while, but you have to understand, I'm a cheerleader for this country. I don't want to create havoc and shock and everything else....I'm not going to go out and start screaming, "This could happen, this could happen." So again, as president, I think a

president has to be a cheerleader for their country. But at the same time I'm cheerleading, I'm also closing down a very highly infected place, specifically the location, as you know, in China that had the problems.

During the April 23 task force briefing—with Task Force Coordinator Dr. Deborah Birx looking on in horror—President Trump made the following somewhat rhetorical inquiry immediately after the DHS science and technology advisor had explained that disinfectants (such as bleach and isopropyl alcohol) and ultraviolet light kill the coronavirus on surfaces:

So I asked Bill a question that probably some of you are thinking of, if you're totally into that world, which I find to be very interesting. So, supposing we hit the body with a tremendous—whether it's ultraviolet or just very powerful light—and I think you said that that hasn't been checked, but you're going to test it. And then I said, supposing you brought the light inside the body, which you can do either through the skin or in some other way, and I think you said you're going to test that too. It sounds interesting....And then I see the disinfectant, where it knocks it out in a minute. And is there a way we can do something like that by injection inside or almost a cleaning? Because you see it gets in the lungs and it does a tremendous number on the lungs. So it'd be interesting to check that, so that you're going to have to use medical doctors with—but it sounds interesting to me. So, we'll see. But the whole

concept of the light, the way it kills it in one minute—
that's pretty powerful.

The following day, in response to the president's comments, the
CDC along with companies that produce disinfectants published
reminders about the proper use of household products, including
a warning from the makers of Lysol that its products should not be
"administered into the human body (through injection, ingestion or
any other route)." On the same day, the FDA cautioned against the
use of hydroxychloroquine after reports of serious cardiac events.

During an interview with Geraldo Rivera, Vice President
Pence engaged in wishful thinking of his own. "I think, honestly,
if you look at the trends today, I think by Memorial Day weekend
we will largely have this coronavirus epidemic behind us." Not to be
outdone, President Trump suggested that the country would soon
exceed five million tests per day, a benchmark some experts suggested
was necessary to safely reopen the country. Admiral Brett Giroir,
responsible for America's testing program, was forced to admit that
"there is absolutely no way on Earth, on this planet or any other
planet, that we can do twenty million tests a day, or even five million
tests a day."

During an April 29 interview on Fox News, Jared Kushner
declared, "We're on the other side of the medical aspect of this and I
think that we've achieved all the different milestones that are needed,
so the federal government rose to the challenge and this is a great
success story. And I think that that's really what needs to be told....
We've done more tests than any other country in the world, so we've
gotta be doing a lot of things right." He went on to say, "I think
you'll see by June a lot of the country should be back to normal, and

the hope is that by July the country's really rocking again.”

The end of April also marked the end of the administration's forty-five-day “Slow the spread” mitigation effort. President Trump's repeated emphasis on the total (cumulative) number of COVID tests administered—especially in the absence of adequate contact tracing—was reminiscent of the misguided emphasis on enemy body counts as an objective measure of success during the Vietnam War. By the last day of April, American COVID-19 fatalities (over sixty-seven thousand) had surpassed the number of Americans who perished during the decade-long conflict in Vietnam.

In early May, the president predicted that America would lose “anywhere from seventy-five, eighty, to one hundred thousand people.” His messaging suggested that the worst had come and gone.

@realDonaldTrump
Exciting to see our Country starting to open up again!
8:33 AM - May 5, 2020

Meanwhile, the administration was announcing its plans to disband the Coronavirus Task Force in a matter of weeks. The vice president described the plan as “a reflection of the tremendous progress we've made as a country.” President Trump was eventually convinced to keep the task force running.

@realDonaldTrump
As you know, I designated this day to be a National Day of Prayer. **As our Nation heals**, our Spirit has never been Stronger!
12:25 PM - May 7, 2020

It was premature for the nation to begin healing when the seven-day moving average for daily deaths still exceeded 1,800 per day and a vaccine was still months away.

> @realDonaldTrump
> Good numbers coming out of States that are opening. America is getting its life back! Vaccine work is looking VERY promising, before end of year. Likewise, other solutions!
> 9:07 AM - May 14, 2020

In mid-May, President Trump announced Operation Warp Speed but simultaneously downplayed the importance of the vaccine: "I just want to make something clear. It's very important: vaccine or no vaccine, we're back."

> @realDonaldTrump
> Now that our Country is "Transitioning back to Greatness", I am considering rescheduling the G-7, on the same or similar date, in Washington, D.C., at the legendary Camp David. The other members are also beginning their COMEBACK. It would be a great sign to all - normalization!
> 10:23 AM - May 20, 2020

> @realDonaldTrump
> Stock Market up BIG, DOW crosses 25,000. S&P 500 over 3000. States should open up ASAP. The Transition to Greatness has started, ahead of schedule. There will be ups and downs, but next year will be one of the best ever!
> 9:45 AM - May 26, 2020

By late May, the U.S. death toll had surpassed one hundred thousand. After a slight downward trend in new cases in May, mid-June ushered in the beginning of America's summer surge in cases that was most evident in the South and West. Vice President Pence urged governors to attribute the rise in case numbers to increased testing. In an opinion piece in the *Wall Street Journal* titled, "There Isn't a Coronavirus 'Second Wave,'" Pence praised President Trump's leadership and suggested that media predictions of a second wave of infections amounted to fearmongering.

After several months without holding a rally, President Trump was making plans for an indoor gathering of his supporters in Tulsa.

@realDonaldTrump
Almost One Million people request tickets for the Saturday Night Rally in Tulsa, Oklahoma!
9:28 AM - Jun 15, 2020

@realDonaldTrump
The Far Left Fake News Media, which had no Covid problem with the Rioters & Looters destroying Democrat run cities, is trying to Covid Shame us on our big Rallies. Won't work!
10:02 AM - Jun 15, 2020

Just prior to the rally, the president suggested that the coronavirus would go away, even without a vaccine. Asked if he was concerned about people getting sick at the upcoming rally, he replied, "No, because if you look, the numbers are very minuscule compared to what it was. It's dying out." During the rally, the president suggested that "testing is a double-edged sword....Here's the bad part. When you do testing to that extent, you're going to find more people, you're going to find more cases. So I said to my people, 'Slow the testing down, please.'" The president's public health officials denied that he had ever made such a request. At least ten Trump staffers and Secret Service agents reportedly tested positive after supporting the Tulsa rally.

> @realDonaldTrump
> WOW! The Trump Rally gives @FoxNews the "LARGEST SATURDAY NIGHT AUDIENCE IN ITS HUSTORY". Isn't it amazing that virtually nobody in the Lamestream Media is reporting this rather major feat!
> 7:35 PM - Jun 22, 2020

President Trump continued to tie rising case numbers to increased testing while appearing obsessed with comparisons to other countries. The WHO reiterated that a worldwide increase in cases was not related to any "testing phenomenon."

> @realDonaldTrump
> Cases are going up in the U.S. because we are testing far more than any other country, and ever expanding. With smaller testing we would show fewer cases!
> 6:54 AM - Jun 23, 2020

President Trump appeared unable to appreciate that hospitalizations and deaths were lagging indicators. Hospitalizations in the

United States began increasing dramatically during the last week of June.

@realDonaldTrump

Coronavirus deaths are way down. Mortality rate is one of the lowest in the World. Our Economy is roaring back and will NOT be shut down. "Embers" or flare ups will be put out, as necessary!

11:54 PM - Jun 25, 2020

The United States set a daily record for new cases on June 25. The next day, during a task force briefing, Vice President Pence expressed sympathy for the 126,000 Americans who had died. He also acknowledged rising case numbers and announced that "all fifty states and territories across this country are opening up safely and responsibly." He acknowledged that some states were struggling more than others. In response, Dr. Fauci emphasized that the states were interconnected. "So, what goes on in one area of the country ultimately could have an effect on the other areas." Three days later, Pence visited a Dallas megachurch with approximately 2,400 people in attendance.

@realDonaldTrump

Have a good time this morning at First Baptist Dallas Church. The wonderful Pastor @robertjeffress will be joined by our GREAT @VP Mike Pence!

8:16 AM - Jun 28, 2020

Texas daily case numbers, hospitalizations, and deaths had all been steadily rising in the previous two weeks.

In early July, a resurgence in new cases was accompanied by the inevitable and continued rise in hospitalizations. President Trump, during an interview on Fox Business, stated, "I think we're going to be very good with the coronavirus. I think that at some point it's going to sort of just disappear, I hope." The president continued to attribute the national increase in confirmed infections to the recent expansion of testing across the country.

> @realDonaldTrump
> There is a rise in Coronavirus cases because our testing is so massive and so good, far bigger and better than any other country. This is great news, but even better news is that death, and the death rate, is DOWN. Also, younger people, who get better much easier and faster!
> 11:44 PM - Jul 2, 2020

Testing does not create cases. It merely confirms their existence. COVID deaths began a steady increase in early July that lasted for thirty days.

> @realDonaldTrump
> For the 1/100th time, the reason we show so many Cases, compared to other countries that haven't done nearly as well as we have, is that our TESTING is much bigger and better. We have tested 40,000,000 people. If we did 20,000,000 instead, Cases would be half, etc. NOT REPORTED!
> 8:39 AM - Jul 9, 2020

During an August 3 interview with Axios's Jonathan Swan, the president suggested that the pandemic in the United States was "under control." When reminded that one thousand people were dying each day, Trump responded, "They are dying. That's true. And it is what it is. But that doesn't mean we aren't doing everything we can. It's under control as much as you can control it." When Swan pointed out that South Korea—a country with over fifty-one million people—had recorded only three hundred deaths, Trump responded, "You don't know that."

Facebook and Twitter removed a video in which the president suggested that "children are almost—and I would almost say definitely, but almost immune from this disease." Referring to the virus, Trump further suggested, "This thing's going away. It will go away like things go away."

In an effort to justify the comments he had made to Bob Woodward in March about his desire to downplay the threat of the virus, President Trump in early September said, "I'm not going to drive this country or the world into a frenzy. We want to show confidence. We want to show strength." The president made similar comments the next day:

> I want to show a level of confidence and I want to show strength as a leader, and I want to show that our country is going to be fine, one way or the other. Whether we lose one person—we shouldn't lose any, because this shouldn't have happened. This is China's fault. This is nobody's fault but China. China should not have allowed it to happen....That doesn't mean I'm going to jump up and down in the air and start saying, "People are going

to die!" No, I'm not going to do that. We're going to get through this. And we're, right now, I hope—really think we're going to—we're rounding the final turn.

While it is important for a leader to remind people that there will be better days ahead, President Trump—likely motivated primarily by self-interest—had been doing so prematurely for months. The president had ignored one of the primary lessons of the 1918 pandemic: the need to tell people the truth.

During a Trump rally in Michigan, a reporter asked some attendees why they were not concerned about the lack of social distancing and mask wearing at the event. One attendee responded, "Because there's no COVID. It's a fake pandemic created to destroy the United States of America."

> @realDonaldTrump
> Congratulations to JPMorgan Chase for ordering
> everyone BACK TO OFFICE on September 21st. Will
> always be better than working from home!
> 6:13 AM - Sep 11, 2020

By mid-September, the U.S. death toll had reached two hundred thousand and case numbers had begun rising again. Vaccines were still months away. During a town hall event moderated by ABC, the president was asked about his previous suggestions that the virus would disappear. He responded, "It is going to disappear. It's going to disappear. I still say that." When asked to clarify that it will disappear only if action is taken, Trump replied, "No, I still say it. It's going to disappear....It's probably going to go away now a lot faster because of the vaccine. It would go away without the vaccine…with time, it goes away.…You'll develop like a herd mentality [herd immunity]. It's going to be herd developed, and that's going to happen. That will all happen. But with the vaccine, I think it will go away very quickly."

On September 26, the White House hosted an event announcing the nomination of Amy Coney Barrett to the Supreme Court. Within a week, this apparent super-spreader event was deemed the likely source of infections for the president and first lady, three Republican senators, former New Jersey governor Chris Christie (who spent seven days in an ICU), the chairwoman of the Republican National Committee, several White House staffers, and the president of the University of Notre Dame, who offered the following public apology to his community:

> I regret my error of judgment in not wearing a mask during the ceremony and by shaking hands with a number of people in the Rose Garden. I failed to lead by example, at a time when I've asked everyone else in the Notre Dame community to do so. I especially regret my mistake in light of the sacrifices made on a daily basis by many, particularly our students, in adjusting their lives to observe our health protocols.

A Cornell University study of over thirty-eight million articles, published during a five-month period in 2020 in English-language media around the world, concluded that President Trump was likely the largest driver of what the WHO termed the COVID-19 misinformation "infodemic."

Case numbers were steadily increasing in early October. After testing positive for COVID-19, the president received a level of care to which virtually no other American had access.

> @realDonaldTrump
> I will be leaving the great Walter Reed Medical Center today at 6:30 P.M. Feeling really good! **Don't be afraid of Covid.** Don't let it dominate your life. We have developed, under the Trump Administration, some really great drugs & knowledge. **I feel better than I did 20 years ago!**
> 2:37 PM - Oct 5, 2020

The president returned to the White House for a dramatic photo op on the balcony of the south lawn. He then filmed a video message that included the following statements:

> Don't let it dominate you. Don't be afraid of it. You're going to beat it. We have the best medical equipment. We have the best medicines, all developed recently. And you're going to beat it. I went, I didn't feel so good. And two days ago—I could have left two days ago—two days ago I felt great, like better than I have in a long time.... Don't let it take over your lives. Don't let that happen....I stood out front. I led. Nobody that's a leader would not do what I did. And I know there's a risk, there's a danger. But that's okay, and now I'm better. Maybe I'm immune. I don't know. But don't let it dominate your lives....The vaccines are coming momentarily.

Vice President Pence was asked during a debate how Americans could be expected to follow the administration's safety guidelines when they were not being followed at the White House. Pence replied, "The difference here is President Trump and I trust the American people to make choices in the best interest of their health."

The following post was flagged by Twitter because it "violated the Twitter Rules about spreading misleading and potentially harmful information related to COVID-19."

> @realDonaldTrump
> A total and complete sign off from White House Doctors yesterday. That means I can't get it (immune), and can't give it. Very nice to know!!!
> 11:39 AM - Oct 11, 2020

In the final three weeks before the election, President Trump crowed about the size of his rally crowds in Pennsylvania, Georgia, Michigan, Nebraska, and California. During a rally in Pennsylvania, the president again suggested that the pandemic was nearing its end:

> We're rounding the turn on the pandemic. We understand it. Hey, I just had it. Here I am. It's actually me....I gotta get out, and I have to meet people, and I have to see people, and I know it's risky to do that. But you have to do what you have to do. I'm the president. I can't sit in the basement and say, "Let's wait this thing out." I'm not going to do that. And now I'm immune. They tell me I'm immune. I could come down and start kissing everybody. I'll kiss every guy—man and woman. Look at that

guy, how handsome he is. And I'll kiss him. Not with a lot of enjoyment, but that's okay....Who has had it here? Who's had it? Yeah, a lot of people. Well, you're the people I want to say hello to because you are right now immune. Or they say that. You know, they hate to admit it because I had it. So in the old days they said, "Well, if you have it, you're immune for life," right? Once I got it, they give you four months....It's anybody else but me, you're immune for life.

By mid-October, hospitalizations and deaths were once again on the rise. By the end of the month, the seven-day averages for new daily cases and daily deaths increased by almost 100 percent and 50 percent, respectively. During an October 23 rally in Florida, the president declared, "We're rounding the turn, with or without the vaccine....We want normal life to fully resume and that's happening."

@realDonaldTrump
The Fake News is talking about CASES, CASES, CASES. This includes many low risk people. Media is doing everything possible to create fear prior to November 3rd. The Cases are up because TESTING is way up, by far the most, and best, in the world. Mortality rate is DOWN 85% plus!
10:55 AM - Oct 24, 2020

@realDonaldTrump
Landed in Wisconsin. BIG CROWD. On my way!
8:40 PM - Oct 24, 2020

Wisconsin was experiencing a surge in cases and deaths.

Vice President Pence announced that he would not quarantine after his chief of staff and four other top aides tested positive. During multiple rallies, President Trump suggested that American COVID-19 deaths were inflated because doctors and hospitals were financially incentivized to attribute deaths to the virus in lieu of other underlying conditions:

> Our doctors get more money if somebody dies from COVID. You know that, right? I mean, our doctors, they're very smart people. So what they do is they say, "I'm sorry, but everybody dies of COVID."…It's like $2,000 more. So you get more money.

Underlying chronic conditions, or comorbidities, were often contributing factors that made people more vulnerable to COVID-19. They were not, however, part of the chain of cause and effect that ultimately caused COVID-19 deaths. As Robert Anderson of the CDC's National Center for Health Statistics explained, those charged with determining the cause of mortality are trying to determine "the condition or disease that started the chain of events leading to the death. For COVID-19, that might be something like acute respiratory distress due to pneumonia due to COVID-19." Excess mortality during 2020 was easily verifiable and further suggested that COVID-19 deaths may have been somewhat undercounted.

@realDonaldTrump
Covid, Covid, Covid is the unified chant of the Fake
News Lamestream Media. They will talk about nothing
else until November 4th., when the Election will be
(hopefully!) over. Then the talk will be how low the
death rate is, plenty of hospital rooms, & many tests
of young people.
8:35 AM - Oct 28, 2020

Dr. Fauci warned of very difficult times ahead for Americans, saying, "All the stars are aligned in the wrong place as you go into the fall and winter season, with people congregating at home indoors. You could not possibly be positioned more poorly." By mid-November, the Coronavirus Task Force was reporting that there was "aggressive, unrelenting, expanding broad community spread across the country, reaching most counties, without evidence of improvement but rather, further deterioration. Current mitigation efforts are inadequate and must be increased to flatten the curve to sustain the health system for both Covid and non-Covid emergencies." Per Fauci, President Trump had not attended a White House Coronavirus Task Force meeting in several months. HHS revealed that more than one thousand American hospitals (approximately 20 percent of those that report staffing status to HHS) were critically short on staff.

In late November, Fauci again warned that "December, January, and early February are going to be terribly painful months."

@realDonaldTrump

Fake News always "forgets" to mention that far fewer people are dying when they get Covid. This is do to both our advanced therapeutics, and the gained knowledge of our great doctors, nurses and front line workers!

5:48 PM - Nov 21, 2020

In early December, just under twenty-five hundred Americans, on average, were dying from COVID every day. New cases were reported at an average of over two hundred thousand per day.

@realDonaldTrump

Big Rally Saturday Night in Georgia!!!

8:05 AM - Dec 4, 2020

The coronavirus killed over three thousand Americans on December 9.

@realDonaldTrump

STOCK MARKETS AT NEW ALL TIME HIGHS!!!

9:42 AM - Dec 9, 2020

By December 5, the cumulative U.S. death toll exceeded three hundred thousand. As they had been for several months, morgues were overflowing in cities and towns across the country, necessitating the use of freezer trucks and trailers.

During the first week of January 2021, deaths were averaging over three thousand per day. America was experiencing a post-holiday surge that on two consecutive days resulted in over four thousand daily deaths.

> @realDonaldTrump
> The number of cases and deaths of the China Virus
> is far exaggerated in the United States because
> of @CDCgov's ridiculous method of determination
> compared to other countries, many of whom report,
> purposely, very inaccurately and low. "When in doubt,
> call it Covid." Fake News!
> 8:14 AM - Jan 3, 2021

By the third week of January, nearly one hundred thousand COVID deaths had been recorded in the previous four weeks. America's health-care system was reeling. Among America's COVID victims were several thousand health-care workers. Many physicians and nurses who had become mentally and physically exhausted or traumatized either retired early or changed careers.

CHAPTER 37

Public Leadership:
A License to Serve

A man dies when he refuses to stand up for that which is right. A man dies when he refuses to stand up for justice. A man dies when he refuses to take a stand for that which is true.

—Martin Luther King Jr.

Just days after the 2021 attack on the U.S. Capitol, former California governor Arnold Schwarzenegger spoke about the urgent need for leaders who have "a public servant's heart…who will serve higher ideals, the ideals in which this country was founded and the ideals that other countries look up to." The attack also compelled Senator Ben Sasse to address the role of servant leaders:

> God gives us rights by nature, and government is just our shared project to secure those rights….We're supposed to be servant leaders who try to maintain a framework for ordered liberty….Sometimes the big things we do

WHAT HANGS IN THE BALANCE

together are governmental, like kicking Hitler's ass or like going to the moon.

The history of the United States is replete with courageous individuals who sacrificed for the common good, for the oppressed, and for the preservation of the ideals enshrined in the Constitution. It is this commitment to serving others that Britain's King George VI referred to as "the highest of distinctions." This selflessness can also be described as "service in spite of self"—the imperative to subdue personal desires and ambitions that betray our own values along with organizational and institutional interests and objectives. Selflessness in public service is the antithesis of the abuse of power or dereliction of duty that surfaces in the absence of discipline, self-control, and a strong ethical foundation.

An enduring legacy of selfless service makes a difference in the lives of others and is built during the course of a lifetime. It is built one day and one choice at a time. Selfless leadership puts principle and duty at the forefront of decision-making.

Most meaningful and successful careers in public service will not culminate in widespread acclaim. They may instead be characterized by faithful service and a series of seemingly understated yet significant acts of selflessness. For example, one can profoundly influence the personal and professional lives of one's subordinates by taking the time to understand them and their challenges. If forced to choose, one can prioritize the welfare of one's subordinates over one's own career progression. One can admit to mistakes and even wrongdoing, avoid gratuitous self-promotion, and give credit to those who truly deserve it. One can practice principled loyalty to a disliked superior and follow lawful and ethical orders that one finds personally objectionable. Finally, one can suppress ego and a fear of adversity when they might compromise principled and objective decision-making.

> *To the sacrifice of time, labor, fortune, a public servant must count*
> *upon adding that of peace of mind, and even reputation.*
> —THOMAS JEFFERSON

"Courage is contagious." Ambassador Marie Yovanovitch spoke those words during her final public remarks in Ukraine at an event honoring a woman who had died fighting corruption. Selfless leadership requires courage. It may also require personal sacrifice. Robert Kennedy proclaimed, "Few men are willing to brave the disapproval of their fellows, the censure of their colleagues, the wrath of their society." In that context, he described moral courage as "a rarer commodity than bravery in battle or great intelligence. Yet it is the one essential, vital quality for those who seek to change the world which yields most painfully to change." As Representative Hakeem Jeffries (D-NY) reminded us, "Doing the right thing and being constant to our principles requires a level of moral courage that is difficult but by no means impossible."

Following the 2019 presidential impeachment hearings, Representative Adam Schiff saluted the courageous public servants who had agreed to testify:

> Some courageous people came forward, courageous people that risked their entire careers…when they had everything to lose, when people senior to them who have every advantage, who sit in positions of power, lack that

same basic commitment, lack that same basic willingness to put their country first and expose wrongdoing....Why is it that they were willing to stick their neck out and answer lawful subpoenas when their bosses wouldn't?

The attorney representing impeachment witness Alexander Vindman made a similar observation:

> In recent months, many entrusted with power in our political system have cowered out of fear. And, yet, a handful of men and women, not endowed with prestige or power, but equipped only with a sense of right borne out of years of quiet service to their country made different choices. They courageously chose to honor their duty with integrity, to trust the truth, and to put their faith in country ahead of fear. And they have paid a price. The truth has cost LTC Alexander Vindman his job, his career, and his privacy. He did what any member of our military is charged with doing every day: he followed orders, he obeyed his oath, and he served his country, even when doing so was fraught with danger and personal peril.

Individuals possessed of character and courage act selflessly despite the inevitable risk of short-term and potentially long-term personal consequences. Representatives Liz Cheney and Adam Kinzinger defied their political party when they chose to serve on the House committee investigating the attack on the U.S. Capitol. They both understood that standing up for the truth could cost them their congressional careers.

For those serving in elected office, service before self regulates the instinct for self-preservation that can falsely equate personal interests with the public interest. Theodore Roosevelt had years earlier described the "dreadful misfortune for a man to grow to feel that his whole livelihood and whole happiness depend on his staying in office. Such a feeling prevents him from being of real service to the people while in office, and always puts him under the heaviest strain of pressure to barter his convictions for the sake of holding office."

Neither Cheney nor Kinzinger bartered their convictions despite relentless attacks from their Republican colleagues and the threat of losing reelection. And lose reelection they did. As Cheney explained, "No House seat, no office in this land, is more important than the principles that we are all sworn to protect. And I well understood the potential political consequences of abiding by my duty." Representative Kinzinger had a similar message:

> Had I known that standing up for the truth would cost me my job, friendships, and even my personal security, I would—without hesitation—do it all over again. I can rest easy at night knowing that I fulfilled my oath to the office. I know many in this institution cannot do the same.

Kinzinger had put that risk into context five months before losing reelection. "If we are going to ask Americans to be willing to die in service to our country, we as leaders must at least be willing to sacrifice our political careers when integrity and our oath requires it. After all, losing a job is nothing compared to losing your life." Taking a principled stand does not always result in losing one's job. Georgia secretary of state Brad Raffensperger was reelected in 2022 after withstanding presidential pressure following the 2020 election.

Principled, selfless leadership is a long game that rewards uncompromised integrity. The necessary courage may also require perseverance, as described by John Lewis:

> There may be some setbacks, some delays, some disappointment. But you must never, ever give up or give in. You must keep the faith and keep your eyes on the prize. That is your calling. That is your mission. That is your moral obligation. That is your mandate. Get out there and do it. Get in the way!...Be bold. Be courageous. Stand up. Speak up. Speak out.

As a leader in public service, be the person who confronts discrimination and abuses of power. Be the person who calls out fearmongering and hate-mongering. Be the person who refuses to carry out unlawful orders, resists undue influence and intimidation, and shields others from their effects.

Be the person who holds themselves and others accountable and who risks personal persecution in the interest of justice. Speak truth to power and choose principled loyalty over loyalty to any one person or group of people.

Be the defender of cherished organizational values and principles under attack. Be the voice of reason in a sea of self-destructive absurdity and indecency and the person who shouts "No" when surrounded by shameless acquiescence. Honor the struggles, sacrifices, and unfinished work of earlier generations through a willingness to risk your life for the cause of preserving liberty and democracy.

Be the leader you aspire to be, the leader you decide to be. Not just to enable the pursuit of noble aims but also to inspire others to pursue the principled and courageous leadership *you* have demonstrated during a lifetime of service to others.

Let it be said that you answered the call to service and met the moment. Be the public servant whose selfless leadership profoundly impacts the lives of others in ways you may never know. Get out there and do it.

Acknowledgments

★ ★ ★

I owe a huge debt of gratitude to the friends and former colleagues who followed through on their commitments to review and provide thoughtful, insightful, and critical feedback on my ridiculously long first draft. To Nikki Johnson, Gerard, Scott, Alex T., Chris D. Bernuth, and Shane D.—thank you for the considerable effort you expended in shaping the final product. My reviewers also included my parents as well as my partner, Erin, whose love, support, and advice on all manner of book-related tasks were essential during what became a six-year journey to publication. A huge thank-you to Cheryl Price for volunteering her time and talents to shoot the author photo and to Aimee Tyreman for graciously volunteering her time to help shape the final version of the book cover. Bleu the Ragdoll cat was also supportive on those occasions when my office was deemed suitable for napping. This project may have never started without Frank McKinney, whose 2016 Aspire event led me to meditate on how I might make the best use of my skills, passions, and experiences.

I was fortunate to have the guidance and support of my outstanding publishing, editing, and design team. To Becky Nesbitt and Kia Harris at Forefront Books—thank you for your belief in my vision for this project, for your assistance with finalizing the title, and for keeping the editing process on track. Forefront's Billie Brownell and Lauren Ward were key to ensuring the timeliness and quality of the production process. I'm indebted to my editors, Sharifa Stevens and Kelsey Mitchener, whose perspectives, attention to detail, and command of the English language resulted in meaningful and substantive changes that certainly improved readability. I'd also like to acknowledge the stellar work of my publicist, Stephen Lee of PR by the Book.

I am very grateful to have benefited from the generosity of the following writers who permitted me to incorporate some of their published works: Timothy Snyder, Malcolm Gladwell, Michael Cohen, Jeffrey Kluger, Kathryn Dunn Tenpas, Robert Draper, Mark Lynas, and Clay T. Buckingham. Similarly, a big thank-you to the following authors, journalists, former public servants, and experts in their fields who allowed me to incorporate their observations, reflections, and expertise: Anne Applebaum, John Bolton, Rutger Bregman, Robert Cardillo, Ron Chernow, James Comey, G. Edward DeSeve, Joseph Dieleman, Noah Feldman, Eddie Glaude, John Hnatio, John I. Jenkins, Bob Johansen, William McRaven, Jon Meacham, Cynthia Miller-Idriss, Mick Mulvaney, Cindy Otis, Chuck Park, David Patrikarakos, Carl D. Rehberg, Mitt Romney, Jason Stanley, Brian Stelter, Douglas Stone, Laurence H. Tribe, Stephen Young, and Fareed Zakaria.

Finally, I want to acknowledge the following media and nongovernmental organizations that allowed me to use excerpts and transcripts: *Air and Space Forces Magazine,* Axios, Center for Creative Leadership, *Christianity Today,* Chicago Project on Security and Threats, Committee to Protect Journalists, Freedom House, MasterClass, *New England Journal of Medicine,* Pew Research Center, PRRI, Rev.com, *Science,* the *Washington Post,* and Yale University Press.

Notes

INTRODUCTION

"to tweet like we need to eat": "How Trump Reshaped the Presidency in Over 11,000 Tweets," Michael D. Shear, Maggie Haberman, Nicholas Confessore, Karen Yourish, Larry Buchanan and Keith Collins, *New York Times*, November 2, 2019. https://www.nytimes.com/interactive/2019/11/02/us/politics/trump-twitter-presidency.html

CHAPTER 1: Defending the Constitution and Key Institutions

"Freedom is never more": President Ronald Reagan, July 6, 1987. https://www.reaganfoundation.org/media/128817/kiwanis.pdf

"There is a reason why people": "Here's every word of the third Jan. 6 committee hearing on its investigation," NPR, June 16, 2022. https://www.npr.org/2022/06/16/1105683634/transcript-jan-6-committee

"a firm commitment to a life of service": Jason Crow, February 3, 2022, Congressional Record, Proceedings and Debates of the 116th Congress, Second Session, Vol. 166, No. 22, S786, 14. https://www.congress.gov/116/crec/2020/02/03/CREC-2020-02-03-pt1-PgS773-2.pdf

South Africa's Nelson Mandela knew that: Richard Stengel, *Mandela's Way: Fifteen Lessons on Life, Love, and Courage,* (New York: Crown Publishers, 2009), 82

"I view it as a covenant I have": "Joseph Maguire Testimony Transcript: Intel Chief Testifies in Hearing Before Congress," *Rev.com*, September 26, 2019. https://www.rev.com/blog/transcripts/joseph-maguire-testimony-transcript-intel-chief-testifies-before-congress

"An oath is also a bond between people": Jason Crow, February 3, 2022, Congressional Record, Proceedings and Debates of the 116th Congress, Second Session, Vol. 166, No. 22, S786, 14. https://www.congress.gov/116/crec/2020/02/03/CREC-2020-02-03-pt1-PgS773-2.pdf

"the founders were not speaking, of course": "Rep. Adam Schiff's full opening statement on whistleblower complaint DNI hearing," *PBS NewsHour*. https://www.youtube.com/watch?v=GN4CJ8MYLTY

"If destruction be our lot": Abraham Lincoln, January 1838, "Fact check: Abraham Lincoln quote is fabricated but Lincoln did once warn against internal threats," Antonio Fins, *USA*

Today, July 14, 2020. https://www.usatoday.com/story/news/factcheck/2020/07/14/fact-check-abraham-lincoln-quote-fabricated/5420062002/

"It is comforting to assume that the institutions": "Final Report, Select Committee to Investigate the January 6th Attack on the United States Capitol," House Report 117-663, December 22, 2022, xvi

"disgraceful situation...total witch hunt": "Trump's full remarks after the FBI raid of his lawyer's office," *Washington Post*, April 9, 2018. https://www.youtube.com/watch?v=Kjpv-vrx2CA8

"an attack on our country": "Trump's full remarks after the FBI raid of his lawyer's office," *Washington Post*, April 9, 2018. https://www.youtube.com/watch?v=Kjpvvrx2CA8

"to corruptly obstruct, impede, or influence": "Final Report, Select Committee to Investigate the January 6th Attack on the United States Capitol," House Report 117-663, December 22, 2022, 99

would have violated both state and federal: "Final Report, Select Committee to Investigate the January 6th Attack on the United States Capitol," House Report 117-663, December 22, 2022, 9

"President Trump falsely declared victory": "Here's every word from the fifth Jan. 6 committee hearing on its investigation," NPR, June 23, 2022. https://www.npr.org/2022/06/23/1106700800/jan-6-committee-hearing-transcript

"a historic and profound abuse": Judge Linda Parker, King v. Whitmer, Case 2:20-cv-13134-LVP-RSW ECF No. 172, PageID.6890, filed August 25, 2021, 1, 108. https://www.scribd.com/document/521719762/King-v-Whitmer-Sanction-Decision-08-25-21

"President Trump claims the election was stolen": "Mitch McConnell Senate Speech Transcript January 6: Rejects Efforts to Overturn Presidential Election Results," *Rev.com*, January 6, 2021. https://www.rev.com/blog/transcripts/mitch-mcconnell-senate-speech-on-election-confirmation-transcript-january-6

"Having failed to make even a plausible case": Mitt Romney, statement posted on Twitter, November 19, 2020. https://twitter.com/MittRomney/status/1329629701447573504/photo/1

"the most reckless, insidious and calamitous": "Here's every word of the third Jan. 6 committee hearing on its investigation," NPR, June 16, 2022. https://www.npr.org/2022/06/16/1105683634/transcript-jan-6-committee

"We're debating a step that has never been taken": "Mitch McConnell Senate Speech Transcript January 6: Rejects Efforts to Overturn Presidential Election Results," *Rev.com*, January 6, 2021. https://www.rev.com/blog/transcripts/mitch-mcconnell-senate-speech-on-election-confirmation-transcript-january-6

"Gravely endangered the security": Impeaching Donald John Trump, President of the United States, for high crimes and misdemeanors, H.R. 24, 117th Cong. (2021). https://www.cnn.com/2021/01/11/politics/house-articles-of-impeachment/index.html

"The U.S. military will obey" : "Memorandum for the Joint Force," The Joint Chiefs of Staff, January 12, 2021. https://www.npr.org/sections/insurrection-at-the-capitol/2021/01/12/956170188/joint-chiefs-remind-u-s-forces-that-they-defend-the-constitution

"Our Constitution only works": "An Open Letter from Congressional Staff to Senate," February 3, 2021. https://stafflettertosenate.medium.com/an-open-letter-from-congressional-staff-to-senate-d8ec5d25af4d

were angry because the election had been stolen: United States of America v. Donald J. Trump (Indictment), Case No. 1:23-cr-00257-TSC, Document 1, August 1, 2023, 39–40. www.justice.gov/storage/US_v_Trump_23_cr_257.pdf

Secret Service radio chatter revealed: "Final Report, Select Committee to Investigate the January 6th Attack on the United States Capitol," House Report 117-663, December 22, 2022, 86

suggested by his daughter Ivanka: "Final Report, Select Committee to Investigate the January 6th Attack on the United States Capitol," House Report 117-663, December 22, 2022, 90

"condem [*sic*] this shit. Asap": "Final Report, Select Committee to Investigate the January 6th Attack on the United States Capitol," House Report 117-663, December 22, 2022, 82

Sometime after 3:05 p.m., the President: "Final Report, Select Committee to Investigate the January 6th Attack on the United States Capitol," House Report 117-663, December 22, 2022, 91

"I know your pain. I know your hurt": "President Trump Video Statement on Capitol Protesters," C-SPAN, January 6, 2021. https://www.c-span.org/video/?507774-1/president-trump-claims-election-stolen-tells-protesters-leave-capitol

At no time on January 6….to check on the welfare of his Vice President: "Final Report, Select Committee to Investigate the January 6th Attack on the United States Capitol," House Report 117-663, December 22, 2022, 94

The President also phoned his personal attorney: "Final Report, Select Committee to Investigate the January 6th Attack on the United States Capitol," House Report 117-663, December 22, 2022, 78

"You know, you're the Commander in Chief": "Final Report, Select Committee to Investigate the January 6th Attack on the United States Capitol," House Report 117-663, December 22, 2022, 95

"The unconscionable behavior did not end": "Senate Minority Leader Mitch McConnell Remarks Following Senate Impeachment Vote," C-SPAN, February 13, 2021. https://www.youtube.com/watch?v=yxRMoqNnfvw

"Betrayal of his office and supporters": "Barr: Trump's Conduct Was a 'Betrayal of His Office and Supporters,'" Mairead McArdle, *National Review*, January 7, 2021. https://news.yahoo.com/barr-trump-conduct-betrayal-office-165807071.html

"There has never been a greater": Liz Cheney, January 12, 2021. https://www.politico.com/f/?id=00000176-f8dc-d367-a17e-fefc40700000

"Donald Trump made a purposeful choice": "Here's every word from the 8th Jan. 6 committee on its investigation," NPR, July 22, 2022. https://www.npr.org/2022/07/22/1112138665/jan-6-committee-hearing-transcript

"pushing for uncertainty in our country": "Jan. 6 Committee Hearing – Day 7 Transcript," *Rev.com*, July 13, 2022. https://www.rev.com/blog/transcripts/jan-6-committee-hearing-day-7-transcript

by invoking the 25ᵗʰ Amendment: "Hearing Before the Select Committee to Investigate the January 6th Attack on the United States Capitol," House Of Representatives, 117th Congress, Second Session, June 28, 2022, 24–25. https://www.govinfo.gov/content/pkg/CHRG -117hhrg49354/pdf/CHRG-117hhrg49354.pdf

"immediately deployed the National Guard": "President Trump on Election and Breach of the U.S. Capitol," C-SPAN, January 7, 2021. https://www.c-span.org/video/?507829-1/ president-trump-election-breach-us-capitol

"the legitimate results of the 2020 presidential": United States of America v. Donald J. Trump (Indictment), Case No. 1:23-cr-00257-TSC, Document 1, August 1, 2023, 2, 3, 4

concluded in a 2021 report that global: "Freedom in the World 2021: Democracy under Siege," Sarah Repucci and Amy Slipowitz. https://freedomhouse.org/report/free-dom-world/2021/democracy-under-siege

"The European history of the twentieth century": Timothy Snyder, *On Tyranny: Twenty Lessons from the Twentieth Century* (New York: Tim Duggan Books, 2017), 11–12

"Sometimes 'No' must be spoken": "Comey deserves to lead FBI, having proven he knows how to say no (Column)," *Washington Post* republished in *Denver Post*, April 29, 2016. https ://www.denverpost.com/2013/05/31/comey-deserves-to-lead-fbi-having-proven-he-knows -how-to-say-no-column/

"return with joy to that state": Thomas Jefferson, edited by Eric S. Petersen, *Light and Liberty: Reflections on the Pursuit of Happiness* (New York: The Modern Library, 2004), 53

"There is a point when caution": Laurence Tribe, May 7, 2019, The Last Word with Laurence O'Donnell, MSNBC

"We are likely to preserve": Thomas Jefferson, edited by Eric S. Petersen, *Light and Liberty: Reflections on the Pursuit of Happiness* (New York: The Modern Library, 2004), 82

"The Constitution is a powerful document": Adam Schiff on Twitter, February 5, 2020. https://twitter.com/RepAdamSchiff/status/1225214701530906624

CHAPTER 2: Promoting Core Values and Principles

People of high ability are important: "Implications of *Dereliction of Duty,*" Carl D. Rehberg, January 2000. http://isme.tamu.edu/JSCOPE00/Rehberg00.html

"Any attempt to invade...summoned in the future": "Federal judge rebukes Trump over Roger Stone jury comments," Darren Samuelsohn and Josh Gerstein, *Politico*, February 25, 2020. https://www.politico.com/news/2020/02/25/judge-rebukes-trump-roger-stone-jury-117442

"not only called into question the integrity": The People of the State of New York against Donald J. Trump, Decision and Order, People's Motion for Contempt, SMZ 71911-24, May 6, 2024, 4. https://www.nycourts.gov/LegacyPDFS/press/PDFs/DOcontempt_5-6-24FINAL.pdf

"not fair...almost ought to be outlawed": Report on the Investigation Into Russian Inter-ference in the 2016 Presidential Election, Volume II of II, U.S. Department of Justice, March 2019, 127

"very brave…flip…break": Report on the Investigation into Russian Interference in the 2016 Presidential Election, Volume II of II, U.S. Department of Justice, March 2019, 128, 132

"sought to leverage his position"…the Russian intelligence services: U.S. Senate Rep. 116-290, Russian Measures Campaigns and Interference in the 2016 U.S. Election, Volume 5, Counterintelligence Threats and Vulnerabilities (2020), 28, 30, 32

"The flames kindled on the 4th of July": Thomas Jefferson, edited by Eric S. Petersen, *Light and Liberty: Reflections on the Pursuit of Happiness* (New York: The Modern Library, 2004), 67

"America remains the beacon of democracy": The Trump-Ukraine Impeachment Inquiry Report: Report of the House Permanent Select Committee on Intelligence, December 2019, 11

"in so doing, the President undermined": The Trump-Ukraine Impeachment Inquiry Report: Report of the House Permanent Select Committee on Intelligence, December 2019, 35

"our leadership depends on": "Impeachment Hearing Transcript Day 2 – Marie Yovanovitch Testimony," *Rev.com*, November 15, 2019. https://www.rev.com/blog/transcripts/impeachment-hearing-transcript-day-2-marie-yovanovitch-testimony

"The question is not right now": Timothy Snyder, July 25, 2019, *The 11th Hour with Brian Williams*, MSNBC

"The U.S. Supreme Court has spoken": "Text of Al Gore's Speech," ABC News, December 13, 2000. https://abcnews.go.com/Politics/story?id=122220&page=1

"Trump probably wouldn't start riots": "Why Losing Candidates Should Concede," Noah Feldman, October 21, 2016. https://www.bloomberg.com/opinion/articles/2016-10-21/why-losing-candidates-should-concede

"Indeed, given my experience working": "Michael Cohen: 'I fear' Trump won't peacefully give up the White House if he loses the 2020 election," Kevin Breuninger and Dan Mangan, CNBC, February 27, 2019. https://www.cnbc.com/2019/02/27/michael-cohen-i-fear-trump-wont-give-up-the-white-house-if-he-loses-in-2020.html

President Trump would be the first American President: "Final Report, Select Committee to Investigate the January 6th Attack on the United States Capitol," House Report 117-663, December 22, 2022, xv

"For more than 200 years": Adam Schiff. www.congress.gov/event/117th-congress/house-event/114923/text

"there will be a smooth transition": "Pompeo Promises 'A Smooth Transition To A Second Trump Administration,'" Bill Chappell, NPR, November 10, 2020. https://www.npr.org/sections/biden-transition-updates/2020/11/10/933516479/pompeo-promises-a-smooth-transition-to-a-second-trump-administration

"That's why Mike was number one": Donald J. Trump on Twitter, @realDonaldTrump, 8:59 PM, November 10, 2020.

The President had requested that his staff: Select Committee to Investigate the January 6th Attack on the U.S. Capitol, U.S. House of Representatives, Interview of: Jared Kushner, Thursday, March 31, 2022, 73. https://s3.documentcloud.org/documents/23559241/transcript-of-jared-kushners-interview-with-house-january-6-committee.pdf

many of the President's senior staff and certain: "Final Report, Select Committee to Investigate the January 6th Attack on the United States Capitol," House Report 117-663, December 22, 2022, 21

"a ground rule of democracy": "Merkel: Trump shares blame for US Capitol storming," Richard Connor, DW, January 7, 2021

"The wisdom of our sages": Thomas Jefferson, edited by Eric S. Petersen, *Light and Liberty: Reflections on the Pursuit of Happiness* (New York: The Modern Library, 2004), 43–44

"we've always been fighting for the soul": "Ron Chernow Stands for Press Freedom at the White House Correspondents' Dinner," Ron Chernow, April 30, 2019, *Pen America*. https://pen.org/ron-chernow-white-house-correspondents-dinner/

"battle between democracy and autocracy": "Full transcript of President Biden's speech in Warsaw on Russia's invasion of Ukraine," ABC News, March 26, 2022. https://abcnews.go.com/Politics/full-transcript-president-bidens-speech-warsaw-russias-invasion/story?id=83690301

CHAPTER 3: Freedom of the Press

"our liberty depends on the freedom": "Selected Quotations from the Thomas Jefferson Papers," Library of Congress. https://www.loc.gov/collections/thomas-jefferson-papers/articles-and-essays/selected-quotations-from-the-thomas-jefferson-papers/

"Freedom of the press ensures": "Free Press Can Act as Voice of People against Tyranny and Oppression, Secretary-General Says in Message on World Press Freedom Day," United Nations, May 1, 2001. https://www.un.org/press/en/2001/sgsm7787.doc.htm

"The fourth estate is absolutely critical": Eddie Glaude, MSNBC, April 27, 2019

"Without the facts, we cannot have": "Ron Chernow Stands for Press Freedom at the White House Correspondents' Dinner," Ron Chernow, April 30, 2019, Pen America. https://pen.org/ron-chernow-white-house-correspondents-dinner/

"a very heavy obligation to seek": "2022 White House Correspondents' Association Dinner Transcript," *Rev.com*, May 1, 2022. https://www.rev.com/blog/transcripts/2022-white-house-correspondents-association-dinner-transcript

"Even though we never like it": "John F. Kennedy and the Press," Presidential Library and Museum. https://www.jfklibrary.org/learn/about-jfk/jfk-in-history/john-f-kennedy-and-the-press

"But I guess that's the whole point": Defense Department Briefing, C-SPAN, May 10, 2022. https://www.c-span.org/video/?520116-1/defense-department-briefing

363 journalists were imprisoned…killed in 2022: Committee to Protect Journalists. cpj.org

"To announce that there must": Theodore Roosevelt, "Sedition, Free Press, and Personal Rule," May 7, 1918. https://www.theodoreroosevelt.org/content.aspx?page_id=22&club_id=991271&module_id=339333

"People love it when": "Mueller's investigation erases line drawn after Watergate," Peter Baker, *New York Times*, March 26, 2019. https://www.bostonglobe.com/news/nation/2019/03/26/mueller-investigation-erases-line-drawn-after-watergate/3kcfFipDtqXeAURLawuE7M/story.html

Within weeks of Russia's invasion: "Russian lawmakers approve prison for what they deem to be 'fake' war reports," *PBS NewsHour*, March 4, 2022. https://www.pbs.org/newshour/world /russian-lawmakers-approve-prison-for-what-they-deem-to-be-fake-war-reports

"Trump's continued attacks on our": Cindy Otis on Twitter, @cindyotis_ 6:14 PM, July 29, 2018

CHAPTER 4: Understanding Your Role

The stewardship activity that allocates: Edward DeSeve, 5-Star Management Model

"The office humbles you": Barack Obama Keynote Address at the Civil Rights Summit, AmericanRhetoric.com, April 10, 2014. https://www.americanrhetoric.com/speeches/PDFFiles/ Barack%20Obama%20-%20Civil%20Rights%20Summit%20LBJ.pdf

"The function of leadership": Ralph Nader, "The 100 Best Leadership Quotes of All Time," Lolly Daskal, Inc. https://www.inc.com/lolly-daskal/the-100-best-leadership-quotes-of-all -time.html

"But though an old man": Thomas Jefferson, edited by Eric S. Petersen, *Light and Liberty: Reflections on the Pursuit of Happiness* (New York: The Modern Library, 2004), 63

found that 38 to 50 percent of executives: "Executive Integration: Equipping Transitioning Leaders for Success," Douglas Riddle (November 2011), Center for Creative Leadership, 1. https://www.ccl.org/wp-content/uploads/2015/04/ExecutiveIntegration.pdf

according to former secretary of state Rex Tillerson: "Trump urged top aid to help Giuliani client facing DOJ charges," Bloomberg News, October 9, 2019. https://www.bloomberg.com /news/articles/2019-10-09/trump-urged-top-aide-to-help-giuliani-client-facing-doj-charges

"When somebody is the president": "Donald Trump: 'When somebody is president of the United States, the authority is total,'" *Guardian News*, April 13, 2020. https://www.youtube .com/watch?v=r3QXrQDTDYo

The defense argues that the Senate: "Full text: Romney's speech on why he'll vote to convict Trump of abuse of power," NBC News, February 5, 2020. https://www.nbcnews.com/politics /trump-impeachment-inquiry/full-text-romney-s-speech-why-he-ll-vote-convict-n1130936

"I'm actually, I guess, the chief law enforcement": "Trump falsely declares himself 'the chief law enforcement officer' of the US," *Guardian News*, February 18, 2020. https://www .youtube.com/watch?v=wjMOs1jHXJw

CHAPTER 5: Understanding Your Organization

"If that's what the law is": "Trump: I like to obey the law, but ...," CNN, January 7, 2020. https://www.youtube.com/watch?v=GebHtdjPza0

"remembered the Nazis also shot people": Jonathan Glover, *Humanity: A Moral History of the Twentieth Century* (New Haven, CT: Yale University Press, 2000), 412

"to affirm West Point's long tradition...our national past deserves": The Naming Commission, Final Report to Congress, Part II: U.S. Military Academy and U.S. Naval Academy, August 2022. https://s3.amazonaws.com/usma-media/inline-images/public_affairs/congressional_naming _commission/Naming_Commission_Final_Report_Part_II.pdf

"I have been clear in my opposition": "Presidential Veto Message to the House of Representatives for H.R. 6395," December 23, 2020. https://trumpwhitehouse.archives.gov/briefings-statements/presidential-veto-message-house-representatives-h-r-6395/

"As nations, and as people": "Barack Obama Reconciliation Address at Pearl Harbor," AmericanRhetoric.com, December 27, 2016. https://www.americanrhetoric.com/speeches/barack-obama/barackobamapearlharbor.htm

CHAPTER 6: Serving Your People

"when brought together in society": Thomas Jefferson, edited by Eric S. Petersen, *Light and Liberty: Reflections on the Pursuit of Happiness* (New York: The Modern Library, 2004), 41

"Leaders in every field need": Theodore Roosevelt, *An Autobiography*, (New York: The MacMillan Company, 1913) 334

A study of executives in senior: "What Makes a Top Executive," *Psychology Today*, Morgan W. McCall Jr. and Michael M. Lombardo of the Center for Creative Leadership, February 1983, 26–31

"Our country needs a commander-in-chief": Colin Powell, Democratic National Convention, August 18, 2020

"If we just take people as they are": "If We Treat People as If They Were What They Ought to Be, We Help Them Become What They Are Capable of Becoming," Quote Investigator, October 9, 2018. https://quoteinvestigator.com/2018/10/09/capable/#:~:text=The%20famous%20poet%20Goethe%20once%20wrote%3A%20%E2%80%9CIf%20we,Salt%20Lake%20Tribune%E2%80%9D%20of%20Salt%20Lake%20City%2C%20Utah

cultivating respect through recognition...regarding those processes: "The Power of Respect," Center for Creative Leadership November 20, 2020. https://www.ccl.org/articles/leading-effectively-articles/the-power-of-respect/

"The attacks against Ambassador Yovanovitch": The Trump-Ukraine Impeachment Inquiry Report: Report of the House Permanent Select Committee on Intelligence, December 2019, 16

"The former ambassador from the United States": The Trump-Ukraine Impeachment Inquiry Report: Report of the House Permanent Select Committee on Intelligence, December 2019, 103

"Every government degenerates when trusted": Thomas Jefferson, edited by Eric S. Petersen, *Light and Liberty: Reflections on the Pursuit of Happiness* (New York: The Modern Library, 2004), 68–69

CHAPTER 7: How *Not* to Undermine Your Organization

sixty-one nominations requiring Senate: "Trump revolving door creates 'unprecedented' vacancy mess in government," Dareh Gregorian, NBC News, May 25, 2019. https://www.nbcnews.com/politics/donald-trump/trump-revolving-door-creates-unprecedented-vacancy-mess-gov-t-n1004566

"I think the White House has": "Trump says media is part of vetting his nominees: 'We save a lot of money that way,'" Brett Samuels, *The Hill*, August 2, 2019. https://thehill.com/homenews/administration/455998-trump-says-media-is-part-of-vetting-his-nominees-we-save-a-lot-of

"The existence of a cadre": U.S. Senate Rep. 116-290, Russian Measures Campaigns and Interference in the 2016 U.S. Election, Volume 5, Counterintelligence Threats and Vulnerabilities (2020), xiii

Trump replaced 35% of his: "Tracking turnover in the Trump administration," Kathryn Dunn Tenpas, Brookings, January 2021. https://www.brookings.edu/research/tracking-turnover-in-the-trump-administration/

"to challenge the department's": "Job Vacancies and Inexperience Mar Federal Response to Coronavirus," Jennifer Steinhauer and Zolan Kanno-Youngs, *New York Times*, March 26, 2020. https://www.nytimes.com/2020/03/26/us/politics/coronavirus-expertise-trump.html

"hollowing-out of the foreign service": "Trump Is Waging War on America's Diplomats," Julia Ioffe, *GQ*, December 3, 2019. https://www.gq.com/story/trump-is-waging-war-on-american-diplomats

fewer applicants taking the foreign service: "Fewer Americans are opting for careers at the State Department," Dan De Luce, NBC News, February 25, 2019. https://www.nbcnews.com/politics/national-security/fewer-americans-are-opting-careers-state-department-n973631

abrupt removal of Ambassador Yovanovitch: The Trump-Ukraine Impeachment Inquiry Report: Report of the House Permanent Select Committee on Intelligence, December 2019, 38, 50

"It makes it hard to be a credible": The Trump-Ukraine Impeachment Inquiry Report: Report of the House Permanent Select Committee on Intelligence, December 2019, 44, 49

"found no evidence that the FBI attempted": Review of Four FISA Applications and Other Aspects of the FBI's Crossfire Hurricane Investigation, Office of the Inspector General, U.S. Department of Justice (December 2019), 411

In August 2020, an attorney: "Ex-FBI lawyer Clinesmith pleads guilty to falsifying email in Russia probe in Durham's first case," Kristine Phillips and Kevin Johnson, *USA Today*, August 19, 2020. https://www.usatoday.com/story/news/politics/2020/08/19/ex-fbi-lawyer-kevin-clinesmith-court-1st-durham-case-russia/3393941001/

it concluded that the FBI was justified: Review of Four FISA Applications and Other Aspects of the FBI's Crossfire Hurricane Investigation, Office of the Inspector General, U.S. Department of Justice (December 2019), 349

"missing in action—can't tell you where they are": "Here's every word from the fifth Jan. 6 committee hearing on its investigation," NPR, June 23, 2022. https://www.npr.org/2022/06/23/1106700800/jan-6-committee-hearing-transcript

"totally obliterate the Deep State": "Former President Trump Holds Rally in Waco, Texas," C-SPAN, March 25, 2023. https://www.c-span.org/video/?526860-1/president-trump-holds-rally-waco-texas

"make it impossible for me to do my job": "AG Barr says Trump tweets 'make it impossible for me to do my job,'" Dareh Gregorian, NBC News, February 13, 2020. https://www.nbcnews.com/politics/donald-trump/ag-barr-says-trump-Tweets-make-it-impossible-me-do-n1136726

"Yeah, I do make his job harder": "Trump praises embattled Attorney General William Barr, says 'I do make his job harder,'" John Fritze, Kevin Johnson and David Jackson, *USA Today*, February 18, 2020. https://www.usatoday.com/story/news/politics/2020/02/18/donald-trump -praises-ag-william-barr-says-i-do-make-his-job-harder/4795212002/

"misleading public statements…lack of candor": "The DOJ under Barr wrongly withheld parts of a Russia probe memo, a court rules," NPR, August 20, 2022. https://www.npr .org/2022/08/20/1118625157/doj-barr-trump-russia-investigation-memo

was initiated on a "bogus narrative": "Barr: FBI's Russia investigation based on 'bogus narrative,'" Eric Tucker and Michael Balsamo, Associated Press, December 10, 2019. https://apnews .com/5c07051effd2a4720a75c2da11ddaa34

"President Trump, you first…in his denial today": "Read the full transcript of the Helsinki press conference," Jenny Neufeld, *Vox*, July 17, 2018. https://www.vox. com/2018/7/16/17576956/transcript-putin-trump-russia-helsinki-press-conference

Trump publicly contradicted and undermined: "Trump smashed months of FBI work to thwart election interference," Darren Samuelsohn and Natasha Bertrand, *Politico*, June 13, 2019. https://www.politico.com/story/2019/06/13/fbi-election-interference-fight-donald-trump-1364597

"Over three tours abroad": "I can no longer justify being part of Trump's 'Complacent State.' So I'm resigning," Chuck Park, *Washington Post*, August 8, 2019. https://www.washingtonpost.com/opinions/i-can-no-longer-justify-being-a-part-of-trumps-complacent-state-so-im -resigning/2019/08/08/fed849e4-af14-11e9-8e77-03b30bc29f64_story.html

"So let them send it in": "Trump encourages North Carolina residents to vote twice to test mail-in system," Lauren Egan and Pete Williams, NBC News, September 2, 2020. https://www.nbcnews.com/politics/2020-election/trump-encourages-north-carolina-residents-vote-twice-test-mail-system-n1239140

"The State Board office strongly discourages": "North Carolina officials reject Trump's call for supporters to vote by mail and in person," Jordyn Phelps, ABC News, September 3, 2020. https://abcnews.go.com/Politics/trump-encourages-supporters-vote-illegal/story?id =72791833

"Needless to say, this is not the message": "Local election official reacts after President Trump suggests people vote twice to test system," Rick Earle, WPXI-TV, September 3, 2020. https:// www.wpxi.com/news/top-stories/local-election-official-reacts-after-president-trump-suggests-people-vote-twice-test-system/L75EZFVH5FFQHPBQBX6HKLX2NI/

refused to publicize peer-reviewed: "Agriculture Department buries studies showing dangers of climate change," Helena Bottemiller Evich, *Politico*, June 23, 2019. https://www.politico. com/story/2019/06/23/agriculture-department-climate-change-1376413

the early dismissal of Acting Director: "Trump angry after House briefed on 2020 Russia election meddling on his behalf," Ken Dilanian, Andrea Mitchell, and Katy Tur, NBC News, February 20, 2020. https://www.nbcnews.com/politics/national-security/trump-anger-cost -joseph-maguire-job-director-national-intelligence-n1140086

"When good men and women": "Opinion: William McRaven. If good men like Joe Maguire can't speak the truth, we should be deeply afraid," *Washington Post*, February 21, 2020.

https://www.washingtonpost.com/opinions/william-mcraven-if-good-men-like-joe-maguire-cant-speak-the-truth-we-should-be-deeply-afraid/2020/02/21/2068874c-5503-11ea-b119-4faabac6674f_story.html

In mid-May 2020, Mr. [Chad] Wolf: Whistleblower Reprisal Complaint, Department of Homeland Security, Office of Inspector General, September 8, 2020, 12–15

"I should not have been there": "West Point grads' letter to class of 2020 calls out one of its most powerful alumni: Esper," Meghann Myers, *Military Times*, June 11, 2020. https://www.militarytimes.com/news/your-military/2020/06/11/west-point-grads-letter-to-class-of-2020-calls-out-one-of-its-most-powerful-alumni-secdef/

CHAPTER 8: Seeking Counsel and Expertise

"One of the great challenges": "Neil deGrasse Tyson Teaches Scientific Thinking and Communication," Official Trailer, MasterClass. https://www.youtube.com/watch?v=0kPINN-hHGNw

"I think the people of this country": "Who needs experts? Richard Portes comes to the defence of an embattled breed," Richard Portes, London Business School, May 9, 2017. https://www.london.edu/think/who-needs-experts

Nelson Mandela often aligned himself: Richard Stengel, *Mandela's Way: Fifteen Lessons on Life, Love, and Courage* (New York: Crown Publishers, 2009), 78

President Mandela was aware that Lincoln: Richard Stengel, *Mandela's Way: Fifteen Lessons on Life, Love, and Courage* (New York: Crown Publishers, 2009), 83

"I'm not the smartest fellow": Franklin D. Roosevelt. https://www.goodreads.com/author/quotes/219075.Franklin_D_Roosevelt

"I watched Lou Dobbs last night": "Donald Trump Press Conference Transcript September 10: Coronavirus, Bob Woodward Recording," *Rev.com*, September 10, 2020. https://www.rev.com/blog/transcripts/donald-trump-press-conference-transcript-september-10-coronavirus-bob-woodward-recording

"You guys may not be following the internet": "Here's every word from the fifth Jan. 6 committee hearing on its investigation," NPR, June 23, 2022. https://www.npr.org/2022/06/23/1106700800/jan-6-committee-hearing-transcript

The President reportedly discussed: The Trump-Ukraine Impeachment Inquiry Report: Report of the House Permanent Select Committee on Intelligence, December 2019, 59–60

The United States has an interest: The Trump-Ukraine Impeachment Inquiry Report: Report of the House Permanent Select Committee on Intelligence, December 2019, 68, 62–63

In late August 2019: "Behind the Ukraine Aid Freeze: 84 Days of Conflict and Confusion," Eric Lipton, Maggie Haberman, and Mark Mazzetti, *New York Times*, December 29, 2019. https://www.nytimes.com/2019/12/29/us/politics/trump-ukraine-military-aid.html?te=1&nl=morning

"A truly effective leader": Lt. Col. Henry Staley, "Feedback: A Unique Key to Leadership," Air University 24, Concepts for Air Force Leadership, Richard I. Lester (Executive Editor), 382. https://www.airuniversity.af.edu/Portals/10/AUPress/Books/AU-24_Concepts_for_Air_

Force_Leadership.pdf

Nelson Mandela was more comfortable: Richard Stengel, *Mandela's Way: Fifteen Lessons on Life, Love, and Courage* (New York: Crown Publishers, 2009), 156

Nelson Mandela understood that there is: Richard Stengel, *Mandela's Way: Fifteen Lessons on Life, Love, and Courage* (New York: Crown Publishers, 2009), 78

Now, why would Donald Trump: "Adam Schiff Closing Argument Transcript: Thursday Impeachment Trial," *Rev.com*, January 24, 2020. https://www.rev.com/blog/transcripts/adam-schiff-closing-argument-transcript-thursday-impeachment-trial

"As an intelligence professional": Robert Cardillo, September 28, 2020, CNN

"I'm speaking with myself": "Donald Trump: 'My Primary Consultant Is Myself,'" *Morning Joe*, MSNBC, March 16, 2016. https://www.youtube.com/watch?v=W7CBp8lQ6ro

money, debt, taxes, trade: "Everything Trump says he knows 'more about than anybody,'" Haley Britzky, Axios, January 5, 2019. https://www.axios.com/2019/01/05/everything-trump-says-he-knows-more-about-than-anybody

"We don't have time": "Remarks by the President on Climate Change," The White House, Office of the Press Secretary, June 25, 2013. https://obamawhitehouse.archives.gov/the-press-office/2013/06/25/remarks-president-climate-change

Representative Elijah Cummings: "Top Democrat sent letter to Mike Pence in November warning of Michael Flynn's Turkey lobbying," Natasha Bertrand, *Business Insider*, March 10, 2017. https://www.businessinsider.com/elijah-cummings-letter-to-mike-pence-about-flynn-turkey-lobbying-2017-3

Flynn had reportedly informed Trump's: "Fact Checking Trump's Tweet on Flynn," Marshall Cohen, CNN, May 17, 2019. https://www.cnn.com/2019/05/17/politics/trump-flynn-tweet

"But the military says": "Transcript: 'Fox News Sunday' Interview with President Trump," Fox News, July 19, 2020. https://www.foxnews.com/politics/transcript-fox-news-sunday-interview-with-president-trump

What is exceptional, though: Robert Cardillo, *The Rachel Maddow Show*, MSNBC, September 25, 2020

Good government depends on: "Volume 663: Debated on Wednesday 10 July 2019," UK Parliament, July 10, 2019. https://hansard.parliament.uk/commons/2019-07-10/debates/08BBDD0D-1A31-4BAD-8FC9-FC175B1D2081/Engagements

"I would say almost everything…he's wrong": "Donald Trump & Joe Biden 1st Presidential Debate Transcript 2020," *Rev.com*, September 29, 2020. https://www.rev.com/blog/transcripts/donald-trump-joe-biden-1st-presidential-debate-transcript-2020

"Wray had also testified that antifa": "FBI director says antifa is an ideology, not an organization," Eric Tucker and Ben Fox, Associated Press, September 17, 2020. https://apnews.com/article/donald-trump-race-and-ethnicity-archive-bdd3b6078e9efadcfcd0be4b65f2362e

CHAPTER 9: Considered Decision-Making

"The triumph of gut over brain": Fareed Zakaria, *Fareed Zakaria GPS*, CNN, October 20, 2019

"because in my heart, I don't know if it is right": "GOP commission refuses to certify New Mexico primary results over distrust of voting machines," *PBS Newshour*, June 14, 2022. https://www.pbs.org/newshour/politics/gop-commission-refuses-to-certify-new-mexico-primary-results-over-distrust-of-voting-machines

"based on any evidence…to base my vote on the elections": "Facing removal from office, criminal charges, Otero County certifies election results," Andy Lyman, *The NM Political Report*, June 17, 2022. https://nmpoliticalreport.com/2022/06/17/facing-removal-from-office-criminal-charges-otero-county-certifies-election-results/

"experience alone brings skill": Thomas Jefferson, edited by Eric S. Petersen, *Light and Liberty: Reflections on the Pursuit of Happiness* (New York: The Modern Library, 2004), 50

"I never submitted the whole": Thomas Jefferson, edited by Eric S. Petersen, *Light and Liberty: Reflections on the Pursuit of Happiness* (New York: The Modern Library, 2004), 47

Dr. John Hnatio described the critical thinker: Dr. John Hnatio

"There was never an indication of interest": "Here's every word of the second Jan. 6 committee hearing on its investigation," NPR, June 13, 2022. https://www.npr.org/2022/06/13/1104690690/heres-every-word-of-the-second-jan-6-committee-hearing-on-its-investigation

"who reflects too much": "Philosophers Squared–Friedrich Schiller," Probaway, August 21, 2013. https://probaway.wordpress.com/2013/08/21/philosophers-squared-friedrich-schiller/

"I don't know him at all": "Taking On the Media: President Trump Full White House News Conference 5/18/20," LiveNOW from Fox, May 18, 2020. https://www.youtube.com/watch?v=cGTfW2gb2SI

Pompeo's conduct was eventually found: "State Department OIG Investigates Former Secretary Pompeo and Wife, Finds Evidence of Ethics Violations," Ana Popovich, *Whistleblower Network News*, April 23, 2021. https://whistleblowersblog.org/government-whistleblowers/state-department-oig-investigates-former-secretary-pompeo-and-wife-find-evidence-of-ethics-violations/

Nelson Mandela believed that most: Richard Stengel, *Mandela's Way: Fifteen Lessons on Life, Love, and Courage* (New York: Crown Publishers, 2009), 53

There are some decisions that benefit: Richard Stengel, *Mandela's Way: Fifteen Lessons on Life, Love, and Courage* (New York: Crown Publishers, 2009), 167

"Perhaps the strongest feature of his": Thomas Jefferson, edited by Eric S. Petersen, *Light and Liberty: Reflections on the Pursuit of Happiness* (New York: The Modern Library, 2004), 30

Soviet leader Nikita Khrushchev understood: Jonathan Glover, *Humanity: A Moral History of the Twentieth Century* (New Haven, CT: Yale University Press, 2000), 213–14

The Iran nuclear agreement: "The Joint Comprehensive Plan of Action (JCPOA) at a Glance," ArmsControl.org. https://www.armscontrol.org/factsheets/JCPOA-at-a-glance

As former secretary of energy Ernest Moniz: *Fareed Zakaria GPS*, CNN, August 28, 2022

Iran was not given $150 billion: "FactChecking Trump's Iran Address," Eugene Kiely, Robert Farley, D'Angelo Gore, and Jessica McDonald, FactCheck.org., January 8, 2020. https://www.factcheck.org/2020/01/factchecking-trumps-iran-address/

"The best illustration of the incoherence": "Opinion: Fareed Zakaria. Trump is strangling Iran. It's raising tensions across the Middle East," *Washington Post*, July 11, 2019. https ://www.washingtonpost.com/opinions/trump-is-strangling-iran-its-sowing-resentment -across-the-middle-east/2019/07/11/511b13c4-a413-11e9-b732-41a79c2551bf_story .html?utm_term=.3bf0b7a1d947

Prior to 2018, Iran had no…tons of enriched uranium: Ernest Moniz, *Fareed Zakaria GPS*, CNN, August 28, 2022

A November 2021 IAEA: "Analysis of IAEA Iran Verification and Monitoring Report— November 2021," David Albright, Sarah Burkhard, and Andrea Stricker, Institute for Science and International Stability, November 19, 2021. https://isis-online.org/isis-reports/detail /analysis-of-iaea-iran-verification-and-monitoring-report-november-2021/

CHAPTER 10: Things You Don't Do Publicly

"too naïve or too stupid": "Acting Navy secretary apologizes for calling ousted aircraft carrier captain 'stupid' in address to ship's crew," Barbara Starr, Evan Perez, and Ryan Browne, CNN, April 6, 2020. https://www.cnn.com/2020/04/06/politics/uss-tr-crozier-modly/index.html

"very active efforts by the Russians": "House Homeland Security Hearing Chris Wray Testimony Transcript September 17: FBI Director Testifies," *Rev.com*, September 17, 2020. https://www.rev.com/blog/transcripts/house-homeland-security-hearing-transcript-september-17-fbi-director-testifies

"Well, then he's not doing a very good job": "Donald Trump NBC Town Hall Transcript October 15," *Rev.com*, October 15, 2020. https://www.rev.com/blog/transcripts/donald -trump-nbc-town-hall-transcript-october-15

FBI Director James Comey learned: "Comey opens up about the shocking way he found out he was fired by Trump," Meghan Keneally, ABC News, April 15, 2018. https://abcnews. go.com/Politics/comey-opens-shocking-found-fired-trump/story?id=54486383

"I just fired the head of the FBI": Report On The Investigation Into Russian Interference In The 2016 Presidential Election, Volume II of II, U.S. Department of Justice (March 2019), 62

CHAPTER 11: Diplomacy and Professional Interpersonal Relationships

2020 Pew Research Center poll: "U.S. Image Plummets Internationally as Most Say Country Has Handled Coronavirus Badly," Richard Wike, Janell Fetterolf, and Mara Mordecai, Pew Research Center, Washington, D.C., September 15, 2020. https://www.pewresearch. org/global/2020/09/15/us-image-plummets-internationally-as-most-say-country-has-handled-coronavirus-badly/

he described as a "strong leader": "80 Times Trump Talked about Putin," Andrew Kaczynski, Chris Massie, and Nathan McDermott, CNN, March 2017. https://www.cnn.com/interactive/2017/03/politics/trump-putin-russia-timeline/

"Very strong control over…has been a leader": "Trump Says Putin Better Leader Than Obama in Military Town Hall," Meghan Keneally, ABC News, September 7, 2016. https:// abcnews.go.com/Politics/trump-putin-leader-obama-military-town-hall/story?id=41936057

"I was really being tough": "President Donald Trump on Kim Jong Un: 'We fell in love' over 'beautiful letters,'" John Bacon, *USA Today*, September 30, 2018. https://www.usatoday.com/story/news/politics/2018/09/30/trump-north-koreas-kim-love-beautiful-letters/1478834002/

"I had rather be the victim": Thomas Jefferson, edited by Eric S. Petersen, *Light and Liberty: Reflections on the Pursuit of Happiness* (New York: The Modern Library, 2004), 17

Malcolm Gladwell described a phenomenon: Malcom Gladwell, *Fareed Zakaria GPS*, CNN, September 22, 2019

looked the man in the eye: "User Clip: Bush Saw Putin's Soul," C-SPAN, June 17, 2001. https://www.c-span.org/video/?c4718091/user-clip-bush-putins-soul

Two of Trump's Cabinet members: "Bolton Was Concerned That Trump Did Favors for Autocratic Leaders, Book Says," Michael S. Schmidt and Maggie Haberman, *New York Times*, January 27, 2020. https://www.nytimes.com/2020/01/27/us/politics/john-bolton-trump-book-barr.html?te=1&nl=morning-briefing&emc=edit_NN_p_20200128&section=topNews?campaign_id=9&instance_id=15509&segment_id=20717&user_id=69760d-127d2ac6d230be6136001f652c&regi_id=93941638tion=topNews

"unwavering faith in President Trump": "Trump thanks North Korea's Kim for 'unwavering faith,'" Caitlin Oprysko, *Politico*, September 6, 2018. https://www.politico.eu/article/donald-trump-thanks-north-koreas-kim-jong-un-for-unwavering-faith/

President Trump reportedly revealed: "U.S. Escalates Online Attacks on Russia's Power Grid," David E. Sanger and Nicole Perlroth, *New York Times*, June 15, 2019. https://www.nytimes.com/2019/06/15/us/politics/trump-cyber-russia-grid.html

CHAPTER 12: Retaliation

addressed an "urgent concern" regarding the President: The Trump-Ukraine Impeachment Inquiry Report: Report of the House Permanent Select Committee on Intelligence, December 2019, 32–33

"I want to know who's the person": The Trump-Ukraine Impeachment Inquiry Report: Report of the House Permanent Select Committee on Intelligence, December 2019, 260–61

in over 100 public statements: The Trump-Ukraine Impeachment Inquiry Report: Report of the House Permanent Select Committee on Intelligence, December 2019, 260–61

"I can't tell you who the whistleblower is": "Impeachment Trial Q&A Day 2 Transcript —Thursday January 30, 2020," *Rev.com*, January 30, 2020. https://www.rev.com/blog/transcripts/impeachment-trial-qa-day-2-transcript-thursday-january-30-2020

"the President's personal retribution tour": "President's Fiscal Year 2021 Budget, Hearing Before the Committee on Finance United States Senate," February 12, 2020. https://www.finance.senate.gov/imo/media/doc/45146.pdf

"I want to take a moment to recognize": Alexander Vindman, The Trump-Ukraine Impeachment Inquiry Report: Report of the House Permanent Select Committee on Intelligence, December 2019, 259

It's an attempt to stoke fear: John Meacham, *The Last Word with Laurence O'Donnell*, MSNBC, May 24, 2019

Trump removed three more inspectors general: "The internal watchdogs Trump has fired or replaced," Melissa Quinn, CBS News, May 19, 2020. https://www.cbsnews.com/news/trump-inspectors-general-internal-watchdogs-fired-list/

serving a three-year prison sentence: "Judge finds Michael Cohen's return to prison 'retaliatory,' orders his release," Pete Williams and Tom Winter, NBC News, July 23, 2020. https://www.nbcnews.com/politics/justice-department/judge-finds-michael-cohen-s-return-prison-retaliatory-orders-his-n1234712

"Respondents' purpose in transferring Cohen": Michael D. Cohen v. William Barr, Case 1:20-cv-05614-AKH, Document 30, July 23, 2020, 1. https://www.courthousenews.com/wp-content/uploads/2020/07/Cohen-rulng.pdf

"I tolerate with the utmost latitude": Thomas Jefferson, edited by Eric S. Petersen, *Light and Liberty: Reflections on the Pursuit of Happiness* (New York: The Modern Library, 2004), 94

The President said he had received: Report On The Investigation Into Russian Interference In The 2016 Presidential Election, Volume II of II, U.S. Department of Justice (March 2019), 72

"completely frivolous…without regard to facts": Donald J. Trump v. Hillary R. Clinton, et al., United States District Court, Southern District of Florida, Case No. 22-14102-CV-MIDDLEBROOKS, June 1, 2023, 6, 1, 10. https://storage.courtlistener.com/recap/gov.uscourts.flsd.610157/gov.uscourts.flsd.610157.302.0.pdf

CHAPTER 13: Communication Befitting a Leader

"elevate the national discourse with comity": "Opinion: Mitt Romney. The president shapes the public character of the nation. Trump's character falls short," *Washington Post*, January 1, 2019. https://www.washingtonpost.com/opinions/mitt-romney-the-president-shapes-the-public-character-of-the-nation-trumps-character-falls-short/2019/01/01/37a3c8c2-0d1a-11e9-8938-5898adc28fa2_story.html

We had a fairly coherent…24/7 professional wrestler: Jon Meacham, *The 11th Hour with Brian Williams*, MSNBC, June 7, 2019

"Great leaders are almost always great simplifiers": "The 100 Best Leadership Quotes of All Time," Lolly Daskal, Inc. https://www.inc.com/lolly-daskal/the-100-best-leadership-quotes-of-all-time.html

"a repost, whether with or without commentary": The People of the State of New York against Donald J. Trump, Decision and Order, People's Motion for Contempt, SMZ 71762-24 and SMZ 71764-24, April 30, 2024, 4–5, 7. https://static01.nyt.com/newsgraphics/documenttools/099a29c4a13b27db/77ba144c-full.pdf

"Truth matters, right matters": "Transcript: Trump Impeachment Trial Monday, February 3, 2020 Key Moments," *Rev.com*, February 3, 2020. https://www.rev.com/blog/transcripts/transcript-trump-impeachment-trial-monday-february-3-2020-key-moments

"Well, it's easier to be a parent": "Van Jones cries on air after Biden victory: 'It's easier to be a parent this morning,'" Kaelan Deese, *The Hill*, November 7, 2020. https://thehill.com/homenews/media/524938-van-jones-on-bidens-projected-win-its-easier-to-be-a-parent-this-morning/

CHAPTER 14: Staying above the Fray

"As president of our country": "Obama at the UN: As president, people call me awful things every day," Charlie Spiering, *Washington Examiner*, September 25, 2012. https://www.washingtonexaminer.com/obama-at-the-un-as-president-people-call-me-awful-things-every-day

"when a thoughtless or unkind word is spoken": "Ruth Bader Ginsburg Quotes: Seven Powerful Lines by the Notorious RBG on Her 85th Birthday," Nicole Rojas, *Newsweek*, March 15, 2018. https://www.newsweek.com/ruth-bader-ginsburg-quotes-7-powerful-lines-notorious-rbg-her-85th-birthday-845820

"take the high road": "Charlie Munger uses this Warren Buffett 'life trick' to get 'more out of life than I deserve,'" Taylor Locke, CNBC, March 5, 2020. https://www.cnbc.com/2020/03/05/charlie-munger-shares-warren-buffetts-favorite-saying-and-life-tricks.html

"mesmerizing and hard for anyone to look away": "Key moments from Pete Buttigieg's Fox News town hall," Allie Caren, *Washington Post*, May 20, 2019. https://www.washingtonpost.com/video/politics/key-moments-from-pete-buttigiegs-fox-news-town-hall/2019/05/20/57dd651b-d664-4514-a7b3-daa18d1ce7c0_video.html

"I feel extraordinary gratification": Thomas Jefferson, edited by Eric S. Petersen, *Light and Liberty: Reflections on the Pursuit of Happiness* (New York: The Modern Library, 2004), 97

"If you're confident about your strength": "Barack Obama Talks about Toxic Masculinity and 'Being a Man,'" Sarah Ruiz-Grossman, *HuffPost*, February 19, 2019. https://www.huffingtonpost.ca/entry/barack-obama-steph-curry-toxic-masculinity_n_5c6cafe6e4b0f40774c9df5c

They cannot degrade Frederick Douglass: Booker T. Washington, *Up from Slavery* (New York: Doubleday, 1906), 100

CHAPTER 15: Patriotism

"the person who can holler": "Directory of Mark Twain's maxims, quotations, and various opinions," twainquotes.com. http://www.twainquotes.com/Patriotism.html

"capable of loving our country": Donald J. Trump, @realDonaldTrump on Twitter, 5:07 a.m., July 21, 2019

"If you are the leader": "UK leadership contenders criticize Trump's lawmaker tweets," Jill Lawless, Associated Press, July 15, 2019. https://apnews.com/article/europe-ap-top-news-donald-trump-united-states-london-292b141b94bb4ff9a93017f040bdc053

Immigration of people from all over: Condemning President Trump's racist comments directed at Members of Congress, H.R. 489, 116th Congress (2019). https://www.congress.gov/bill/116th-congress/house-resolution/489/text

"Send her back...incredible patriots": "Trump: Rally attendees were 'incredible patriots,'" CNN. https://www.cnn.com/videos/politics/2019/07/19/president-trump-defends-supporters-criticizes-ilhan-omar-crn-vpx.cnn

This country will not be a permanently: "Quotations from the Speeches and Other Works of Theodore Roosevelt," Theodore Roosevelt Association. https://www.theodoreroosevelt.org/content.aspx?page_id=22&club_id=991271&module_id=339333

Against every law of society and nature: "President Trump's Full Speech at Mount Rushmore," *USA Today*, July 3, 2020. https://www.youtube.com/watch?v=mXD4zPY4Ai0

"a definitive chronicle of the American": "1776 Commission Takes Historic and Scholarly Step to Restore Understanding of the Greatness of the American Founding," The White House, January 18, 2021. https://trumpwhitehouse.archives.gov/briefings-statements/1776-commission-takes-historic-scholarly-step-restore-understanding-greatness-american-founding/

CHAPTER 16: Humility, Validation, and Recognition

Humility is essential to good character: Paul D. Ryan, praise for David J. Bobb, *Humility: An Unlikely Biography of America's Greatest Virtue* (Nashville, TN: Nelson Books, 2013)

The chapter's introductory quote: David J. Bobb, *Humility: An Unlikely Biography of America's Greatest Virtue* (Nashville, TN: Nelson Books, 2013), 131, 207–8

"the favor with which they have been pleased": Thomas Jefferson, edited by Eric S. Petersen, *Light and Liberty: Reflections on the Pursuit of Happiness* (New York: The Modern Library, 2004), 19

The succession to Doctor Franklin: Thomas Jefferson, edited by Eric S. Petersen, *Light and Liberty: Reflections on the Pursuit of Happiness* (New York: The Modern Library, 2004), 23

"The higher we are placed": "35 Inspirational Marcus Tullius Cicero Quotes on Success," Asad Meah, *Awaken the Greatness Within*. https://www.awakenthegreatnesswithin.com/35-inspirational-marcus-tullius-cicero-quotes-on-success/

"To possess self-confidence and humility": "Humility, a Leadership Attribute Throughout the Ages," David Shedd, *Business Insider*, April 1, 2011. https://www.businessinsider.com/humility-a-leadership-attribute-throughout-the-ages-2011-4

And whosoever shall exalt himself: Matthew 23:12, Holy Bible, King James Version

He gave himself a ten out of ten: "Trump gives himself 10 out of 10 on coronavirus response," Morgan Chalfant, *The Hill*, March 16, 2020. https://thehill.com/homenews/administration/487883-trump-gives-himself-10-out-of-10-on-coronavirus-response/

Oh! That I could wear out of my mind: John Adams diary 1, November 18, 1755–August 29, 1756, Massachusetts Historical Society, masshist.org. https://www.masshist.org/digitaladams/archive/doc?id=D1&hi=1&query=Oh!%20That%20I%20could%20wear%20out%20of%20my%20mind&tag=text&archive=diary&rec=5&start=0&numRecs=51

From the private circle of assent: "James Comey: How Trump Co-opts Leaders like Bill Barr," *New York Times*, May 1, 2019. https://www.nytimes.com/2019/05/01/opinion/william-barr-testimony.html

"I have ever found in my progress": Thomas Jefferson, edited by Eric S. Petersen, *Light and Liberty: Reflections on the Pursuit of Happiness* (New York: The Modern Library, 2004), 45

I would be glad to know: Thomas Jefferson, edited by Eric S. Petersen, *Light and Liberty: Reflections on the Pursuit of Happiness* (New York: The Modern Library, 2004), 22

A good leader takes a little more: Arnold H. Glasow, "The 100 Best Leadership Quotes of All Time," Lolly Daskal, Inc. https://www.inc.com/lolly-daskal/the-100-best-leadership-quotes-of-all-time.html

"The greatest leader is not necessarily": "Ronald Reagan on Leadership," *Leading Now*, February 6, 2011. https://www.leadershipnow.com/leadingblog/2011/02/ronald_reagan_on_ leadership.html

Avoid putting yourself before others: "Leaders, Honor Thy People," Terrence Seamon, *About Leaders*, March 2, 2022. https://aboutleaders.com/leaders-honor-thy-people/#gs.jjfese

CHAPTER 17: Respecting the Dignity of Others

"He believed that in all of us": "Former President Barack Obama delivers a rousing eulogy: 'America was built by John Lewises,'" Joshua Bote, *USA Today*, July 30, 2020. https://www. usatoday.com/story/news/politics/2020/07/30/barack-obama-eulogy-john-lewis-funeral-full-transcript/5544048002/

"lived and worked with urgency": "The voice of the late Rep. John Lewis echoes in the Capitol during ceremony," Libby Cathey, ABC News, July 27, 2020. https://abcnews.go.com/ Politics/procession-begins-late-rep-john-lewis-lies-state/story?id=71999770

The last line of President Obama's: *The Way I See It*, Dawn Porter, MSNBC Films, 2020

"Though we have political differences": "Statement by President George W. Bush," George W. Bush Presidential Center, November 8, 2020. https://www.bushcenter.org/about-the-center/newsroom/press-releases/2020/11/president-george-w-bush-statement-joe-biden.html

"I'm not joking when I say this": "Biden tells appointees 'I will fire you on the spot' for showing disrespect to colleagues," *Yahoo News*, January 20, 2021. https://www.yahoo.com/ news/biden-tells-appointees-fire-spot-000137278.html

I see too many proofs of the imperfection: Thomas Jefferson, edited by Eric S. Petersen, *Light and Liberty: Reflections on the Pursuit of Happiness* (New York: The Modern Library, 2004), 86

"You can easily judge the character": quoteinvestigator.com, October 28, 2011. https:// quoteinvestigator.com/2011/10/28/judge-character/

"We should be too big to take offense": "Suffering an Offense Is Better Than Committing One," Donald DeMarco, *The Wanderer*, June 16, 2014. https://thewandererpress.com/cath-olic/news/featured-today/suffering-an-offense-is-better-than-committing-one/

civility in professional relationships: "President John F. Kennedy's Inaugural Address (1961)," National Archives. https://www.archives.gov/milestone-documents/president-john-f-kenned-ys-inaugural-address#:~:text=On%20January%2020%2C%201961%2C%20President,sur-vival%20and%20success%20of%20liberty.%22

In *Humility*, David J. Bobb explained: David J. Bobb, *Humility: An Unlikely Biography of America's Greatest Virtue* (Nashville, TN: Nelson Books, 2013), 100

"He is a criminal": "'CAUGHT COLD' Trump says 'criminal' Joe Biden 'should've been locked up weeks ago' and says Bill Barr had mercy on him," Nicole Darrah, *The Sun*, October 19, 2020. https://www.thesun.co.uk/news/12969942/trump-arizona-reporter-biden-crimi-nal-election/

executives who "derailed": "What Makes a Top Executive," *Psychology Today*, Morgan W. McCall

Notes

Jr. and Michael M. Lombardo of the Center for Creative Leadership, February 1983, 26–31

"one of the greatest barriers against atrocity": Jonathan Glover, *Humanity: A Moral History of the Twentieth Century* (New Haven, CT: Yale University Press, 2000), 36–37, 146, 150

"Human kindness has never weakened": FDRLibrary.marist.edu. http://www.fdrlibrary.marist.edu/daybyday/event/october-1940-10/

CHAPTER 18: Discipline and Self-Control

One [of] the most important responsibilities: "READ: Navy Secretary Richard Spencer's letter to the President acknowledging his termination," CNN, November 24, 2019. https://www.cnn.com/2019/11/24/politics/read-navy-secretary-richard-spencer-resignation-letter/index.html

"Laws control the lesser man": https://www.marktwainperforms.com/quotes.html#II

"You can tell the greatness of a man": "Abraham Lincoln's Most Inspirational Quotes," Benjamin Spall. https://benjaminspall.com/lincoln-quotes/

His propensity to blurt out sensitive: "Officials cringed as Trump spilled sensitive details of al-Baghdadi raid," Courtney Kube and Carol E. Lee, NBC News, October 29, 2019. https://www.nbcnews.com/news/world/officials-cringe-trump-spills-sensitive-details-al-baghdadi-raid-n1073001

posted a photo of an explosion: "The Poisoned Relationship Between Trump and the Keepers of U.S. Secrets," Mark Mazzetti, *New York Times*, August 11, 2022. https://www.nytimes.com/2022/08/11/us/politics/trump-fbi.html?te=1&nl=the-morning&emc=edit_nn_20220812

CHAPTER 19: Empathy

What more sublime delight: Thomas Jefferson, edited by Eric S. Petersen, *Light and Liberty: Reflections on the Pursuit of Happiness* (New York: The Modern Library, 2004), 91

Affective empathy allows us: "Are Leaders Learning How to Be More Empathetic? If Not Now, When?," Stephen Young, Ph.D., and Cathleen Swody, Ph.D., September 1, 2020. https://trainingindustry.com/articles/leadership/are-leaders-learning-how-to-be-more-empathetic-if-not-now-when/

as the moral resources and human: Jonathan Glover, *Humanity: A Moral History of the Twentieth Century* (New Haven, CT: Yale University Press, 2000), 22

"moral emergencies": Jonathan Glover, *Humanity: A Moral History of the Twentieth Century* (New Haven, CT: Yale University Press, 2000), 408

"These small acts reinforce the ordinary": Jonathan Glover, *Humanity: A Moral History of the Twentieth Century* (New Haven, CT: Yale University Press, 2000), 393

"We are sorry for all the dead": "Brazil is easing restrictions even though coronavirus deaths are at their highest, with President Bolsonaro saying death is 'everyone's destiny,'" Bill Bostock, *Business Insider*, June 4, 2020. https://www.businessinsider.com/brazil-eases-lockdown-coronavirus-deaths-peak-bolsonaro-ignores-2020-6

Let me hurt some feelings: "Texas mayor resigns after telling residents desperate for power and heat 'only the strong will survive,'" Christopher Brito, CBS News, February 18, 2021. https://www.cbsnews.com/news/tim-boyd-texas-mayor-colorado-city-resigns-power-outages/

choke like a golfer: "Trump tells Ingraham some officers 'choke' during shootings, saying 'They miss a 3-foot putt,'" William Cummings, *USA Today*, September 1, 2020. https://www.usatoday.com/story/news/politics/2020/09/01/trump-missed-putt-analogy-kenosha/3454010001/

"Please don't be too nice": "Trump to police: 'Please don't be too nice' to suspects," Meghan Keneally, ABC News, July 28, 2017. https://abcnews.go.com/Politics/trump-police-nice-suspects/story?id=48914504

"From Jamestown forward, our story": Jon Meacham, August 20, 2020, "2020 Democratic National Convention (DNC) Night 4 Transcript," *Rev.com*, August 21, 2020. https://www.rev.com/blog/transcripts/2020-democratic-national-convention-dnc-night-4-transcript

CHAPTER 20: Responsibility and Accountability

"If any blame or fault attaches": Dwight Eisenhower, June 5, 1944, National Archives. https://www.archives.gov/education/lessons/d-day

"When you say me, I didn't do it...take responsibility at all": "Trump: 'I Don't Take Responsibility at All,'" Jonathan Chait, *New York Magazine*, March 13, 2020. https://nymag.com/intelligencer/2020/03/trump-i-dont-take-responsibility-at-all-coronavirus.html

We've fought horrific wars: "Ron Chernow Stands for Press Freedom At The White House Correspondents' Dinner," Ron Chernow, April 30, 2019, Pen America. https://pen.org/ron-chernow-white-house-correspondents-dinner/

"I failed, nobody else failed": "'I failed': Operation Warp Speed leader takes responsibility for Covid-19 vaccine distribution confusion," Erin Brodwin, *STAT News*, December 19, 2020. https://www.statnews.com/2020/12/19/operation-warp-speed-leader-takes-sole-responsibility-for-covid-19-vaccine-distribution-confusion/

My dear General—I do not remember: Letter from President Abraham Lincoln to General Ulysses S. Grant, July 13, 1863, Abraham Lincoln Online. http://www.abrahamlincolnonline.org/lincoln/speeches/grant.htm

"admitted the mistake, forewarned others": "What Makes a Top Executive," *Psychology Today*, Morgan W. McCall Jr. and Michael M. Lombardo of the Center for Creative Leadership, February 1983, 26–31

"Blaming outside circumstances...outperform the stock market year to year": Jeffrey Kluger, *The Narcissist Next Door* (New York: Riverhead Books, 2014), 149

"Inflexible leaders limit the workplace adaptability...to run the business or organization": "Adapting to Change Requires Flexibility: How to Be a More Flexible Leader," Center for Creative Leadership, August 24, 2021. https://www.ccl.org/articles/leading-effectively-articles/adaptability-1-idea-3-facts-5-tips/

When Nelson Mandela reverses himself: Richard Stengel, *Mandela's Way: Fifteen Lessons on Life, Love, and Courage* (New York: Crown Publishers, 2009), 205–6

mutual cooperation, and empowerment: "A Commander's First Challenge: Building Trust," Jesper R. Stubbendorff and Robert E. Overstreet, Courtesy of *Air and Space Power Journal*, (Summer 2019), 16. https://www.airuniversity.af.edu/Portals/10/ASPJ/journals/Volume-33_Issue-2/F-Stubbendorff_Overstreet.pdf

Congress and the Nation have placed: "Leadership and Ethics across the Continuum of Learning: The Ethical Leadership Framework," Courtesy of *Air and Space Power Journal*, (Winter 2019), 50

Shifting from *blame* to *contribution*: Douglas Stone, Bruce Patton, and Sheila Heen, *Difficult Conversations: How to Discuss What Matters Most*, 3rd ed. (New York: Penguin Books, 2023), 76–77, 82, 84

"did not establish that members of the Trump": Report on The Investigation Into Russian Interference in The 2016 Presidential Election, Volume I of II, U.S. Department of Justice (March 2019), 2

If we had confidence after a thorough: Report on The Investigation Into Russian Interference in The 2016 Presidential Election, Volume II of II, U.S. Department of Justice (March 2019), 2

Having witnessed the degree to which: The Trump-Ukraine Impeachment Inquiry Report: Report of the House Permanent Select Committee on Intelligence, December 2019, 10

"I never in my wildest dreams": @realDonaldTrump on Twitter, 8:08 AM, November 21, 2019

"It was inappropriate for the President": "Sen. Lamar Alexander's full statement on impeachment trial witnesses," WATE ABC, January 31, 2020. https://www.wate.com/news/national-world/sen-lamar-alexanders-full-statement-on-impeachment-trial-witnesses/

The Framers provided for impeachment: Noah Feldman, Prepared Statement for testimony to the House Judiciary Committee, December 4, 2019

"A triumphant Mr. Trump emerges": Peter Baker, as quoted by @realDonaldTrump on Twitter, 8:04 AM, February 15, 2020

"accountability, for truth and justice": "Romney says he thinks Senate impeachment trial of Trump is constitutional, important for unity," Kenneth Singletary, *Boston Globe*, January 24, 2021. https://www.bostonglobe.com/2021/01/24/nation/romney-says-he-thinks-senate-impeachment-trial-trump-is-constitutional-important-unity/

"Some people ask: Why would you impeach": Bernie Sanders, January 8, 2021. https://www.instagram.com/p/CJ09-lkBdjQ/

"There's no question—none—that President Trump": "After not-guilty vote, McConnell says Trump 'morally responsible' for Capitol riot," Makini Brice and David Morgan, Reuters, February 13, 2021. https://www.reuters.com/article/us-usa-trump-impeachment-republicans-idUSKBN2AD0OG

"we have a common interest in making clear": Congressional Record, Proceedings and Debates of the 117th Congress, First Session, February 9, 2021, S596. https://www.congress.gov/117/crec/2021/02/09/CREC-2021-02-09.pdf

"President Trump's lack of remorse": Congressional Record, Proceedings and Debates of the 117th Congress, First Session, February 11, 2021, S650. https://www.govinfo.gov/content/

pkg/CREC-2021-02-11/pdf/CREC-2021-02-11-pt1-PgS645-2.pdf

"Impeachment is not to punish": Congressional Record, Proceedings and Debates of the 117th Congress, First Session, February 11, 2021, S654. https://www.govinfo.gov/content/pkg/CREC-2021-02-11/pdf/CREC-2021-02-11-pt1-PgS645-2.pdf

"Remind them that the seeds they plant": Congressional Record, Proceedings and Debates of the 117th Congress, First Session, February 11, 2021, S645. https://www.govinfo.gov/content/pkg/CREC-2021-02-11/pdf/CREC-2021-02-11-pt1-PgS645-2.pdf

"a President has unbounded authority": United States Court of Appeals for the District of Columbia, No. 23-3228, United States of America v. Donald J. Trump, 40

"would undermine our nation's foundational": No. 23-939, Brief of Retired Four-Star Admirals and Generals, and Former Secretaries of the U.S. Army, Navy, And Air Force as Amici Curiae in Support of Respondent," April 8, 2024, 1, 8, 10, 16. https://www.supremecourt.gov/DocketPDF/23/23-939/307029/20240408130715170_No.%2023-939bsacRetiredFour-StarAdmiralsAndGenerals.pdf

"in dividing official from unofficial conduct": Opinion of the Court, Supreme Court of the United States, No. 23-939, Donald J. Trump v. United States, 18

"this new official-acts immunity now": Sotomayor, J., dissenting, Supreme Court of the United States, No. 23-939, Donald J. Trump v. United States, 29–30

"the majority has concocted something entirely": Jackson, J., dissenting, Supreme Court of the United States, No. 23-939, Donald J. Trump v. United States, 5, 17

Without accountability, it all becomes normal: "Here's every word from the 9th Jan. 6 committee hearing on its investigation," NPR, October 13, 2022. https://www.npr.org/2022/10/13/1125331584/jan-6-committee-hearing-transcript

CHAPTER 21: Promises and Commitments

Undertake not what you cannot perform: "The Rules of Civility," MountVernon.org. https://www.mountvernon.org/george-washington/rules-of-civility/#:~:text=George%20Washington%20wrote%20out%20a,popularly%20circulated%20during%20Washington's%20time

I believe that this nation should commit: "The Decision to Go to the Moon: President John F. Kennedy's May 25, 1961 Speech before a Joint Session of Congress." https://www.nasa.gov/history/the-decision-to-go-to-the-moon/

CHAPTER 22: Perceptions and Conflicts of Interest

he could give the award to himself: "Trump jokes that he wanted to give himself the Medal of Honor while speaking at national veterans convention," Savannah Behrmann, *USA Today*, August 21, 2019. https://www.usatoday.com/story/news/2019/08/21/donald-trump-jokes-he-wanted-give-himself-medal-honor/2077813001/

Clark did not inform his boss...violated the policy: "Final Report, Select Committee to Investigate the January 6th Attack on the United States Capitol," House Report 117-663,

December 22, 2022, 50

during a phone call with the President: United States of America v. Donald J. Trump (Indictment), Case No. 1:23-cr-00257-TSC, Document 1, August 1, 2023, 28, 30

"We must especially beware of that small group": "Transcript of President Franklin Roosevelt's Annual Message (Four Freedoms) to Congress (1941)," National Archives. https://www. archives.gov/milestone-documents/president-franklin-roosevelts-annual-message-to-congress

My public proceedings were always directed: Thomas Jefferson on a candidate's qualifications: Thomas Jefferson, edited by Eric S. Petersen, *Light and Liberty: Reflections on the Pursuit of Happiness* (New York: The Modern Library, 2004), 91

Trump attorney Michael Cohen recalled conversations: Report on the Investigation Into Russian Interference in The 2016 Presidential Election, Volume I of II, U.S. Department of Justice, March 2019, 72

As president, he visited…on over 415 of his approximately 1460: "Tracking the President's Visits to Trump Properties," Karen Yourish and Troy Griggs, *New York Times*, November 23, 2020. https://www.nytimes.com/interactive/2017/04/05/us/politics/tracking-trumps-visits-to-his-branded-properties.html

had documented 3,403 conflicts of interest: "President Trump's 3,400 Conflicts of Interest," CREW, September 24, 2020. https://www.citizensforethics.org/reports-investigations/crew -reports/president-trumps-3400-conflicts-of-interest/

President Trump received, through entities he owned: "White House for Sale: How Princes, Prime Ministers, and Premiers Paid Off President Trump," Staff Report, Committee on Oversight and Accountability, Democratic Staff, January 4, 2024, 9. https://oversightdemocrats. house.gov/sites/democrats.oversight.house.gov/files/2024-01-04.COA%20DEMS%20-%20 Mazars%20Report.pdf

"the exact kinds of presidential corruption and conflicts": White House for Sale: How Princes, Prime Ministers, and Premiers Paid Off President Trump," Staff Report, Committee on Oversight and Accountability, Democratic Staff, January 4, 2024, 13

four U.S. senators were urged to explain: "4 U.S. senators sold stock after getting coronavirus threat briefings in January," David Kocieniewski and Bloomberg, *Fortune*, March 20, 2020. https://fortune.com/2020/03/20/senators-burr-loeffler-sold-stock-coronavirus-threat-briefings-in-january/

the President encouraged a state agency: "President Trump and Allies Push to Save a Very Specific Coal Plant," Jeff Brady, NPR, February 12, 2019. https://www.npr. org/2019/02/12/693966847/president-trump-and-allies-push-to-save-a-very-specific-coal -plant

I love to see honest and honorable men: Thomas Jefferson, edited by Eric S. Petersen, *Light and Liberty: Reflections on the Pursuit of Happiness* (New York: The Modern Library, 2004), 25

CHAPTER 23: Dishonesty and Deception

It is of great importance to set: Thomas Jefferson, edited by Eric S. Petersen, *Light and Liberty: Reflections on the Pursuit of Happiness* (New York: The Modern Library, 2004), 53

Notes

He who permits himself to tell a lie once: Thomas Jefferson, edited by Eric S. Petersen, *Light and Liberty: Reflections on the Pursuit of Happiness* (New York: The Modern Library, 2004), 53

"the truth is found when men are free": "Address at Temple University, Philadelphia, on Receiving an Honorary Degree," The American Presidency Project. https://www.presidency.ucsb.edu/documents/address-temple-university-philadelphia-receiving-honorary-degree

"America believes in a thing called truth": Adam Schiff, February 3, 2020. https://www.congress.gov/116/crec/2020/02/03/CREC-2020-02-03-pt1-PgS790-4.pdf

"Will facts actually continue to be": Jon Meacham, *The 11th Hour with Brian Williams*, MSNBC, March 22, 2019

"to abandon facts is to abandon freedom": Timothy Snyder, *On Tyranny—Twenty Lessons from the Twentieth Century* (New York: Tim Duggan Books, 2017), 65

"When people don't believe in truth": Timothy Snyder, *Fareed Zakaria GPS*, CNN, January 18, 2021

"Politics depends on our ability": "Obama's 2006 Speech on Faith and Politics," *New York Times*, June 28, 2006. https://www.nytimes.com/2006/06/28/us/politics/2006obamaspeech.html

The truth still matters: Judge Amy Berman Jackson, United States of America v. Roger J. Stone, Jr., Case 1:19-cr-00018-ABJ Document 334, February 24, 2020, 87–88, 72, 83. https://storage.courtlistener.com/recap/gov.uscourts.dcd.203583/gov.uscourts.dcd.203583.334.0_1.pdf

"the tension involved in conscious deception": Jonathan Glover, *Humanity: A Moral History of the Twentieth Century* (New Haven, CT: Yale University Press, 2000), 281

Above all, do not lie to yourself: Fyodor Dostoyevsky, *The Brothers Karamazov* (1879). https://www.goodreads.com/quotes/29218-above-all-don-t-lie-to-yourself-the-man-who-lies

As self-deception feeds on itself: Jonathan Glover, *Humanity: A Moral History of the Twentieth Century* (New Haven, CT: Yale University Press, 2000), 282

You submit to tyranny: Timothy Snyder, *On Tyranny—Twenty Lessons from the Twentieth Century* (New York: Tim Duggan Books, 2017), 66

a prominent former governor argued: "Ruhle interviews Jeff Sessions and Chris Christie at the SALT conference," MSNBC, May 8, 2019. https://www.msnbc.com/msnbc/watch/msnbc-s-stephanie-ruhle-interviews-jeff-sessions-and-chris-christie-at-the-salt-conference-in-las-vegas-59252293820

This president [Trump], because he's an amoral: Town Hall Meeting with Former FBI Director James Comey, CNN, May 9, 2019. http://edition.cnn.com/TRANSCRIPTS/1905/09/se.01.html

"We're going to be pretty soon": "Donald Trump Coronavirus Press Conference Transcript: Trump and CDC Give Coronavirus Updates," *Rev.com*, February 26, 2020. https://www.rev.com/blog/transcripts/donald-trump-coronavirus-press-conference-transcript-trump-and-cdc-give-coronavirus-updates

Truman suggested that people who make mistakes: Harry S. Truman, *Mr. Citizen* (New York: Bernard Geis Associates, 1960), 27

"it is not truth which matters, but victory": Adolf Hitler, Biography.com. https://www.biography.com/political-figures/adolf-hitler

653

the total had reached 30,573: "Trump's false or misleading claims total 30,573 over 4 years," Glenn Kessler, Salvador Rizzo, and Meg Kelly, *Washington Post*, January 24, 2021. https:// www.washingtonpost.com/politics/2021/01/24/trumps-false-or-misleading-claims-total-30573-over-four-years/

"His intent is always to give": "Press Secretary Kayleigh McEnany Press Conference Transcript May 28," *Rev.com*, May 28, 2020. https://www.rev.com/blog/transcripts/press-secretary-kayleigh-mcenany-press-conference-transcript-may-28

"Steele's reports played no role": Review of Four FISA Applications and Other Aspects of the FBI's Crossfire Hurricane Investigation, Office of the Inspector General, U.S. Department of Justice (December 2019), ii

"exercise of discretion in opening": Review of Four FISA Applications and Other Aspects of the FBI's Crossfire Hurricane Investigation, Office of the Inspector General, U.S. Department of Justice (December 2019), 410

"established that several individuals affiliated": Report On The Investigation Into Russian Interference In The 2016 Presidential Election, Volume I of II, U.S. Department of Justice (March 2019), 9

The Russians made outreach to the Trump campaign: "Full transcript: Mueller testimony before House Judiciary, Intelligence committees," NBC News, July 24, 2019. https://www.nbcnews.com/politics/congress/full-transcript-robert-mueller-house-committee-testimony-n1033216

In early 2018, the press reported: Report on The Investigation Into Russian Interference In The 2016 Presidential Election, Volume II of II, U.S. Department of Justice (March 2019), 5–6

Shortly after the FBI opened the Crossfire: Review of Four FISA Applications and Other Aspects of the FBI's Crossfire Hurricane Investigation, Office of the Inspector General, U.S. Department of Justice (December 2019), 411

"no evidence that Comey or his attorneys": Report of Investigation of Former Federal Bureau of Investigation Director James Comey's Disclosure of Sensitive Investigative Information and Handling of Certain Memoranda, Office of the Inspector General, U.S. Department of Justice (August 2019), 2

His campaign manager, Bill Stepien, understood: "Here's every word of the second Jan. 6 committee hearing on its investigation," NPR, June 13, 2022. https://www.npr.org/2022/06/13/1104690690/heres-every-word-of-the-second-jan-6-committee-hearing-on-its-investigation

"This is a fraud on the American public": "Donald Trump 2020 Election Night Speech Transcript," *Rev.com*, November 4, 2020. https://www.rev.com/blog/transcripts/donald-trump-2020-election-night-speech-transcript

the Trump Campaign's lead data analyst: "Final Report, Select Committee to Investigate the January 6th Attack on the United States Capitol," House Report 117-663, December 22, 2022, 12

"this flight from fact": Jon Meacham, *The 11th Hour with Brian Williams*, MSNBC, January 8, 2021. https://www.msnbc.com/transcripts/transcript-11th-hour-brian-williams-january-8-2021-n1259054

And insofar as he gets people to believe: Timothy Snyder, MSNBC, November 13, 2020

"I think the Trump presidency risks": Town Hall Meeting with Former FBI Director James Comey, CNN, May 9, 2019. http://edition.cnn.com/TRANSCRIPTS/1905/09/se.01.html

"There is truth and there are lies": "Inaugural Address by President Joseph R. Biden, Jr. January 20, 2021." https://www.whitehouse.gov/briefing-room/speeches-remarks/2021/01/20/inaugural-address-by-president-joseph-r-biden-jr/

That night, the White House Press Office: Report on The Investigation Into Russian Interference in the 2016 Presidential Election, Volume II of II, U.S. Department of Justice (March 2019), 62, 70–71

CHAPTER 24: Disinformation (Trafficking in Bullshit)

"It organizes your followers": Anne Applebaum, January 10, 2021, MSNBC

it aims to sow confusion: *TIME*, December 24–31, 2018, 57

"The ideal subject of totalitarian rule": From *The Origins of Totalitarianism* by Hannah Arendt published by Penguin Classics. Copyright © Hannah Arendt, 1966, 1968. Copyright renewed © Hannah Arendt, 1948, 1951. Copyright renewed © Hannah Arendt, 1976. Copyright renewed © Mary McCarthy West, 1979. Copyright renewed © Lotte Kohler, 1994. Reprinted by permission of Penguin Books Limited

falsehood diffused significantly farther: "The spread of true and false news online," Soroush Vosoughi, Deb Roy, and Sinan Aral, *Science* 359 (March 9, 2018): 1147. http://fsnagle.org/papers/vosoughi2018spread.pdf

"well-staged insinuation": "Ukraine war: Putin's spokesman Dmitry Peskov denies war crimes but admits 'significant' Russian losses," Alix Culbertson, Sky.com, April 8, 2022. https://news.sky.com/story/ukraine-war-putins-spokesman-denies-war-crimes-but-admits-significant-russian-losses-12584552

"simply a well-directed—but tragic—show": "Kremlin says Bucha is 'monstrous forgery' aimed at smearing Russia," Guy Faulconbridge, Reuters, April 5, 2022. https://www.reuters.com/world/europe/putin-ally-says-bucha-killings-are-fake-propaganda-2022-04-05/

"presents one of the most serious": "Final Report, Select Committee to Investigate the January 6th Attack on the United States Capitol," House Report 117-663, December 22, 2022, 808

Russian President Putin authorized: Foreign Threats to the 2020 US Federal Elections (March 10, 2021), National Intelligence Council, i, 2

"If a nation expects to be ignorant": Thomas Jefferson, edited by Eric S. Petersen, *Light and Liberty: Reflections on the Pursuit of Happiness* (New York: The Modern Library, 2004), 114

As of 2019, it had on its payroll: "Trump's New Favorite Channel Employs Kremlin-Paid Journalist," Kevin Poulsen, *Daily Beast*, November 2, 2019. https://www.thedailybeast.com/oan-trumps-new-favorite-channel-employs-kremlin-paid-journalist?ref=scroll

"He's breaking down factuality": Jason Stanley, *All In with Chris Hayes*, MSNBC, May 6, 2019

"You're the president. You're not like someone's": "Donald Trump NBC Town Hall Transcript October 15," *Rev.com*, October 15, 2020. https://www.rev.com/blog/transcripts/donald -trump-nbc-town-hall-transcript-october-15

The dangerous implication of this conspiracy: "President Barack Obama and Maria Ressa on Disinformation and the Erosion of Democracy," *The Atlantic*, April 6, 2022. https://www. youtube.com/watch?v=guO3_7pn7FI&t=183s

So I just heard that…very talented lawyer: "Trump promotes false conspiracy claiming Kamala Harris ineligible for White House," Aamer Madhani, Sara Burnett, Amanda Seitz, and Jill Colvin, Associated Press, August 13, 2020. https://globalnews.ca/news/7274280/ trump-kamala-harris-conspiracy/

"The President was asking questions": *The Situation Room*, CNN, June 10, 2020. https:// transcripts.cnn.com/show/sitroom/date/2020-06-10/segment/01

"these are people that love our country": "Trump on QAnon conspiracy believers: 'They love our country,'" CTV News, August 19, 2020. https://www.youtube.com/watch?v=XWVNkH-Qtdbw

"I know nothing about QAnon": "Donald Trump NBC Town Hall Transcript October 15," *Rev.com*, October 15, 2020. https://www.rev.com/blog/transcripts/donald-trump-nbc-town-hall-transcript-october-15

"allowed to believe things that weren't true": "Marjorie Taylor Greene: 'I Was Allowed to Believe Things That Weren't True,'" *MTP Daily*, MSNBC, February 4, 2021. https://www. youtube.com/watch?v=llbltxLBsN8

A national survey conducted in March 2021: "Understanding QAnon's Connection to American Politics, Religion, and Media Consumption," PRRI-IFYC, May 27, 2021. www. prri.org/research/qanon-conspiracy-american-politics-report

"No ma'am. No ma'am. He's a decent…and that's the point": "Watch John McCain Strongly Defend Barack Obama During the 2008 Campaign," Lisa Marie Segarra, *TIME*, August 25, 2018. https://time.com/4866404/john-mccain-barack-obama-arab-cancer/

John believed in honest argument: "Full Transcript Of Obama Eulogy At McCain's Funeral," Lady Steele, *Love Peace & Slander*, September 1, 2018. https://lovepeacenslander.com/index. php/2018/09/01/full-transcript-of-obama-eulogy-at-mccains-funeral/

Rational people check their beliefs: Jonathan Glover, *Humanity: A Moral History of the Twentieth Century* (New Haven, CT: Yale University Press, 2000), 364

"He who knows nothing is nearer the truth": Thomas Jefferson, edited by Eric S. Petersen, *Light and Liberty: Reflections on the Pursuit of Happiness* (New York: The Modern Library, 2004), 112

CHAPTER 25: Creating Distrust: The 2020 Election Disinformation Campaign

The spirit of 1776 is not dead: Thomas Jefferson, edited by Eric S. Petersen, *Light and Liberty: Reflections on the Pursuit of Happiness* (New York: The Modern Library, 2004), 82–83

"built on the widespread mistrust the Defendant was creating": United States of America v. Donald J. Trump (Indictment), Case No. 1:23-cr-00257-TSC, Document 1, August 1, 2023, 2

Notes

"the only way they can take this election": "Donald Trump 2020 RNC Speech Transcript August 24," *Rev.com*, August 24, 2020. https://www.rev.com/blog/transcripts/donald-trump-2020-rnc-speech-transcript-august-24; Trump "rigged election" quote—August 24, 2020, press briefing in Charlotte, NC

"If it were able to be legally shut down": "Remarks by President Trump Announcing an Executive Order on Preventing Online Censorship," May 28, 2020. https://trumpwhitehouse.archives.gov/briefings-statements/remarks-president-trump-announcing-executive-order-preventing-online-censorship/

campaign manager Bill Stepien and House Minority: "Here's every word of the second Jan. 6 committee hearing on its investigation," NPR, June 13, 2022. https://www.npr.org/2022/06/13/1104690690/heres-every-word-of-the-second-jan-6-committee-hearing-on-its-investigation

Foreign actors and cybercriminals: "Foreign Actors and Cybercriminals Likely to Spread Disinformation Regarding 2020 Election Results," FBI/CISA, Alert # I-092220PSA, September 22, 2020. https://www.ic3.gov/Media/Y2020/PSA200922

"Russia is likely to continue amplifying": "Final Report, Select Committee to Investigate the January 6th Attack on the United States Capitol," House Report 117–663, December 22, 2022, 808

We have not seen, historically: "FBI has not seen evidence of widespread voter fraud, Director Wray tells senators," Hannah Miao, CNBC, September 24, 2020. https://www.cnbc.com/2020/09/24/fbi-has-not-seen-evidence-of-widespread-voter-fraud-director-wray-tells-senators.html

the Russian government was also amplifying: "Intelligence bulletin warns Russia amplifying false claims mail-in voting will lead to widespread fraud," Zachary Cohen, CNN, September 4, 2020. https://www.cnn.com/2020/09/03/politics/russia-intel-bulletin-mail-in-voting-warning/index.html;

Russia's disinformation engine used President Trump's: "Final Report, Select Committee to Investigate the January 6th Attack on the United States Capitol," House Report 117-663, December 22, 2022, 808

suggesting the complicity of DOJ and FBI officials: "Trump Suggests FBI and Justice Department Led By His Own Appointees May Be 'Involved' With Rigging Election Against Him," Jason Lemon, *Newsweek*, November 29, 2020. https://www.newsweek.com/trump-suggests-fbi-justice-department-led-his-own-appointees-may-involved-rigging-election-1551010

votes were somehow being counted outside: "The President Is Acting Crazy, So Why Are We Shrugging It Off?," Susan B. Glaser, *The New Yorker*, December 3, 2020. https://www.newyorker.com/news/letter-from-trumps-washington/the-president-is-acting-crazy-so-why-are-we-shrugging-it-off

the threats became much more specific and graphic: "Here's every word of the second Jan. 6 committee hearing on its investigation," NPR, June 13, 2022. https://www.npr.org/2022/06/13/1104690690/heres-every-word-of-the-second-jan-6-committee-hearing-on-its-investigation

"the most secure in American history...in any way compromised": "Foreign Actors and Cybercriminals Likely to Spread Disinformation Regarding 2020 Election Results," FBI/CISA, Alert # I-092220PSA, September 22, 2020. www.cisa.gov/news-events/news/

joint-statement-elections-infrastructure-government-coordinating-council-election

President Trump replaced the head of his campaign's legal: "Here's every word of the second Jan. 6 committee hearing on its investigation," NPR, June 13, 2022. https://www.npr.org/2022/06/13/1104690690/heres-every-word-of-the-second-jan-6-committee-hearing-on-its-investigation

The president had appointed eleven of the judges: "Final Report, Select Committee to Investigate the January 6th Attack on the United States Capitol," House Report 117-663, December 22, 2022, 19

"filed this lawsuit in bad faith": U.S. District Judge Linda Parker, Timothy King v. Gretchen Whitmer, Case 2:20-cv-13134-LVP-RSW, ECF No. 172, PageID.6890, filed August 25, 2021, 3, 103–4. https://www.scribd.com/document/521719762/King-v-Whitmer-Sanction-Decision-08-25-21

"deceiving a federal court and the American people": U.S. District Judge Linda Parker, Timothy King v. Gretchen Whitmer, Case 2:20-cv-13134-LVP-RSW, ECF No. 172, PageID.6890, filed August 25, 2021, 1, 3. https://www.scribd.com/document/521719762/King-v-Whitmer-Sanction-Decision-08-25-21

"found no evidence of widespread or systematic": Report on the November 2020 Election in Michigan, Michigan Senate Oversight Committee, 3

There is uncontroverted evidence that respondent: Supreme Court of the State of New York, Appellate Division, First Judicial Department, Motion No. 2021-00491, May 3, 2021, 2. https://int.nyt.com/data/documenttools/giuliani-law-license-suspension/1ae5ad6007c0ebfa/full.pdf

On November 23, Attorney General Barr: "Here's every word of the second Jan. 6 committee hearing on its investigation," NPR, June 13, 2022. https://www.npr.org/2022/06/13/1104690690/heres-every-word-of-the-second-jan-6-committee-hearing-on-its-investigation

"This was a massive fraud": "Speech: Donald Trump Addresses Troops Worldwide on Thanksgiving—November 26, 2020," C-SPAN (Factbase Videos). https://www.youtube.com/watch?v=NMQ8jGBkSg4

"To date, we have not seen fraud on a scale": "Barr says no evidence of widespread voter fraud, defying Trump," Lauren Egan, NBC News, December 1, 2020. https://www.nbcnews.com/politics/white-house/barr-says-no-evidence-widespread-voter-fraud-defying-trump-n1249581

Trump had told his advisors in private: United States of America v. Donald J. Trump (Indictment), Case No. 1:23-cr-00257-TSC, Document 1, August 1, 2023, 12

Barr debunked the various fraud claims; "a grave disservice to the country": "Here's every word of the second Jan. 6 committee hearing on its investigation," NPR, June 13, 2022. https://www.npr.org/2022/06/13/1104690690/heres-every-word-of-the-second-jan-6-committee-hearing-on-its-investigation

"crazy stuff": "Here's every word of the first Jan. 6 committee hearing on its investigation," NPR, June 10, 2022. https://www.npr.org/2022/06/10/1104156949/jan-6-committee-hearing-transcript

We have a company that's very suspect: "Here's every word of the second Jan. 6

committee hearing on its investigation," NPR, June 13, 2022. https://www.npr.org /2022/06/13/1104690690/heres-every-word-of-the-second-jan-6-committee-hearing-on-its -investigation

The President posted or reposted: "Final Report, Select Committee to Investigate the January 6th Attack on the United States Capitol," House Report 117-663, December 22, 2022, 25

"The biggest vulnerability in democracy": Chris Krebs, CNN, August 17, 2022

"there is no world, there is no option": United States of America v. Donald J. Trump (Indictment), Case No. 1:23-cr-00257-TSC, Document 1, August 1, 2023, 30

Giuliani made false claims...False Statements and Writings: Fulton County Superior Court Indictment, Che Alexander, Clerk of Court, August 14, 2023, 72

over 1500 former prosecutors: "1,500 attorneys say Trump's lawyers are a 'disgrace' and a threat to democracy," Amy Lieu, *The American Independent*, December 8, 2020. https://americanindependent.com/1500-attorneys-open-letter-trump-lawyers-election-rudy-giuliani-bill-barr/

"detached from reality if he really believes": "Here's every word of the first Jan. 6 committee hearing on its investigation," NPR, June 10, 2022. https://www.npr.org /2022/06/10/1104156949/jan-6-committee-hearing-transcript

who had objected to the President's peddling: "Final Report, Select Committee to Investigate the January 6th Attack on the United States Capitol," House Report 117-663, December 22, 2022, 379

Mark Meadows, personally observed: United States of America v. Donald J. Trump (Indictment), Case No. 1:23-cr-00257-TSC, Document 1, August 1, 2023, 14

On almost every day between December 23...for over ninety minutes: "Final Report, Select Committee to Investigate the January 6th Attack on the United States Capitol," House Report 117-663, December 22, 2022, 49

The two men debunked: "Here's every word from the fifth Jan. 6 committee hearing on its investigation," NPR, June 23, 2022. https://www.npr.org/2022/06/23/1106700800/jan-6-committee -hearing-transcript

Donoghue even walked the President...not sufficiently credible for litigation: "Here's every word of the second Jan. 6 committee hearing on its investigation," NPR, June 13, 2022. https://www.npr.org/2022/06/13/1104690690/heres-every-word-of-the-second-jan-6-committee-hearing-on-its-investigation

On December 29, President Trump falsely: United States of America v. Donald J. Trump (Indictment), Case No. 1:23-cr-00257-TSC, Document 1, August 1, 2023, 33

no evidence of malfeasance or fraud...only four votes in his state: "Here's every word from the fourth Jan. 6 committee hearing on its investigation," NPR, June 21, 2022. https://www.npr.org/2022/06/21/1105848096/jan-6-committee-hearing-transcript

"not sufficient to be outcome determinative": "Here's every word of the second Jan. 6 committee hearing on its investigation," NPR, June 13, 2022. https://www.npr.org/2022/06/13/1104690690/heres-every-word-of-the-second-jan-6-committee-hearing-on-its-investigation

It has to stop. Mr. President: "Someone's Going to Get Killed': Ga. Official Blasts GOP Silence on Election Threats," Stephen Fowler, NPR, December 1, 2020. https://www.npr.org /sections/biden-transition-updates/2020/12/01/940961602/someones-going-to-get-killed -ga-official-blasts-gop-silence-on-election-threats

"professional vote scammer and hustler": "Read the full transcript and listen to Trump's audio call with Georgia secretary of state," CNN, January 3, 2021. https://www.cnn. com/2021/01/03/politics/trump-brad-raffensperger-phone-call-transcript/index.html

"all just conspiracy shit beamed down": United States of America v. Donald J. Trump (Indictment), Case No. 1:23-cr-00257-TSC, Document 1, August 1, 2023, 13–14

Rudy Giuliani had accused Freeman: United States of America v. Donald J. Trump (Indictment), Case No. 1:23-cr-00257-TSC, Document 1, August 1, 2023, 14

Several individuals (eventually charged in August 2023: Fulton County Superior Court Indictment, Che Alexander, Clerk of Court, August 14, 2023, 17, 43

After their contact information was published: "Final Report, Select Committee to Investigate the January 6th Attack on the United States Capitol," House Report 117-663, December 22, 2022, 45

Reuters had documented over 850: "Anatomy of a Death Threat," Peter Eisler, Jason Szep, Linda So, and Sam Hart, Reuters, December 30, 2021. https://graphics.reuters.com/ USA-ELECTION/THREATS/mopanwmlkva/

Recent polling shows that 39 percent: "Ted Cruz Senate Speech on Election Certification Transcript January 6," *Rev.com*, January 6, 2021. https://www.rev.com/blog/transcripts /ted-cruz-senate-speech-on-election-certification-transcript-january-6

When you look at other democracies: Senator Gary Peters, *The Rachel Maddow Show,* MSNBC, December 16, 2020. www.msnbc.com/transcripts/transcript-rachel-maddow-show -december-16-2020-n1260818

would be an "illegitimate president" if he took office: "Final Report, Select Committee to Investigate the January 6th Attack on the United States Capitol," House Report 117-663, December 22, 2022, 28

The Trump campaign—along with: "Trump, RNC raise over $200M on vote fraud claims, but some big-money donors aren't backing his fight," Brian Schwartz, CNBC, December 4, 2020. https://www.cnbc.com/2020/12/04/trump-gop-fundraising-election-vote-fraud-claims.html

raised over $250 million…Save America political action committee: "Here's every word of the second Jan. 6 committee hearing on its investigation," NPR, June 13, 2022. https:// www.npr.org/2022/06/13/1104690690/heres-every-word-of-the-second-jan-6-commit-tee-hearing-on-its-investigation; "Trump Raised $250 Million Since Election to Challenge Outcome—Here's Where Most of the Money Will Actually Go," Jemima McEvoy, *Forbes*, January 31, 2021. https://www.forbes.com/sites/jemimamcevoy/2021/01/31/trump-raised-250-million-since-election-to-challenge-outcome-heres-where-most-of-the-money-will-actu-ally-go/?sh=536a02238824

"sudden disaster that requires": Timothy Snyder, *On Tyranny—Twenty Lessons from the Twentieth Century* (New York: Tim Duggan Books, 2017), 103

"A Massive Fraud of this type": Donald J. Trump on Truth Social, 7:44 AM, December 3, 2022

The basis of our political systems: "Washington's Farewell Address," Senate Document No. 106–21, 2000. https://www.govinfo.gov/content/pkg/GPO-CDOC-106sdoc21/pdf/ GPO-CDOC-106sdoc21.pdf

CHAPTER 26: Fomenting Fear

"Our fate is contingent upon": Jon Meacham, *The Soul of America: The Battle for Our Better Angels* (New York: Random House, 2018), 7

"cold, calculating, unimpassioned reason": Abraham Lincoln, "Address before the Young Men's Lyceum of Springfield, Illinois," in Basler, ed., *Collected Works*, vol. 1, 115

"Army for Trump's election security operation": "Trump's Calls For Poll Watchers Raise Fears about Voter Intimidation," Pam Fessler, NPR, September 30, 2020. https://www.npr. org/2020/09/30/918766323/trumps-calls-for-poll-watchers-raises-fears-about-voter-intimi- dation

"travel is fatal to prejudice": "The Reports of Mark Twain's Travel Quotes Are Somewhat Exaggerated," Craig Thompson, *Clearing Customs*, September 18, 2019. https://clearingcustoms. net/2019/09/08/the-reports-of-mark-twains-travel-quotations-are-somewhat-exaggerated/

the term "invasion" to describe migrants: "Trump referred to immigrant 'invasion' in 2,000 Facebook ads, analysis reveals," Peter Andringa, *The Guardian*, August 5, 2019. https://www. theguardian.com/us-news/2019/aug/05/trump-internet-facebook-ads-racism-immigrant-in- vasion

A 2020 FBI report indicated: "Hate Crimes Under Trump Surged Nearly 20 Percent Says FBI Report," Daniel Villarreal, *Newsweek*, November 16, 2020. https://www.newsweek.com/ hate-crimes-under-trump-surged-nearly-20-percent-says-fbi-report-1547870

"Hispanic invasion of Texas": "The Manifesto of the El Paso Terrorist," Farid Hafez, *Bridge*, August 26, 2019. https://bridge.georgetown.edu/research/the-manifesto-of-the-el-paso-terrorist/

"fight to protect me and to protect you": "Donald Trump Rally Speech Transcript Scranton, PA November 2," *Rev.com*, November 2, 2020. https://www.rev.com/blog/transcripts/donald- trump-rally-speech-transcript-scranton-pa-november-2

He's going to do things that nobody ever: "President Trump delivers remarks on economic prosperity—8/6/2020," CNBC. https://www.youtube.com/watch?v=gX2jtownpWo

"bring on NEGRO EQUALITY, more DEBT": *Heritage Auctions.* https://historical.ha.com/ itm/political/posters-and-broadsides-pre-1896-/george-mcclellan-fabulous-1864-racist- broadside/a/6092-38111.s

In similar posts, the President suggested: @realDonaldTrump Tweets 4:08 PM January 23, 2020; 12:43 PM October 18, 2018; and 9:53 PM September 10, 2020

Kamala [mispronounced] will not be your: "Donald Trump Rally Speech Transcript The Villages, Florida October 23," *Rev.com*, October 23, 2020. https://www.rev.com/blog/tran- scripts/donald-trump-rally-speech-transcript-the-villages-florida-october-23

CHAPTER 27: Ethics in Public Leadership

Labor to keep alive in your breast: "The Rules of Civility," MountVernon.org. https://www. mountvernon.org/george-washington/rules-of-civility/#:~:text=George%20Washington%20 wrote%20out%20a,popularly%20circulated%20during%20Washington's%20time

"Let us have faith that right": Abraham Lincoln, Cooper Union Address, New York, February 27, 1860. http://www.abrahamlincolnonline.org/lincoln/speeches/cooper.htm

If right doesn't matter, it doesn't matter how good: "Adam Schiff Closing Argument Transcript: Thursday Impeachment Trial," *Rev.com*, January 24, 2020. https://www.rev.com/blog/ transcripts/adam-schiff-closing-argument-transcript-thursday-impeachment-trial

"The presidency is not merely an administrative office": Anne O'Hare McCormick, "Roosevelt's View of the Big Job: The Presidency Is 'a Superb Opportunity for Applying the Simple Rules of Human Conduct,' Says the Democratic Candidate, Interviewed in the Midst of a Whirl of Varied Activity," *New York Times*, September 11, 1932

I gather that you believe that knowingly: "Mueller Testimony live stream: Watch Special Counsel Robert Mueller's Congressional hearing today," CBS News, July 24, 2019. https:// www.youtube.com/watch?v=8db5lriRfwM

"A character of good faith is": Thomas Jefferson, edited by Eric S. Petersen, *Light and Liberty: Reflections on the Pursuit of Happiness* (New York: The Modern Library, 2004), 66

Viewing ethical leadership as central...as one's career progressed: "Leadership and Ethics across the Continuum of Learning: The Ethical Leadership Framework," Courtesy of *Air and Space Power Journal* (Winter 2019), 43, 44, 47–48, 51

Become an honest and useful man: Thomas Jefferson, edited by Eric S. Petersen, *Light and Liberty: Reflections on the Pursuit of Happiness* (New York: The Modern Library, 2004), 11

CHAPTER 28: Principled Loyalty

an unswerving allegiance: Merriam-Webster, s.v. "loyal *(adj.)*," March 2022. https://www. merriam-webster.com/dictionary/loyal

When you put your life on the line: "2020 Democratic National Convention (DNC) Night 4 Transcript," *Rev.com*, August 20, 2020. https://www.rev.com/blog/transcripts/2020-democratic-national-convention-dnc-night-4-transcript

The man who loves his country: Thomas Jefferson, edited by Eric S. Petersen, *Light and Liberty: Reflections on the Pursuit of Happiness* (New York: The Modern Library, 2004), 66

"natural human inclination to encapsulate ourselves": Jimmy Carter, *Christianity Today*

"If you look at history": Rutger Bregman, *Fareed Zakaria GPS*, CNN, July 5, 2020

To sin by silence, when we should protest: Ella Wheeler Wilcox, "Protest" (1914). https:// checkyourfact.com/2019/08/12/fact-check-abraham-lincoln-sin-silence-protest-cowards-men/

"widespread human tendency to give uncritical": Jonathan Glover, *Humanity: A Moral History of the Twentieth Century* (New Haven, CT: Yale University Press, 2000), 333

Cohen said that…he believed: Report on The Investigation Into Russian Interference In The 2016 Presidential Election, Volume II of II, U.S. Department of Justice (March 2019), 147

"My party's leadership has chosen": "GOP Sen. Burr censured by North Carolina GOP after Trump conviction vote," Myah Ward, *Politico*, February 15, 2021. https://www.politico.com/news/2021/02/15/richard-burr-north-carolina-censure-469027

"We did not send him there to vote": "GOP County Chair Blasts Pat Toomey Vote: 'We Did Not Send Him There to Do the Right Thing,'" Darragh Roche, *Newsweek*, February 16, 2021. https://www.newsweek.com/gop-county-chair-blasts-pat-toomey-impeachment-vote-1569478

Your commitment to your oath will be tested: "A Letter to the West Point Class of 2020, from Fellow Members of the Long Gray Line," United Members of the Long Gray Line, June 11, 2020. https://concernedwestpointgrads.medium.com/a-letter-to-the-west-point-class-of-2020-from-fellow-members-of-the-long-gray-line-f8b4862babda

Comey said that when he arrived: Report on The Investigation Into Russian Interference In The 2016 Presidential Election, Volume II of II, U.S. Department of Justice (March 2019), 33–35

After Flynn withdrew from a joint: Report on The Investigation Into Russian Interference In The 2016 Presidential Election, Volume II of II, U.S. Department of Justice (March 2019), 6

"Mark [Meadows]wants me to let you know": Select Committee To Investigate The January 6th Attack On The U.S. Capitol, U.S. House Of Representatives, Interview Of: Cassidy Hutchinson, Wednesday, September 14, 2022, 70. https://s3.documentcloud.org/documents/23506040/cassidy-hutchinson-january-6-transcript-september-14-2022.pdf

protect who she needed to protect: "Final Report, Select Committee to Investigate the January 6th Attack on the United States Capitol," House Report 117-663, December 22, 2022, 122

Sessions believed the decision…He did not unrecuse: Report On The Investigation Into Russian Interference In The 2016 Presidential Election, Volume II of II, U.S. Department of Justice (March 2019), 5, 49–51, 108

"I made a bad decision": "Transcript: 'Fox News Sunday' Interview with President Trump," Fox News, July 19, 2020. https://www.foxnews.com/politics/transcript-fox-news-sunday-interview-with-president-trump

Associate yourself with men of good quality: "The Rules of Civility," MountVernon.org. https://www.mountvernon.org/george-washington/rules-of-civility/#:~:text=George%20Washington%20wrote%20out%20a,popularly%20circulated%20during%20Washington's%20time

"His integrity was most pure": Thomas Jefferson, edited by Eric S. Petersen, *Light and Liberty: Reflections on the Pursuit of Happiness* (New York: The Modern Library, 2004), 30

What a revolutionary notion, this idea: "Former President Barack Obama delivers a rousing eulogy: 'America was built by John Lewises,'" Joshua Bote, *USA Today*, July 30, 2020. https://www.usatoday.com/story/news/politics/2020/07/30/barack-obama-eulogy-john-lewis-funeral-full-transcript/5544048002/

directed White House Counsel Don McGahn: Report on The Investigation Into Russian Interference In The 2016 Presidential Election, Volume II of II, U.S. Department of Justice (March 2019), 113

Comey did not end the investigation: Report on The Investigation Into Russian Interference In The 2016 Presidential Election, Volume II of II, U.S. Department of Justice (March 2019), 158

CHAPTER 29: Abuse of Authority

when authority is used strictly in the conduct: Clay T. Buckingham, *Ethics and the Senior Officer: Institutional Tensions*, 1985.

there were only four things for which: General Creech anecdote courtesy of *Air and Space Forces Magazine*: Walter J. Boyne, "Creech," *Air and Space Forces Magazine* 88, no. 3 (March 2005). https://www.airforcemag.com/article/0305Creech/

"It is when the President commits crimes": Jackson, J., dissenting, Supreme Court of the United States, No. 23-939, Donald J. Trump v. United States, 19

"strikes at the core of the government's effort": "Full transcript: Mueller testimony before House Judiciary, Intelligence committees," NBC News, July 24, 2019. https://www.nbcnews.com/politics/congress/full-transcript-robert-mueller-house-committee-testimony-n1033216

"When corrupt motives take root": House of Representatives Judiciary Committee report, *Constitutional Grounds for Presidential Impeachment*, 116th Congress (December 2019), 1

"A bold president who knew himself to be supported": James Bryce, *The American Commonwealth*, 1:68

One of the letter writers said: "Judge while sentencing Trump campaign aide: 'If people don't have the facts, democracy doesn't work,'" Katelyn Polantz, CNN, December 17, 2019. https://www.cnn.com/2019/12/17/politics/amy-berman-jackson-gates-barr/index.html

"a classic organized crime...trying to communicate": "WATCH: Rep. Adam Schiff's full opening statement on whistleblower complaint: DNI hearing," *PBS NewsHour*. https://www.youtube.com/watch?v=GN4CJ8MYLTY

The President asked a foreign government: "Full text: Romney's speech on why he'll vote to convict Trump of abuse of power," NBC News, February 5, 2020. https://www.nbcnews.com/politics/trump-impeachment-inquiry/full-text-romney-s-speech-why-he-ll-vote-convict-n1130936

a corrupt abuse of the power..."spare no efforts": Noah Feldman Prepared Statement for the House Intelligence Committee, December 4, 2019. https://docs.house.gov/meetings/JU/JU00/20191204/110281/HHRG-116-JU00-Wstate-FeldmanP-20191204.pdf

the head of the DOJ's Civil Division...and the Justice Department: "Here's every word from the fifth Jan. 6 committee hearing on its investigation," NPR, June 23, 2022. https://www.npr.org/2022/06/23/1106700800/jan-6-committee-hearing-transcript

At this time we have identified...President of the Senate: Jeffrey Clark draft letter, "Pre-Decisional & Deliberative/Attorney-Client or Legal Work Product Georgia Proof of Concept," December 28, 2020. https://www.documentcloud.org/documents/21087991-jeffrey-clark-draft-letter

The intended effect...replace the DOJ leadership: "Here's every word from the fifth Jan. 6 committee hearing on its investigation," NPR, June 23, 2022. https://www.npr.org/2022/06/23/1106700800/jan-6-committee-hearing-transcript

"a grave step for the department": "Final Report, Select Committee to Investigate the January 6th Attack on the United States Capitol," House Report 117-663, December 22, 2022, 92

the president suggested that the DOJ: "Final Report, Select Committee to Investigate the January 6th Attack on the United States Capitol," House Report 117-663, December 22, 2022, 396

The president told Rosen...not going to change: "Here's every word from the fifth Jan. 6 committee hearing on its investigation," NPR, June 23, 2022. https://www.npr.org/2022/06/23/1106700800/jan-6-committee-hearing-transcript

Clark informed Rosen...constitutional crisis: : "Final Report, Select Committee to Investigate the January 6th Attack on the United States Capitol," House Report 117-663, December 22, 2022, 397, 402

"One thing we know...murder-suicide pact": "Here's every word from the fifth Jan. 6 committee hearing on its investigation," NPR, June 23, 2022. https://www.npr.org/2022/06/23/1106700800/jan-6-committee-hearing-transcript

I appreciate your willingness to do it: "Final Report, Select Committee to Investigate the January 6th Attack on the United States Capitol," House Report 117-663, December 22, 2022, 54

a Georgia grand jury in August 2023: Fulton County Superior Court Indictment, Che Alexander, Clerk of Court, August 14, 2023, 83

"You know, I don't think people should be allowed": The Trump-Ukraine Impeachment Inquiry Report: Report of the House Permanent Select Committee on Intelligence, December 2019, 246

His constant attacks on the FBI: "Democratic National Convention (DNC) 2020 Night 2 Transcript: Speeches by Bill Clinton, AOC, Jill Biden & More," *Rev.com*, August 18, 2020. https://www.rev.com/blog/transcripts/democratic-national-convention-dnc-2020-night-2-transcript

CHAPTER 30: The Spectrum of Undue Influence

41 percent of non-Christian cadets: "Air Force Cadets Cite Christian Proselytizing," CBS News, October 28, 2019. https://www.cbsnews.com/news/air-force-cadets-cite-christian-proselytizing/

Research conducted by the U.S. Merit Systems: The Merit Systems Principles—Keys to Managing the Federal Workforce, October 2020, 2

Roger Stone was found guilty: United States Attorney's Office, District of Columbia, November 15, 2019. https://www.justice.gov/usao-dc/pr/roger-stone-found-guilty-obstruction-false-statements-and-witness-tampering

"never seen political influence...afraid of the President": Assistant United States Attorney Aaron S. J. Zelinsky, Statement for the Record, House Judiciary Committee, June 24, 2020

"excessive and unwarranted": United States of America v. Roger J. Stone, Jr., Case 1:19-cr-00018-ABJ, Document 286, February 11, 2020, 4. https://www.politico.com/f/?id=00000170-3639-d66b-ad7e-3e3b62380000

"government's initial memorandum was well researched": Assistant United States Attorney Aaron S. J. Zelinsky, Statement for the Record, House Judiciary Committee, June 24, 2020

This case also exemplifies: Judge Amy Berman Jackson, United States of America v. Roger J. Stone, Jr., Case 1:19-cr-00018-ABJ Document 334, February 24, 2020, 83–84. https://storage.courtlistener.com/recap/gov.uscourts.dcd.203583/gov.uscourts.dcd.203583.334.0_1.pdf

"interference in the fair administration of justice...face of unlawful directives": DOJ Alumni Statement on the Events Surrounding the Sentencing of Roger Stone, February 16, 2020. https://medium.com/@dojalumni/doj-alumni-statement-on-the-events-surrounding-the-sentencing-of-roger-stone-c2cb75ae4937

A related White House statement: "Statement from the Press Secretary Regarding Executive Grant of Clemency for Roger Stone, Jr.," July 10, 2020. https://trumpwhitehouse.archives.gov/briefings-statements/statement-press-secretary-regarding-executive-grant-clemency-roger-stone-jr/

In so doing, and despite the fact: The Trump-Ukraine Impeachment Inquiry Report: Report of the House Permanent Select Committee on Intelligence, December 2019, 36

"effectuated through direct efforts to produce false": Report on The Investigation Into Russian Interference In The 2016 Presidential Election, Volume II of II, U.S. Department of Justice, March 2019, 173

The President's position as the head: Report on The Investigation Into Russian Interference In The 2016 Presidential Election, Volume II of II, U.S. Department of Justice, March 2019, 7, 157

Our investigation found multiple...or his family: Report on The Investigation Into Russian Interference In The 2016 Presidential Election, Volume II of II, U.S. Department of Justice, March 2019, 7, 157

"the President's conduct toward Michael Cohen": Report On The Investigation Into Russian Interference In The 2016 Presidential Election, Volume II of II, U.S. Department of Justice, March 2019, 6

"The President's effort to have [Attorney General] Sessions": Report On The Investigation Into Russian Interference In The 2016 Presidential Election, Volume II of II, U.S. Department of Justice, March 2019, 97

"reports that the President was being investigated": Report On The Investigation Into Russian Interference In The 2016 Presidential Election, Volume II of II, U.S. Department of Justice, March 2019, 89

"an unrecused Attorney General would play": Report On The Investigation Into Russian Interference In The 2016 Presidential Election, Volume II of II, U.S. Department of Justice, March 2019, 113

"The President's efforts to influence": Report on The Investigation Into Russian Interference In The 2016 Presidential Election, Volume II of II, U.S. Department of Justice, March 2019, 158

President Trump engaged in a brazen effort: The Trump-Ukraine Impeachment Inquiry Report: Report of the House Permanent Select Committee on Intelligence, December 2019, 257

"prevent, delay, or influence the testimony": The Trump-Ukraine Impeachment Inquiry Report: Report of the House Permanent Select Committee on Intelligence, December 2019, 36

While it may be more difficult: Report on The Investigation Into Russian Interference In The 2016 Presidential Election, Volume II of II, U.S. Department of Justice, March 2019, 157

The founders really let us down: Michael Beschloss, *The Rachel Maddow Show*, MSNBC, December 22, 2020. www.msnbc.com/transcripts/transcript-rachel-maddow-show-december -22-2020-n1260845

On February 13, 2017: Report on The Investigation Into Russian Interference In The 2016 Presidential Election, Volume II of II, U.S. Department of Justice, March 2019, 38

According to Comey's account: Report on The Investigation Into Russian Interference In The 2016 Presidential Election, Volume II of II, U.S. Department of Justice, March 2019, 40

"did not have a basis for a counterintelligence": "Justice Department drops criminal case against Michael Flynn," Katelyn Polantz, CNN, May 7, 2020. https://www.cnn .com/2020/05/07/politics/michael-flynn-prosecution/index.html

"newly minted definition of materiality": "Judge takes final shots at Trump, Flynn as he agrees to dismiss case," Pete Williams and Tom Winter, NBC News, December 8, 2020. https://www.nbcnews.com/politics/justice-department/judge-take-final-shots-trump-flynn -he-agrees-dismiss-case-n1250415

The Department of Justice has a solemn: United States of America v. Michael T. Flynn, Case No. 17-cr-232 (EGS), Document 223-2, June 10, 2020, 71

"an injustice against an innocent": "Statement from the Press Secretary Regarding Executive Grant of Clemency for General Michael T. Flynn," November 25, 2020. https://trump whitehouse.archives.gov/briefings-statements/statement-press-secretary-regarding-executive-grant-clemency-general-michael-t-flynn/

Michael Flynn was asked if: "Final Report, Select Committee to Investigate the January 6th Attack on the United States Capitol," House Report 117-663, December 22, 2022, 118

"intended Manafort to believe": Report on The Investigation Into Russian Interference In The 2016 Presidential Election, Volume II of II, U.S. Department of Justice, March 2019, 132–33

I think the whole Manafort trial: Report on The Investigation Into Russian Interference In The 2016 Presidential Election, Volume II of II, U.S. Department of Justice, March 2019, 126

[Rudy] Giuliani told the Washington Post: Report on The Investigation Into Russian Interference In The 2016 Presidential Election, Volume II of II, U.S. Department of Justice, March 2019, 127

"perhaps the greatest witch hunt": "Statement from the Press Secretary Regarding Executive Grants of Clemency," December 23, 2020. https://trumpwhitehouse.archives.gov/briefings-statements/statement-press-secretary-regarding-executive-grants-clemency-122320/

CHAPTER 31: Undue Influence in the 2020 Election

"White House Chief of Staff Mark Meadows": Subverting Justice: How the Former President and His Allies Pressured DOJ to Overturn the 2020 Election, Senate Committee on the Judiciary (Majority Staff Report), October 2021, 3

"Just say the election was corrupt": "Final Report, Select Committee to Investigate the January 6th Attack on the United States Capitol," House Report 117-663, December 22, 2022, 49

"prior efforts to subvert and obstruct": Impeaching Donald John Trump, President of the United States, for high crimes and misdemeanors, H.R. 24, 117th Congress (2021), 4. https://www.cnn.com/2021/01/11/politics/house-articles-of-impeachment/index.html

Bowers explained to Giuliani: "Final Report, Select Committee to Investigate the January 6th Attack on the United States Capitol," House Report 117-663, December 22, 2022, 46–47

During a second call from Trump to Bowers: Fulton County Superior Court Indictment, Che Alexander, Clerk of Court, August 14, 2023, 45

President Trump focused on Republican Senate: "Final Report, Select Committee to Investigate the January 6th Attack on the United States Capitol," House Report 117-663, December 22, 2022, 47

In a November 17 phone call: "Trump recorded pressuring Wayne County canvassers not to certify 2020 vote," Craig Mauger, *Detroit News*, December 21, 2023. https://www.detroitnews.com/story/news/politics/2023/12/21/donald-trump-recorded-pressuring-wayne-canvassers-not-to-certify-2020-vote-michigan/72004514007/?utm_campaign=atlantic-daily-newsletter&utm_source=newsletter&utm_medium=email&utm_content=20231222&lct-g=6050e64f4c8a1e4095f6a39a&utm_term=The%20Atlantic%20Daily

He phoned both Kemp and Ralston: Fulton County Superior Court Indictment, Che Alexander, Clerk of Court, August 14, 2023, 27, 30

On December 8, Trump phoned...to support those claims: United States of America v. Donald J. Trump (Indictment), Case No. 1:23-cr-00257-TSC, Document 1, August 1, 2023, 13

January 2, 2021, hour-long phone call: "Read the full transcript and listen to Trump's audio call with Georgia secretary of state," CNN, January 3, 2021. https://www.cnn.com/2021/01/03/politics/trump-brad-raffensperger-phone-call-transcript/index.html

Trump forced Pak's resignation: Subverting Justice: How the Former President and His Allies Pressured DOJ to Overturn the 2020 Election, Senate Committee on the Judiciary (Majority Staff Report), October 2021, 5

In Georgia, your secretary of state: "Transcript of Trump's Speech at Rally Before US Capitol Riot," Associated Press, January 13, 2021. https://www.usnews.com/news/politics/articles/2021-01-13/transcript-of-trumps-speech-at-rally-before-us-capitol-riot

Because I knew that we had followed the law: "Here's every word from the fourth Jan. 6 committee hearing on its investigation," NPR, June 21, 2022. https://www.npr.org/2022/06/21/1105848096/jan-6-committee-hearing-transcript

a Georgia grand jury charged former president Trump: Fulton County Superior Court Indictment, Che Alexander, Clerk of Court, August 14, 2023, 74, 87

charged former president Trump: Fulton County Superior Court Indictment, Che Alexander, Clerk of Court, August 14, 2023, 1–3

"the most basic principles of a strong democracy": "Brad Raffensperger's Two-Sentence Response to Trump Indictment," Anna Skinner, *Newsweek*, August 15, 2023. https://www. newsweek.com/brad-raffenspergers-two-sentence-response-trump-indictment-1819945#:~:-text=%22The%20most%20basic%20principles%20of,or%20you%20don%27t.%22&tex-t=Trump%27s%20campaign%20maintains%20that%20the,chances%20in%20the%20 2024%20election

When Pence phoned the President on December 25…lawsuit the previous day: United States of America v. Donald J. Trump (Indictment), Case No. 1:23-cr-00257-TSC, Document 1, August 1, 2023, 33

Pence was summoned to the Oval Office…for further deliberation: "Final Report, Select Committee to Investigate the January 6th Attack on the United States Capitol," House Report 117-663, December 22, 2022, 444–45

"I hope Mike Pence comes through for us": "Final Report, Select Committee to Investigate the January 6th Attack on the United States Capitol," House Report 117-663, December 22, 2022, 449

the President again demanded…alone, without staff present": "Final Report, Select Committee to Investigate the January 6th Attack on the United States Capitol," House Report 117-663, December 22, 2022, 452

When Pence once again refused…Secret Service detail": United States of America v. Donald J. Trump (Indictment), Case No. 1:23-cr-00257-TSC, Document 1, August 1, 2023, 36

"in total agreement"…for one State tabulation: "Final Report, Select Committee to Investigate the January 6th Attack on the United States Capitol," House Report 117-663, December 22, 2022, 454

"the legal authority to send the electoral…wimp": "Final Report, Select Committee to Investigate the January 6th Attack on the United States Capitol," House Report 117-663, December 22, 2022, 457–58

Mike Pence is going to have to: "Transcript of Trump's Speech at Rally Before US Capitol Riot," Associated Press, January 13, 2021. https://www.usnews.com/news/politics/arti-cles/2021-01-13/transcript-of-trumps-speech-at-rally-before-us-capitol-riot

"This may be the most important": "Final Report, Select Committee to Investigate the January 6th Attack on the United States Capitol," House Report 117-663, December 22, 2022, 462

It is my considered judgment that my oath: "Read: Vice President Mike Pence's statement breaking with Trump on Electoral College vote count," CNN, January 6, 2021. https://www .cnn.com/2021/01/06/politics/pence-trump-electoral-college-letter/index.html

President Trump said I had the right: "Here's every word of the third Jan. 6 committee hearing on its investigation," NPR, June 16, 2022. https://www.npr.org/2022/06/16/1105683634/ transcript-jan-6-committee

CHAPTER 32: Deepening Division

Yet hear me clearly: Disagreement must: "Inaugural Address by President Joseph R. Biden, Jr.," The White House, January 20, 2021. https://www.whitehouse.gov/briefing-room/speeches-remarks/2021/01/20/inaugural-address-by-president-joseph-r-biden-jr/

"If you have to win a campaign": "Barack Obama rebukes Donald Trump in all but name—video," *The Guardian*, October 19, 2017. https://www.theguardian.com/us-news/video/2017/oct/20/barack-obama-calls-for-unity-as-he-returns-to-campaign-trail-in-virginia-video

first president in his lifetime: "Read: The Full Statement from Jim Mattis," NPR, June 4, 2020. https://www.npr.org/2020/06/04/869262728/read-the-full-statement-from-jim-mattis

Trump identified issues he could exploit: Michael Cohen, *Disloyal: A Memoir* (New York: Skyhorse Publishing, 2020), 114–15

The Russians have new tools available: H.R. McMaster, *The 11th Hour with Brian Williams*, MSNBC, September 23, 2020

"cultivating and supporting...inimical to Russia's interests": Michael Cohen, *Disloyal: A Memoir* (New York: Skyhorse Publishing, 2020), 407–8

happy people avoid toxic tribalism: "Four secrets from the world's longest happiness Study," Kara Baskin, *Boston Globe*, September 16, 2022. https://www.bostonglobe.com/2022/09/16/lifestyle/four-secrets-worlds-longest-happiness-study/

facing too many crises..."hate and division": "Biden calls for national unity in his own Gettysburg address," MSNBC, October 6, 2020. https://www.msnbc.com/11th-hour/watch/biden-calls-for-national-unity-in-his-own-gettysburg-address-93302853984

In his final Sunday sermon: "2020 Democratic National Convention (DNC) Night 4 Transcript," *Rev.com*, August 20, 2020. https://www.rev.com/blog/transcripts/2020-democratic-national-convention-dnc-night-4-transcript

To reassume our leadership in world politics: "Opinion: Mitt Romney. The president shapes the public character of the nation. Trump's character falls short," *Washington Post*, January 1, 2019. https://www.washingtonpost.com/opinions/mitt-romney-the-president-shapes-the-public-character-of-the-nation-trumps-character-falls-short/2019/01/01/37a3c8c2-0d1a-11e9-8938-5898adc28fa2_story.html

When he urged South Africans: Richard Stengel, *Mandela's Way: Fifteen Lessons on Life, Love, and Courage* (New York: Crown Publishers, 2009), 125

constructive depolarizing...toward constructive engagement: "Leadership Skills in an Uncertain World," November 11, 2020, Center for Creative Leadership. https://www.ccl.org/articles/leading-effectively-articles/leadership-skills-for-an-uncertain-world/#:~:text=Constructive%20depolarizing.%20Ability%20to%20bring%20people%20from%20divergent,and%20improve%20tense%20situations%20where%20people%20cannot%20agree

CHAPTER 33: Inciting Violence: The Attack on the Capitol

History has taught us: Congresswoman Liz Cheney, 7:14 AM, May 16, 2022, @Liz_Cheney on Twitter

racially or ethnically motivated violent extremists: "Live Coverage of Senate Hearing on the January 6th Insurrection," CNN, March 3, 2021. http://edition.cnn.com/TRAN-SCRIPTS/2103/03/cnr.04.html

2019 was the most lethal year: "FBI Reports an Increase in Hate Crimes in 2019: Hate-Based Murders More Than Doubled," Southern Poverty Law Center, November 16, 2020. https://www.splcenter.org/news/2020/11/16/fbi-reports-increase-hate-crimes-2019-hate-based-murders-more-doubled

"Terrible job"; "any extreme violence": Donald J. Trump via @realDonaldTrump Twitter account, multiple Tweets at 9:30 PM, October 8, 2020

"The Defendant had a right, like every American": United States of America v. Donald J. Trump (Indictment), Case No. 1:23-cr-00257-TSC, Document 1, August 1, 2023, 2

"stand back and stand by": "Donald Trump & Joe Biden 1st Presidential Debate Transcript 2020," *Rev.com*, September 29, 2020. https://www.rev.com/blog/transcripts/donald-trump-joe-biden-1st-presidential-debate-transcript-2020

membership in the group probably tripled: "Here's every word of the first Jan. 6 committee hearing on its investigation," NPR, June 10, 2022. https://www.npr.org/2022/06/10/1104156949/jan-6-committee-hearing-transcript

The rabid attacks kindle the conspiracy mongers: Senator Mitt Romney, October 13, 2020, via @MittRomney on Twitter. https://www.dailydot.com/debug/mitt-romney-political-discourse-tweet/

"This is a case where they're trying": "Donald Trump White House Press Conference as Election Counts Continue," *Rev.com*, November 5, 2020. https://www.rev.com/blog/transcripts/donald-trump-white-house-press-conference-as-election-counts-continue-transcript-november-5

"This is now our greatest fight": "Actor Jon Voight says fighting 'lie' that Biden won is 'greatest fight since the Civil War,'" *The Hill*, November 11, 2020. https://www.youtube.com/watch?v=eL43dp58P3w

"You can't let another person steal": "Donald Trump Speech on Election Fraud Claims Transcript December 2," *Rev.com*, December 2, 2020. https://www.rev.com/blog/transcripts/donald-trump-speech-on-election-fraud-claims-transcript-december-2

"very gracious loser": "Donald Trump Georgia Rally Transcript Before Senate Runoff Elections December 5," *Rev.com*, December 5, 2021. https://www.rev.com/blog/transcripts/donald-trump-georgia-rally-transcript-before-senate-runoff-elections-december-5

"The Electoral College has spoken": "McConnell recognizes Biden as president-elect," Burgess Everett, *Politico*, December 15, 2020. https://www.politico.com/news/2020/12/15/mcconnell-recognizes-biden-as-president-elect-445450

The leadership of the Proud Boys…Three Percenter groups: "Final Report, Select Committee to Investigate the January 6th Attack on the United States Capitol," House Report 117-663, December 22, 2022, 56–60

patriotic duty and civic responsibility: "Final Report, Select Committee to Investigate the January 6th Attack on the United States Capitol," House Report 117-663, December 22, 2022, 2–3

"We won this election by a magnificent landslide": "Donald Trump Vlog: Contesting Election Results—December 22, 2020," *Factbase Videos.* https://www.youtube.com/watch?v=Y-J8LfWC1Wks

"This is not a rally": "Final Report, Select Committee to Investigate the January 6th Attack on the United States Capitol," House Report 117-663, December 22, 2022, 62

"things might get real, real bad": "Final Report, Select Committee to Investigate the January 6th Attack on the United States Capitol," House Report 117-663, December 22, 2022, 64

the President intended to direct: "Final Report, Select Committee to Investigate the January 6th Attack on the United States Capitol," House Report 117-663, December 22, 2022, 66

"supporters of the current president see January 6": "Capitol Police intelligence report warned three days before attack that 'Congress itself' could be targeted," Carol D. Leonnig, *Washington Post,* January 15, 2021. https://www.washingtonpost.com/politics/capitol-police-intelligence-warning/2021/01/15/c8b50744-5742-11eb-a08b-f1381ef3d207_story.html

"there is no way we lost Georgia"…We will never, ever surrender: "Donald Trump Rally Speech Transcript Dalton, Georgia: Senate Runoff Election," *Rev.com,* January 4, 2021. https://www.rev.com/blog/transcripts/donald-trump-rally-speech-transcript-dalton-georgia-senate-runoff-election

Hope Hicks…January 6 must remain peaceful: "Final Report, Select Committee to Investigate the January 6th Attack on the United States Capitol," House Report 117-663, December 22, 2022, 65–66

"Get violent…stop calling this a march": "Final Report, Select Committee to Investigate the January 6th Attack on the United States Capitol," House Report 117-663, December 22, 2022, 62

for use by a "quick reaction force": "Final Report, Select Committee to Investigate the January 6th Attack on the United States Capitol," House Report 117-663, December 22, 2022, 63

A Secret Service briefing mentioned: "Here's every word from the 9th Jan. 6 committee hearing on its investigation," NPR, October 13, 2022. https://www.npr.org/2022/10/13/1125331584/jan-6-committee-hearing-transcript

"all hell is going to break loose": "Jan. 6 Committee Hearing—Day 7 Transcript," *Rev.com,* July 13, 2022. https://www.rev.com/blog/transcripts/jan-6-committee-hearing-day-7-transcript

as later described by FBI Director: "FBI Director Christopher Wray Testifies on Capitol Attack, Domestic Terrorism Full Hearing Transcript March 2," *Rev.com,* March 2, 2021. https://www.rev.com/blog/transcripts/fbi-director-christopher-wray-testifies-on-capitol-attack-domestic-terrorism-full-hearing-transcript-march-2

they were mobilized by a sense of precarity: Cynthia Miller-Idriss, *Fareed Zakaria GPS,* CNN, January 18, 2021

"dead man walking": "Final Report, Select Committee to Investigate the January 6th Attack on the United States Capitol," House Report 117-663, December 22, 2022, 429

About half of the approximately 53,000; "to the Capitol from here": "Final Report, Select Committee to Investigate the January 6th Attack on the United States Capitol," House Report 117-663, December 22, 2022, 68–70, 585

"Today is the day American patriots": "Rep. Mo Brooks on Incendiary Jan. 6th Speech: Trump Made Me Do It," Ryan Bort, *Rolling Stone*, July 6, 2021

All of us here today do not want...down Pennsylvania Avenue: "Transcript of Trump's Speech at Rally Before US Capitol Riot," Associated Press, January 13, 2021. https://apnews .com/article/election-2020-joe-biden-donald-trump-capitol-siege-media-e79eb-5164613d6718e9f4502eb471f27

Pence had "caved"..."Hang Mike Pence": "Final Report, Select Committee to Investigate the January 6th Attack on the United States Capitol," House Report 117-663, December 22, 2022, 37–38

The President nonetheless continued...the proposed movement: "Final Report, Select Committee to Investigate the January 6th Attack on the United States Capitol," House Report 117-663, December 22, 2022, 75

feared for their own lives: "Final Report, Select Committee to Investigate the January 6th Attack on the United States Capitol," House Report 117-663, December 22, 2022, 86

secure location in an underground...mere forty feet: "Here's every word of the third Jan. 6 committee hearing on its investigation," NPR, June 16, 2022. https://www.npr. org/2022/06/16/1105683634/transcript-jan-6-committee

Twitter employees became concerned...24,000 likes within two minutes: "Here's every word from the 9th Jan. 6 committee hearing on its investigation," NPR, October 13, 2022. https://www.npr.org/2022/10/13/1125331584/jan-6-committee-hearing-transcript

Pottinger decided immediately to resign: "Final Report, Select Committee to Investigate the January 6th Attack on the United States Capitol," House Report 117-663, December 22, 2022, 87

precipitated an increased level of violence: "Final Report, Select Committee to Investigate the January 6th Attack on the United States Capitol," House Report 117-663, December 22, 2022, 86

"exploited the disruption [the attack]": United States of America v. Donald J. Trump (Indictment), Case No. 1:23-cr-00257-TSC, Document 1, August 1, 2023, 6

They tried to disrupt our democracy: "Mitch McConnell's Statement to the Senate on the Storming of the Capitol," *U.S. News*, January 6, 2021. https://www.usnews.com/news/elec-tions/articles/2021-01-06/read-mitch-mcconnells-statement-to-the-senate-on-the-storming-of-the-capitol

Now we gather due to a selfish: "Sen. Mitt Romney Remarks following Capitol Lock Down," C-SPAN, January 6, 2021. https://www.youtube.com/watch?v=4H6N0lqkvS8

Today's violent assault on our Capitol: "Former SecDef Jim Mattis Denounces Pro-Trump 'Violent Assault' on US Capitol," Hope Hodge Seck, *Military.com*, January 6, 2021. https:// www.military.com/daily-news/2021/01/06/former-secdef-jim-mattis-denounces-pro-trump-violent-assault-us-capitol.html

"January sixth was a culmination": "Rep. Jamie Raskin Speech Trump Impeachment Trial Transcript: 'Trump's Continuing Pattern and Practice of Inciting Violence,'" *Rev.com*, February 11, 2021. https://www.rev.com/blog/transcripts/rep-jamie-raskin-speech-trump-im-peachment-trial-transcript-trumps-continuing-pattern-and-practice-of-inciting-violence

The most combustible thing: "Senate Impeachment Trial Day 2, Part 1," C-SPAN, February 10, 2021. https://www.c-span.org/video/?508741-5/senate-impeachment-trial-day-2-part-1&event=508741&playEvent

January sixth was a disgrace: "Mitch McConnell Speech Transcript After Vote to Acquit Trump in 2nd Impeachment Trial," *Rev.com*, February 13, 2021. https://www.rev.com/blog/transcripts/mitch-mcconnell-speech-transcript-after-vote-to-acquit-trump-in-2nd-impeachment-trial

"We properly planned for a mass": "Senate Hearing on January 6 Capitol Attack Transcript February 23," *Rev.com*, February 23, 2021. https://www.rev.com/blog/transcripts/senate-hearing-on-january-6-capitol-attack-transcript-february-23

"amplify narratives in furtherance": "DHS-FBI-USSS Joint Threat Assessment: 59th Presidential Inauguration," January 16. 2021. https://publicintelligence.net/dhs-fbi-usss-inauguration-threats-2021/

"It emboldened our enemies": "Here's every word from the 8th Jan. 6 committee on its investigation," NPR, July 22, 2022. https://www.npr.org/2022/07/22/1112138665/jan-6-committee-hearing-transcript

more than 700 individuals…convicted at trial: "The Jan. 6 Riot Inquiry So Far: Three Years, Hundreds of Prison Sentences," Alan Feuer and Molly Cook Escobar, *New York Times*, January 3, 2024. https://www.nytimes.com/interactive/2024/01/04/us/january-6-capitol-trump-investigation.html?te=1&nl=the-morning&emc=edit_nn_20240104

Trump had publicly accused of treason: @realDonaldTrump Tweet, 10:27 PM, October 6, 2019

conduct constituted an official act of terrorism: "Proud Boys Leader Sentenced to 22 Years in Prison on Seditious Conspiracy and Other Charges Related to U.S. Capitol Breach," The United States Attorney's Office, District of Columbia, September 5, 2023

"persecution of ordinary citizens engaged": "Resolution to Formally Censure Liz Cheney and Adam Kinzinger and to No Longer Support Them as Members of the Republican Party," Republican National Committee. https://int.nyt.com/data/documenttools/rnc-jan6-resolution/2d6a07e7cf8d8cfb/full.pdf

"We saw it happen. It was a violent": "McConnell Denounces R.N.C. Censure of Jan. 6 Panel Members," Jonathan Weisman and Annie Karni, *New York Times*, February 8, 2022. www.nytimes.com/2022/02/08/us/politics/republicans-censure-mcconnell.html

"Those who think political ends justify": United States District Court for the District of Columbia, United States of America v. Taylor James Johnatakis, Case No. 1:21-cr-91-RCL-3, Notes for Sentencing, 5. www.washingtonpost.com/documents/1923dd68-27cc-4b1f-90d2-0e6e0f183008.pdf

"the problem of incitement to political violence": "Jan. 6 Committee Hearing—Day 7 Transcript," *Rev.com*, July 13, 2022. https://www.rev.com/blog/transcripts/jan-6-committee-hearing-day-7-transcript

In 2016, the Capitol Police…tenfold the number in 2016: "Capitol Police investigated more than 7,500 threats against lawmakers last year," Zoë Richards, NBC News, January 17, 2023. https://www.nbcnews.com/politics/congress/capitol-police-investigated-7500-threats-lawmakers-last-year-rcna66214

"in-person engagement between DVEs...violent action is necessary": Joint Intelligence Bulletin: "Domestic Violent Extremists Emboldened in Aftermath of Capitol Breach, Elevated Domestic Terrorism Threat of Violence Likely Amid Political Transitions and Beyond," January 13, 2021, 5. https://info.publicintelligence.net/DHS-FBI-NCTC-CapitolBreachViolence.pdf

A survey conducted in June 2023: "July 2023 Survey Report: Dangers to Democracy: Tracking Deep Distrust of Democratic Institutions, Conspiracy Beliefs, and Support for Political Violence Among Americans," Robert Pape, Chicago Project on Security & Threats, July 10, 2023, 2–3. https://d3qi0qp55mx5f5.cloudfront.net/cpost/i/docs/2023-06_CPOST-NORC_Political_Violence_Survey_Report.pdf

Peña had attended President Trump's: "He Cheered Trump on Jan. 6. Now He's Accused of Targeting Political Rivals," Simon Romero and Alan Feuer, *New York Times*, January 17, 2023. https://www.nytimes.com/2023/01/17/us/solomon-pena-new-mexico-shootings.html

The top prosecutors in each...The FBI created a special unit: "As Trump Prosecutions Move Forward, Threats and Concerns Increase," Michael S. Schmidt, Adam Goldman, Alan Feuer, Maggie Haberman, and Glenn Thrush, *New York Times*, September 24, 2023. https://www.nytimes.com/2023/09/24/us/politics/trump-prosecutions-threats-violence.html?te=1&nl=the-morning&emc=edit_nn_20230925

the Chairman of the Joint Chiefs of Staff: "Trump and GOP Rep. Gosar suggest Joint Chiefs boss Mark Milley deserves death," Amanda Macias, CNBC, September 25, 2023. https://www.cnbc.com/2023/09/25/trump-paul-gosar-suggest-gen-mark-milley-deserves-death.html?utm_campaign=atlantic-daily-newsletter&utm_source=newsletter&utm_medium=email&utm_content=20230926&lctg=6050e64f4c8a1e4095f6a39a&utm_term=The%20Atlantic%20Daily

"root out the Communists, Marxists": "Trump's ramped-up rhetoric raises new concerns about violence and authoritarianism," *PBS NewsHour*, November 13, 2023. https://www.pbs.org/newshour/show/trumps-ramped-up-rhetoric-raises-new-concerns-about-violence-and-authoritarianism

CHAPTER 34: Leadership Is Not a Popularity Contest

"an amazing gift to the future generations": "Chuck Schumer Speech Transcript after Senate Acquits Trump in 2nd Impeachment," *Rev.com*, February 13, 2021. https://www.rev.com/blog/transcripts/chuck-schumer-speech-transcript-after-senate-acquits-trump-in-2nd-impeachment

"politics isn't about the weird worship": "Sasse hits back at state GOP amid censure attempt: 'Politics isn't about the weird worship of one dude,'" Paul Steinhauser, Fox News, February 5, 2021. https://www.foxnews.com/politics/sasse-hits-back-at-state-gop-amid-censure-attempt-politics-isnt-about-the-weird-worship-of-one-dude

"You can't promote principled anticorruption": The Trump-Ukraine Impeachment Inquiry Report: Report of the House Permanent Select Committee on Intelligence, December 2019, 15

"Our part is to pursue with steadiness": Thomas Jefferson, edited by Eric S. Petersen, *Light and Liberty: Reflections on the Pursuit of Happiness* (New York: The Modern Library, 2004), 53

"With public sentiment, nothing can fail": Abraham Lincoln, from debate at Ottawa, August 21, 1858, AbrahamLincoln.org. https://abrahamlincoln.org/features/speeches-writings/abraham-lincoln-quotes/#:~:text=%E2%80%9CPublic%20sentiment%20is%20everything.,without%20it%20nothing%20can%20succeed.%E2%80%9D

CHAPTER 35: Personality Disorders

DSM-5-TR™ references: Reprinted with permission from the *Diagnostic and Statistical Manual of Mental Disorders*, Fifth Edition, Text Revision (Copyright © 2022). American Psychiatric Association. All Rights Reserved

Having been one of those who: Thomas Jefferson, edited by Eric S. Petersen, *Light and Liberty: Reflections on the Pursuit of Happiness* (New York: The Modern Library, 2004), 41

I did something good: "Transcript of President Trump's Interview With The Wall Street Journal," *Wall Street Journal*, June 18, 2020

happy people are not self-absorbed: "Four secrets from the world's longest happiness study," Kara Baskin, *Boston Globe*, September 16, 2022. https://www.bostonglobe.com/2022/09/16/lifestyle/four-secrets-worlds-longest-happiness-study/

"We had an amazing day": "Remarks in an Exchange With Reporters Prior to a Meeting With Law Enforcement Personnel at the Emergency Operations Center in El Paso, Texas," The American Presidency Project, August 7, 2019. https://www.presidency.ucsb.edu/documents/remarks-exchange-with-reporters-prior-meeting-with-law-enforcement-personnel-the-emergency

Former Iraqi president Saddam Hussein: Jonathan Glover, *Humanity: A Moral History of the Twentieth Century* (New Haven, CT: Yale University Press, 2000), 171

"I don't get it. All these other Republicans": Donald J. Trump, "The Inside Story of Michigan's Fake Voter Fraud Scandal," Tim Alberta, *Politico*, November 24, 2020. https://www.politico.com/news/magazine/2020/11/24/michigan-election-trump-voter-fraud-democracy-440475

approximately 28,000 Georgians declined to vote: "Here's every word from the fourth Jan. 6 committee hearing on its investigation," NPR, June 21, 2022. https://www.npr.org/2022/06/21/1105848096/jan-6-committee-hearing-transcript

he was personally involved with packing boxes...not authorized for their storage: United States of America v. Donald J. Trump and Waltine Nauta (Indictment), Case No. 23-cr-80101-AMC, Document 3, June 8, 2023, 2–3, 5–7, 10, 14, 20

As the head of the executive branch: United States of America v. Donald J. Trump and Waltine Nauta (Indictment), Case No. 9:23-cr-80101-AMC, Document 3, June 8, 2023, 9

further claimed through his attorneys...False Statements and Representations: United States of America v. Donald J. Trump and Waltine Nauta (Indictment), Case No. 23-cr-80101-AMC, Document 3, June 8, 2023, 3, 21, 27–28, 34, 40

corruptly concealing, altering: United States of America v. Donald J. Trump, Waltine Nauta and Carlos De Oliveira (Indictment), Case No. 23-cr-80101-AMC, July 27, 2023, 57

Swan: John Lewis is lying in State in the U.S. Capitol: "Donald Trump Interview Transcript With Jonathan Swan of Axios on HBO," *Rev.com*, August 3, 2020. https://www.rev.com/blog/transcripts/donald-trump-interview-transcript-with-axios-on-hbo

"No. I won't be going": "John Lewis's Own Words Highlight Ceremony As He Lies In State At U.S. Capitol; Donald Trump Says He Won't Visit," Ted Johnson, Deadline.com, July 27, 2020. https://deadline.com/2020/07/john-lewis-lies-in-state-capitol-funeral-1202996142/

"arbitrary and capricious manner": "Supreme Court Overturns Trump Administration's Termination of DACA," National Immigration Law Center, June 22, 2020. https://www.nilc.org/issues/daca/alert-supreme-court-overturns-trump-administrations-termination-of-daca/

to embarrass him by delegitimizing: Report On The Investigation Into Russian Interference In The 2016 Presidential Election, Volume II of II, U.S. Department of Justice, March 2019, 25

accused his attorney general of "hating Trump": "Here's every word of the second Jan. 6 committee hearing on its investigation," NPR, June 13, 2022. https://www.npr.org/2022/06/13/1104690690/heres-every-word-of-the-second-jan-6-committee-hearing-on-its-investigation

The virtues are lost in self-interest: François de La Rochefoucauld. https://www.goodreads.com/quotes/1270727-virtues-are-lost-in-self-interest-as-rivers-are-lost

"Take from man his selfish propensities": Thomas Jefferson, edited by Eric S. Petersen, *Light and Liberty: Reflections on the Pursuit of Happiness* (New York: The Modern Library, 2004), 50

"He is an unprincipled person": "Trump Proposed Launching Missiles Into Mexico to 'Destroy the Drug Labs,' Esper Says," Maggie Haberman, *New York Times*, May 5, 2022. https://www.nytimes.com/2022/05/05/us/politics/mark-esper-book-trump.html

The evidence shows that the President was focused: Report On The Investigation Into Russian Interference In The 2016 Presidential Election, Volume II of II, U.S. Department of Justice (March 2019), 61

"A complete aberration in the American system": "This Was Trump Pulling a Putin," Robert Draper, *New York Times Magazine*, April 11, 2022. www.nytimes.com/2022/04/11/magazine/trump-putin-ukraine-fiona-hill.html

"This trial was about the final acts": "Chuck Schumer Speech Transcript After Senate Acquits Trump in 2nd Impeachment," *Rev.com*, February 13, 2021. https://www.rev.com/blog/transcripts/chuck-schumer-speech-transcript-after-senate-acquits-trump-in-2nd-impeachment

a fifteen-year global trend in democratic deterioration: *Freedom in the World 2021: Democracy under Siege*, Sarah Repucci and Amy Slipowitz. https://freedomhouse.org/report/freedom-world/2021/democracy-under-siege

CHAPTER 36: The Art of Exacerbating a Crisis: The COVID-19 Pandemic

Chronic underfunding, longstanding health: "House Coronavirus Subcommittee Issues and Discusses Final Report," Lily Murphy and Kerry Allen, The National Association of County Health Officials, December 16, 2022. https://www.naccho.org/blog/articles/house-coronavirus-subcommittee-issues-and-discusses-final-report

a culture of resisting authority: "The Plague Year," Lawrence Wright, *The New Yorker*, December 28, 2020. https://www.newyorker.com/magazine/2021/01/04/the-plague-year?-campaign_id=154&emc=edit_cb_20210105&instance_id=25678&nl=coronavirus-briefing&regi_id=93941638&segment_id=48438&te=1&user_id=69760d127d2ac6d-230be6136001f652c

public health guidance must be transparent: "Written testimony: Summary of lessons learned and the path forward," Deborah Birx, June 23, 2022

killed over 450,000 Americans: All COVID death statistics referenced in this chapter: CDC COVID Data Tracker. https://covid.cdc.gov/covid-data-tracker/#trends_totaldeaths _select_00

Birx estimated that 130,000: "Hearing with Former Trump White House Coronavirus Response Coordinator Dr. Deborah Birx," Select Subcommittee on the Coronavirus Crisis, June 23, 2022. https://www.youtube.com/watch?v=jpNKbd240Ng

In a single day, he used the term in four posts: Donald J. Trump on Twitter, @realDonaldTrump, 6:41 AM March 18, 2020; 7:12 AM March 18, 2020; 7:46 AM March 18, 2020; 5:37 PM March 18, 2020

at least 1,000 hate crimes: "Attacks on Asian Americans skyrocket to 100 per day during coronavirus pandemic," Alexandra Kelley, *The Hill*, March 31, 2020. https://thehill.com/ changing-america/respect/equality/490373-attacks-on-asian-americans-at-about-100-per-day-due-to/

150 percent in sixteen of America's largest cities: "Anti-Asian hate crimes increased by nearly 150% in 2020, mostly in N.Y. and L.A., new report says," Kimmy Yam, NBC News, March 9, 2021. https://www.nbcnews.com/news/asian-america/anti-asian-hate-crimes-increased-nearly-150-2020-mostly-n-n1260264

"No, I haven't"…I love that world. I really do: WATCH: Trump's full remarks on coronovirus during March 6 visit to the CDC in Atlanta," *PBS NewsHour*. https://www.youtube.com /watch?v=yUP9IF387MA

'I'd rate it a ten. I think we've done a great job": "Remarks by President Trump, Vice President Pence, and Members of the Coronavirus Task Force in Press Briefing," March 16, 2020. https://trumpwhitehouse.archives.gov/briefings-statements/remarks-president-trump-vice-president-pence-members-coronavirus-task-force-press-briefing-3/

"The FDA Commissioner, Stephen Hahn": "Donald Trump Coronavirus Task Force Briefing Transcript March 19: Trump Takes Shots at the Media," *Rev.com*, March 19, 2020. https://www.rev.com/blog/transcripts/donald-trump-coronavirus-task-force-briefing-transcript-march-19-trump-takes-shots-at-the-media

"It's going to disappear and I'll be right": "Transcript: 'Fox News Sunday' Interview with President Trump," Fox News, July 19, 2020. https://www.foxnews.com/politics/transcript-fox -news-sunday-interview-with-president-trump

So it's interesting. He's got a very good: "Donald Trump Coronavirus Press Conference Transcript July 28: Talks Kodak, Vaccine, DACA," *Rev.com*, July 28, 2020. https://www.rev.com/ blog/transcripts/donald-trump-coronavirus-press-conference-transcript-july-28

Hi. Perhaps you recognize me: "Donald Trump Vlog: Coronavirus COVID-19 Update—October 7, 2020," Factbase videos, October 7, 2020. https://www.youtube.com/watch?v=teEFlKoXESU

distrust in public health expertise, harassment: "House Coronavirus Subcommittee Issues and Discusses Final Report," Lily Murphy and Kerry Allen, The National Association of County Health Officials, December 16, 2022. https://www.naccho.org/blog/articles/ house-coronavirus-subcommittee-issues-and-discusses-final-report

She warned that community spread: "Transcript for the CDC Telebriefing Update on COVID-19," Centers for Disease Control and Prevention, February 26, 2020. https://archive .cdc.gov/#/details?q=https://www.%20cdc.gov/media/releases/2020/t0225-cdc-telebriefing

-covid-19.html&start=0&rows=10&url=https://www.cdc.gov/media/releases/2020/ t0225-cdc-telebriefing-covid-19.html

"What do you have to lose…fifteen times": "Donald Trump Coronavirus Task Force Briefing Transcript April 5," *Rev.com*, April 5, 2020. https://www.rev.com/blog/transcripts/ donald-trump-coronavirus-task-force-briefing-transcript-april-5

"it was terrible what he did, to write a letter": "President Trump with Coronavirus Task Force Briefing," C-SPAN, April 4, 2020. https://www.c-span.org/video/?470970-1/president-trump-comments-firing-intelligence-community-inspector-general

An HHS IG report revealed: "Hospital Experiences Responding to the COVID-19 Pandemic: Results of a National Pulse Survey March 23–27, 2020," U.S. Department of Health and Human Services, Office of the Inspector General, April 3, 2020. https://oig.hhs.gov/oei/ reports/oei-06-20-00300.asp

"getting the country back from the doctors": "Kushner Told Woodward Trump 'Got the Country Back from the Doctors' in Discussing U.S. COVID Response," Daniel Villarreal, *Newsweek*, October 28, 2020. https://www.newsweek.com/kushner-told-woodward-trump-got-country-back-doctors-discussing-us-covid-response-1543070

recommendations in a CDC report: "The CDC softened a report on meatpacking safety during the pandemic. Democrats say they want to know why," Eli Rosenberg, *Washington Post*, September 30, 2020. https://www.washingtonpost.com/business/2020/09/30/cdc-meatpacking-smithfield/

Despite polls showing broad support: "Public Attitudes, Behaviors, and Beliefs Related to COVID-19, Stay-at-Home Orders, Nonessential Business Closures, and Public Health Guidance—United States, New York City, and Los Angeles, May 5–12, 2020," Centers for Disease Control and Prevention, June 19, 2020. https://www.cdc.gov/mmwr/volumes/69/wr /mm6924e1.htm

"should think of themselves as warriors": "Trump calls Americans 'warriors' in fight to open the economy," Chris Megerian, *Los Angeles Times*, May 6, 2020. https://www.latimes.com/ politics/story/2020-05-06/trump-americans-warriors-fight-to-open-economy

"frankly, overrated. Maybe it is": "President Trump Delivers Remarks at Distribution Center in Allentown, Pennsylvania," C-SPAN, May 14, 2020. https://www.c-span.org/video/?472143-1 /president-trump-delivers-remarks-distribution-center-allentown-pennsylvania

"I think it's good—I've heard a lot of good stories": "Trump says he's taking hydroxychloroquine, unproven drug he's touted for COVID-19," Libby Cathey, Ben Gittleson, and Jordyn Phelps, ABC News, May 19, 2020. https://abcnews.go.com/Politics/trump-taking-hydroxychloroquine-unproven-drug-touted-covid-19/story?id=70751728

"an aberrancy that I haven't seen": "'Science Was Distorted & Rejected': Dr. Fauci On Working With Trump Admin," Rachel Maddow, MSNBC. https://www.youtube.com /watch?v=Z9sv9yWlTs4

"an abdication of America's role": "Senator Murray: President Trump's Move to Exit WHO 'Is The Opposite of Putting America First—It Will Put America at Risk'"

Trump reposted a former gameshow host's: "Donald Trump Retweets Chuck Woolery's COVID-19 Conspiracy Theory," Ron Dicker, *Huffpost*, July 13, 2020. https://www.huffpost .com/entry/chuck-woolery-covid-19-conspiracy_n_5f0c37a0c5b6480493d2a13a

"No. When I repost a Tweet": "Transcript: Trump on masks, reopening schools, race and pardoning Roger Stone," CBS News, July 15, 2020. https://www.cbsnews.com/news/trump-race-face-mask-school-roger-stone/

In a peer-reviewed study of 177 countries: "Pandemic preparedness and COVID-19: an exploratory analysis of infection and fatality rates, and contextual factors associated with preparedness in 177 countries, from Jan 1, 2020, to Sept 30, 2021," *The Lancet*, February 1, 2022. https://doi.org/10.1016/S0140-6736(22)00172-6

A high level of trust in science: "How Australia Saved Thousands of Lives While Covid Killed a Million Americans," Damien Cave, *New York Times*, May 15, 2022. https://www.nytimes.com/2022/05/15/world/australia/covid-deaths.html

"No matter what we do…very overrated": "Hearing with Former Trump White House Coronavirus Response Coordinator Dr. Deborah Birx," Select Subcommittee on the Coronavirus Crisis, June 23, 2022. https://www.youtube.com/watch?v=jpNKbd240Ng

"due to ongoing health and safety…to compete this fall": "Big Ten Statement on 2020-21 Fall Season," BigTen.org, August 11, 2020. https://admin.bigten.org/news/2020/8/11/general-al-big-ten-statement-on-2020-21-fall-season.aspx

"have taken a crisis…dangerously incompetent": "Dying in a Leadership Vacuum," *The New England Journal of Medicine*, 383 (October 8, 2020): 1479–80. DOI: 10.1056/NEJMe2029812. https://www.nejm.org/doi/full/10.1056/NEJMe2029812

"decisions to authorize or approve any such vaccine": "COVID-19: An Update on the Federal Response—FDA Opening Remarks September 23, 2020," U.S. Food and Drug Administration, September 23, 2020. https://www.fda.gov/news-events/congressional-testimony/covid-19-update-federal-response-fda-opening-remarks-09232020

62 percent of Americans were concerned: "Poll: Most Americans Worry Political Pressure Will Lead to Premature Approval of a COVID-19 Vaccine; Half Say They Would Not Get a Free Vaccine Approved Before Election Day," Kaiser Family Foundation, September 10, 2020, accessed March 24, 2023. https://www.kff.org/coronavirus-covid-19/press-release/poll-most-americans-worry-political-pressure-will-lead-to-premature-approval-of-a-covid-19-vaccine-half-say-they-would-not-get-a-free-vaccine-approved-before-election-day/

"Don't tell anybody, but let me wait": "Donald Trump Rally Speech Transcript Opa-locka, Florida November 1," *Rev.com*, November 1, 2020. https://www.rev.com/blog/transcripts/donald-trump-rally-speech-transcript-opa-locka-florida-november-1

"the ominous politicization…and coordinated control": "Open Letter by Epidemic Intelligence Service Officers Past and Present—in Support of CDC," NIH National Library of Medicine, October 14, 2020. https://www.ncbi.nlm.nih.gov/pmc/articles/PMC7748252/

over 81 percent of the state's COVID-19 deaths: "COVID-19 Cases, Hospitalizations, and Deaths by Vaccination Status," Washington State Department of Health, December 8, 2021, 11. https://www.doh.wa.gov/Portals/1/Documents/1600/coronavirus/data-tables/421-010-CasesInNotFullyVaccinated.pdf

"consistent and factual communication from the President": "Written testimony: Summary of lessons learned and the path forward," Deborah Birx, June 23, 2022

Trump's Presidential Daily Briefs began highlighting: "Trump reportedly ignored intel briefings on coronavirus threat," Steve Benen, *The Rachel Maddow Show*, MSNBC, April 28, 2020.

https://www.msnbc.com/rachel-maddow-show/trump-reportedly-ignored-intel-briefings-coronavirus-threat-n1194106

"No. Not at all…great relationship with President Xi": "Full interview: President Trump discusses trade, impeachment, Boeing and Elon Musk with CNBC in Davos," Mike Calia, CNBC, January 22, 2020. https://www.cnbc.com/2020/01/22/davos-2020-cnbcs-full-interview-with-president-trump.html

"all countries should be prepared for containment": "Statement on the first meeting of the International Health Regulations (2005) Emergency Committee regarding the outbreak of novel coronavirus (2019-nCoV)," World Health Organization, January 23, 2020

"We think we have it very well": "Timeline of Trump's COVID-19 Comments," Eugene Kiely, Lori Robertson, Rem Rieder, and D'Angelo Gore, FactCheck.org, October 2, 2020. https://www.factcheck.org/2020/10/timeline-of-trumps-covid-19-comments/

"this virus is probably with us beyond": "CDC director: Novel coronavirus 'is probably with us beyond this season, beyond this year,'" Jacqueline Howard, CNN, February 13, 2020. https://www.cnn.com/2020/02/13/health/coronavirus-cdc-robert-redfield-gupta-intv/index.html

When you have fifteen people…"We're really prepared": "Press Conference: Donald Trump Provides an Update on the Coronavirus Outbreak—February 26, 2020," Factbase videos, February 26, 2020. https://www.youtube.com/watch?v=eoJlNEmxf0w

"It's going to disappear. One day": "Trump says coronavirus will 'disappear' eventually," Maegan Vazquez and Caroline Kelly, CNN, February 28, 2020. https://edition.cnn.com/2020/02/27/politics/trump-coronavirus-disappear/index.html

"They said one-tenth of 1 percent…tests are all perfect": "Remarks: Donald Trump Has a Briefing during a Tour of the CDC in Atlanta—March 6, 2020," Factbase, March 6, 2020. https://factba.se/transcript/donald-trump-remarks-cdc-briefing-tour-atlanta-march-6-2020

"created a sense among…across our agencies": "Hearing with Former Trump White House Coronavirus Response Coordinator Dr. Deborah Birx," Select Subcommittee on the Coronavirus Crisis, June 23, 2022. https://www.youtube.com/watch?v=jpNKbd240Ng

"And it will go away": "A timeline of what Trump has said on coronavirus," Kathryn Watson, CBS News, April 3, 2020. https://www.cbsnews.com/news/timeline-president-donald-trump-changing-statements-on-coronavirus/

Fauci informed Congress: "Dr. Fauci and Other CDC & NIH Officials Testify on Coronavirus—March 11," *Rev.com*, March 11, 2020. https://www.rev.com/blog/transcripts/dr-fauci-and-other-cdc-nih-officials-testify-on-coronavirus-march-11

"This is a very contagious virus": "Donald Trump and Coronavirus Task Force News Conference Transcript: March 15," *Rev.com*, March 15, 2020. https://www.rev.com/blog/transcripts/donald-trump-and-coronavirus-task-force-news-conference-transcript-march-15

"I say that you're a terrible reporter": "Donald Trump & Coronavirus Task Force March 20 Press Conference Transcript: Trump Spars with Reporters in Fiery Briefing," *Rev.com*, March 20, 2020. https://www.rev.com/blog/transcripts/donald-trump-coronavirus-task-force-march-20-press-conference-transcript-trump-spars-with-reporters-in-fiery-briefing

"if we can hold that down": "Donald Trump Coronavirus Task Force Briefing Transcript March 29: Trump Extends Task Force Guidelines to April 30," *Rev.com*, March 29, 2020.

https://www.rev.com/blog/transcripts/donald-trump-coronavirus-task-force-briefing-tran-script-march-29-trump-extends-task-force-guidelines-to-april-30

"I want every American to be prepared": "'Very, very painful two weeks ahead': Donald Trump warns Americans to be prepared," *Hindustan Times*, April 1, 2020. https://www.youtube.com/watch?v=PUVINBonAuM

Which I was right about: "Donald Trump Coronavirus Task Force Briefing April 7," *Rev.com*, April 7, 2020. https://www.rev.com/blog/transcripts/donald-trump-coronavirus-task-force-briefing-april-7

So I asked Bill a question: "President Trump with Coronavirus Task Force Briefing," C-SPAN, April 23, 2020. https://www.c-span.org/video/?471458-1/president-trump-corona-virus-task-force-briefing

"administered into the human body": "Lysol warns against injecting disinfectant after Trump speculates on coronavirus cure," Dalvin Brown, *USA Today*, April 24, 2020. https://www.usatoday.com/story/money/2020/04/24/lysol-warns-against-injecting-disinfectant-af-ter-trumps-comments/3018425001/

"I think honestly, if you look at the trends": "Pence says coronavirus could be 'largely' behind us by Memorial Day weekend," Morgan Phillips, Fox News, April 23, 2020. https://www.foxnews.com/politics/pence-says-coronavirus-could-be-largely-behind-us-by-memo-rial-day-weekend

"there is absolutely no way on earth": "Trump Says U.S. Will Run 5 Million Tests 'Very Soon'. His Testing Chief Says That's Impossible," W.J. Hennigan, *TIME*, April 28, 2020. https://time.com/5828843/trump-coronavirus-testing-giroir/

"We're on the other side of the medical": "Jared Kushner: 'We have all the testing we need' to start reopening the country," Julia Musto, Fox News, April 29, 2020. https://www.foxnews.com/media/jared-kushner-we-have-all-the-testing-we-need-to-start-reopening

"anywhere from seventy-five, eighty": "Donald Trump Virtual Town Hall Transcript May 3," *Rev.com*, May 3, 2020. https://www.rev.com/blog/transcripts/donald-trump-virtual-town-hall-transcript-may-3

"a reflection of the tremendous progress": "Winding down Coronavirus Task Force is under discussion by Trump administration," Ben Tracy, Kathryn Watson, and Paula Reid, CBS News, May 6, 2020. https://www.cbsnews.com/news/coronavirus-task-force-winding-down-discus-sions/

"I just want to make something clear": "Donald Trump Speech Transcript on Vaccine Development for Coronavirus," *Rev.com*, May 15, 2020. https://www.rev.com/blog/transcripts/donald-trump-speech-transcript-on-vaccine-development-for-coronavirus

Vice President Pence urged governors: "Pence Tells Governors to Repeat Misleading Claim on Outbreaks," *New York Times*, June 15, 2020. https://www.nytimes.com/2020/06/15/world/coronavirus-usa-world.html

"testing is a double-edged sword": "President Trump Campaign Rally in Tulsa, Oklahoma," C-SPAN, June 20, 2020. https://www.c-span.org/video/?473015-1/president-trump-cam-paign-rally-tulsa-oklahoma

"all fifty states and territories...areas of the country": "Mike Pence, Dr. Fauci & Coronavirus Task Force Press Conference June 26," *Rev.com*, June 26, 2020. https://www.rev.com/blog/transcripts/mike-pence-dr-fauci-coronavirus-task-force-press-conference-june-26

"I think we're going to be very good": "Trump wants to incentivize Americans to go back to work," Fox Business, July 1, 2020. https://video.foxbusiness.com/v/6168640717001#sp=-show-clips

"They are dying. That's true...you don't know that": "Donald Trump Interview Transcript With Jonathan Swan of Axios on HBO," *Rev.com*, August 3, 2020. https://www.rev.com/blog/transcripts/donald-trump-interview-transcript-with-axios-on-hbo

"children are almost...like things go away": "Interview: Donald Trump Calls In to Fox and Friends for an Interview—August 5, 2020," Factbase. https://factba.se/transcript/donald-trump-interview-fox-and-friends-august-5-2020

"I'm not going to drive this country": "'I don't want to create panic': Trump defends coronavirus remarks he made to Bob Woodward—video," *The Guardian*, September 9, 2020. https://www.theguardian.com/us-news/video/2020/sep/09/trump-coronavirus-bob-woodward-book-rage

I want to show a level of confidence: "Donald Trump Press Conference Transcript September 10: Coronavirus, Bob Woodward Recording," *Rev.com*, September 10, 2020. https://www.rev.com/blog/transcripts/donald-trump-press-conference-transcript-september-10-coronavirus-bob-woodward-recording

"It is going to disappear": "Donald Trump ABC News Town Hall Transcript with George Stephanopoulos in Philadelphia," *Rev.com*, September 16, 2020. https://www.rev.com/blog/transcripts/donald-trump-abc-news-town-hall-transcript-with-george-stephanopoulos-in-philadelphia

I regret my error of judgment: "A Message from Rev. John I. Jenkins, C.S.C.: I regret my error of judgment in not wearing a mask," University of Notre Dame, Office of the President. https://president.nd.edu/homilies-writings-addresses/a-message-from-rev-john-i-jenkins-c-s-c-i-regret-my-error-of-judgment-in-not-wearing-a-mask/

A Cornell University study: "Coronavirus misinformation: quantifying sources and themes in the COVID-19 'infodemic,'" Sarah Evanega, Mark Lynas, Jordan Adams, and Karinne Smolenyak, The Cornell Alliance for Science, Department of Global Development, Cornell University, Ithaca, NY; Cision Global Insights, Ann Arbor, MI. https://int.nyt.com/data/documenttools/evanega-et-al-coronavirus-misinformation-submitted-07-23-20-1/080839ac-0c22bca8/full.pdf

Don't let it dominate you: "'Maybe I'm immune': Trump posts video from White House after returning from Walter Reed," NBC News, October 5, 2020. https://www.nbcnews.com/video/trump-posts-video-from-white-house-after-returning-from-walter-reed-93199941665

"The difference here is President Trump": "Kamala Harris & Mike Pence 2020 Vice Presidential Debate Transcript," *Rev.com*, October 7, 2020. https://www.rev.com/blog/transcripts/kamala-harris-mike-pence-2020-vice-presidential-debate-transcript

We're rounding the turn on the pandemic: "Donald Trump Rally Johnstown, PA Transcript October 13," *Rev.com*, October 13, 2020. https://www.rev.com/blog/transcripts/donald-trump-rally-johnstown-pa-transcript-october-13

"We're rounding the turn, with or without": "Donald Trump Rally Speech Transcript

Pensacola, FL October 23," *Rev.com*, October 24, 2020. https://www.rev.com/blog/transcripts/donald-trump-rally-speech-transcript-pensacola-fl-october-23

Our doctors get more money: "Donald Trump Rally Speech Transcript Waterford Township, Michigan October 30," *Rev.com*, October 30, 2020. https://www.rev.com/blog/transcripts/donald-trump-rally-speech-transcript-waterford-township-michigan-october-30

"the condition or disease that started": "Debunking the False Claim That COVID Death Counts Are Inflated," Christie Aschwanden, *Scientific American*, October 20, 2020. https://www.scientificamerican.com/article/debunking-the-false-claim-that-covid-death-counts-are-inflated1/

"All the stars are aligned in the wrong place": "Fauci Says Americans Should Expect 'A Whole Lot of Hurt' from COVID-19 in Coming Days," Darragh Roche, *Newsweek*, November 1, 2020. https://www.newsweek.com/fauci-americans-hurt-covid-19-coming-days-1543833

"aggressive, unrelenting, expanding broad community": "Task force warns of 'further deterioration' as pandemic worsens," Betsy Klein, CNN, November 17, 2020. https://www.cnn.com/2020/11/17/politics/white-house-coronavirus-task-force-state-reports/index.html

President Trump had not attended: "Dr. Fauci: Trump Hasn't Attended a Coronavirus Task Force Meeting in 'Several Months,'" Justin Baragona, *Daily Beast*, November 15, 2020. https://www.thedailybeast.com/dr-fauci-says-trump-hasnt-attended-coronavirus-task-force-meeting-in-several-months

HHS revealed that more than 1,000: "1,000 U.S. Hospitals Are 'Critically' Short On Staff— And More Expect To Be Soon," Sean McMinn and Selena Simmons-Duffin, NPR, November 20, 2020. https://www.npr.org/sections/health-shots/2020/11/20/937152062/1-000-u-s-hospitals-are-short-on-staff-and-more-expect-to-be-soon

"December, January, and early February": "Dr. Fauci Sees 'Terribly Painful Months' Ahead," Jonathan Wolfe and Adam Pasick, *New York Times*, November 20, 2020. https://www.nytimes.com/2020/11/20/us/coronavirus-today.html

CHAPTER 37: Public Leadership: A License to Serve

A man dies when he refuses: "Selma March 1965. Martin Luther King on Standing Up. Archive film 99319," Huntley Film Archives, October 10, 2017. https://www.youtube.com/watch?v=O46ugLRvQkc

"a public servant's heart": "Governor Schwarzenegger's Message Following This Week's Attack on the Capitol," Arnold Schwarzenegger, January 10, 2021. https://www.youtube.com/watch?v=x_P-0I6sAck&feature=youtu.be

God gives us rights by nature: "Sasse: America Can't Do Big Things If We Hate Our Neighbors," U.S. Senator for Nebraska, Ben Sasse, January 6, 2021. https://www.youtube.com/watch?v=df6Mf5Q4Gmc

"the highest of distinctions": "The 100 Best Leadership Quotes of All Time," Lolly Daskal, Inc. https://www.inc.com/lolly-daskal/the-100-best-leadership-quotes-of-all-time.html

To the sacrifice of time, labor, fortune: Thomas Jefferson, edited by Eric S. Petersen, *Light and Liberty: Reflections on the Pursuit of Happiness* (New York: The Modern Library, 2004), 44

"Few men are willing to brave...most painfully to change": Day of Affirmation Address, University of Cape Town, Cape Town, South Africa, June 6, 1966, John F. Kennedy Presidential Library and Museum. https://www.jfklibrary.org/learn/about-jfk/the-kennedy-family/ robert-f-kennedy/robert-f-kennedy-speeches/day-of-affirmation-address-university-of-cape-town-capetown-south-africa-june-6-1966

"Doing the right thing and being constant": "User Clip: Hakeem Jeffries Closing Argument," C-SPAN, February 3, 2020. https://www.c-span.org/video/?c4851756/user-clip-hakeem-jeffries

Some courageous people came forward: "The best of Adam Schiff from the impeachment trial," David Knowles, Yahoo! News, January 24, 2020. https://news.yahoo.com/the-best-of-adam-schiff-from-the-impeachment-trial-225950957.html

"In recent months, many entrusted with power": "Vindman, Sondland Removed as Trump Purges Impeachment Witnesses," Roberta Rampton, Amita Kelly, and Franco Ordonez, NPR, February 7, 2020. https://www.npr.org/2020/02/07/803904417/lt-col-alexander-vindman-escorted-out-of-the-white-house-his-lawyer-says

"dreadful misfortune for a man to grow": *Theodore Roosevelt, An Autobiography*, 56.

"No House seat, no office in this land": "Rep. Liz Cheney Primary Night Remarks," C-SPAN, August 16, 2022. https://www.c-span.org/video/?522338-1/rep-cheney-loses-wyoming-republican-primary-harriet-hageman

Had I known that standing up for the truth: Adam Kinzinger's Final Floor Speech, country1st.com, December 15, 2022. https://www.country1st.com/finalspeech?utm_campaign=last_speech_d&utm_medium=email&utm_source=country1st

"If we are going to ask Americans to be willing": "Here's every word from the fifth Jan. 6 committee hearing on its investigation," NPR, June 23, 2022. https://www.npr.org/2022/06/23/1106700800/jan-6-committee-hearing-transcript

There may be some setbacks, some delays: "John Lewis Commencement Speech at Emory University," ABC News. https://abcnews.go.com/Politics/video/john-lewis-commencement-speech-emory-university-23739630